D0267428

The European Union as a Global Actor

When trade, global warming, human rights, local conflicts, or indeed most of the major global issues are addressed in the news, it is likely that the European Union will be involved. It is not a state, yet in some of its roles it rivals the United States. This poses a problem for international relations theory, which is more accustomed to dealing with sovereign state actors.

This new and substantially re-written edition of *The European Union as a Global Actor* seeks to address this issue, develops a theoretical approach to understanding the European Union as an actor in the global system, and applies the theory across the range of the EU's external activities.

This new edition includes:

- A new emphasis on the construction of identity and its relation to actor capability
- An investigation of external constructions of the EU, including a wide range of interviews with the staff of third country missions
- A substantive analysis of the dimensions of EU external action based on new research which provides a wide coverage of recent developments in economic, environmental, development, foreign and now military policy
- Up-to-date material on the structures, procedures and content of EU external action.

The European Union as a Global Actor builds upon the ground-breaking constructivist approach to defining and explaining the development of the European actor formulated within the first edition. This book provides an invaluable and comprehensive resource for students with interests in European Studies, International Relations and Politics.

Charlotte Bretherton is Senior Lecturer in European Studies and International Relations at Liverpool John Moores University. Her main interests are in the contemporary European Union, development and gender issues.

John Vogler is Professor of International Relations at Keele University and Chair of the British International Studies Association Environment Group. He is the author of numerous publications on the environment in world politics and international cooperation including *The Global Commons* (2000).

The European Union as a Global Actor

Second edition

Charlotte Bretherton and John Vogler

LONDON AND NEW YORK

Second edition published 2006
by Routledge
2 Park Square, Milton Park, Abingdon, Oxon OX14 4RN

Simultaneously published in the USA and Canada
by Routledge
270 Madison Ave, New York, NY 10016

First published 1999 by Routledge
Reprinted 2000, 2002, 2003, 2005

Routledge is an imprint of the Taylor & Francis Group

Typeset in Garamond by
HWA Text and Data Management, Tunbridge Wells
Printed and bound in Great Britain by
TJ International Ltd, Padstow, Cornwall

British Library Cataloguing in Publication Data
A catalogue record for this book is available from the British Library

Library of Congress Cataloging-in-Publication Data
Bretherton, Charlotte.
    The European Union as a global actor / Charlotte Bretherton & John
    Vogler.–2nd ed.
        p.   cm.
    "Simultaneously published in the USA and Canada."
    Includes bibliographical references and index.
    1. European Union countries—Foreign relations. 2. European Union
    countries–Foreign economic relations. I. Vogler, John. II. Title.
D1060.B735 2006
341.2422′2–dc22   2005017285

ISBN10: 0–415–28244–6 (hbk)
ISBN10: 0–415–28245–4 (pbk)

ISBN13: 9–78–0–415–28244–4 (hbk)
ISBN13: 9–78–0–415–28245–3 (pbk)

Contents

Illustrations

Figures

Tables

Preface to the second edition

A far greater time has elapsed, since publication of the first edition, than we had originally anticipated. During that period the European Union has undergone very significant alterations, necessitating rather more fundamental revisions than we had envisaged when undertaking to produce a second edition. Indeed, in most respects this is an entirely new book, although it retains and extends the model of actorness developed in the first edition. In researching it, from 2001 to 2005, we were once again indebted to the many officials of EU institutions and external missions who gave of their time to answer our questions about the changes in which they were immersed.

Very shortly after completion of the first edition we saw the launch of the euro which, despite its mixed performance, has inevitably enhanced the Union's international presence, and entry into force of the Treaty of Amsterdam, which brought important innovations in the field of Common Foreign and Security Policy. Subsequently there have been unprecedented developments in the field of security. The European Security and Defence Policy, which saw EU involvement in two small-scale operations in 2003 (in Macedonia and the Democratic Republic of Congo) and a continuing policing operation in Bosnia-Herzegovina, was unimaginable at the time of writing the first edition. 2003 also saw the production of a European Security Strategy that responded, in part, to the terrorist attacks on the USA of 11 September 2001. It also raised questions about the international roles and identity of the Union that must necessarily concern us in this volume.

The Amsterdam Treaty also initiated a process of 'communitarising' the Justice and Home Affairs policy area, particularly in relation to immigration and border control matters. Progress in this area has also been rapid, introducing a new dimension to EU external policy that doubtless merits its own chapter in a work claiming to cover all areas of EU external policy. Nevertheless we have chosen to integrate this policy area into those dealt with in the first edition, but also to discuss it more fully in a completely new chapter dealing with meanings of EU identity.

The most significant change affecting the Union since the first edition was, of course, its enlargement, in May 2004, to include ten new Member States from Eastern and Southern Europe. This has substantially changed the internal dynamics and external borders of the Union, necessitating a new approach to 'neighbours' which as yet remains in embryonic form. Meanwhile further candidates await accession.

Primarily to accommodate enlargement, the Treaty of Nice (which entered into force in February 2003) introduced interim changes to the Union's decision-making procedures. This was followed by establishment of a Convention on the future of Europe, charged with revising and consolidating the founding Treaties and, *inter alia*, ensuring the Union is equipped to play a major role in twenty-first century international affairs. The Constitutional Treaty that finally emerged did, indeed, include provisions intended to facilitate decision-making and to strengthen the Union's capacity for external action. The rotating presidency and the entire pillar structure were to be removed while the EU was to acquire its own legal personality, foreign minister and External Action Service. The Treaty's rejection by popular referenda in France and the Netherlands (in mid-2005) inevitably raises questions about the future direction of the EU.

These recent, momentous events impacted upon the process of completing this book. In order that it should not be outdated immediately upon publication, we decided to await the successful completion of the 2004 enlargement. It was clearly not practical, however, to await ratification of the Constitutional Treaty. Initially we included references to the Treaty's provisions wherever they had relevance. Latterly, as it became clear that the Treaty faced rejection, we removed many of these references. However, we have retained discussion of those provisions, for example in relation to the proposed External Action Service, that have particular relevance; and that are likely to reappear in some form once the current 'period of reflection' is completed. From a purely selfish viewpoint, delivery of a manuscript during such a period may mean that its contents will not be too quickly outdated. Events may prove us wrong.

Charlotte Bretherton, Liverpool
John Vogler, Keele
June 2005

Acknowledgements

We gratefully acknowledge the generosity of the many external Mission staff and NGO representatives who spared time to talk with us, and whose insights proved invaluable. We are deeply indebted, also, to the officials we interviewed at the European Commission and the General-Secretariat of the Council of Ministers, at Member State Permanent Representations, the UK Foreign Office and the Department of the Environment.

Authors' note

It has become customary, in recent years, for commentators to refer exclusively to the European Union (EU) – despite the continuing existence of the European Community (EC). Since this makes matters simpler for all concerned, we have referred to the European Union when speaking in general terms about external action. Nevertheless, in some contexts, the differing responsibilities of the Community and the Union have considerable significance for the arguments we are making. Thus, in circumstances where we wished to emphasise that the policy area under discussion falls within Community competence, we found it necessary to continue referring to the European Community.

Abbreviations

AAMS	Associated African and Malagasy States
ACP	African, Caribbean and Pacific Group
ALA	Asian and Latin American countries
AMCHAM	American Chamber of Commerce
AOSIS	Association of Small Island States
APEC	Asia-Pacific Economic Cooperation
ASEAN	Association of South East Asian Nations
ASEM	Asia-Europe Meetings
CAP	Common Agricultural Policy of the EU
CARDS	Community Assistance for Reconstruction, Development and Stabilization (programme for Western Balkans)
CCAMLR	Convention on the Conservation of Antarctic Marine Living Resources
CCP	Common Commercial Policy of the EU
CCT	Common Customs Tariff of the EU
CDM	Clean Development Mechanism (of the Kyoto Protocol to the FCCC)
CEEC	Central and East European Countries
CEFTA	Central European Free Trade Area
CFC	Chlorofluorocarbon
CFSP	Common Foreign and Security Policy
CIS	Commonwealth of Independent States (of the former Soviet Union)
CIVCOM	Committee for Civilian Crisis Management (of the EU)
CJTF	Combined Joint Task Force
CMEA	Council for Mutual Economic Assistance (also known as Comecon)
CoP	Conference of the Parties
COREPER	Committee of Permanent Representatives (to the EU)
CSCE	Conference on Security and Cooperation in Europe (now OSCE)
CSD	Commission for Sustainable Development
DAC	Development Assistance Countries (of the OECD)

DDA	Doha Development Agenda (of the WTO)
DDR	Doha Development Round
DG	Directorate-General (of the European Commission)
DSACEUR	Deputy Supreme Allied Commander, Europe (of NATO)
DTI	Department of Trade and Industry (of UK government)
EAGGF	European Agricultural Guidance and Guarantee Fund
EAPC	Euro-Atlantic Partnership Council
EBA	Everything but Arms (concessionary trade provision for LDCs)
EBRD	European Bank for Reconstruction and Development
EC	European Community
ECAP	European Capability Action Plan
ECB	European Central Bank
ECHO	European Community Humanitarian Office
ECJ	European Court of Justice
ECOFIN	Economic and Financial Affairs Council
ECOSOC	Economic and Social Council of the United Nations
ECSC	European Coal and Steel Community
ECU	European currency unit
EDC	European Defence Community
EDF	European Development Fund
EEA	European Economic Area
EEC	European Economic Community
EFTA	European Free Trade Association
EIB	European Investment Bank
EMP	Euro–Mediterranean Partnership
EMU	Economic and Monetary Union
ENP	European Neighbourhood Policy
EP	European Parliament
EPA	Economic Partnership Agreement (with ACP countries)
EPC	European Political Cooperation
ERDF	European Regional Development Fund
ERTA	European Road Transport Agreement
ESDI	European Security and Defence Identity (within NATO)
ESDP	European Security and Defence Policy
EU	European Union
EUFOR	EU Force (military deployment)
EUJUST	EU justice mission
EUMC	European Union Military Committee
EUMS	European Union Military Staff
EUPM	EU Police Mission to Bosnia and Herzogovina
EUPOL	EU police mission
FAO	Food and Agricultural Organization of the United Nations
FCCC	Framework Convention on Climate Change
FCO	Foreign and Commonwealth Office
FDI	Foreign direct investment

FTA	Free Trade Area
GAERC	General Affairs and External Relations Council (of the EU)
GATS	General Agreement on Trade in Services
GATT	General Agreement on Tariffs and Trade
GDP	Gross domestic product
GMES	Global Monitoring for Environment and Security
GMP	Global Mediterranean Policy (of the EU)
GSP	Generalized System of Preferences
HDI	Human Development Index (of United Nations Development Programme)
ICJ	International Court of Justice (the World Court)
ICTY	International Criminal Tribunal for Yugoslavia
IFOR	Implementation Force (NATO led deployment in Bosnia)
IGC	Intergovernmental Conference
IGO	Intergovernmental Organization
IMF	International Monetary Fund
IMO	International Maritime Organization
INC	Intergovernmental Negotiating Committee
INF	Intermediate Nuclear Forces
IPCC	Intergovernmental Panel on Climate Change
IPPC	Integrated Pollution and Prevention Control
IR	International Relations
ITO	International Trade Organization
JHA	Justice and Home Affairs
JI	Joint implementation (provision for the Kyoto Protocol of the FCCC)
JUSCANZ	Japan, the United States, Canada and New Zealand
LDC	least developed countries
LRTAP	Long Range Transboundary Air Pollution Convention
MAI	Multilateral Agreement on Investment
MEA	Multilateral environmental agreement
MEDA	MEsures D'Accompagnement (programme of the EU)
MEPP	Middle East Peace Process
Mercosur	Mercado Común del Sur (Southern cone common market)
MFA	Multifibre Agreement
MFN	most favoured nation
MNC	Mediterranean non-member countries (of the EU)
NACC	North Atlantic Cooperation Council
NAFTA	North American Free Trade Agreement
NATO	North Atlantic Treaty Organization
NGDO	non-governmental development organization
NGO	non-governmental organization
NIC	newly industrializing countries
NIEO	new international economic order
NIS	new independent states (of the former Soviet Union)

NTA	New Transatlantic Agenda (US–EU)
NTB	non-tariff barrier
ODA	official development assistance
ODI	Overseas Development Institute
OECD	Organization for Economic Cooperation and Development
OPEC	Organization of Petroleum Exporting Countries
OSCE	Organization for Security and Cooperation in Europe
PCA	Partnership and Cooperation Agreement (between EU and NIS)
PfP	Partnership for Peace
Phare	Poland–Hungary: Aid for Reconstruction of the Economy (subsequently extended to other countries)
PIC	prior informed consent
PPEWU	Policy Planning and Early Warning Unit (of the EU)
PSC	Political and Security Committee (of the EU)
QMV	qualified majority voting (in EU Council of Ministers)
REIO	Regional Economic Integration Organization
SAA	Stabilization and Association Agreement (with Western Balkans countries)
SADC	South African Development Community
SAP	Stabilization and Association Process (in Western Balkans)
SEA	Single European Act
SEM	Single European Market
SFOR	Stabilization Force (NATO led replacement for IFOR)
SHAPE	Supreme Headquarters Allied Powers, Europe (of NATO)
SIA	sustainability impact assessment
SITCEN	Situation Centre (of the EU)
Stabex	System for the stabilization of export earnings (in ACP countries)
Sysmin	System for the promotion of mineral production and exports (in ACP countries)
Tacis	Technical Assistance to the Commonwealth of Independent States
TEC	Treaty establishing the European Communities
TEU	Treaty on European Union
TNC	Transnational Business Corporation
TOA	Treaty of Amsterdam
TRIMS	trade related investment measures
TRIPS	trade related intellectual property measures
TRNC	Turkish Republic of Northern Cyprus
UNCED	United Nations Conference on Environment and Development
UNCHE	United Nations Conference on the Human Environment
UNCTAD	United Nations Conference on Trade and Development
UNDP	United Nations Development Programme
UNEP	United Nations Environment Programme
UNGA	United Nations General Assembly

UNGASS	United Nations General Assembly Special Session
UNPROFOR	United Nations Protection Force (in ex-Yugoslavia)
USTR	United States Trade Representative
VER	voluntary export restraint
WEU	Western European Union
WSSD	World Summit on Sustainable Development
WTO	World Trade Organization

Introduction

Our principal aim, in the first edition of this book (published in 1999), was to establish the extent to which the European Union was capable of functioning as an effective actor across the full range of its external activities. Our conclusion was that the importance of the Union in international affairs was greater than we had anticipated, but that its capacity as an actor was limited, in some policy areas more than others, by its distinctive character. That assessment remains valid. We also concluded that, in view of the challenges it then faced, the Union would be unlikely to develop further as an external policy actor.[1]

At the time of submitting this second edition (May 2005), the Union is again at a turning point. Enlarged to a membership of twenty-five, and confronted by numerous further demands for membership, but seemingly unable to agree the reforms necessary to accommodate such numbers, real questions are raised about the Union's future. Nevertheless, in the period since 1999, a number of important developments combined to strengthen the Union's capacity as an actor. In consequence, this second edition, while maintaining a focus on actor capability, also addresses questions concerning the *nature* of the EU as an actor. These include the extent to which the Union has attained a distinctive collective identity that informs the broad direction of its external activities; and, more specifically, the extent to which there has developed a capacity and willingness to provide strategic direction for external policy. A final question must concern the extent to which the enlarged Union can operate effectively in the absence of fundamental reform.

Our initial interest in the EU stemmed from a gradual realization that, in our areas of research (global environmental diplomacy, development policy), the activities of the Union impinged significantly. We were thus encouraged to develop an approach that, when we began researching the first edition in 1996, differed considerably from contemporary studies dealing with the external policies of the EU. Such studies, focusing almost exclusively upon the Union's halting attempts to develop conventional foreign policy capabilities, and explicitly or implicitly using the state as comparator, inevitably concluded that the EU had yet to develop a significant role in international affairs. Traditional analyses, we believed, were unable fully to capture the external impact of EU activities.

Hence, our second aim was to engage with contemporary debates within the discipline of International Relations (IR). Divergent approaches to the entities that may be considered actors in international politics have long characterized the discipline. While traditional (Realist) analyses have prioritized states as actors, pluralist approaches have conceptualized a multi-actor system that includes, *inter alia*, intergovernmental organizations and non-governmental organizations. None, however, has effectively conceptualized the EU as an international actor.

Our approach has self-consciously avoided entering into debates that seek to categorize the Union. The EU is not an intergovernmental organization as traditionally understood, nor is it a partially formed state. While it is clearly a regional organization, its degree of integration, and the range of policy competences and instruments it possesses, render comparison with other regional organizations such as the North American Free Trade Agreement (NAFTA) meaningless. We thus concluded that the Union should be treated as *sui generis*; and that our study would focus upon the extent to which the EU had acquired qualities of actorness. In particular we were and are interested in the processes through which such qualities might be constructed.

We have found a process-oriented approach to be invaluable, both because the Union is, itself, a project under construction; and because it is our view that actorness cannot be fully understood through study of the behaviour of the entity in question. Rather, actorness is constructed through the interplay of many factors, both internal to the Union and in the external environment of ideas and events that permit or constrain EU action. Our approach to actorness, which we develop in Chapter 1, comprises three elements – opportunity, which denotes the external context; presence, which captures the ability of the EU, by virtue of its existence, to exert influence beyond its borders; and capability, which signifies the ability to exploit opportunity and capitalize on presence.

In developing our model of actorness we have attached great importance to the understandings of those closely involved with the Union as an international actor, whether in the formulation and implementation of EU policy or as its interlocutors. To elicit these understandings, an intensive programme of interviews was undertaken between January 1996 and July 1997 (for the first edition) and, for this second edition, intermittently between March 2001 and April 2005. Interviewees involved with the internal policy process comprised officials of the European Commission and the Council Secretariat, staff of Member State Permanent Representations to the EU and national officials. To elicit understandings from the Union's external interlocutors, we interviewed third country diplomats from all regions of the world and representatives of non-governmental organizations. We are, of course, very much aware that the insights gained (with the exception of those from nationally based officials) reflect the view from Brussels, and are thus likely to accord greater prominence to EU activities than might otherwise be the case. Nevertheless several of the third country diplomats interviewed had been in post only a short time. While they knew their way around the complex EU system less well than their more experienced colleagues, their views on key points relating to EU actorness were not substantially different.

These exercises proved highly productive, giving insights concerning the manner in which shared understandings are constructed. We refer to our interview material in all the chapters that follow. Of particular interest, for this second edition, is the evolution of understandings over time – a matter we return to below. First, however, we provide a brief overview of the evolution of the EU itself as an external policy actor.

Evolution of the EU as an external policy actor

Since its creation in 1958 the European Community, and subsequently the Union, has evolved considerably. It has expanded, through a series of enlargements, from six to twenty-five members. Four additional states (Bulgaria, Croatia, Romania and Turkey) are candidates for membership and others have been offered membership in the future (the Western Balkans countries) or are actively seeking candidate status (Ukraine and other former Soviet Republics). Alongside this continuing expansion of membership, the years since 1958 have also witnessed a considerable increase in the scope of the Union's policy competences, most recently with the introduction of Economic and Monetary Union and the launch of the euro in 2002. The tensions between these processes of widening and deepening, and the institutional changes required to accommodate them, remain very much a current issue.

The early phases of community building in Europe took place in the aftermath of the Second World War, at a time when Cold War tensions were increasingly evident. Thus European policy elites faced two major challenges – the need to reconstruct their economies and societies; and the need to ensure a stable and secure external environment in which the processes of reconstruction might prosper. In 1950 this latter concern was largely met through the creation of the North Atlantic Treaty Organization (NATO), which effectively linked United States military capabilities to the defence of Western Europe. Nevertheless, the need to secure peaceful relations between the states of Western Europe remained, as did aspirations to create a strong, united (Western) Europe capable of playing an important role in the post-War world.

To this end, two 'community-building' proposals were launched in the early 1950s. The European Coal and Steel Community (ECSC), established in 1952, aimed to initiate a process of economic integration, sector by sector, which would gradually reconfigure the political landscape of Europe. Alongside the ECSC proposals, ambitious plans were launched for a European Defence Community (EDC). This essentially federalist proposal envisaged a fully integrated European army under supranational control. The defeat of this proposal, after more than two years of debate, was a major setback for federalist aspirations. It ensured that the traditional subject matter of International Relations – foreign and security policy and defence – were excluded from the formal policy agenda of the European Community. They remained so for decades.

The European Community, established in 1958, was an exclusively civilian body. The Treaty establishing the European Communities (TEC) made no mention of foreign or security policy; nor, indeed, of the environment, an area of external policy where the Union has become an important global player. Responsibility for 'external economic relations', however, was entrusted to the Community. This flowed directly from the aspiration to create a common internal market, which necessitated formation of a customs union and levying a Common Commercial Tariff (CCT). In consequence the EC was accorded responsibility for formulation and implementation of external trade policy – a responsibility which was to include external representation and negotiation by the Commission (on behalf of the Member States) in matters of international trade.

A further sphere of external activity accorded to the Community by the TEC was the creation of association agreements with third countries, 'involving reciprocal rights and obligations, common action and special procedures' (TEC Article 310). This provision formed the basis for the construction of a vast network of differentiated and multi-faceted agreements between the EC and countries and regional organizations in all parts of the world. More specifically, it provided the foundation for a distinctive 'Community' approach to development cooperation. Chapters 5 and 6 consider in some detail the development and current scope of the Union's complex networks of external relations.

This significant growth of the Community's external economic activities was strengthened by the provisions of the 1987 Single European Act (SEA). The SEA, in providing for completion of the internal market, greatly increased its attractiveness to third parties, bringing demands for privileged market access from all regions of the world. The ability to grant, deny or withdraw such access remains among the most important policy instruments available to the Union. Moreover the magnetic effect of the single market continues to generate demands for membership or closer association, thus providing the Union with its most important source of external influence. Undoubtedly it is the economic strength of the Union that provides the foundation for all its external activities, and Chapter 3 carries a heavy burden in establishing the Union's roles as economic power and trade actor.

The SEA had significance, also, for the growth of the Union's roles as foreign policy actor and in global environmental diplomacy. Both these policy areas had developed outside the TEC provisions but were formally incorporated by the SEA. In relation to environmental diplomacy, the SEA explicitly recognized the importance of this policy area. It also provided for qualified majority voting, thus enabling the Community to participate more effectively in international negotiations on ozone depletion in the late 1980s (see Chapter 4).

In terms of foreign policy, the SEA began a process of institutionalizing a system of foreign policy coordination between Member States, known as European Political Cooperation (EPC), that had begun in 1970. In this 'high politics' area of traditional international relations, however, the EPC process remained outside the Community framework. While habits of cooperation were established among Member State foreign ministers, diplomats and officials, it was not until the end of the Cold War, followed by entry into force of the Treaty on European Union in 1993, that attempts were made to develop a Common Foreign and Security Policy (CFSP) for the newly created European Union, and thus to give overall political direction to external policy.

The TEU undoubtedly had importance for the development of the Union's roles as a global actor. It incorporated the aim that the Union should 'establish its identity on the international scene' (Article 2) and provided, for the CFSP, a set of general objectives (Article 12) and policy instruments (Articles 13–15). For the first time, too, an institution to support the formulation of foreign policy was established within the EU framework, in the form of Directorate-General E of the Council Secretariat.

In practice, however, these innovations proved largely symbolic. The Pillar structure created by the TEU placed CFSP firmly in the intergovernmental Pillar II, where Member State unanimity is required. It thus formally separated the political direction to be provided by CFSP from the Community's economic instruments in Pillar I. Hence, in its early years of operation, the CFSP was impeded not only by the need for consensus among the Member States, but also by tensions and turf battles between the European Commission and the Council. Neither of these problems has yet been fully resolved, as we shall see in future chapters.

Disappointment with the functioning of the CFSP led to Treaty reform, most notably through the 1999 Treaty of Amsterdam (TOA). The TOA provided for a new position, of High Representative for the CFSP, which was filled by Javier Solana. Charged with oversight of the CFSP, Solana proved an able appointee. He has made an important contribution to the effectiveness and visibility of the Union as a foreign policy actor. Subsequently the 2003 Treaty of Nice strengthened the institutional structure of the CFSP and formalized arrangements that would give effect to the military and policing instruments of the ESDP. The draft Constitutional Treaty, agreed by all Member States in June 2004, would have contributed further to the evolution of these policy areas. As we shall see in Chapter 7, its provisions will form a basis for future reform.

Much of the impetus for this process of strengthening the Union's foreign policy capacity has derived from changes in the external environment since the end of the Cold War. As will be apparent from the chapters that follow, we have attached considerable importance to the external policy context, or opportunity structure, in the construction of EU actorness. The end of the Cold War had great significance for the evolution of the EU as a global actor, most evidently in terms of the new and unprecedented demands emanating from Central and East European countries (CEEC), eight of which became Member States in 2004.

The ending of East/West tensions also produced a policy environment that was, in principle, conducive to development of the Union's roles as a civilian actor. In practice, however, the outbreak of violent conflict in (former) Yugoslavia in the early 1990s, and the failure of the Union's exclusively civilian approach, underlined the inadequacies of the nascent CFSP. This initiated a process that would lead, by 1999, to the unprecedented decision to develop a military capability for the Union, through the ESDP. Given its novelty, and the reluctance of Member States to accord a role to the Union in this most sensitive of policy areas, the ESDP has developed surprisingly rapidly – as we shall see in Chapter 8. Subsequently, the September 2001 terrorist attacks on the United States provided impetus to external policy developments in the area of Justice and Home Affairs (border management issues) and the Pillar III area of cooperation on criminal matters, which are discussed in Chapters 2 and 8 respectively.

In the context of this increasingly visible and proactive external activity, the deep divisions between Member States, in 2003, over the invasion of Iraq, inevitably cast a shadow. Nevertheless, during that year, the Union's first ESDP operations were conducted. 2003 also saw publication of the European Security Strategy, a document that aims to provide an overarching framework for the Union's roles as a global actor;

and guidance for use of the full range of policy instruments to which it now has access. This reminds us that, while the novelty of ESDP instruments inevitably attracts the attention of commentators, the economic instruments falling within Pillar I continue to provide the foundations of EU actorness. To assist understanding of policy-making within and between the Pillars, we provide a brief outline of the policy processes.

The making of external policy

The ability to formulate policy is among the basic requirements for actorness discussed in Chapter 1. Formulation of EU external policy is complicated by the Pillar structure, which formally separates economic from political dimensions of policy and provides for different decision processes in each Pillar.

Policy in Pillar I is formulated according to the Community method. Here, the Commission has sole right of initiative, although the Council of Ministers, in conjunction with the European Parliament, ultimately decides upon the fate of measures proposed. An important role is played by the Committee of (Member State) Permanent Representatives to the EU (COREPER) and numerous Working Groups, comprising national officials and experts, which report to COREPER. Policy dossiers are discussed in the Working Groups and channelled to the Council via COREPER, whose recommendations are regularly adopted. The Council itself discusses only the more controversial items. In Pillar I, Council decisions are frequently taken by qualified majority voting. Hence, in external policy areas within Community competence – such as trade, development and humanitarian assistance, and aspects of environmental policy – there is not an automatic Member State right of veto.

In Pillar I policy areas the role of the Commission is significant, both in initiating policy proposals and managing policy instruments. The Commission also negotiates, on behalf of the Member States, in multilateral forums such as the World Trade Organization, in aspects of global environmental policy, and with third parties seeking various forms of trade or association agreement. Here it should be noted that the European Community (but not the Union) enjoys formal legal personality and is thus empowered to enter into binding international agreements on behalf of the Member States. In Chapters 3 and 4, where the Commission's role as negotiator is discussed, we will see that its officials are considered to be formidable interlocutors by the third party representatives with whom they interact.

In order to formulate and implement policy in the various Pillar I areas of external activity, the Commission is organized into a number of Directorates-General (DGs). The DG structure has been the subject of frequent reorganization and, at the time of writing the first edition, there was considerable geographical fragmentation of the Commission's external efforts, as Table 0.1 shows. The major reorganization undertaken for the 2000–4 Commission produced a more rational structure, which has been maintained by the Barroso Commission (and is also shown in Table 0.1). Nevertheless the coordination problems experienced in the past have persisted, albeit to a lesser extent – an obvious example being the separation of African, Caribbean and Pacific countries from other developing countries in Asia and Latin America. Again issues concerning the structure of the Commission, and its implications for

Table 0.1 Directorates-General with responsibility for external relations

1995–2000 (the Santer Commission)	1999–2004 (The Prodi and Barroso Commissions)
Directorate-General I Common Commercial Policy. Responsible for multilateral trade negotiations at the World Trade Organization (WTO). Relations with North America, Japan, China, South Korea, Hong Kong, Macao and Taiwan.	**Directorate-General Trade** Common Commercial Policy. Responsible for multilateral trade relations at the WTO. Responsible for bilateral trade negotiations with all third countries.
Directorate-General IA Common Foreign and Security Policy. Relations with Central and East European Countries and New Independent Sates. Relations with Turkey, Cyprus and Malta. Responsible for Commission Delegations to third countries.	**Directorate-General External Relations** Common Foreign and Security Policy. Relations with all developed countries and Asian and Latin American countries. Responsible for European Neighbourhood Policy. Responsible for Commission Delegations to third countries.
Directorate-General IB Relations with the Southern Mediterranean countries, Middle and Near East and most of developing Asia.	**Directorate-General Enlargement** Relations with candidate countries and prospective candidates in the Western Balkans.
Directorate-General VIII Relations with African, Caribbean and Pacific countries.	**Directorate-General Development** Relations with African, Caribbean and Pacific countries.
European Community Humanitarian Office Humanitarian assistance.	**European Community Humanitarian Office** Humanitarian assistance.
	EuropeAid Cooperation Office Implementation of all long-term assistance programmes.

policy-making, will be revisited throughout the book. A further, related problem that emerged from our interviews is the uncertainty and lowered morale among officials who have been subject to frequent reorganization.

Despite its significance in Pillar I, the potential for the Commission to play a leadership role in external policy is limited by its relative marginalization within Pillar II (CFSP), where the Commission has no special right of initiative and is merely considered to be 'associated' with the policy process. In the past this has caused considerable resentment among Commission officials, and has resulted in delays in implementation of CFSP decisions requiring Pillar I policy instruments. While habits of cooperation have developed over time, tensions still arise in new policy areas, as we shall see in Chapter 7.

The CFSP Pillar is intergovernmental in character – that is policy formulation takes place outside the Community framework, within the Council of Ministers and its various Working Groups, on the basis of unanimity.[2] Originally CFSP matters, alongside many others, were dealt with in the General Affairs Council. With the explicit aim of enhancing external policy formulation, the Council structure was reformed in 2002. Foremost among the reforms was creation of a General Affairs and External Relations Council which meets in two formations. Thus the External Relations Council considers trade and development policy alongside CFSP and ESDP. This change explicitly recognized the interconnections between the political and economic dimensions of external policy.

Institutional support for CFSP within the Council framework was initially modest, and much depended upon the capacity and commitment of each successive six-monthly Presidency.[3] However, amendments to the TEU since its entry into force in 1993 have considerably strengthened the Pillar II policy process. Within the Council Secretariat the most important innovations are the appointment of the High Representative and the creation of a Policy Planning and Early Warning Unit (in 1999) and, subsequently, the development of military committees and structures. Of great importance, too, has been establishment of the Political and Security Committee (comprising senior Member State diplomats based in Brussels) as the operational hub of CFSP and ESDP.

Questions for the second edition

Several of the changes outlined above have, of course, occurred since publication of our first edition. They raise issues that impinge directly upon the new questions addressed by this present edition. Thus, in Chapters 2 and 8 we consider whether access to military instruments undermines the civilian identity that has been constructed for the Union. A related question concerns the potential for the European Security Strategy to provide strategic direction for the Union. And to what extent would prioritization of security issues jeopardize the Union's established commitment to development and humanitarian assistance and to protection of the natural environment?

These questions are addressed throughout the book. Here, since we place great emphasis upon shared understandings in the construction of EU actorness, we briefly review the changing perceptions and expectations of those interviewed for the first and second editions, placing particular emphasis upon evolving understandings among third party representatives.

In our early interviews (1996–7) a number of persistent themes emerged. Third party interviewees referred, without exception, to the considerable challenges involved in interacting with the EU, which is 'quite unlike dealing with an individual state government'. The complexity of the EU, and the related difficulty of ascertaining the cause of policy blockages, was one theme; a second the extremely hard bargaining positions adopted by Commission negotiators. Moreover, distinctions were frequently drawn between the effectiveness of the Commission and the uncertainty and inconsistency attending dealings with the Presidency. There is no doubt that the Commission's relative permanence and more ready access to economic policy instruments was seen as providing considerable advantages over the rotating Presidency.

While a number of interviewees commented upon the lack of overall political direction and impetus to external policy, the absence of military capability was not identified as an issue by any of the third party representatives interviewed – all of whom nevertheless considered the EU to be a significant actor. Frequent reference was made, however, to the Union's failure to derive political benefits, in terms of recognition and influence, commensurate with its economic investment. The EU's role in the Middle East was most commonly identified in this respect, although there were other areas, including humanitarian aid, where the Union's contribution was considered to have been largely unacknowledged. The overall thrust of these comments indicates that the EU was perceived, by those knowledgeable third party representatives whom we interviewed, to be more significant as an actor than is generally apparent; despite the failure fully to realize the political potential of its economic presence.

In our interviews for this second edition the first themes above remained very much to the fore. 'The complexity is daunting and the institutional balance is always shifting' typifies comments from third country diplomats. Such comments reflect both continuity and change. New factors include the greater complexity of the trade agenda as a consequence of the introduction of new trade issues (see Chapter 3) and a perception that the European Parliament had become more important to external relations. In consequence many third country diplomats considered that it had become necessary to develop contacts with Members of the European Parliament in addition to Commission, Council and Member State officials.

When asked about the principal changes that had occurred since 1999 a typical comment was – 'There has been intensification and diversification of relations'. The reference, here, was to a perceived increase in political significance of the Union. This was evident even among third country diplomats whose principal preoccupation was with issues of market access. For example, a view from the Antipodes was that 'serious discussions' take place on 'regional issues, climate change, development assistance, Iraq, the Asia-Pacific'. Viewed more closely, from its Eastern border, the Union was 'a very important player, an exporter of stability'. And, from the same region, 'the Union is a growing force in international relations … we look at it very closely to safeguard ourselves from negative consequences'.

Perceptions of the increased political role of the Union were complemented by views on the role of Javier Solana, the High Representative for the CFSP. Solana was considered by several third country diplomats to have increased the effectiveness and visibility of the Union's foreign policy. However, the 'Solana effect' was striking in comments from officials of the Council Secretariat and the Member State Permanent Representations. Without exception they referred to Solana's appointment when asked about the principal changes in the Union's role as a political actor since 1999. Here, commentary from Commission officials reflected their sense of marginalization from key processes and events. 'Solana is always ahead of [External Relations Commissioner] Patten when there is a photo-opportunity', it was claimed.

Despite this general sense of the Union as a more effective political actor in recent years, numerous impediments to actorness remain – as we shall see in the chapters that follow.

Organization of the book

In attempting to provide an assessment of the capacity and character of the European Union as a global actor we have been concerned to explore the continuities and discontinuities between actorness in different issue areas. In consequence our chapters are organized 'horizontally' according to policy area – an approach that departs from the more traditional focus upon the Union's bilateral relations with third countries or regions.

The first two chapters address our principal research questions. Chapter 1 focuses upon the construction of actorness. It proceeds from a survey of approaches to actorness in International Law and the International Relations literature to an examination of the social construction of the Union's various external roles. Here, the focus is upon the interaction of opportunity (the external context of ideas, events and expectations), presence (representing the structural power of the Union) and internal capability. Chapter 2 considers competing collective identities offered to the Union and their implications for its role(s) in international affairs. Is the Union an inclusive or exclusive actor; can it be seen as having a dominant identity that is value-based, as a civilian or normative power, which distinguishes it from other global actors, notably the USA?

Chapters 3, 4 and 5 discuss the relatively well-established 'Community' policy areas of trade, environment, and development and humanitarian assistance. In discussing the Union as an economic power, Chapter 3 charts the development of the Union as global trade actor and leading member of the World Trade Organization, rivalled only by the USA. It discusses the regulatory effects of the Single Market upon outsiders and considers the Union's policies on agriculture, services and monetary affairs. The economic presence and actor capabilities of the Union provide the framework and instruments through which it continues to conduct most of its external relations, detailed in subsequent chapters. Chapter 4 considers the way in which the environmental implications of the European market led the Union to become the most significant actor in the new politics of the global environment. There are a number of difficulties with this policy area because the conduct of external environmental policy is shared between the Community and the Member States. However, this has not prevented the Union's engagement with a broad spectrum of international environmental regimes, including that for climate change. Chapter 5 begins with a consideration of the Union's long established and distinctive model of development cooperation with African, Caribbean and Pacific countries. It then discusses the more traditional pattern of relations with Asia and Latin America before considering the role and activities of the European Community Humanitarian Office.

Chapter 6 considers the Union as a regional actor. Relations with candidates and neighbours are a key policy priority and it is here that (in relation to the Western Balkans) the full range of the Union's policy instruments has been employed. The offer of a membership perspective to several countries of the region may prove to be the source of considerable EU influence. However, non-candidate neighbours to the East and South are included in a new initiative, the European Neighbourhood Policy, which may prove less effective as a policy tool. Ultimately, the reputation of the Union as an external actor depends upon the success of its regional policies.

Chapters 7 and 8 consider the relatively less developed (and essentially intergovernmental) Pillar II areas of foreign and security policy. Chapter 7 considers the evolution of a foreign policy capability for the Union from its modest beginnings in the 1970s. It discusses the contemporary CFSP structures and the policy instruments at the Union's disposal. Finally, there is an assessment of the potential for the European Security Strategy to provide an overarching framework that would guide EU external activity as a whole. Chapter 8 can be regarded as a continuation of the previous chapter because its subject, the European Security and Defence Policy, provides a new and controversial set of military and police capabilities for the CFSP. The relationship between the Union and military force is discussed, from the Cold War through the Balkan problems of the 1990s to the formation of the ESDP. Its structures and instruments are described and its emergent and limited roles considered. Finally we consider whether these new actor capabilities have compromised the essentially civilian external identity of the Union.

1 Conceptualizing actors and actorness

> It is because foreign policy is widely associated with nation states that the EU is overlooked as an international political actor by many who study international relations.
>
> (Ginsberg 2001: 12)

It is true that, in the International Relations (IR) literature, there has been both a neglect and an underestimation of the EU's role in world politics. This reflects two factors. First, the considerable influence of traditional state-centric approaches to IR, which has served to direct research and shape the perceptions of researchers. Second, a related tendency to focus attention upon a limited range of external activities considered to comprise the 'high politics' of traditional foreign policy – encompassing, primarily, the activities of foreign ministries, diplomats and militaries. A state-centric worldview, combined with a focus upon those policy areas where the EU might be considered least effective, would inevitably lead to the conclusion that the EU is not (or not yet) an actor. And, over the years, many commentators have so concluded (Bull 1983; Hill 1993; Zielonka 1998).

Recently, however, a number of authors have explicitly rejected the state-centric approach and narrow focus of traditional IR, with its concentration on the formal institutions and policy outcomes of the CFSP process. Hazel Smith, for example, highlights the 'staggering effect' of state-centric approaches, which succeed in excluding all that is significant and distinctive in the EU's external activity (Smith 2002: 9). Similarly, Karen Smith focuses upon 'what the EU actually does in international relations' – which she identifies as promotion of regional cooperation, human rights, and democracy/good governance; conflict prevention and the fight against international crime (Smith 2003: 2 and *passim*). Roy Ginsberg, too, in his evaluation of 'the extent of the EU's international political influence', departs significantly from traditional IR approaches (Ginsberg 2001: 15). The empirical findings of Ginsberg's extensive research accord with our own initial hypothesis concerning the cumulative impact of the EU. Ginsberg found the EU's external political influence to be substantial, leading him to the conclusion that conventional depictions of the EU, by IR scholars, as 'economic giant – political pygmy' are invalid (Ginsberg 2001: 277–9).

These important studies provide a relatively comprehensive overview of the scope and impact of EU external activity. Nevertheless, significant omissions remain. In particular they retain an approach to external policy which is 'primarily political and security-related (as opposed, for example, to international environmental protection or the promotion of sustainable development)' (Smith 2003: 13). Given the extensive discussion of notions of environmental security in recent years, this exclusion of environmental issue areas from the domain of politics/security is still redolent of the traditional foreign policy agenda.[1] Moreover, as we shall see in Chapter 4, it is in the field of environmental diplomacy that particularly strong claims are made for the importance and effectiveness of EU action. Hence, our concern to assess the cumulative impact of the EU's external activities, demands that we examine all of the policy areas in which the Union is involved.

Our central concern, however, is not to analyse the scope and influence of EU external activity, important and demanding as these tasks are, but to consider the extent to which the Union has become an actor in global politics. Since the EU is a unique, non-traditional and relatively new contender for this status, conceptualizing its international roles, or 'actorness', presents many challenges. We develop an approach to actors and actorness that enables us to treat the EU as unique, in terms of its character and its identity, and also as part of an evolving multi-actor global system. In particular, given the relative novelty and rapid development of the EU's external activity, we are concerned with processes of change. Key questions thus become – which internal and external factors have permitted, promoted or constrained the development of the EU's roles in global politics; how and to what extent is the EU perceived as an actor by its various 'audiences'?

In attempting to answer these questions we have found particularly useful a social constructivist approach that conceptualizes global politics in terms of the processes of social interaction in which actors engage. These formal and informal processes shape the evolution of actors' identities and provide contexts within which action is constrained or enabled.[2] Before elaborating upon this approach, however, we locate our arguments within the wider, historical debates in International Relations – which have in turn contributed to the construction of understandings about the roles and identity of the EU.

Our discussion begins with a brief examination of the relatively formal approach to actorness in International Law. Subsequently, treatments of actorness in the IR literature are reviewed, and an assessment made of behavioural (agency focused) and structural approaches to analysis. We then consider the contribution of social constructivist explanations focusing upon the co-constitution of structure and agency in a process of structuration (Giddens 1984). Finally, drawing upon constructivist approaches, we outline our approach to analysis of EU actorness based upon the interrelated concepts of opportunity, presence and capability.

Actorness in International Law

A formal answer to the question 'how do we recognize an actor?' is provided by Public International Law. This, by definition, focuses upon the inter-state system, and has developed its own formal concept of actorness in terms of the notion of legal personality. As Coplin (1965: 146) argued, International Law has too often been treated exclusively as a system of restraints upon state activity, rather than as 'a quasi-authoritative system of communicating the assumptions of the state system to policy-makers'. Foremost amongst these assumptions, since the Treaty of Westphalia in 1648 formally inaugurated the modern state system, has been the notion of the sovereign territorial state as the subject of International Law, and associated recognition doctrines. Only states could make treaties, join international organizations and be held to account by other states. Legal actorness confers a right to participate, but also to be held responsible by other actors, and to incur obligations.

Whereas for several hundred years there may have been a reasonable correspondence between the legal framework and the political realities of international life, by the mid twentieth century the 'Westphalian assumptions' were under challenge. The first formal recognition of this came with the 1948 International Court of Justice (ICJ) decision on the legal status of the United Nations, in the context of the organization's right to present a claim for damages in respect of the assassination of its mediator in Palestine, Count Folke Bernadotte. The Court established that the UN had inter-national legal status, but that this was not equivalent to that of a state:

> By applying the well-known principle of the 'specificity' of corporate persona, the UN and by extension all international organizations are recognized as having the necessary and sufficient capacity to exercise the functions which have been devolved to them by their charters. If IGOs (Intergovernmental Organizations) are in fact governed by international law, distinct from the members which constitute them, they do not enjoy the whole range of competencies which are accorded by law to states.
>
> (Merle 1987: 293–4)

On this basis the European Community achieved legal personality, although its formal status has been that of an intergovernmental organization and it is entitled to act only in areas of legally established competence.

Creation of the European Union, upon entry into force of the Treaty of European Union (TEU) in November 1993, introduced complications for the accordance of actorness in formal, legal terms. The TEU established the Union as an overarching framework comprising three 'Pillars', a political compromise which facilitated partial integration of foreign and security policy (Pillar II) and aspects of internal state security (Pillar III), alongside the existing European Community (Pillar I). As a consequence of the political sensitivity of the Pillar II and III policy areas, the TEU did not accord legal personality to the Union. Hence the Union, unlike the Community, cannot conclude international agreements. Not surprisingly this has proved a source of confusion to third parties. However, the Constitutional Treaty, agreed by Member States in June 2004, accorded legal personality to the Union (Article I-7).

This dynamic process of attaining legally sanctioned actorness might be described in terms of the interaction of institutional/legal structures and political agency, in a process of 'structuration', where International Law both reflects and shapes the evolution of practice. Certainly there has been an ongoing dialectic between the assertion of rights by bodies such as the EU and the understandings that inform the responses of other members of the international community. This process is evident, too, from the manner in which the EC came to be accepted as the successor to the Member States as a party to certain international agreements. Under the General Agreement on Tariffs and Trade (GATT) it was informally accepted as a player representing the contracting parties. It only became a party in its own right, alongside the Member States, with the creation of the World Trade Organization in 1994 (Macleod *et al.* 1996: 235–6). In other areas where a common policy applies, such as international fisheries agreements, the EC is a direct successor to the Member States.

A similar dynamic can also be seen to operate in reverse, in that there is a tension between external demands that the EU should play an active role in the international system and reluctance on the part of Member State governments to accord competence to the EC in areas considered sensitive domestically. Competence is the EC term for 'powers', and can be defined as:

> … the authority to undertake negotiations, conclude binding agreements, and adopt implementation measures. Where competence is exclusive it belongs solely to the Community to the exclusion of the Member States. Where it is concurrent either the Community or the Member States may act but not simultaneously.
>
> (Macrory and Hession 1996: 183)

Disputes relating to the extent of competence have been evident, to a greater or lesser degree, in all the policy areas we discuss.

The importance of evolving practices in the complex and dynamic processes surrounding attribution of formal legal status reminds us that, while it is necessary to have an understanding of actorness as ascribed by International Law, it is hardly sufficient. Moreover, there is no necessary correspondence between the achievement of legal personality and actorness in behavioural terms. Weak states may have full legal status but are insignificant as actors, while bodies such as the European Union can fulfil important functions without possessing legal personality. Nonetheless, the law continues to have significance in so far as it provides an institutional context which contributes to shared understandings concerning who may act and the appropriateness (or otherwise) of actors' behaviour.

Actors and actorness in International Relations

In conventional International Relations the answer to the question 'how do we recognize an actor?' is essentially the same as that given by the lawyers: statehood. The question of actorness has always been a fundamental one for students of IR, even if the concept itself has not been subject to the kind of scrutiny that its significance would seem to merit. It is fundamental because the term actor is used as a synonym for the units that constitute political systems on the largest scale. Actors, here, are akin to the players in a theatre – the *dramatis personae*. The attribution of actorness in this sense will determine what is studied.

The classical, or Realist, approach is state-centric, leading to a focus on the international (really inter-state) political system. Other actors, such as intergovernmental organizations and transnational business corporations, may be admitted but their functions are seen as essentially subordinate to those of states. While, in some respects, this approach resembles that of International Law, it departs from it in significant ways. Thus Realism provides an essentially political analysis in which power differentials between states are a central focus. Ultimately, the actors of interest to Realists are powerful states.

From the 1970s pluralist approaches challenged the simplicities of Realism. By identifying a range of significant units, in which non-state actors were not necessarily always subordinated to states, they portrayed an alternative 'mixed actor' (Young 1972) or even a 'world' or 'global' political system (McGrew and Lewis 1992; Bretherton and Ponton 1996).[3] The relative inclusiveness of such approaches reflects the condition of world politics at a time when Realist state-centric analyses, with their focus upon 'superpower' relations, appeared inadequate to conceptualize a world greatly complicated by the emergence of what Keohane and Nye (1977) describe as complex interdependence.

During the post-Vietnam period, when United States economic and even military predominance appeared to be in question, policy-makers within the European Community began actively seeking to enhance the external policy capabilities of the EC, in particular through a system of foreign policy coordination, known as European Political Cooperation (EPC), initiated in 1970. The abrupt ending of the Cold War, which posed a major challenge to IR scholars and, indeed, to practitioners, exposed the inadequacies of the EPC system. The re-emergence of armed conflict in Europe in the early 1990s, and fears of widespread political instability in Eastern Europe, suggested a significant role for the EU as a regional security actor. For scholars in the fields of IR and Foreign Policy analysis, this aspect of the Union's external activity has subsequently been the primary focus of investigation. In principle, at least, the EU's emerging external role could be accommodated in a mixed actor system.

In practice, however, attempts in the IR literature to categorize the actors in world politics have not been notably successful in accommodating the EU. It has been categorized as an intergovernmental organization (Keohane and Nye 1973: 380; Rosenau 1990) in ways that failed to capture the Union's multi-dimensional character. In other similar exercises the EU has been disaggregated; in effect, appearing as several actors. Alternatively actorness may explicitly be attributed to the European Commission, an approach utilized by Hocking and Smith in discussing 'the new variety of international actors' (1990: 75). This approach captures an element of the present reality and is in line with legal competence, where the Commission acts on behalf of the European Community. However it prevents us from assessing the overall impact of the EU – which is our central purpose. A solution may lie in abandoning formal organizational and legal criteria in favour of a behavioural approach.

Behavioural criteria of actorness

The attribution of actorness does more than simply designate the units of a system. It implies an entity that exhibits a degree of autonomy from its external environment, and indeed from its internal constituents, and which is capable of volition or purpose.

Hence a minimal behavioural definition of an actor would be an entity that is capable of formulating purposes and making decisions, and thus engaging in some form of purposive action.

In IR approaches to actorness, the concept of autonomy has been accorded central importance (Cosgrove and Twitchett 1970: 12; Hopkins and Mansbach 1973: 36; Merle 1987: 296) This requirement tends to highlight the internal procedures of the Union and it has been possible to arrive at different conclusions concerning autonomy dependent upon the voting arrangements in the Council of Ministers and the competences exercised by the Commission.[4]

Alongside autonomy, the ability to perform 'significant and continuing functions having an impact on inter-state relations' and the importance accorded to the would-be international actor both by its members and by third parties have also been stressed as behavioural criteria (Cosgrove and Twitchett 1970: 12). Achievement of actorness requires that these criteria must be met 'in some degree for most of the time', a formula which allowed Cosgrove and Twitchett (1970: 49) to conclude, even in the late 1960s, that the EC was 'a viable international actor'.

We return, later, to behavioural criteria of actorness in relation to the contemporary EU. In particular, we address the issue of actor capability, which both contributes to and overlaps with autonomy. Defined by Gunnar Sjöstedt (1977: 16) as 'capacity to behave actively and deliberately in relation to other actors in the international system', actor capability is regarded by Sjöstedt as a function of internal resources. As already indicated, however, we consider an exclusive focus on internal factors – and, indeed, on behavioural criteria generally – to be inadequate in assessing actorness. In consequence, before examining the internal factors which contribute to (or inhibit) EU actorness, we question the extent to which its external activities are the product of purposive action, or agency; or are shaped or constrained by structural factors.

Structural approaches to actorness

Explanations of social phenomena which rely upon action or agency make up one side of the agency/structure debate that has long been evident in most of the social sciences. During the 1960s there was considerable discussion in the IR literature of the 'level of analysis problem' – whether attention should be confined to a 'state as actor' focus or to the structure of the system.[5] While the 1970s saw the scope of International Relations broaden to admit 'new' international actors, the predominant approaches to analysis continued to privilege the state; moreover they remained primarily focused on behaviour. However, the end of the decade was to be marked by a new structural direction in the Realist tradition in the form of Waltz's neo-Realism.

The assumptions of structural Realism, as developed by Waltz (1979), are primarily political. Waltz's focus is the international political system, the organizing principle of which (anarchy) determines the behaviour of the units (states). In consequence the sources of behaviour are to be found not in the differing characteristics, or volition, of state actors but in their fundamental need, in an anarchical system, 'to compete with and adjust to one another if they are to survive and flourish' (Waltz 1979: 72). In these circumstances relative power capability is the only significant factor differentiating between states. Hence the interests of states, and ultimately their behaviour, are externally given and, in principle, predictable; they derive from the distribution of power in the international system.

From this perspective, the emergence of the European Community was permitted because the Cold War bipolar structure served both to diminish the importance of the West European 'powers' and mitigate the conditions of anarchy in which they operated. While other obstacles remained, an important impediment to cooperation was removed – that is 'the fear that the greater advantage of one would be translated into military force to be used against the others' (Waltz 1979: 70). Such an analysis might provide useful insights into the creation of the EC, but seems of little relevance to the post-Cold War situation where a plausible prediction following the ending of bipolarity, would have been dissolution of the EU and renationalization of security by its Member States, in some 'back to the future' scenario (Mearsheimer 1990).[6]

Undoubtedly the ending of the Cold War bipolar system has had a significant impact upon the EU. In particular the emergence of conflict and instability in Eastern Europe in the early 1990s posed major challenges. However, these were not met by individual Member State responses, but by a range of EC-led financial assistance and diplomatic initiatives which led, eventually, to the incorporation of eight former Eastern bloc countries into the Union in May 2004, with the prospect of further Eastern enlargements in the future. Moreover, the potential for instability in Europe did not induce Member State governments to increase national defence expenditure, rather it was met by proposals for the development of an EU military capability. Nevertheless, there have been and remain significant divisions between Member States on the issue of military security. These divisions, however, are not easily explained from the perspective of structural Realism. While it might be predicted that an EU military capability would be supported only by the smaller, 'less powerful' Member States, in practice the situation is very much more complex. Divisions on this issue, for example between the UK and France (or indeed between Ireland and Belgium), do not reflect power differentials, rather they reflect a complex mixture of national traditions and attitudes. A final concern over the relevance of structural Realism arises from its starkly one dimensional character; it takes no account of those economic structures most significant for a political entity founded upon a Customs Union and a Common Market.

A primary focus of Marxist and neo-Marxist accounts of the global system is the structure of a capitalist economy which has become increasingly integrated in its operation, and extensive in its scope. From this perspective the state retains a significant, although not fully autonomous, role; subordinate to the needs and interests of capital. As with neo-Realism, international politics is portrayed as a struggle for power; but here power is conceived in terms of economic advantage or dominance. There are considerable divergences between theorists adopting a broadly neo-Marxist perspective, and here we briefly examine the implications, for EU actorness, of two such approaches – the 'world-systems theory' of Immanuel Wallerstein and the neo-Gramscian approach of Robert Cox.

Wallerstein (1984) discerned the roots of a 'capitalist world-economy' in the sixteenth and seventeenth centuries and considers the capitalist economy to have become global in scope by the end of the nineteenth century. His concern is to explain the broad historical evolution or 'cyclical rhythm' of the world-system (1991: 8). This perspective encourages us to see significant events, such as the end of the Cold War, in the context of phases of expansion and stagnation in the world-economy. Here a contemporary role for the EU emerges in maximizing the potential of Western European states in challenging US hegemony. Attempts by the Union to compete with the US and Japan in high technology, through the Single Market programme and subsequently the Lisbon Strategy,[7] may be portrayed in Wallerstein's terms (1991: 55) as a struggle 'to gain monopolistic edges that will guarantee the direction of flows of surplus ... clearly it must be of concern to Europe that she will come a poor second in the race'.[8]

While also focusing upon economic structures at the highest level, Robert Cox (1993) sees the emergence of a global capitalist economy as a contemporary and still incomplete phenomenon. In consequence his attention focuses more directly upon the specifics of contemporary change in Europe, rather than upon its location in the panorama of world historical events. In this sense the perspectives of Cox and Wallerstein are complementary. In Wallerstein's analysis, however, the determining role attributed to economic structures is almost complete; little space is left for creative political action and, as in the case of neo-Realism, differences between states are unimportant. For Cox differences in domestic political arrangements, or forms of state, are highly significant (Cox 1986). A central concern is that state autonomy, and the related ability to maintain alternatives to the neoliberal state form, has been eroded through a process of 'internationalization'. Thus, increasingly, 'states must become the instruments for adjusting national economic activities to the exigencies of the global economy' (Cox 1993: 260). In consequence, in the context of Europe, he is concerned with the ability of the social democratic state to withstand the pressures of economic globalization.

Cox's analysis has considerable relevance for our discussion. The emergence of 'macro-regional economic spheres' has been in part a response to economic globalization. It has been associated, in turn, with the emergence of complex, multi-layered systems of governance which challenge Westphalian assumptions of sovereignty and territoriality and which might be considered as a new form of state, or 'international state' (Cox 1986, 1993). Of particular significance, here, is the increasing disjuncture between political/military power, which remains territorially based (the latter most particularly in the USA), and economic power, which is both more widely dispersed and less amenable to regulation at the level of the state. For the EU the consequences of this disjuncture are particularly acute: their impact is twofold.

First, economic globalization has generated considerable pressure for the transfer of economic management functions to the EU level. Here, tensions between neoliberal and social democratic forms of governance can be resolved in circumstances largely divorced from public scrutiny. This separation of economic oversight from domestic political systems has been a crucial factor in disrupting a strong European tradition of political control over economic processes; in consequence it is likely to be maintained (Cox 1993: 284). The implication for our discussion of actorness is that there is no impetus, emanating from structural factors, towards the provision of overall political direction for EU external activities. On the contrary, the interests of global economic liberalism are best served by a continued separation of 'political' foreign policy and external economic relations. Clearly the increased formalization of this separation inherent in the EU's Pillar structure accords with this analysis. Nevertheless it fails to capture the subtle processes by which this has been partially overcome, for example in the evolution of practice in relations to political use of economic instruments.[9]

Second, the increasing separation between the economic and political/military dimensions has resulted in an implicit division of global management tasks between the USA and the EU. Thus major policy decisions at the global level on non-military matters such as trade or environment require, at minimum, US acquiescence; where military enforcement is at issue the US plays a leading role. The EU, for its part, is increasingly expected to pay a large proportion of the cost, while gaining little political advantage. This has been evident in the Middle East, former Yugoslavia and in the broader area of humanitarian assistance. It is not well known, for example, that the European Community Humanitarian Office (ECHO) has become the world's largest single donor of humanitarian aid.

In this analysis, the EU's role as a 'civilian power' paymaster is assigned rather than chosen. We shall argue below, however, that structural determinants cannot alone account for EU actions, rather they reflect the complex interplay of a number of factors which combine to shape EU collective identity. Here, EU reluctance to play a 'paymaster' role in relation to Iraq's reconstruction following the 2003 invasion is instructive. It is indicative not only of agency, but of the importance of normative commitment to preservation of peace and respect for the rule of law embedded in EU treaties (TEU, Article J.1). These norms, which were violated by the invasion and occupation of Iraq, are important contributory factors in the construction of the Union's collective identity.

Ultimately structural explanations alone prove inadequate for a conceptualization of EU actorness. Nevertheless, through their focus on the EU's position within global political and economic structures, such analyses contribute in important ways to our understanding. Their emphasis on the constraints which structural factors impose upon the identities, roles and policy options available to the EU provides a necessary antidote to behavioural approaches which conceive of actorness as primarily a function of political will and the availability of resources. Nevertheless, structural explanations provide insufficient scope for differentiation between the units in a system, and hence the singularity of the EU. Moreover, they provide only one side of a complex story. Bipolarity doubtless permitted, and economic globalization encouraged, the development of cooperation in Europe. However, the European Union as a political form is unique; its creation reflects a combination of external demands and opportunities, and political will and imagination on the part of its founders. The subsequent development of the EU also reflects, we believe, a complex yet dynamic relationship between structure and agency. In short, there is a need for an approach which emphasizes neither structure, nor agency, but the relationship between them. Here social constructivism can help us.

The social construction of actorness

Constructivist accounts that seek to reconcile structural and behavioural approaches to explanation are largely derived from sociological theory.[10] They arise from, and attempt to resolve, what Alvin Gouldner (1971: 54) has termed 'the unique contradiction distinctive of sociology'; that human beings inhabit a social world, which they have themselves created but to which they are also subject. In addressing this contradiction, constructivists seek explicitly to redress the determinism of structural analyses. Thus, for constructivists, structures are seen as providing opportunities as well as constraints – they are potentially enabling; at the same time actors have agency – that is they are rule makers as well as rule takers.

In constructivist analyses, structures are not defined in material terms (as neo-Marxists and neo-Realists would maintain); rather they are intersubjective. Thus, in relation to the international system:

> Intersubjective systemic structures consist of shared understandings, expectations and social knowledge embedded in international institutions. … Intersubjective structures give meaning to material ones, and it is in terms of meanings that actors act.
>
> (Wendt 1994: 389)

In this analysis, structures alone do not determine outcomes, rather they provide 'action settings' or distinct patterns of opportunity and constraint within which agency is displayed. Actors are, to varying extents, knowledgeable about the settings within which they are located and are potentially able to change them (Hay 1995: 200). Hence space is provided for differentiation between actors, in that construction of distinctive identities, and the effectiveness of agency, reflect a number of factors at both the actor and the structural levels.

At the actor level differentiation could reflect availability of resources, although decisions concerning when and how to deploy resources will be shaped by the complex interplay of a range of factors, some of them structural, as we saw in the Iraqi case above. Here, resources include not only economic and military instruments; of great importance, also, are access to knowledge and political will/skill. Indeed the creation of the European Community itself, and its 'relaunch' via the 1987 Single European Act, provide clear evidence of the importance of political energy and creativity in responding to opportunities afforded by international structures.

At the structural level, differentiation reflects the extent to which actors are strategically well placed – in that structures are selective, that is they are more open to some types of strategy (and by implication actor) than others. Hence, in the sphere of external economic activity, EU market opening strategies and imposition of a range of conditionalities (see Chapter 3) accord well with dominant understandings about the efficacy of neoliberal economics. Here the EU is not seen to be 'swimming against the tide' (Bretherton 2001). Conversely, the understandings embedded in the international legal system privilege state actors, as we have seen, and there has frequently been reluctance in international fora to accord recognition to a hybrid entity (more than an intergovernmental organization, less than a state). Despite this, the statements and everyday practices of third party representatives we interviewed showed, repeatedly, that the EU is already considered to be an important global actor – a further demonstration of the dynamic processes through which intersubjective understandings evolve. Thus, in considering the evolving practices that constitute EU external policy, our research has placed particular emphasis upon the perceptions and actions of third parties. These, we believe, contribute significantly to the shared understandings that frame the policy environment, shaping practices of Member State governments, EU officials and third parties alike.

Constructivists, then, posit a dialectical relationship between agency and structure, and it is to this process of construction and reconstruction that we refer in employing the concept of structuration. Actions, which include discursive practices, have consequences, both intended and unintended, and structures evolve through the renegotiation and reinterpretation of international rules and practices. However, constructivists see structure and agency as essentially intertwined, indeed mutually constitutive, and hence only '*theoretically* separable' (Hay 1995: 200, original emphasis). It is precisely the interconnection between structure and agency which is of interest in a study of the evolving identity, roles and actorness of the EU.

As we have observed, the EU is unique, both in conception and evolution. Its creation reflected the dynamic interaction between innovative political actors and the opportunities and constraints afforded by changing international and domestic structures. The subsequent evolution of its external roles reflects a similar dynamic – with the added dimension that the Union's emergence as an international actor itself contributed to the evolution of the meanings and practices which constitute intersubjective international structures. The EU's contribution, in this respect, has been a function not only of intentional decisions or purposive actions but also of its existence, or presence, as a new form of international actor which has defied categorization.[11]

Inevitably, the development of the EU has engendered considerable academic debate about the evolving meanings of international practices and principles – a debate which, of course, also contributes to this evolution. It has, for example, become commonplace for academics, and for politicians, to conceive of sovereignty as divisible. For Keohane and Hoffman (1991: 13) the EU is 'essentially organized as a network that involves the pooling or sharing of sovereignty'. This network analogy, which is commonly applied to the EU, also has the effect of challenging territoriality. Indeed the availability of multiple, shifting meanings of 'Europe' encourages one author to conclude that 'Europe really isn't there' (Walker 2000: 29).

For our purpose, we have found useful John Ruggie's notion of the EU as a 'multiperspectival polity', which captures something of the complexity of the EU's external personality (Ruggie 1993: 172). As we shall see in the chapters which follow, the EU is a multifaceted actor; indeed it can appear to be several different actors, sometimes simultaneously. It has, moreover, a confusing propensity to change its character, or the persona it presents to third parties – as we shall see from the discussion of environmental negotiations in Chapter 4. Thus, in some circumstances the EU resembles an international organization (indeed, as already indicated, it is regarded by International Lawyers as an international organization *sui generis*). In other circumstances it has state-like qualities that cannot be divorced from territoriality, in the sense that stringent rules operate in relation to the flow of goods, and of people, into its space. Moreover, as representatives of states applying for EU membership would confirm, the EU as a 'network' can be remarkably impenetrable. Undoubtedly the eligibility criteria constructed by the EU both contribute to and reflect aspects of its emerging collective identity.

The complexity of the EC/EU as a 'multiperspectival polity' is, of course, experienced on a daily basis by third party representatives. From our interviews it was evident that they encounter (or employ) a range of practices that reflect understandings about the complexity of the EC/EU as an actor. Thus, for example, Commission negotiators, in dealing with third parties, exploit the dense and uncertain characteristics of EC decision processes as a bargaining asset. While our interview material suggests that this ploy contributes to the reputation of Commission officials as formidable negotiators, there is also evidence of reciprocity, in this respect, on the part of the Commission's interlocutors. Thus, in the course of negotiations:

> ... some third parties, while having a very clear idea of the state of affairs at any given time, nevertheless professed '*faux naif*' bewilderment in an endeavour to draw diplomatic advantage from the Community's uncertainties and ambiguities.
> (Nuttall 1996: 130)

Here an excellent example of the evolution of international practices is provided in a speech by then French Prime Minister, Alain Juppé, to a Conference of Ambassadors, in September 1994:

> It is your role as ambassadors of France, both to assert the identity of the European Union and to explain the specific positions defended by France within the institutions thereof. It is without reservations, therefore, that you will endeavour, wherever you are, to affirm the political identity of the Union.
> (Quoted in de La Serre 1996: 36–7)

Similar processes of discursive construction apply to the internal dynamics of policy formulation – as we shall see (in Chapters 3, 5 and 6) from the Commission's unacknowledged but very evident involvement in foreign policy under the guise of external economic relations.

In a very real sense, then, understandings about the EU, its roles, responsibilities and limitations, form a part of the intersubjective international structures that provide the 'action settings' of global politics. At the same time the EU contributes to the processes of constructing international structures, both as a purposive actor exploiting opportunities presented, and through its unique presence. It is to these issues that we now turn.

Opportunity, presence, capability: EU actorness under construction

Our approach to the EU as an actor 'under construction' envisages a complex set of interacting processes, based on the notions of presence, opportunity and capability, that combine in varying ways to shape the Union's external activities:

- Opportunity denotes factors in the external environment of ideas and events which constrain or enable actorness. Opportunity signifies the structural context of action.
- Presence conceptualizes the ability of the EU, by virtue of its existence, to exert influence beyond its borders. An indication of the EU's structural power, presence combines understandings about the fundamental nature, or identity of the EU and the (often unintended) consequences of the Union's internal priorities and policies.
- Capability refers to the internal context of EU external action – the availability of policy instruments and understandings about the Union's ability to utilize these instruments, in response to opportunity and/or to capitalize on presence.

Opportunity

Opportunity denotes the external environment of ideas and events – the context which frames and shapes EU action or inaction. While opportunity is a structural attribute it should not be seen as an 'inert background'; rather it conceptualizes a dynamic process where ideas are interpreted and events accorded meaning (Jacobsen 2003: 56). Thus, while shared understandings constitutive of intersubjective structures shape the context of action, these understandings are not divorced from material conditions; rather they interpret (reflect/distort) them in various ways. The EU itself, in acting or refraining from action, is a participant in the social interaction that characterizes international relations, thus contributing to understandings of the meaning of opportunity. Our approach to EU action includes the discursive practices which contribute, for example, to the construction of the Union's collective identity.

Our concern is with the external environment of ideas/events since the early 1980s. From this time, changes in perceptions of the international system and its operation have interacted with changes in the ideological climate, to produce understandings of unfolding events which have been conducive to increased EC/EU involvement in global politics. Here we refer to notions of interdependence and globalization, and to the impact of the ending of the Cold War. More recently, too, the events of the 11 September 2001 and their aftermath have been accompanied by competing discourses which offer very different understandings of the Union's identity and roles.

From the mid-1970s the international system was increasingly perceived in terms of its (primarily economic) interdependence. In circumstances where the ability of states to govern effectively was deemed to be in question, the EC, a partially integrated regional policy system, appeared well placed to act on behalf of its members in the management of interdependence. Subsequently notions of interdependence have largely been supplanted by an insistent discourse of globalization, in which the individual state is depicted as relatively impotent in the face of non-territorial economic actors operating in a system of globalized production and exchange relationships. More than ever before, the strong economic focus of globalization discourses, and the emphasis upon the inadequacy of the state to regulate the activities of globally oriented economic actors, appeared to present opportunities, indeed imperatives, for the EU to act externally on behalf of its members. Certainly this interpretation has enjoyed wide currency among politicians and officials within the EU, not least in the European Commission, where globalization discourses have been routinely invoked in the 'construction of Europe as a valid space in the light of external challenge' (Rosamond 2001: 168).

In policy terms the neoliberal underpinnings of (dominant) globalization discourses, involving reconceptualization of the relationship between states and markets – to prioritize the latter – has resonated with a policy orientation already embedded at the Community level. This has been reflected internally, in the Single Market programme and the subsequent Lisbon Process, and externally in the Union's trade relations and market opening strategies. Dominant (neoliberal) discourses of globalization, have interacted with, and been greatly encouraged by, the series of events that constituted the definitive ending of the Cold War. These events significantly altered, in a number of ways, the patterns of opportunity and constraint which contextualize EU action.

Most fundamentally, the end of the Cold War brought into question what had appeared to be the more or less fixed boundaries of the European project, thus challenging the appropriation of the concept 'European', by the European Community. This was initially manifested in the removal of impediments to membership of the West European neutral countries, in particular Finland, which had long been prevented, by its closeness to the Soviet Union, from pursuing an independent foreign policy.

Of greater significance, however, was the chorus of demands to 'return to Europe' emanating from Central and East European Countries (CEEC). This initiated a discourse of 'return' – of reuniting Europe – which incorporated notions of Western betrayal of and responsibility towards the East.[12] Again, prominent commentators within the EU contributed to this discourse through frequent reference to a sense of historical and moral responsibility consequent upon the West's abandonment of Eastern Europe at the end of the Second World War (Sjursen 2002: 505). Here Fierke and Wiener (1999) argue persuasively for the importance of discursive commitments, or promises, made to the East during and after the Cold War. Failure to honour these promises would have impacted negatively, not on its material interests, but on the collective identity of the EU.

The consequences of these processes of reconstructing Europe's identity (and borders) have been profound. Inevitably the 2004 enlargement of the EU, which saw the accession of ten new members (eight of which were CEE countries), has changed the Union's character. Moreover the process of enlargement is not complete. Hence, for Schimmelfennig and Sedelmeier (2002: 500), a further consequence of the 'reuniting Europe' discourse has been acceptance of enlargement as 'a permanent and continuous item on the EU's agenda'. Indeed it seems clear that overlapping discourses of responsibility and inclusiveness (through enlargement) were central to the offer of future EU membership to the five countries of the Southern Balkans in 1999.[13]

A final area where the ending of the Cold War presented new opportunities for EU actorness proved particularly challenging. The Soviet Union's (and subsequently Russia's) diminished ability to exert control, or even influence, over its former empire generated fears of political instability in countries close to the EU's borders. The outbreak of armed conflict in former Yugoslavia initially provoked attempts to employ a discourse of responsibility. Thus, as conflict broke out in June 1991, Jacques Poos (Luxembourg Foreign Minister speaking for the EC Presidency) was moved to declare 'This is the hour of Europe'. This discourse of responsibility, however, was quickly superseded by a discourse of 'tragic failure' (Buchan 1993). As Brian White has observed (2001: 106), 'No other area of international activity to date has attracted more adverse publicity for either the Community or the EU'. So pervasive has been this discourse of failure that it has almost totally eclipsed the 'considerable and significant political impact' of EU activities during the Yugoslav conflicts – 'given the constraints of its capabilities' (Ginsberg 2001: 83).

This evocation of a 'capability-expectations' gap affecting the Union (Hill 1993) reminds us that, while opportunity may be discursively constructed, the processes of construction cannot be divorced from material conditions. In circumstances where continued US military commitment to Europe has been uncertain, concerns about potential security risks on the borders of the Union have been very evident since the early 1990s. They have been accompanied by a new discourse of EU responsibility which envisages the Union abandoning its 'civilian power' identity and developing 'all the necessary tools' to deal with crises and conflicts near its borders and beyond.[14] Developments in the sphere of military capability have been quite rapid. But, as we shall see in Chapter 2, constructions of the Union as a (potentially) conventional superpower are inconsistent with dominant understandings of EU identity, and have been strongly contested. 'We don't do war', it is claimed (Black 2003).

The context of EU external action was significantly changed by the terrorist attacks of 11 September 2001 and the ensuing, US-led 'war on terror'. In the immediate aftermath of 9/11 the Union employed a range of civilian instruments in a coherent and proactive manner. However, the 2003 invasion and subsequent occupation of Iraq fundamentally challenged norms, such as commitment to multilateralism and the rule of law, that are constitutive of EU identity. The use of military means without a clear United Nations mandate, while supported by some Member State governments (most notably the UK, Spain and Poland), was vociferously opposed by publics across the EU, several Member State governments and prominent spokespersons representing EU institutions.[15]

The significant differences between Member State governments on the Iraq issue undoubtedly impinged on the Union's presence. Nevertheless a new discourse of 'responsibility' has derived from the desire to distance the Union from US interpretations of the 'war on terror'. The US post-9/11 doctrine of pre-emptive defence, and subsequent military action, was seen within the EU as part of a regrettable pattern of US unilateralism, and abdication of responsibility, across a range of policy areas from traditional diplomacy to climate change. Inevitably, US 'irresponsibility' contributes to discourses of EU responsibility, manifested in the ambition to establish an alternative, EU approach to the threat of terrorism. In a communication seeking to define 'the common objectives of outside action', the European Commission makes a clear statement of this position:

> The Union must be in a position to take more resolute and more effective action in the interests of sustainable development and to deal with certain new risks, associated in most cases with the persistent and growing economic and social imbalances in the world. It must therefore stick up for a strategy of sustainable development, based on a multilateral and multipolar organisation of the world economy, to offset any hegemonic or unilateral approach.
>
> (Commission 2002a: 11)

In the absence of a dominant understanding of appropriate responses to 'new' security challenges, the events of 9/11 and their aftermath have provided an opportunity for the EU to adopt new roles and responsibilities. This is acknowledged in the European Security Strategy produced in response to these events – 'Europe should be ready to share in the responsibility for global security and in building a better world' (European Council 2003: 1). The Union's security roles cannot simply be chosen, however, they will be constructed through a process that takes account of its capabilities and its international presence.

Presence

It is our contention, broadly following Allen and Smith (1990), that the Union's growing presence in international affairs has been of great significance. By presence we refer to the ability to exert influence externally; to shape the perceptions, expectations and behaviour of others. Presence does not denote purposive external action, rather it is a consequence of being. In particular, presence reflects two intimately interconnected sets of factors that determine the reputation and status accorded to the EU by external audiences.

First, the character and identity of the EU. Character refers to the Union's material existence, that is the political system comprising the Member States and the common institutions of the EU. Identity attempts to capture the fundamental nature of the EU; it refers to shared understandings that give meaning(s) to what the EU is and what it does. Identity is, we believe, of great importance to actorness. Not only do identities suggest roles, and associated policy priorities, it is in terms of understandings about identity that policy is evaluated. Consequently we deal with identity at some length in Chapter 2, and our treatment below of this aspect of presence is relatively brief.

The second element of presence refers to the external, often unanticipated or unintended, consequences of the Union's internal priorities and policies. Here, the relationship between the EU's presence and actorness can be relatively direct, in that EU internal policy initiatives may generate responses from affected/aggrieved third parties which, in turn, necessitate action by the EU.

In terms of the Union's character, a particularly strong attribution of presence is provided by Charles Kupchan (2002: 145): 'An EU that encompasses Western and

Central Europe and whose wealth rivals that of the United States is *in and of itself* a counterpoise to America' (emphasis added). Certainly the successive enlargements of the EU, and the attractiveness evident from the plethora of further membership applications, contributes to its international presence. In economic terms, too, Kupchan's claim has credibility. In terms of overall influence in international affairs, however, the multifaceted and often disputatious character of the EU political system, with its proliferation of derogations and opt-outs, serves to diminish its presence.[16] Nevertheless, we consider that important processes of influence are associated with the character of the EU as, for example, a model of regional economic integration and a 'Community of security' (Commission 1997a); 'a stabilising factor and a model in the new world order' (European Convention 2003: 1). We return to these matters in Chapter 2.

In relation to the second, more specifically policy-related aspect of presence, the most fundamental sources of the Union's influence are, inevitably, economic. Here we focus on three areas (which are discussed more fully in Chapter 3) – the important but largely unintended external impacts of the Common Agricultural Policy (CAP) and of the Single Market, and the impact of the introduction of the euro.

The CAP provides an excellent example of the processes by which actorness can be induced when third parties respond to the Union's presence in ways which necessitate, in turn, a response by the EU. The mechanisms through which agricultural policy has been managed, and its success in stimulating domestic agricultural production, have impacted significantly on world market prices for temperate agricultural products; prompting political reactions from aggrieved third parties affected by loss of export earnings. The accession of Greece, Spain and Portugal in the 1980s greatly increased the quantity of Mediterranean products affected by the CAP. This impacted negatively upon the export potential of the Maghreb countries, triggering a reaction which, in combination with other factors, led the EC to negotiate a new relationship with non-member Mediterranean countries. Here, the EC's presence initiated a process through which actorness was constructed.

The impact of the Single Market has been of even greater significance. In particular it has had a magnetic effect in attracting foreign investment and in stimulating demands, from a wide range of third countries, for privileged access. Thus the notion of the Commission as 'gatekeeper of the Single Market' is developed in Chapter 3. Here, again, increased presence prompted reactions to which the EC was ultimately obliged to respond actively. One of the most important effects of the Single Market was the initiation of a process that led to the creation of the European Economic Area, and ultimately the accession of three new members (Austria, Finland and Sweden) in 1995. This enlargement further increased the size and attractiveness of the Single Market, and hence the EC's presence in the international economy. The much more substantial 2004 enlargement has also enhanced the presence of the EU, not least through expansion of the Single Market into areas where economic growth is rapid and consumer demand vibrant.

Unlike the CAP and Single Market programme, introduction of the euro in 1999 (followed by physical circulation of coins and notes in 2002) did not prompt fears of significant, negative implications for third party economies. Nevertheless it represents both an important symbol of political commitment to the European project and a major deepening of the integration process. Thus, despite the decision of the UK, Denmark and Sweden to remain outside the eurozone, it might be anticipated that the Union, equipped with the second largest currency after the US dollar, would attain a major additional source of external influence. It might also be anticipated that introduction of the euro would generate responses from third parties, in particular expectations that the Union would assume the responsibilities associated with a major international currency (Bretherton 2004: 201).

In practice, however, international responses to the launch of the euro were muted, and have remained so. Initially there was an insistent discourse of failure, characterized by somewhat gleeful, derisive comments. Goldstein (2001: 1) provides a nice example: 'the first government venturing to stash its national reserves in unreliable euros was that of Saddam Hussein'. Juxtaposed with this has been a (less insistent) discourse of potential, wherein the euro is considered as a future rival to the dollar (Feldstein 1997; Kupchan 2002: 137). This reminds us that the meanings attributed to EU activities by third parties are important, not least in relation to currency issues, where shared understandings about credibility and confidence are crucial. Moreover it is evident that such understandings are not universal – dominant and subordinate actors have different stories to tell about the significance of the Union's presence. Thus, while experienced globally to some extent, it impacts with particular intensity in circumstances where third party expectations are focused primarily upon the EU – that is, where there is heavy dependence upon access to the Single Market or an aspiration to achieve membership status.

Overall, however, the Union's presence has undoubtedly increased over time as a consequence of the expansion of its size and policy scope. It has been mitigated, nevertheless, by internal factors, associated with understandings concerning the efficacy and legitimacy of the EU's policy processes, which have tended to influence third party expectations of the EU's ability to act. It is to these issues of capability that we now turn.

Capability

Capability refers to the internal context of EU action or inaction – those aspects of the EU policy process which constrain or enable external action and hence govern the Union's ability to capitalize on presence or respond to opportunity. Here our focus will be on those aspects of the Union's character that impinge most particularly upon the possibilities for external action – the ability to formulate effective policies and the availability of appropriate policy instruments.

Much of our discussion is concerned with the material conditions of the EU policy environment. Nevertheless, here as elsewhere, the meanings attached to these conditions are of great significance. Understandings among third parties about the effectiveness of the Union's policy process, or the appropriateness/availability of policy instruments, contribute in important ways to its international presence. Internally, too, competing discourses attribute distinctive meanings to the components of capability, in that Euro-sceptics and Euro-enthusiasts tell very different stories about how the Union works and what it should (or should not) do. These competing discourses, and a range of pragmatic positions in between, have impacted significantly upon the Union's construction as a multiperspectival polity with elements both of intergovernmentalism and supranationalism.

Our treatment of capability draws upon the work of Gunnar Sjöstedt (1977). However, Sjöstedt's complex scheme is not elaborated here, rather we propose four basic requirements for actorness:

- Shared commitment to a set of overarching values.
- Domestic legitimation of decision processes and priorities relating to external policy.
- The ability to identify priorities and formulate policies – captured by the concepts of consistency and coherence, where:

    – consistency indicates the degree of congruence between the external policies of the Member States and of the EU;
    – coherence refers to the level of internal coordination of EU policies.

- The availability of, and capacity to utilize, policy instruments – diplomacy/ negotiation, economic tools and military means.

European values?

The first of these requirements is relatively unproblematic. The Common Provisions of the Treaty on European Union set out very clearly the values and principles to which the EU and its Member States claim to be committed, and which contribute to understandings of the Union's identity. These range from economic and social progress and sustainable development, to democratic governance and the rule of law.[17]

Domestic legitimation?

The second requirement is more evidently problematic. Inclusion of domestic legitimacy in a consideration of external policy reflects the growing significance of policy-making at the EU level. This raises issues of legitimacy for two reasons. First, there is a perception that, despite insistence upon adherence to democratic principles on the part of Member States and third parties, the EU itself suffers a democratic deficit. Second, it is evident that, as EU policies impinge more directly upon the daily lives of individuals, policy implementation will increasingly be dependent upon public consent, forbearance and even active support.

Over the past decade a number of commentators have expressed concern that the EU is suffering a 'legitimacy crisis' (García 1993; Laffan 1996; Obradovic 1996). Despite these concerns, there appears to have been sustained public acceptance of the need for EU action in areas where Member State initiatives are perceived to be inadequate. Overwhelmingly these are external policy areas (Taylor 1996; Leonard 1997; Commission 2001a, 2003a). Particularly strong approval has been expressed for a Union role in 'maintaining peace and security in Europe', which was seen as the second highest priority (after combating unemployment) for the Union as a whole (Commission 2001a: 35). There has also been sustained approval of an EU role in foreign and defence policy, and in relation to overseas development and global environmental issues.

Clearly the meanings of such survey material are open to construction. One interpretation is that they indicate a broad understanding that collective representation, via the EU, maximizes Europe's influence in international affairs. While this may prove a fragile basis for legitimation of EU external policy, it is significant that, in October 2003, 81 per cent of respondents to a Eurobarometer survey considered that the EU should play an enhanced role in the Middle East peace process (Commission 2003a: 59).

Identification of priorities, formulation of policies?

As will be evident from the chapters which follow, the ability, *in principle*, to identify policy priorities and formulate coherent policies is not in question. In question, rather, is the extent to which this ability is realized; and this varies considerably according to issue area and policy sector. Inevitably, as in any complex decision making system, divergent understandings of interest generate tensions over the identification and prioritization of goals. Nevertheless policy coordination within the EU system is affected by difficulties which flow from its unique character. We refer to these as the problems of consistency and coherence.

Consistency denotes the extent to which the bilateral external policies of Member States are consistent with each other, and complementary to those of the EU.[18] Hence consistency is a measure both of Member State political commitment to common policies and of the overall impact of the EU and its Member States. Enlargement of the Union to 25 Member States, with more to follow, has inevitably exacerbated problems of consistency.

In those areas of external economic relations where there is exclusive Community competence (see our discussion of International Law above), and common policies are entrenched, consistency has not been a major problem. However, in areas of environmental policy, where competence is shared between the Community and Member States, consistency becomes very much an issue, as we shall see in Chapter 4. In relation to development policy and foreign policy, where Member State bilateral policies maintain a prominent role alongside EU efforts, consistency is of central importance. Put another way, claims that the EU is the world's largest trading bloc have a rather different meaning from claims that it is the world's largest donor of development assistance. In this latter case (which should not be confused with EC humanitarian aid), the development assistance total on which this claim is based amalgamates Community aid with Member States' bilateral aid. As we shall see in Chapter 5, while Member State governments have made a specific commitment to ensure consistency in this area, this has been pursued to only a limited extent in practice. Clearly, in this and other areas, lack of consistency impinges negatively upon EU presence. The bitter divisions over policy towards Iraq in 2003 remind us that the Union can be paralysed, and its reputation undermined, by problems of consistency.

In an effort to overcome problems associated with lack of consensus among Member States, there has been, in recent years, increasing tolerance of 'flexibility' within the EU. This has been manifested in a growing discourse of differentiated integration. Thus the TEU permitted the UK and Denmark to opt out of important policy areas, notably Economic and Monetary Union (EMU) – a provision that Sweden appropriated following accession in 1995. Subsequently, the Treaty of Amsterdam provided for 'constructive abstention' in an attempt to strengthen the Union's Common Foreign and Security Policy and the Nice Treaty elaborated 'General Principles' (Articles 43–5 TEU) for 'enhanced cooperation'. This would permit groups of Member States to move forward (rather than opt out) in policy areas encompassing all three of the Union Pillars.[19] In practice, however, the Member States have been reluctant to utilize these provisions.[20]

Coherence refers to the internal policy processes of the Union. In many respects the problems here are analogous to those affecting any pluralistic political system. Tensions between trade policy and environment policy, for example, are endemic; as are controversies over the extent to which sectors of the economy, in particular agriculture, can or should be protected from external competition. Nevertheless there are aspects of the EU policy system that have generated particular coherence problems.

The first of these is the Pillar structure itself, which has impinged negatively upon the coherence of external policy as a whole. In the early period after creation of the Pillar structure (by the TEU in 1993) tensions were very evident between the Commission, with its responsibility for the economic aspects of external policy (Pillar I), and the Council Secretariat, which is responsible for administration of CFSP and ESDP matters in Pillar II. Over the past decade, however, habits of cross-pillar cooperation have developed in many policy areas (Christiansen 2001). Nevertheless, our interviews with officials (between March 2001 and March 2005) indicated that resentments remain, particularly in areas of potential civilian/military interface such as civil emergencies or crisis management. While habits of cooperation are developing here too, for example in relation to civilian policing, the area is sensitive because it has normative as well as 'turf war' dimensions. Thus, in the Commission, there is uncertainty about a military capability for the Union, and a preference for its 'civilian power' identity.

An attempt to address coherence problems was made in 2002 when the Council structure was rationalized. Creation of the General Affairs and External Relations Council, with the latter configuration dealing with CFSP, ESDP, external trade and development cooperation, was intended to ensure overall coherence of the Union's external action. Within the institutions themselves, coordination problems are also evident. The General-Secretariat of the Council has been subject to momentous changes since the introduction of CFSP and ESDP. While new structures were created to deal with these issue areas, and additional personnel recruited, their functions were initially not clearly established. This led to divisions between new and established officials, and a number of 'futile turf wars' ensued (Interview, Council Secretariat, March 2003). However, as the new structures became more established, and ESDP became operational, these problems diminished (ibid.).

In the Community Pillar, despite frequent reforms and changes to its structure, aspects of the operation of the Commission have been an impediment to coherence.[21] The fragmentation of external policy between several Directorates-General (DGs) has been a particular problem. In an attempt to remedy this, the Prodi Commission (1999–2004) created DG External Relations which was intended, under the leadership of Commissioner Chris Patten, to provide overall coordination of EC external policies. Nevertheless, our interviews revealed widespread dissatisfaction with the performance of DG External Relations in the early years. It was considered to have yielded its principal functions to DG Trade, on the one hand, and EuropeAid on the other.[22] External Relations officials were said to be 'fed up, marginalized' (Interview, DG External Relations, September 2001); 'External Relations is in the process of being eviscerated completely' (Interview, DG Enlargement, September 2001). Our interviews revealed, also, that the frequency of past changes, and uncertainty about the future, had been harmful to morale. Tensions between DGs are reflected within the College of Commissioners, where the problem is exacerbated by the absence of a satisfactory mechanism for resolving disputes between Commissioners. In the absence of strong leadership from recent Commission Presidents, there has been a tendency for the most powerful DGs, and Commissioners, to prevail.[23]

Availability of policy instruments?

The instruments traditionally employed in pursuit of external policy objectives include political (diplomacy/negotiation), economic (incentives/sanctions) or military means. The Union has access, albeit to a varying extent, to all three types of instrument. As we shall see in Chapter 8 it is also developing the capacity to deploy externally a range of civilian policing and judicial measures. The ability to *utilize* all or any of these instruments depends, however, upon a number of factors – not least the extent to which problems of coherence and consistency are overcome.

The traditional diplomatic tools of declarations and démarches have been much deployed in the context of CFSP, and indeed its predecessor, European Political Cooperation (EPC). An example of proactive EU diplomacy is provided by the series of Troika démarches to Washington, Moscow, Pakistan, Iran, Saudi Arabia, Egypt and Syria in October 2001, in an effort to coordinate responses to the terrorist attacks of 9/11.[24] To facilitate more sustained diplomacy on behalf of the Union, the practice has developed of appointing EU Special Representatives to areas of particular concern such as the Balkans, the Middle East, the Great Lakes region of Africa and Afghanistan.

In addition to these CFSP instruments, the Commission operates an external service with some 130 delegations in third countries. They do not operate as a traditional foreign service, however. Political reporting is often 'very weak' and the focus of delegations, reflecting the principal areas of Community competence, has been 'first on trade, second on aid and only third on CFSP' (Interview, DG External Relations, July 2001).

The ability to negotiate with other actors in the international system is fundamental; indeed it is a condition of entry to the system itself. Accordance to the EC of international legal status, or personality, provides a formal right of entry in policy areas where the Community enjoys exclusive competence internally, particularly trade in goods. Elsewhere, however, the unwillingness of Member State governments to transfer competence to the Community in policy areas considered 'sensitive' means that competence can be mixed (shared between the EC and the Member States), disputed or unclear. This is a troublesome issue in environmental negotiations, as Chapter 4 will demonstrate. It should also be noted that particular problems apply to external aspects of monetary policy, in that no formal provision has been made for representation of the eurozone in international negotiations.

Negotiation is central to most EU external activity – whether in the multilateral setting of the World Trade Organization or in agreeing association or cooperation agreements bilaterally with third parties. Here competence to negotiate is not the issue; rather it is the effectiveness of negotiators operating within the constraints of the Union's singular system. Initially, the internal impediments (problems of consistency and coherence) to agreeing a mandate for negotiation are almost invariably apparent. A particular problem has been the lack of flexibility accorded to Commission negotiators in circumstances where changes to the mandate have to be renegotiated internally between 25 Member States. While this can delay or even jeopardize conclusion of negotiations, it can also have the effect of strengthening the Commission's negotiating position. Thus, in circumstances where the Community's economic presence looms large, and third parties are unwilling to take risks, the Community as a negotiator appears truly formidable. Indeed it was evident from interviews both with Commission officials and third parties that the EU uses its structural inflexibility as a negotiating ploy. Typical perceptions of the Commission's approach among third party representatives were: 'there are no free lunches'; 'we've cooked up a deal, take it or leave it'. Even among representatives of large third countries there was a sense of the Commission as a formidable negotiating partner. Without doubt, in circumstances where the economic weight of the EU can be utilized, the Commission is an effective negotiator.

In terms of economic instruments, routine use of the economic presence of the Union in the furtherance of broad policy aims is evident from most of the chapters that follow. The accordance of various forms of privileged access to the Single Market reflects political priorities to a considerable extent; moreover, insertion of explicit political conditionalities into aid and trade agreements has become routine, and increasingly intrusive. Non-compliance has, in a number of cases, led to full or partial suspension of privileges. As Piening has observed (1997: 10), the weight of the EU can be formidable when its displeasure is incurred.

The imposition of formal economic sanctions in the context of joint actions under the CFSP, and in order that the EU can speedily comply with UN decisions to impose sanctions, is an area that straddles the Pillars of the Union – in that the decision to impose sanctions falls within Pillar II and the instruments of policy within Pillar I. To address this issue the TEU introduced specific provision for the imposition of economic sanctions (Article 30 TEC) and financial sanctions (Article 60 TEC).[25] Subsequently, here as elsewhere, habits of cross-Pillar cooperation have led to the institutionalization of practice. This has been supported by decisions of the European Court of Justice (ECJ), whose judgements have illustrated 'in both practical and legal terms, that there is a direct link between the EC and CFSP' (Koutrakos 2001: 223). This rather nicely illustrates the interaction of internal practices and external expectations in constructing EU actorness.

The final set of policy instruments, and the most controversial, involves access to military means. ESDP was formally launched at the Cologne Summit in June 1999 and progress since then has been surprisingly rapid. As we shall see in Chapter 8, both Member States and non-members have made formal commitments of military forces and equipment, and of civilian personnel (police officers, prosecutors, judges and prison officers), for participation in EU crisis management operations. At the same time access to various NATO assets has been negotiated. As a result the ESDP was involved in its first (suitably modest) operations in 2003 – a police mission in Bosnia-Herzegovina and brief military missions in Macedonia and the Democratic Republic of Congo. In this sensitive policy area, however, a number of problems are likely to persist. Not least among these are the consistency problems associated with differing Member State perspectives on security matters.

Conclusion

This chapter has surveyed a range of approaches to actors and actorness from International Law and from International Relations. The attempt to apply these approaches to the EU has revealed two interconnected sets of problems. The first relates to ontological and epistemological questions concerning the nature of, and criteria for, actorness. The second flows from the unique and complex character of the EU itself.

We have defined an actor as an entity that is capable of agency; of formulating and acting upon decisions. Nevertheless we do not see agency as unlimited, rather we consider that the capacity to act reflects the interaction between understandings about internal character and capabilities and external opportunities. In examining the patterns of constraint and opportunity which contextualize agency, consideration was given to structural analyses that conceive of actors as subordinate to economic or political structures. Ultimately, however, our preference is for a social constructivist perspective that conceives of structure and agency as interacting dialectically. From this perspective structures are intersubjective; they comprise shared understandings that provide the context for and give meaning to agency. Since structures provide opportunities as well as constraints, and continually evolve, in response both to unfolding events and proactive action, a constructivist analysis can accommodate change and even permits novelty. Clearly this is a major advantage when considering the EU.

The unique character of the EU has proved a major challenge to IR scholars. Despite the development, from the 1970s, of a 'mixed actor' focus to analysis, it has proved difficult to accommodate a hybrid entity which is neither an intergovernmental organization nor a state, but which operates globally across a range of policy areas. Consequently the temptation to use the state as comparator when discussing the EU has proved difficult to resist. In our view, however, comparisons between the EU and other actors in the global system are likely to produce only limited insights. The EU is an actor *sui generis*. We conceive of it as a multiperspectival polity whose construction reflects both the experimentation of policy entrepreneurs and the opportunities afforded by the changing structures of the international system. Essentially, therefore, the EU remains in the course of construction. This approach accommodates its evolution over time and its shifting character at any one time; it also leaves open the question of its future destination.

In the following chapters we examine, across a range of policy areas, the complex interconnections between three sets of factors in the construction of EU actorness. First, capability, with particular emphasis upon internal coherence/consistency (which to a significant extent reflects political will to act). Second, understandings about the Union's presence, and the mechanisms by which presence contributes to the construction of actorness. Third, the patterns of opportunity and constraint that contextualize EU agency. This enables us to think in overall terms about the status of the EU in the global system, the sources of its influence and the impact of the understandings and expectations of third parties. Thus are the identity and roles of the EU as a global actor socially constructed and reconstructed.

2 Nature of the beast

The identity and roles of the EU

According to the existentialist school of philosophy 'existence precedes essence'. In foreign policy one might say that identity precedes interest.

(Cooper 2004: 190)

Our concern in this chapter is with constructions of the Union's collective identity and its associated roles in international affairs. These, we believe, impact significantly upon practices towards third parties. The relationship between identities, interests and behaviour, however, is neither simple nor linear. Identities do not directly determine interests, rather they perform a mediating function. Thus understandings about the external context of ideas and events, or the appropriateness or feasibility of alternative courses of action, are shaped by identity constructions that are themselves shifting and contested.

Since the EU is a political system under construction, with constantly evolving internal institutions and practices, and expanding membership, it is inevitable that its identity will be relatively fluid when compared with that of established states or international organizations.[1] Where EU Europe is, in terms of its geographical boundaries, remains uncertain (Christiansen *et al.* 2000; Walker 2000). And what it is, in terms of the values, principles and practices which constitute the Union's essence, is contested (Manners 2002; Nicolaïdis and Howse 2002). This sense of the Union as an unfinished project does not necessarily imply that its identity is indistinct; rather, as we shall argue below, the singularity of the EU is an important element of (some) understandings of its identity. Below we explore two facets of the Union's collective identity which impact differently on its prospective roles.

First, we consider a potentially inclusive identity based primarily upon understandings of the EU as a value-based community. Potentially, this provides opportunities for non-members, through approximating the Union's declared values, to draw closer to the Union – in order to gain privileged access to its market; to achieve closer association; or to accede to membership.[2] Here, outsiders are seen in relative terms – as more or less European. Understandings of the Union as inclusive, we believe, reflect a persistent, perhaps dominant, discourse, which is strongly promoted within the Union (in the founding Treaties and by EU representatives). They are also the subject of much scholarly debate, as we shall see.

Second, we consider alternative understandings of the Union as an exclusive community; as 'fortress Europe'. While not part of the dominant (inclusive) discourses emanating from within the EU, they reflect understandings of EU practices in policy areas ranging from market protection to immigration and asylum. Exclusive identities for the Union are associated with placing relatively fixed geographical and cultural boundaries around what is considered to be European. Here, outsiders tend to be seen, not as less European, but as non-European, or alien (Rumelili 2004: 37).

Both these inclusive and exclusive facets of the Union's identity are reflected in the Treaty on European Union. The TEU stipulates that any *European* state 'which respects the principles set out in Article 6(1) may apply to become a member of the Union' (Article 49, TEU). Article 6(1) states that:

> The Union is founded on the principles of liberty, democracy respect for human rights and fundamental freedoms, and the rule of law.

Before examining more fully these distinct facets of the Union's identity, and associated roles that may be proposed for the EU, we briefly consider the processes involved in identity construction.

Constructing the Union's collective identity

Identity is attained in the course of social interaction; through encounters with other actors and in the context of the external environment of institutions and events which enable or constrain EU action and which we have referred to as 'opportunity'. Collective identity is constituted by shared understandings, both within the EU and among third parties, about what the EU is, in terms of its character and its values, and what it should (or should not) do, in terms of its external policies and actions. Identity is, thus, an important aspect of the Union's international presence.

The processes through which identity is constructed are complex, and contested. Central, of course, is the ability to differentiate the (EU) self from others. Commentators disagree, however, about the extent to which the processes of differentiation have exclusionary connotations associated with negative stereotyping of others. Thus Anthony Smith (1992: 75–6) has warned of an EU collective identity constructed 'through opposition to the identities of significant others', with attendant dangers of 'cultural and racial exclusion'. In contrast, Ole Wæver (2004: 210) finds that EU identity construction relies 'to a surprisingly limited degree' on processes of negative othering.[3] Rather, Wæver has proposed Europe's own violent past as the other of the contemporary European Union. More generally, the singularity of the EU, in terms of its evolution and character, has been stressed as an important factor in constructing its difference from other actors, and hence its distinctive identity (Manners and Whitman 2002: 399; Smith 2003: 197–8). In this analysis, the EU's conduct is in part a function of its character; and its other is the traditional Westphalian state.

Both these negative/exclusive and relatively positive/inclusive forms of differentiation contribute to the processes of EU identity construction, as we shall see below. It is less easy to discern, however, the mechanisms by which this is achieved.

Identities, we have argued, reflect shared understandings about the essential nature of an entity, which are constructed through social interaction. For many constructivists, these understandings are gained through socialization, or social learning. These subtle learning processes can lead to internalization – that is 'the adoption of social beliefs and practices into the actor's own repertoire of cognitions and behaviours' (Schimmelfennig 2000: 112). Internalization is by no means automatic. It reflects the degree of congruence between values and beliefs already held by an actor and those encountered during interaction. In the case of the EU, it is frequently argued that internalization of understandings can occur through increased familiarity with EU institutions and practices, especially in the context of relatively small group interaction (Checkel 2001).[4]

Some support for the contention that internalization is associated with relative closeness and endurance of interaction is provided by our own interviews, which indicated gradations of recognition of, or commitment to, dominant (value-based) understandings of the Union's identity. Thus permanent EU officials showed greater commitment than seconded Member State representatives, who in turn showed greater commitment than Member State officials based in London.[5] Third party representatives similarly showed varying degrees of commitment, awareness or scepticism concerning the identity discourses emanating from within the Union. Again, understandings tended to reflect relative depth of interaction with the EU. Thus representatives of states on the brink of accession spoke positively of the Union as, *inter alia*, 'an exporter of stability' (Interview, CEEC Mission, January 2003).

Third party representatives involved in multi-faceted relations with the Union also made statements congruent with the Union's declared values – on human rights and climate change, for example, 'the EU is very clearly the leader' (Interview, External Mission, January 2003). Conversely, third party representatives whose experience of interacting with the Union was almost exclusively trade related made no reference to the EU's declared values. Their comments reflected understandings of the Union's identity as both exclusive and powerful – determined, for example, to impose its own internal trade regimes as the 'international standard'. These practices were seen as indicative of the Union as 'a major economic power'; 'almost a trade superpower' (Interviews, External Missions, September and October 2002).

It is important to note that, alongside the relatively subtle processes of social learning emphasised by many constructivists, EU representatives are actively involved in various practices of 'purposeful construction', intended to initiate and/or strengthen understandings about EU identity (Webber *et al.* 2004: 23). Statements asserting the values claimed to be constitutive of EU identity are frequently reiterated. They are enshrined in the Treaties, as is commitment to promote them externally – 'In its relations with the wider world, the Union shall uphold and promote its values' (Constitutional Treaty, Title I, Article I-3.4). They are also regularly proclaimed by prominent EU representatives. Thus, for example, Javier Solana speaking about 'Europe's place in the world' :

> Our common foreign policy cannot just be interest-based. Protecting and promoting values, which are part of our history and very dear to the hearts of

our citizens, must continue to be a priority. The values of solidarity, of tolerance, of inclusiveness, of compassion are an integral part of European integration. We cannot give up on them, especially now that ugly racist pulsions are surfacing again; and that fighting against poverty is becoming critically important to prevent whole societies falling prey to radical and terrorist tensions.

(Solana 2002: 2)

These identity claims are, in turn, acknowledged, contested or confirmed by the Union's audiences – by third party interlocutors, NGO representatives, the media and, not least, academic commentators, whose interventions also contribute to EU identity construction.[6] We are thus, ourselves, implicated in this process.[7]

The potential for numerous, competing contributions to identity construction raises a central question – to what extent do sets of *shared* understandings emerge from these various constructions of EU identity? In attempting to answer this question, and in selecting the two broad understandings of EU identity discussed below, our approach has been twofold. First, we have considered the prevalence of various identity discourses, both in published documents and literature, and from our own interview material. Second, we have assumed that condemnation of the Union for failure to act in accordance with proclaimed values demonstrates recognition of these values as constitutive of EU identity.[8] This latter is, of course, problematic. In particular it raises a further, central question concerning the relationship between identities and interests in constructivist analyses.

Should the Union consistently fail to act in accordance with proclaimed values, this would suggest that value-based identity is not a decisive factor in shaping behaviour. Thus it may be that the Union's external action is determined primarily by self-interested pursuit of advantage or material gain. An example, here, would be the argument that the European Neighbourhood Policy (ENP), which makes strong claims concerning promotion of the Union's values (see Chapter 6), was launched primarily in order to ensure security of energy supplies from peripheral countries (Gault 2004). Nevertheless, claims concerning the importance of the Union's value-based identity are not necessarily invalidated by the intrusion of interests. In shaping behaviour, values and interests are not mutually exclusive, rather they interact in a variety of ways according to context.[9] Thus, while the practices of well-resourced, purposeful and self-interested actors contribute to the construction of shared understandings, they do so within a context shaped in part by the Union's identity claims. The values so frequently expressed are very public. In consequence actors (including Member State governments), who would not necessarily subscribe fully to the values indicated by dominant understandings of EU identity, are nevertheless identified with these values by others. Expectations are important, and behaviour judged to be incongruent or cynical can result in a loss of credibility. Over time, the benefits of conforming may leave little incentive for deviant behaviour (Schimmelfennig 2000: 119).

Whether through internalization, or as a significant and insistent frame of reference, identity, we believe, is influential in shaping EU action and offering, or circumscribing, the roles available to the Union as an actor. In consequence, the content of the Union's collective identity matters. It is to this issue that we now turn.

Inclusive identities: the EU as singular actor

An EU identity as a singular actor, we have argued, implies that the processes of differentiation between self and other, which are central to identity construction, are based primarily on the characteristics of the (EU) self deemed to distinguish it from others. While this can involve constructing the self as superior to others, as the various 'narratives of projection' of the Union's characteristics and values demonstrate (Nicolaïdis and Howse 2002: 769), it is not dependent upon attribution to others of negative characteristics or stereotypes. Hence, an identity based upon the singular characteristics and/or proclaimed values of the Union is, in principle, inclusive – it is open (or partially open) to those who demonstrate 'commitment to shared values' (Commission 2004a: 12).[10]

Civilian power Europe?

The most enduring characterization of the EU as a singular actor has been François Duchêne's (1972) notion of 'civilian power Europe'. This encompasses both the characteristics and the values of the (then) Community, thus:

> The EC will only make the most of its opportunities if it remains true to its inner characteristics. They are primarily: civilian ends and means and a built-in sense of collective action, which in turn express, however imperfectly, social values of equality, justice and tolerance.
>
> (Duchêne 1972: 20)

This notion of civilian power implies, as Nicolaïdis and Howse argue, both the use of civil (as opposed to military) means to support policy objectives and the external, 'civilising' influence of the Community. Thus Duchêne saw the EC as 'an exemplar of a new stage in political civilisation' in which the Member States, having renounced the use of military means among themselves, can legitimately encourage others to do likewise (Duchêne 1973 quoted in Nicolaïdis and Howse 2002: 770).

Duchêne's formulation proved controversial from the outset, not least due to its contention that civilian power could substitute for military power in providing a basis for the Community's influence in world affairs. In recent years, however, a new debate has arisen – precisely because of the Union's evolving European Security and Defence Policy and related ability to gain access to military means. A number of key questions arise. To what extent does the availability of military capability herald the demise of important aspects of the Union's singularity? Is loss of 'civilian power' status, of itself, a 'cause for concern' (Smith 2000)?

In terms of the Union's collective identity, Zielonka has argued (1998: 229) that eschewing use of military means would 'represent one of the basic strategic choices that could help the Union acquire a distinct profile – so important in terms of identity and legitimacy.' Nevertheless, loss of strictly civilian status may be of relatively less significance than the uses to which military means might be put. As former Swedish Prime Minister, Carl Bildt has observed – 'We have crossed the Rubicon – but where are we heading next?' (quoted in Biscop 2004a: 6).

Contributors to this ongoing debate have identified various principles which must be observed if the Union's singular (value-based) identity is to be retained. First, that military means should be used by the Union only when sanctioned by International Law, through a United Nations Security Council mandate (Royal Institute for International Relations 2003: 12). And, second, that use of military means must be associated with a comprehensive approach to security that reflects and supports the Union's 'civilizing' influence. Eurostep, a network of non-governmental development organizations, has put it thus:

> As a military dimension is added to its foreign policy capacities, security threats need to be understood by the EU holistically rather than militaristically – in terms of human security, rather than in terms of strategic interests and military responses.
>
> (Eurostep 2004)

This approach is reflected, to some extent, in the 2003 European Security Strategy, which explicitly links security with human development issues such as poverty eradication (European Council 2003).[11] In consequence some commentators have argued that, precisely because of its newly acquired access to military capability, the Union could, for the first time, fully assert its civilian identity globally, perhaps becoming a 'civilian superpower' (Biscop and Coolsaet 2003: 31). We consider, however, that the notion of civilian power in the presence of military capability has truly become, as Hedley Bull argued (on very different grounds) in 1983, 'a contradiction in terms'; and that conceptualization of the Union as a value-based community requires an alternative approach.

Normative power Europe?

Such an approach is provided by Ian Manners (2002), who proposes a collective identity for the Union as a 'normative power'. This notion seeks to avoid the civilian/military dichotomy in favour of a focus upon the 'ideational impact of the EU's international identity/role' (Manners 2002: 238). Normative power thus both encompasses and complements the Union's civilian power and 'fledgling military power' through an ideational dimension which (potentially) provides the 'ability to shape conceptions of "normal" in international relations' (Manners 2002: 239).

The EU collective identity proposed by Manners emanates from three sources: its genesis as an explicit rejection of the divisive nationalisms, imperialism and war of Europe's past; its unique character as a 'hybrid polity'; and the development, over the past 50 years, of a body of values which are firmly embedded in successive Treaties and in the Union's practices (Manners 2002: 240). Manners identifies five core values – peace, liberty, democracy, the rule of law and respect for human rights – and four subsidiary values – social solidarity, anti-discrimination, sustainable development and good governance – as contributing to the Union's presence. It is in projecting these values, and in promoting the establishment of related norms for the governance of international behaviour, that the EU might be said to exercise normative power.

Undoubtedly, the Union's proclaimed values feature frequently in documentation and in the rhetoric of EU representatives. An interesting identity construction, which refers to most of the values identified by Manners, can be found in the draft Constitutional Treaty (Title I, Article I-3):

> In its relations with the wider world, the Union shall uphold and promote its values and interests. It shall contribute to peace, security, the sustainable development of the Earth, solidarity and mutual respect among peoples, free and fair trade, eradication of poverty and protection of human rights, in particular the rights of the child, as well as to the strict observance and the development of international law, including respect for the principles of the United Nations Charter.

Not only does this text set out various core values which the Union claims to observe and seeks to project, it also makes implicit identity statements based upon its difference from and superiority over other global actors, most notably the USA. This is evident, given the context of the Treaty's framing during the 2003 Iraq war, from the strong statements regarding respect for International Law and the United Nations. The emphasis upon children's rights 'in particular' appears also to be directed at the USA, which shares with Somalia the dubious distinction of having failed to ratify the 1989 Convention on the Rights of the Child. Constructions of a 'normative power' identity for the EU, it can be argued, conceptualize the USA as the Union's other.

The practices of EU representatives in constructing a value-based identity distinct from that of the USA have been noted by Charles Kupchan (2002). He cites differences with the USA over the Kyoto Protocol on climate change, the International Criminal Court and the death penalty as evidence of EU 'resistance' to US leadership (Kupchan 2002: 157).[12] While several additions could be made to Kupchan's list of EU/US differences, we consider that policy towards Turkey is particularly noteworthy. Here, in insistently pressing for early accession of Turkey to the EU, the US administration has attached scant importance to human rights issues and the treatment of the Kurdish minority, thus potentially undermining the Union's efforts to influence the processes of reform in Turkey.

That the Union attempts to assert and project its values, and to shape the practices of many of the third parties with which it interacts, was evident from our interviews.[13] In the case of the Russian Federation, Rontoyanni (2003: 818) notes the administration's 'irritation' at 'persistent EU pressures regarding media pluralism in Russia and human rights observance in the Chechen conflict'. While such responses contribute to understandings about the Union's collective identity, particular significance should be attributed to attempts to distance the EU from the USA on the basis of superior commitment to core values – precisely because these are claimed to be shared Western values. To construct the Union as morally superior asserts its independent identity. The Union, it is implied, is not simply a junior partner of the USA; indeed it has a responsibility to admonish the US government for its use of practices, such as execution, considered to violate basic human rights.

In his discussion of the EU as a normative power, Ian Manners identifies opposition to the death penalty as an important example of the Union's commitment to project its values externally. As Manners' study demonstrates, the Union has acted, in this policy area, with great consistency and some degree of success. It has raised the profile of the death penalty issue in international fora, attempted to shame the 'super-executioners' (the USA and China) and strongly influenced decisions to abolish the death penalty in a number of states, including Cyprus, Poland, Albania, Ukraine, Turkey and Russia (Manners 2002: 249–50). EU activity in relation to human rights generally, and the death penalty in particular, suggests that:

> … not only is the EU constructed on a normative basis, but importantly that this predisposes it to act in a normative way in world politics. It is built upon the crucial and usually overlooked observation that the most important factor shaping the international role of the EU is not what it does or what it says, but what it is.
>
> (Manners 2002: 251)

Here we have a useful reminder that understandings about the Union's identity are an important aspect of its presence, as are related understandings about its capability. So far we have considered constructions of the EU as a value-based community (whether as a civilian power or a normative power) which have been strongly promoted internally. We now turn to alternative constructions, which have not been the subject of active promotion and which propose relatively weaker identities for the Union, based solely upon its character as a singular, or peculiar, polity.

The Union as a peculiar polity

Treatments which construct the Union's identity and roles as primarily or exclusively a function of its singular character are not new. While varying considerably in many respects, they are united in emphasizing those aspects of the Union's character which differentiate it from a conventional state. However, if identity mediates between opportunity and action, as we have claimed, then an identity for the EU as 'other than a state' provides insufficient basis for construction of understandings about the Union's potential roles or practices. Nevertheless, we cannot exclude from our enquiry approaches that construct the EU, by virtue of its character, as a non-actor, potentially an actor, or a peculiar, but relatively effective, actor in global politics.

In some intergovernmentalist formulations, particularly those which posit the 'European rescue of the nation state' (Milward 1992), the EU is seen primarily as a tool of or adjunct to its Member States. Clearly such constructions propose an identity for the Union that is insufficiently distinct for it to be characterized as an actor in international affairs. While we may conclude that this formulation fails adequately to capture the complexity of the Union's multi-faceted character, it remains an important, if negative, contribution to discourses of EU identity.

Further 'negative' contributions have considered, but substantially rejected, the possibility that the EU is or might become an actor in international affairs. Thus the Community/Union has been considered in terms of its perceived inadequacies – in particular the requirement to reach consensus between Member States in most areas of traditional foreign policy and the Union's lack of assured access to military instruments. Implicitly or explicitly, such treatments contrast the Union with (powerful) states; and find it wanting. On this basis, Hedley Bull (1983: 151) concluded that 'the Europe Community is not an actor in international politics and does not seem likely to become one'. A decade later, Christopher Hill, in his discussion of the 'capabilities-expectations gap' maintained that the EU might 'conceivably reach the position of being able to act purposefully and as one' (Hill 1993: 318). These arguments construct the Union as, at best, a potential actor. More recent contributions, however, have constructed the EU as an actor – but have differed considerably on the meaning and effectiveness of its actions.

A prominent and controversial contributor has been Robert Kagan (2002). Kagan insists that the Union's posture in international affairs derives, not from the desire to project core values, but directly from its 'weakness'. By this he refers specifically to the inability to muster military power comparable to that of the United States. Consequently, 'Europe's military weakness has produced a perfectly understandable aversion to the exercise of military power' (Kagan 2002: 10). Related to this, according to Kagan, is the desire to concentrate external policy efforts on areas where the Union can play to its strengths, exercising influence in relation to human rights or environmental issues through 'such soft-power tools as economics and trade' (Kagan 2002: 13). The Union's relations with the USA are dominated, it is argued, by fears that US unilateralism will destroy the multilateral world order upon which the EU depends for its existence. Consequently, criticisms of the USA for, *inter alia*, retention of the death penalty, simply reflect a desire, born out of weakness, 'to control the behemoth by appealing to its conscience' (Kagan 2002: 11).

Kagan's intervention has provoked considerable debate, most of which has focused upon the issue of military capability. Consequently, despite his references to areas of EU strength, Kagan's work has contributed to constructions of the Union as an ineffective 'non-state'. Interestingly our interviews (in July 2001) with Council-Secretariat officials involved with ESDP issues revealed divergent views on this issue. Thus one civilian official appeared to support Kagan's position – 'ESDP was originally thought of in terms of power projection to frighten Milosevic. Now we are talking about peacekeeping. How are we going to frighten Milosevic?'. More typical, however, was the relatively positive construction of EU efforts by a military officer – 'We are tying to build a global crisis management organization including military and civil assets. Nothing like it exists anywhere in the world'. A nice construction of the Union as a singular actor.

This more positive understanding of the relationship between the Union's peculiar character and its various roles is shared by some academic commentators. Thus Hazel Smith (2002: 271) argues:

> What is structurally important about the ethics of EU foreign policy is its visibility. In an organisation of 15 or more states which are constantly watching the Union for signs of overreach it is difficult to engage in the worst types of foreign policy *realpolitik*. Such actions require secrecy and activity by small groups of people who are protected from public scrutiny – often through claims that such clandestinity is in the national interest.

In this construction, the Union's (relatively) value-based external policy is a function, not of military weakness, but of transparency. Deviations from declared values can be prevented by Member State governments which subscribe to these values. Karen Smith (2003: 198) similarly notes the Union's inability to employ punitive measures in pursuit of policy goals, and its related preference for use of positive incentives. She illustrates ways in which 'the common interest is upgraded' through processes of 'reshaping' the preferences of Member State governments which had previously shown little commitment to value-based external policy (Smith 2003: 197). This accords with the notions of socialization and internalization discussed above. Ultimately, Smith concludes that the Union's identity as a singular actor depends, not upon the values it seeks to promote (as 'normative power' constructions would imply), but upon the means used to pursue its objectives. These, she argues, stem primarily 'from the special nature of the EU itself' (Smith 2003: 199).

With the exception of those who would reject any understanding of an EU identity independent from its Member States, the constructions of EU identity discussed above have all, to a greater or lesser extent, emphasized the importance of the values claimed by the Union. We now turn to alternative and quite different constructions of exclusive identities for the Union.

Exclusive identities: the EU as fortress

Constructions of an exclusive identity for the EU contrast starkly with the value-based identities which were the principal focus of our discussion above. Exclusive identities tend to be associated with negative practices towards outsiders, including, potentially, processes of active othering (Neumann 1996: 168).

Centred around the concepts of access and eligibility, and the complex rules and criteria devised by the Union to regulate or deter those who seek opportunities within its borders, exclusive identities generate understandings of the Union as unwelcoming, even hostile – as 'fortress Europe'. Access refers to the aspiration, on the part of third parties, to trade goods and services into the vast and lucrative Single European Market. Eligibility refers both to the desire of neighbouring states to attain membership status and the hopes of third country migrants seeking security and prosperity within the European Union. Attempts to legitimate the Union's exclusionary practices employ a discourse of protection from external challenge or threat. 'Crime does not respect borders' we are frequently reminded (Commission 2001b).

Access to a fortified market

The notion of 'fortress Europe' originated in the context of the 1987 Single European Act and the aspiration to complete the Single Market by 1992. It was essentially a construction by third parties, in particular the USA, intended to characterize the Union as an increasingly important but self-interested economic power, determined to protect its burgeoning market through a range of exclusionary practices. And there is no doubt that the Union employs such practices – in the form, *inter alia*, of rules of origin, anti-dumping and anti-subsidy provision, even against its poorest trading partners. Indeed these measures have recently been strengthened in order to protect EU companies allegedly suffering from unfair trading practices. 'Strengthening rules on trade defence is in the overall interests of an open trade system' (then Trade Commissioner Pascal Lamy, in International Euromail 1295, June 2004).

The mechanisms and impacts of the Union's trade protectionism are discussed more fully in Chapter 3. In the context of our discussion of EU collective identity, however, it is important to note that the Union's trade policies undermine the commitments to poverty reduction and human rights (in particular the economic and social aspects of the human rights agenda), which are central to understandings of the Union as a value-based community. Trade policy, in addition, is directly linked to the issues of eligibility (of migrants) discussed below, in that 'EU protectionism in labour-intensive sectors has created a demand-pull immigration pressure from south to north, where European producers need the kind of low-cost "informal" labour that illegal immigration provides' (Christiansen *et al.* 2000: 406). While the impact of EU trade policies on third country economies encourages inward migration, the immigration regime, as we shall see, is exclusive.

Eligibility for an exclusive club

The Union's construction of rules and criteria governing eligibility applies both to third country migrants seeking to live and work within the EU and to states wishing to attain membership status. Initially we deal with these issue areas separately. There are important links between them, however, which will become evident from our final area of discussion in this section – establishment of the Union's external borders.

Eligibility and the individual

While understandings about 'fortress Europe' originated from concerns about protectionist impulses arising from the single market programme, they are most evident, today, in relation to immigration and asylum issues (Geddes 2000; Lavenex 2001; Guild 2002; Guiraudon 2004). These policy areas are themselves, of course, associated with the single market provisions, in that establishment of freedom of movement of people within the Union was seen to necessitate development of coordinated policies on immigration and asylum. In short, a common approach was sought to management of flows of people across the Union's external borders.

From the outset, in the context of the 1985 Schengen Agreement and the 1986 Ad Hoc Group on Immigration, the policy focus was upon control and restriction of migration flows.[14] Moreover, within these strictly intergovernmental fora, which were established outside the Treaties and comprised home affairs officials meeting in some secrecy, issues of immigration and asylum were consistently juxtaposed with measures to combat international drug trafficking and other forms of organized crime. Issues of human rights and the treatment of third country nationals resident in the Community were not a focus of attention. Subsequently, a number of factors have combined to ensure that, in the development of this policy area, these negative and exclusionary orientations, and associated processes of othering, have been maintained and strengthened.

The ending of the Cold War, and the accompanying relaxation of internal controls on population movement within and from Eastern Europe, were followed by a new climate of anxiety concerning immigration. This was largely generated by alarmist predictions, on the part of some Western politicians and news media, of an imminent 'invasion' of up to 50 million migrants from the East (Thränhardt 1996: 227–9). While these concerns proved unfounded, they indicate processes of constructing a new external enemy – 'The end of the Cold War had banished traditional fears and dangers, and this new evil was, it seemed, to take their place' (Thränhardt 1996: 228). Subsequently, the arrival within the EU of substantial numbers of refugees displaced by the conflicts in former Yugoslavia increased the salience of these issues, as did growing popular support for xenophobic far-Right political parties in several Member States. Finally, and most significantly, the 9/11 terrorist attacks on the USA greatly heightened anxieties about security matters, heralding a restrictive, security-oriented approach to migration control which seemed, on occasion, 'to imply that all asylum-seekers were terrorists in disguise' (Guiraudon 2004: 171). In this policy area, processes of active othering are clearly evident.

In the context of these growing discourses of fear and exclusion, the development of the immigration and asylum policy areas within the Union began with the TEU, which incorporated Justice and Home Affairs (JHA) as an intergovernmental 'third pillar' of the newly created EU. Within a single Article (then K1) the Treaty proposed as 'matters of common interest' issues ranging from asylum and immigration to drug trafficking and terrorism. Having been made public in the TEU, this unfortunate juxtaposition of immigration/asylum with terrorism/crime caused outrage among civil liberties groups and Members of the European Parliament, amongst others.

The Treaty of Amsterdam (TOA) appeared to end this unhappy issue linkage by providing for the phased transfer, by May 2004, of immigration and asylum matters to the Community pillar, thus potentially providing for input from the European Parliament and the European Court of Justice on these areas of great significance for human rights and individual liberties.[15] The tenor of the TOA provisions is relatively positive. Article 61 (TEC) begins with the aspiration 'to establish progressively an area of freedom, security and justice ...'. Subsequently reference is made to the rights and status of third country nationals resident in the EU – a still neglected issue at the Union level.

Since entry into force of the TOA in May 1999, however, the promise of these provisions has not been realized in practice. While, even before 9/11, issues of security were prioritized over those of freedom and justice, the strengthening of restrictive measures since 9/11 has caused the Union's area of freedom, security and justice to 'look very much like an area of exclusion and stigmatisation' (Guild 2002: 2). Here, the June 2002 Seville European Council marked a turning point, in that its conclusions concerning the treatment of migrants were uniformly negative and restrictive. At Seville, immigration 'became virtually synonymous with illegality and threat' (ibid.). A brief examination of exclusionary measures recently introduced by the Union is instructive.

The focus of EU measures in the areas of immigration and asylum has been upon preventing 'undesirable migrants' from reaching the Union's borders, thus avoiding lengthy and intrusive border controls which might discommode 'desirable' tourists and business people (Guiraudon 2004: 176). A number of measures contribute to these 'beyond border' controls. Nationals of 135 states are required to obtain visas to enter the Schengen area.[16] To do so, they must convince immigration officials that they are able to support themselves during their visit and intend to leave at its conclusion. In addition, an EU directive on carrier sanctions obliges airlines, shipping and coach companies to check the validity of documentation prior to departure. Repatriation of undocumented migrants and failed asylum seekers became a new policy emphasis following the Seville Council (Monar 2003: 123). To facilitate their return, formal readmission agreements have been concluded or are in the course of negotiation.[17] Agreement on return of nationals was included in the Cotonou Agreement, signed in June 2000, between the Union and 77 African, Caribbean and Pacific (ACP) countries. Immigration control is also a focus of Euro-Med agreements with North African countries.

In relation specifically to asylum, measures have been introduced to limit claims for asylum status and to facilitate rejection and expulsion of asylum seekers. Central to this has been the controversial designation of 'safe' third countries of origin or transit, to which claimants can be returned, and the notion of 'manifestly unfounded' requests, in accordance with which claims are not given consideration.

It is undoubtedly in the areas of immigration and asylum that negative and exclusionary discourses, and associated practices, are most evident. As a study by Gallya Lahav has demonstrated, these discourses originate within the Member States and are manipulated by populist/nationalist political parties which, despite opposition to the EU, 'skilfully carry the banner across Europe, and ironically get maximal exposure at the EU level' (Lahav 2004: 208).[18] These exclusionary discourses are not confined to uninformed sectors of EU publics and opportunistic politicians, however. Lahav found that, throughout the EU, on immigration issues, 'elites and general publics embrace similar priorities and are driven by fears that converge considerably' (ibid.).

In these circumstances, pursuit of negative, exclusionary immigration and asylum policies at the EU level is facilitated by the dominance, in JHA policy areas, of national officials whose operation within EU intergovernmental committees is 'Screened from traditional humanitarian forums dealing with asylum seekers and immigrants' (Lavenex 2001: 27). Here it is of interest to note that, in our interviews (in July and September 2001) with seconded Member State officials dealing with JHA issues within the EU institutions, reference was frequently made to the lack of experience of Commission officials in the (then) newly created DG JHA.

Practices in the area of immigration and asylum are evidently inconsistent with the inclusive, value-based understandings of EU identity which have been so strongly promoted by EU officials. Undoubtedly there has been sensitivity to this inconsistency. Thus the Commission, in a publication entitled *Living in an Area of Freedom, Security and Justice* argued that the measures introduced at that time 'Far from trying to create a fortress … make entry into and circulation or travel within the European Union easier for any legitimate person' (Commission 2001b: 7). It was concluded, nevertheless, that the key to 'moving freely in security' is effective policing of external borders (ibid.: 8). We return to the issue of borders below.

Eligibility for accession

EU policy on accession does not demonstrate the acute inconsistencies with value-based understandings of identity that were evident in relation to immigration and asylum. It is in relation to accession, however, that tensions between inclusive and exclusive facets of the Union's identity are most apparent.

Inclusiveness is clearly demonstrated by the accession in May 2004 of a heterogeneous set of new members – three former republics of the Soviet Union, one of the Federal Republic of Yugoslavia, four Central European states which were formerly part of the Soviet bloc, the tiny island of Malta and the still-divided Cyprus. All of these states, after varying periods of negotiation and adaptation, were considered to have sufficiently adopted EU values and practices to be accorded membership. Romania and Bulgaria are deemed to require further time for adaptation before accession (scheduled for 2007) and the further five non-members in the Western Balkans – Albania, Bosnia and Herzegovina, Croatia, Macedonia and Serbia and Montenegro – have been promised membership when readiness is achieved. Turkey has also been accorded candidate status, albeit in the context of considerable ambivalence, as we shall see.

Undoubtedly this inclusiveness is impressive. It reflects, as we argued in the previous chapter, insistent discourses of 'return' (to the centre of Europe of 'Eastern' countries) and 'responsibility' (of Western Europe for its abandonment of Eastern Europe at the end of the Second World War). In consequence, consideration of the limits to EU inclusiveness must examine, not so much a definition of what comprises a European state (as the TEU formula – any European state may apply – might suggest), but the extent to which shared understandings of responsibility and belonging pertain to aspirant states. To exemplify the tensions between inclusive and exclusive understandings of the Union's identity, we consider below the Union's responses to the membership aspirations of Turkey, Ukraine and Morocco. In these cases, active construction of discourses of belonging has been evident within the potential candidate countries, but has not resulted in development of *shared* understandings of a European vocation.

In the case of Turkey, eligibility for membership (and hence 'European' status) was confirmed, in principle, by the 1964 Ankara (Association) Agreement. It has since been reconfirmed – in the Commission's (negative) Opinion on Turkey's original membership application (Commission 1989) and in *Agenda 2000*. In this document Turkey was treated differently from all other applicants (at that time ten Central and East European states and Cyprus), in that Turkey was not considered as a formal candidate for membership. Alone of the twelve applicants, Turkey qualified only for 'deepening relations' with the EU (Commission 1997a: 51–2). Following the Turkish government's outrage at this differential treatment, strong lobbying for Turkish candidacy from some Member States and *rapprochement* with Greece (largely as a result of devastating earthquakes earlier in 1999), Turkey was formally recognized as a candidate at the Helsinki European Council in December 1999.

Candidacy represents an important change in Turkey's status. Not only does it accord with understandings of the Union's inclusive identity, it marks a turning point in the construction of Turkey's identity as a European state committed to embracing the Union's values. Hence, as we shall see in Chapter 6, accordance of candidate status gave considerable impetus to the processes of reform in Turkey. Nevertheless reluctance within the EU to fully embrace Turkey as a prospective member has persisted. The controversy associated with the decision of the December 2004 European Council to open accession negotiations (in October 2005) attests to this.

The Union's enduring ambivalence towards Turkey has ancient roots; indeed debates about the European credentials of 'the Turk' date back at least to the seventeenth century. The construction of Turkey as different – as 'the non-European barbarian' at the gate – reinforces understandings of what 'Europe' is, by constantly demonstrating what it is not (Neumann and Welsh 1991: 329). These constructions of Turkey as non-European, as Europe's other, have persisted. A relatively recent example is provided by a notorious intervention in November 2002 by former French President, Valéry Giscard d'Estaing, who was at that time President of the Convention on the Future of Europe. Giscard declared that Turkey has 'a different culture, a different approach, and a different way of life. It is not a European country'. Furthermore, EU membership for Turkey would signal 'the end of Europe' (quoted in Teitelbaum and Martin 2003: 98). This emphasis 'to the point of obsession' upon Turkey's cultural incompatibility (Müftüler-Bac 1997: 11) reflects an exclusive understanding of EU identity which coexists with the inclusive identity evoked by the Union's decision to open accession negotiations and insistent supervision of Turkey's internal process of reform.

Should the tensions between the inclusive and exclusive facets of EU identity be resolved in favour of Turkey's inclusion, this will in part reflect, as Helen Sjursen has argued (2002: 504), Turkey's strategic importance to the West. Rather than discourses of return and responsibility, with their implications of a shared fate, there has long been, in the case of Turkey, a discourse of strategic partnership, implying cooperation 'without duty or kinship' (ibid.). Turkey has been seen as 'a buffer against everything' – from Soviet expansionism to Islamic militancy (Interview with Turkish diplomat, June 1996). In the aftermath of 9/11 and the invasion of Iraq, this discourse has both intensified and shifted. While an emphasis on security has been maintained, a new, inclusive discourse of 'reaching out' to Turkey has emerged. This has focused upon Turkey's closeness to Europe, as a Western oriented, secular and democratic Muslim country, and has been constructed in terms of inclusive and value-based understandings of EU identity. Thus, for example:

> By reaching out to a mostly Muslim country with almost 70 million inhabitants, the Union's leaders would be proving that pluralism is not just a value to which they pay lip-service, but something they actually cherish. They would also be sending a message to Osama bin Laden and his fellow extremists that there is no reason why Islam and Christianity cannot coexist peacefully.
>
> (Cronin 2004: 16)

This new discourse of inclusion may finally resolve the Union's ambivalence towards Turkey.

In the case of Morocco's aspirations to EU membership, the Union's response has not been characterized by the ambivalence noted above. Morocco's membership application in 1987 was met with outright rejection; indeed the normal procedures for dealing with applications were not even invoked. No opinion was issued by the Commission, nor were there proposals for an enhanced relationship with Morocco, as had been the case when Turkey's application was rejected. Within the EU, it was considered that 'Morocco was so clearly not-Europe that its claim to a European identity seemed totally incomprehensible, even ludicrous' (Rumelili 2004: 40).[19]

Morocco's position is less clear-cut than EU 'incomprehension' would imply, however. The Spanish enclaves of Ceuta and Melilla on the North African coast are formally part of the EU, and Morocco has long defined itself as a bridge between Europe and Africa (ibid.). Morocco has maintained its claims to European status, with an adviser to King Mohammed VI stating in 2000: 'Geographically, historically and culturally, Morocco is closer to Western Europe than most of Eastern Europe. The Strait of Gibraltar is just a geographical accident' (quoted in Rumelili 2004: 42–3).

Attempts to construct a European identity for Morocco have not succeeded in creating shared understandings, however. Morocco was excluded from EU narratives of enlargement during the 1990s, but since 2003 has been included in the Union's European Neighbourhood Policy. The ENP 'offers a means to reinforce relations between the EU and partner countries, which is distinct from the possibilities under Article 49 of the Treaty on European Union' (Commission 2004a: 3). Put bluntly, this means 'you can't join' (Interview, DG Relex, September 2003). In employing the rhetoric of partnership, and denying membership to 'partners', the ENP is a manifestation of the Union's exclusive identity – not least because of the wide range of non-member states included within its ambit.

In the case of Ukraine, its status as an ENP partner falls far short of aspirations for a close relationship with the EU and, ultimately, membership. While Ukraine is one of four 'new outsiders' – along with Belarus, Moldova and Russia – identified by White *et al.* (2002), it is distinguished from the others by claims to EU membership based, *inter alia*, upon its geographical location. 'In 1891 it was established that West Ukraine is the centre of Europe' (Interview, Ukrainian official, January 2003).

Ukraine was the first former Soviet Republic to conclude a Partnership and Cooperation Agreement (PCA) with the Union, in June 1994. Following entry into force of the PCA in 1998, the Ukrainian President issued a Decree on the Strategy of Integration into the European Union. Thus Ukraine 'proclaimed full-fledged membership in the European Union as a strategic goal' (Burakovsky *et al.* 2000: 17) and in 2002 adopted a bill on the harmonization of its laws with those of the EU.[20] Ukraine has also been eager to participate in other EU initiatives – for example deploying officers to the EU Police Mission in Bosnia-Herzegovina in 2003 and participating in Operation Althea, also in Bosnia-Herzegovina, in late 2004.

Despite these efforts, understandings of Ukraine as central to Europe are not widely shared within the EU. While recognizing 'the European aspirations of Ukraine', and welcoming Ukraine's 'European choice', the EU Common Strategy on Ukraine, agreed by the December 1999 Helsinki Council, focused on full implementation of the existing PCA provisions (European Council 1999b). No commitment to future membership for Ukraine was made at this time, nor subsequently; indeed within the EU there has been great reluctance even to discuss eventual membership for Ukraine (Zagorski 2004: 88). The incorporation of Ukraine in the ENP, alongside Middle-Eastern states such as Syria and Lebanon, appeared to signify categorical rejection of Ukraine's candidacy. Ukraine differs from these countries in important respects, however. It now directly borders the Union and has close historical, cultural and other ties with EU Member States, most notably Poland. It may be that, through representations from Poland and other new members, and in the context of accelerated reform processes within Ukraine following the 2004 'Orange Revolution' that brought President Victor Yushchenko to power, shared understandings of Ukraine's place in Europe will be constructed.

In the meantime, however, fresh exclusionary practices have been introduced by imposition of the Schengen visa regime, and associated border controls, by the new Member States. The sealing of Ukraine's previously porous borders with Poland, Slovakia and Hungary, in the context of these countries' accession processes, has impacted significantly upon cross-border trade, tourism and cultural cooperation. The border with Romania will be similarly affected. 'We've been cut off from Europe' has been the reaction in Kiev (Horakik 2004: 15). It is to the issue of borders that we now turn.

Establishing the Union's external borders

Since borders differentiate between insiders and outsiders, they are, by definition, exclusionary. Here, we refer to two sets of practices which contribute to processes of differentiation; and to understandings of the Union's exclusive identity – control of the Union's external borders and the sensitive issue of finally establishing its geographical limits. In the context of the 2004 Eastern enlargement, these matters became inextricably linked. Thus concerns were raised about the ability to function of a constantly enlarging and increasingly heterogeneous Union and, as we saw above, about the potential for significant population movements into established Member States from the less prosperous new Member States, and their even less prosperous neighbours. Three issues are raised by these concerns – movement of people from new to established Member States following the 2004 accession; movement of people from neighbouring states such as Ukraine; and determining the physical limits of the Union. This last potentially involves excluding from candidacy states other than those already promised membership at some future point – that is Romania, Bulgaria, Turkey and the five states of the Western Balkans.

Since internal free movement of persons is one of the fundamental freedoms associated with the Single European Market, movement of people between new and established Member States should not, in principle, have been an issue. In practice, however, the Accession Treaty permitted existing Member States to introduce transitional arrangements restricting movement of people from the new Member States for up to seven years. For an initial period of two years (to May 2006) national measures restricting movement can be taken without any obligation to give reasons for their use. With the exception of Ireland, all Members States introduced some initial restrictive measures. These can be extended for a further two years, and potentially three years more, provided that the Commission is notified of Member States' intentions. In consequence complete freedom of movement for citizens of the new Member States will be delayed until May 2011. It is interesting to note the exceptions to these exclusionary measures, which apply only to the eight new Member States from Central and Eastern Europe. Due to their small size and relative prosperity, Cyprus and Malta are exempt. Of interest too, is the extension, from June 2002, of full free movement rights to Swiss nationals – despite the status of Switzerland outside both the EU and the European Economic Area (EEA).[21]

The exclusion of those EU citizens who stand the most to gain from access to the opportunities afforded by the Single Market is related to the requirement that the new Member States implement in full all aspects of JHA policy, including the Schengen *acquis*, as a condition of accession. This involved, first, implementation of the Schengen visa regime, a requirement which implies classifying citizens of non-candidate countries such as Ukraine as 'undesirable illegal migrants' (Jileva 2003: 79). Second, meeting the technical requirements of the Schengen Information System (SIS), which has proved particularly expensive and demanding.[22] Pending implementation of this requirement by all new Member States, full internal freedom of movement is unlikely to be granted to their citizens. Finally, new Member States were required to strengthen control of their external borders, a process which began prior to accession.

Strengthening the external borders of the Union, and moving towards common control practices, became a priority following the 1985 Schengen Agreement, which provided for the removal of internal borders between signatories. By the late 1990s, when it had become clear that the external borders of the Union would shift substantially Eastwards, the border management systems of candidate states became a matter of great concern within the EU. As a Commission official commented, 'The political focus of enlargement is now on tightening borders' (Interview, DG JHA, July 2001).

Historically, in the context of the Cold War, the emphasis within the candidate countries had been upon control of their Western borders using military personnel. A shift of control to the Eastern borders necessitated creation of additional border crossings, recruitment and training of professional border guards and installation of expensive equipment to meet the standards required by the EU. Despite funding and technical support from the EU, these measures were not fully in place at the time of accession. Meantime, the terrorist attacks of 9/11 had generated pressure for further strengthening of border controls.

In its communication, *Towards an Integrated Management of External Borders*, the Commission made a number of recommendations, including establishment of a European Corps of Border Guards (Commission 2002b). These led to the establishment (in November 2002) of the Union's Agency for the Management of Operational Cooperation at the External Borders, which has an oversight role. The further strengthening of policy on external borders again drew attention to deficiencies in candidate countries, in that their border arrangements did not accord with the Union's post-9/11 security priorities. Despite reservations concerning the impact on relations with their Eastern neighbours, the new Member States have implemented much of the Schengen *acquis*. Indeed Bulgaria moved forward in this policy area, well in advance of accession, as a condition for removal (in 2001) from the EU's negative list of countries whose citizens require a visa for entry into the Schengen area (Jileva 2003: 81).[23]

Does the perceived need to strength the Union's external borders indicate that the time has now come to firmly establish the geographical limits of the European Union? In 1992 the Delors Commission was clear that it did not:

> The term European … combines geographical, historical and cultural elements which all contribute to the European identity. The shared experience of proximity, ideas, values and historical interaction cannot be condensed into a simple formula, and is subject to review by each succeeding generation … it is neither possible nor opportune to establish now the frontiers of the European Union, whose contours will be shaped over many years to come.
>
> (Commission 1992b: 11)

Since 1992, the progressive strengthening of the Union's external borders has contributed significantly to the process of excluding adjacent non-members such as Belarus, Moldova, Russia and Ukraine. The European Neighbourhood Policy, with its rhetoric of 'partnership not membership', compounds the impact of exclusionary border management practices. While not necessarily signifying final determination of the Union's geographical limits, these processes of active othering indicate the current absence of widely shared understandings about the 'European' credentials of outsiders.

External roles of the EU

As we shall see in the chapters that follow, the EU, as a global actor, engages in a variety of external activities. These reflect understandings of identity and a range of associated, overarching roles offered to, or claimed by, the Union.

The relationship between identities and roles is, we believe, important but indirect. In the context of the ideas, expectations and events which constitute the policy environment, identities offer understandings of appropriate and inappropriate behaviour. To the extent that these understandings are widely shared within the Union, they promote or constrain action. In circumstances where one or a few Member State governments reject certain understandings of EU identity, these understandings nevertheless continue to provide a frame of reference, and hence a source of influence, for EU action – for it is in terms of these understandings that the Union may be judged by others.

Above we have discussed two distinct facets of the Union's identity. The first, which we see as dominant, provides understandings of the Union as singular in character and relatively inclusive. Prominent here, because of their strong promotion internally, are notions of the EU as a value-based community. The second, or alternative, facet of the Union's identity is negative and exclusive, potentially involving processes of constructing stereotypes of alien outsiders – of active othering. Here, notions of the EU as fortress are prominent. Both sets of understandings are constitutive of the Union's hybrid identity. Each proposes distinct sets of overarching roles for the Union. Since these roles are reflected in each of the chapters that follow, our discussion here provides only a brief overview.

The Union's roles as a singular and inclusive actor

Understandings of the Union as a singular, inclusive and/or value-based actor suggest three broad, complementary roles for the EU in international affairs – as a model; as a promoter of its (proclaimed) internal values; and as a counterweight to the USA.

The first of these roles reflects identity understandings emanating from the Union's character and its international presence. These project the EU as a model – of integration on a regional scale and as an island of peace and prosperity – which others aspire to join or to emulate (Tunander 1997). The impacts of the Union as model do not simply reflect its presence, however. Through its 'narratives of projection' the Union actively promotes understandings of its character and practices as a positive model for others (Nicolaïdis and Howse 2002). Thus the Preface to the draft Constitutional Treaty considered 'how to develop the Union into a stabilising factor and a model in the new world order' (European Convention 2003).

Beyond these discursive projections, the Union takes measures actively to export aspects of its internal practices. Thus, in the context of the wider European region, the Union has imposed its model of integration through the requirement that candidate countries implement the *acquis* in its entirety, and through the conditionalities inserted in the plethora of association agreements entered into with CEE countries since the end of the Cold War. This practice continues in the context of the European Neighbourhood Policy, which similarly emphasizes adherence to the Union's values and practices as a condition for closer partnership. More widely again, there has been active promotion of regional cooperation – through, for example, the 1995 Interregional Framework Agreement between the EU and Mercosur (Mercado Común del Sur), which supports regional economic cooperation in Latin America. Thus, the EU insists on dealing with Mercosur as a common entity, obliging its members (Argentina, Brazil, Uruguay and Paraguay) to negotiate as a bloc. This is seen, in the Commission, as 'a model for EU relations with other regional groupings' (Interview, DG Relex, September 2001). In the context of its relations with the African, Caribbean and Pacific Group (ACP), too, the Union actively promotes development of regional groupings – as we shall see in Chapter 5.

A second, broad role available to the Union reflects understandings of its identity as a value-based community; that is as a promoter of norms associated with protection of human rights, extension of democratic governance and safeguarding the natural environment. We have referred, above, to Ian Manners' (2002) discussion of the Union's active promotion of an abolitionist international norm in relation to the death penalty. In several of the chapters that follow we will be reviewing EU practices in the promotion of human rights, in particular the inclusion of conditionalities in negotiations and agreements with third parties. Also of importance, here, is the Union's (proclaimed) singular role in development cooperation and humanitarian assistance, which is the subject of Chapter 5. Finally the Union claims, with some justification, to have played not only a singular role, but also to have exerted leadership, in global environmental negotiations. In Chapter 4 we consider the Union's achievements, and aspirations, in relation to protection of the global environment.

The final role suggested by understandings of the Union's identity as a singular actor – as an alternative source of global influence, or counterweight, to the USA – combines its roles as model and as promoter of norms and values. Here the EU serves as model in terms both of its internal arrangements, which have prevented conflict and promoted prosperity among its Member States, and its external practices of cooperative engagement with third countries and international organizations. Engaged multilateralism, Robert Keohane has argued, can serve as an effective alternative to power politics :

> The point is that accepting a matrix of norms, rules, practices and organizations is not necessarily a mark of weakness. On the contrary it can be a sign of strength, self-confidence and sophistication about how to achieve security and welfare for one's citizens in a globalizing world.
>
> (Keohane 2002: 755)

We have referred, above, to discourses that construct the EU's difference from the USA in terms of the Union's superior commitment to shared Western values, manifested in a range of areas from the death penalty to climate change. Significant, also, is the Union's relatively holistic approach to international security (see Chapter 8). Whether in its approach to regional conflict or to international terrorism, the Union has focused upon prevention – emphasizing the need to address fundamental causes rather than deal only with symptoms; and hence to employ a wide range of primarily civilian policy instruments.[24] The distinctiveness of the EU approach to conflict management (when contrasted with that of the USA) is summarized by Andrew Moravcsik (2003: 85):

> ...with regard to each of the policy instruments that could make a difference – trade, aid, peacekeeping, monitoring and multilateral legitimation – Europeans are better prepared than Americans to do what has to be done.

The Union's roles as an exclusive actor

The roles suggested by understandings of the Union's identity as exclusive can be constructed in terms of the EU as protector, of its Member States and citizens, from some form of external threat. For the Union to assume this role, there is a need both for identification of potential threats and for the development of shared understandings that these threats can most effectively be dealt with through common action at the EU level (Rosamond 2001: 168). Three types of threat which evoke the Union's role as protector can be suggested – threats to prosperity; threats to stability and security; and threats to the Union, itself, as provider of protection.

In terms of prosperity, a relatively specific threat is seen to emanate from the potentially unfair trading practices of external competitors. Here, as we shall see in Chapter 3, the Commission acts as vigilant gatekeeper of the Single Market. A more diffuse threat (but potentially also opportunity) is associated with notions of globalization, constructed in terms of radical change, turbulence and unpredictability; and, again, increased pressure from external competitors. The assertive posture of Union negotiators in multilateral and bilateral trade negotiations, whether in opening markets to EU-sourced goods or gaining access to the fish stocks of weaker partners, ensures that the Union is both defended against the depredations associated (rhetorically) with globalization, and well positioned to take advantage of the opportunities. These matters are further discussed in Chapter 3.

The second threat, to societal stability and security, is deemed to emanate from unregulated influxes of external migrants, cross-border crime or terrorist incursions. Here, while Member State governments continue to act as the principal protectors of their citizens, the Union, through the common visa regime and supervision of border management systems, has increasingly become involved in protecting the Union's external borders. Even before 9/11, the Member States had accepted that, in this policy area, 'common problems need common solutions' (Commission 2001b: 8).

The third potential threat is less explicit. It is to the EU itself. Should the Union fail, the Commission informs us darkly:

> Europe, a mere geographical entity, will come under the influence of outside powers which will extort the price of its dependence and its need for protection.
> (Commission 1990a: 5)

Understandings of danger associated with failure of integration are widespread. Among Danes, for example, there is a belief that their 'comfortable situation depends upon the current European order being upheld' (Wæver 1996: 119–20). Fears of failure are reflected, *inter alia*, in concern that successive enlargements threaten the Union's capacity to function and, hence, in exclusionary practices (exemplified by the ENP) intended to restrict or prevent further enlargement. The *record* of enlargement, however, illustrates tensions and inconsistencies associated with the Union's hybrid identity.

Hybrid identity – inconsistent activity?

Inclusive and exclusive constructions of EU identity, as we have seen, offer contrasting roles for the Union in international affairs. Inevitably this leads to inconsistencies in EU behaviour and, in particular, criticism that EU practices deviate from those which might be expected were it to act in accordance with value-based understandings of identity so frequently claimed on behalf of the Union.

As we shall see in the chapters which follow, the Union's exclusionary/'protective' practices in relation to the Single Market undermine value-based commitments such as poverty reduction and environmental protection. The progressive strengthening of the Union's external borders, and associated restrictive practices in relation to immigration and asylum, also impact negatively on commitments to human rights and a range of inclusive values frequently reiterated in EU rhetoric, such as tolerance, respect for diversity and pluralism. Moreover, the Union's role as model (of successful regional integration) is also implicated in this policy area. The requirement that the new Member States in Central and Eastern Europe strengthen their external borders, and implement in full the Schengen visa regime, is entirely inconsistent with EU exhortations that CEE countries should (in the interest of security and stability in the wider Europe) promote regional economic cooperation and maintain or develop cordial relations with their neighbours (Jileva 2003: 86; Lavenex 2001: 37).

In relation to EU enlargement, however, inclusive understandings of identity have tended to guide practice. The 2004 enlargement, the promise of future membership made to eight further candidates and more recent constructions of Ukraine's European vocation, demonstrate ways in which discourses of belonging and responsibility have prevailed over exclusionary, threat-related discourses – thus supporting inclusive practices that could endanger the integration process itself.

Undoubtedly there are numerous areas where the hybrid identity of the Union is associated with tensions and inconsistencies between roles and associated practices. Nevertheless, there is not *necessarily* a fundamental contradiction between inclusive and exclusive facets of EU identity. The Union's economic power, for example, is used in the context of trade negotiations to pursue value-based goals such as protection of workers' rights and the natural environment (see Chapter 3). Moreover, despite the increased prevalence, post-9/11, of discourses of threat and exclusion, the Union has continued to emphasize the importance of poverty reduction and democracy promotion in combating terrorism. Even if these discourses of 'comprehensive security' were absent, however, the singular nature of the Union impedes use of punitive or aggressive measures against third parties. As Chris Patten (then Commissioner for External Relations) has argued:

> If there is any institution in the world that can demonstrate the benefits of multilateralism, of arguing about fish quotas or budgets rather than murdering each other, it is the European Union.
>
> (Patten 2001: 3)

An American scholar makes even stronger claims for the Union as civilian power; indeed he posits a direct link between inclusive and exclusive facets of EU identity:

> Arguably the single most powerful policy instrument for promoting peace and security in the world today, is the ultimate in market access: admission to or association with the EU trading bloc.
>
> (Moravcsik 2003: 85)

Conclusion

Our discussion of identity has attempted to capture shared understandings which give meaning to what the EU is and what it does. In the construction of actorness, identity mediates between opportunity and action. It links the Union's presence, and understandings about its capabilities, in constructing expectations concerning EU practices. In this chapter we have reviewed two facets of the Union's identity and briefly considered the various overarching roles, and the parameters of appropriate and inappropriate behaviour, suggested by these very different constructions of identity.

We considered, first, a relatively inclusive identity, which is based (primarily) upon constructions of the Union as a value-based community. Within the EU, these constructions represent the dominant approach to the Union's identity. An inclusive identity does not depend upon attribution of negative stereotypes to non-European outsiders, but upon understandings that the Union's roles and behaviour are associated with its singular character and/or its proclaimed values. Here the Union's other may be Europe's violent past; or perhaps the USA. Certainly, in recent years, EU discourses of identity have included reference to the Union's superior commitment to supposedly shared Western values in the conduct of external policy. Contributions to these debates range from constructions which depict the Union's roles and practices as a function of its inherent (military) weakness (Kagan 2002) to constructions of the Union as a 'normative power' (Manners 2002).

Appropriate, broad roles suggested by inclusive understandings of the Union's identity include the EU as model (of internal arrangements and external actions conducive to peace and prosperity); and the EU as promoter and exporter of the values to which it claims commitment. A final role suggested for the Union – as counterweight to the USA – combines elements of the EU as model and as promoter of values. It proposes the EU as exemplar of an alternative approach to international relations, based upon networks of communication and cooperation rather than expressions of military power and political domination.

Second, we considered constructions of the Union as 'fortress'. This reflects understandings of a range of practices, centred around the concepts of access and eligibility, which serve to restrict or exclude participation in the prosperity and security which the Union itself claims to offer. An exclusive identity implies processes of active othering, through which outsiders are characterized as alien, 'non-European' and potentially threatening.

Exclusionary practices associated with the Union's identity as fortress can be found in relation to trade; immigration, asylum and border control; and accordance of candidate status to aspirant members. Here, appropriate roles for the EU are associated with constructions of the Union as protector. The threats from which the Member States and citizens of the EU are to be protected include, *inter alia*, the unfair trading practices of others and illegal cross-border activities. A final threat, to the EU itself as protector of a secure and prosperous Europe, reflects concerns about the future size and viability of the EU, manifested in exclusionary practices towards aspirant non-members among the Union's neighbours.

It is to be expected that the hybrid identity of the Union will be associated with inconsistencies of role and behaviour, and we have shown this to be the case. Nevertheless, the Union, through its practices, maintains links between the exclusive and inclusive facets of its identity – demonstrating, for example, a comprehensive approach to security and using its economic power to impose conditionalities in the spheres of human rights and environmental protection. In the chapters which follow, the implications of the overarching and potentially competing roles suggested by the Union's hybrid identity will be more fully explored in relation to the policy areas in which the Union acts externally.

3　The EU as an economic power and trade actor

The EU is above all an economic power, and trade provides the foundations of its actorness. Underlying this is the presence of the Single Market. Within its tariff walls live 455 million consumers with an aggregate GDP of €9.6 trillion. Comparable figures for the USA show a significantly smaller population of 291 million people but a somewhat larger economy with a GDP of 11 trillion euros (Eurostat 2004). Although the US and EU currently constitute the largest economic entities on earth they have only 4.6 per cent and 7 per cent of global population respectively.[1]

Europe's economic presence, as it has developed from a customs union of six nations to a single market of 25, has not been entirely matched by the development of a capacity to behave as a single purposive actor in the world system. The foundations of such a capacity were legally provided by the Treaty of Rome, which granted exclusive Community competence in the management of external trade in goods as a necessary corollary to the creation of a customs union with a Common Commercial Tariff (CCT). Since 1961 the EU has fully developed its potential as a trade policy actor in ways that were extensively determined by the structural influence of the world trade regime. However, trade in goods is only one aspect of the contemporary global economy, and one which has declined in relative significance since the establishment of the Community. In these other areas – services, investment and monetary affairs – the burgeoning presence of the EU has not been reflected in an equivalent capacity to act as a single player. The relationship between economic presence and different forms and degrees of external actorness are the subject of the first part of this chapter.

Based, at least initially, on its position as a trade policy actor, the Union has developed a repertoire of roles in the world political economy. Most evident, to the very large number of states that rely upon trading access to the single market, is its role as gatekeeper and negotiator of access to the markets of others. The utilization of various degrees of preferential access to the single market, discussed in the second part of this chapter, positions the Union at the centre of a web of bilateral links. For those outsiders at the periphery of this system the EU can appear as a very potent, sometimes inscrutable, and on occasion domineering, single actor.

The EU is also a key contestant in the often conflictual relations between the major blocs in the world economy. 'With the end of the Cold War', wrote the Director of Economic Studies at the US Council for Foreign Relations, 'US trade policy is becoming high foreign policy even if policy-makers in Washington do not always recognise it' (Aho 1993: 19). If this was so for the only remaining military superpower, it is likely to be an even more relevant observation for Europeans. The third section of this chapter thus considers the role of the EU as a 'big power' in relation to Asia and, most significantly, the United States. A notable element of transatlantic interaction is the way in which US administrations, despite continuing quarrels over the specifics of trade policy, have increasingly 'constructed' the European actor as an equal with whom to conduct a whole range of economic and political business. The final part of this chapter considers the Union as a multilateral negotiator on the expanding and controversial trade agenda of the World Trade Organization (WTO).

Trade: foundation of presence and actorness

This most fundamental aspect of Community presence derives from the initial creation of a customs union. The method employed, under General Agreement on Tariffs and Trade (GATT) rules, was to establish a Common Customs Tariff (CCT) calculated by taking the average of all the existing tariffs of the original six members.[2] As soon as this was put in place it had real impacts for outsiders in terms of what economists describe as trade diversionary effects. Trade statistics indicate that the customs union was effective in bringing about a reversal of the ratio between internal and external trade.[3] Successive enlargements greatly added to the presence of the EC in the world economy and the accession of Britain in 1973, with its high dependence on overseas trade and its extensive system of ex-imperial preference, which necessitated a new EC relationship with the African, Caribbean and Pacific countries (ACP), was particularly significant.

The Union can lay claim to being the 'world's biggest trading power' (Commission 2003b: 11). Despite all the shifts in the volume and composition of world merchandise trade, its share of global imports and exports has remained relatively stable at around 20 per cent (Figures 3.1 and 3.2). The composition and direction of EU merchandise trade is described in Figure 3.3 and in the accompanying list of the EU's top 20 trading partners (Table 3.1). In the context of the rapid de-industrialization of the advanced economies, the Union is the largest trader in services, responsible for nearly 30 per cent of the world total. The EU is the foremost exporter of capital and 'dominated world foreign direct investment outflows … accounting for forty-seven per cent of the total' (WTO 2002a: 2).

A key set of indicators of presence measure the dependence of trading partners on the EU market. This can be very extensive indeed for some European and African economies. In 1995 the ten accession countries were conducting some 63 per cent of their foreign trade with the EU (Commission 1997a: 5–7). In 2003 a similar pattern was observable for Romania (75 per cent) and Bulgaria (59 per cent). However, they accounted for a mere 1.6 per cent and 0.4 per cent respectively of the total external trade of the EU 25. Turkey, already part of a customs union with the EU, conducts 56.5 per cent of its trade with the Union representing 3 per cent of the EU total. Russia, the most significant neighbour of the Union, displays equivalent figures of 64 per cent and 6 per cent (Commission 2004j).

Africa is another region of high trade dependence. In the late 1990s Uganda conducted 75 per cent of its trade with the EU, Mauritania 79 per cent and Equatorial

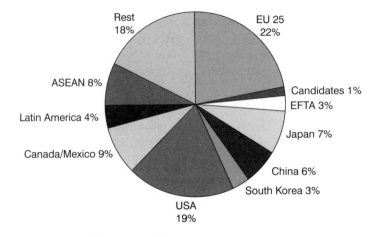

Figure 3.1 Share of world trade in goods 2002

Source: Commission 2004m.

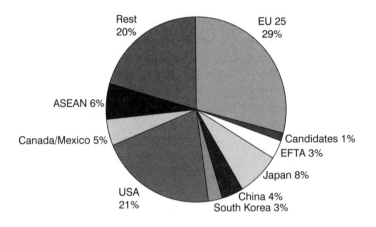

Figure 3.2 Share of world trade in services 2002

Source: Commission 2004m.

Guinea 99 per cent (Commission 1997d: 56–7). The entire ACP, which comprises 78 developing countries joined in a preferential trade and aid relationship with the Union, only accounted for a tiny and diminishing share of EU trade. In 1980, 7.9 per cent of EU imports were sourced from ACP countries and by 2001 this figure had fallen to 3.1 per cent. The export figures are similarly depressing, reducing from 8.9 to 2.9 per cent (Commission 2004j).

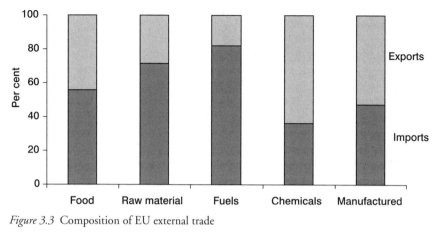

Figure 3.3 Composition of EU external trade

Source: Eurostat 2003: 143, 145.

Table 3.1 Top 20 trading partners of the EU, 2004

Rank	Exports	%	Imports	%
1	United States	24.3	United States	15.3
2	Switzerland	7.8	China	12.3
3	China	5.0	Japan	7.2
4	Russia	4.7	Switzerland	6.0
5	Japan	4.5	Norway	5.4
6	Turkey	3.9	Russia	4.7
7	Norway	3.2	Turkey	3.0
8	Canada	2.3	Korea	2.9
9	Australia	2.1	Taiwan	2.3
10	Hong Kong	2.0	Brazil	2.1
11	United Arab Emirates	1.9	Singapore	1.6
12	Romania	1.9	Canada	1.6
13	Korea	1.8	India	1.6
14	India	1.8	Saudi Arabia	1.6
15	South Africa	1.7	Malaysia	1.5
16	Singapore	1.7	South Africa	1.5
17	Mexico	1.5	Algeria	1.5
18	Brazil	1.5	Romania	1.4
19	Taiwan	1.3	Libya	1.3
20	Thailand	1.2	Israel	1.3

Source: Commission 2005b.

Actorness and the international trade regime

A customs union required consistency amongst its members and necessarily involved the granting of exclusive competence to the Commission to negotiate tariff levels with third parties. This continues to provide the basis for the oldest and most potent manifestation of the EU as an actor, the Common Commercial Policy, effective since

1961. At that time the EC, in the shape of the Commission, was almost immediately involved in developing its role as a trade actor, as its trading partners sought to negotiate on the effects of the customs union. The GATT 'Dillon Round' of 1960–1 was largely devoted to this.

The evolution of the Common Commercial Policy and the EU as a trade actor can only be understood with reference to the trade regime, initiated in 1947. For half a century the GATT provided the basis of a multilateral rule-based regime. Its fundamental norms have been 'most favoured nation treatment' (Article I) in terms of the tariffs set by members against each other and 'national treatment' of imported goods once customs duties at the border have been paid (Article III). Other important GATT provisions, sometimes honoured in their breach rather than observance, are the outlawing of quotas, non-tariff barriers (Articles XI–XIV) and trade distorting subsidies (Article XVI).

The Common Commercial Policy of the EC was something of a *tabula rasa*. Its development and the understandings and practices adopted by the Community as it emerged as a trade actor were the outcome of a mutual process of structuration. That is to say, EC agency was constructed in terms of the disciplines and institutional setting of the GATT regime, but equally the regime itself was moulded to the requirements of one of its most powerful participants. Of primary significance here is GATT Article XXIV concerning the creation of customs unions and free trade areas (FTAs).[4] This provides the international legal justification for the EU itself and for its many non-MFN agreements with third parties. EU practice across the whole range of its trade activities and policy instruments has been framed, not only by the legal 'disciplines', but also by the common intersubjective understandings of the regime. Thus in the words of a Commission report to the WTO:

> The WTO's system of rules, negotiated market access commitments and its commitment to future progressive liberalisation and strengthened rules constitutes, in a sense, an external framework for agreement on and implementation of the right economic policies, comparable to the EU's own internal market programme, its own experience of international cooperation and rule-making and its commitment to sustainable development.
>
> (WTO 2002a: 4)

The original 1947 GATT was an agreement between 'contracting parties', not an international organization – indeed an International Trade Organization had been explicitly rejected by the US Congress.[5] After the creation of the Common Market this gave rise to the anomaly that only the Member State contracting parties had full legal status and responsibility for carrying out obligations, while at the same time in terms of internal Community law the EC had succeeded them as participants in the GATT (Macleod *et al.* 1996: 179). Notwithstanding, the Commission exercised its exclusive competence in trade matters in the decision-making procedures of the regime – where the Community from the beginning has operated and been accepted as a single actor, a position that was regularized when the EC was given full membership, alongside the Member States, of the new WTO in 1995.[6]

Trade policy-making

As the Common Commercial Policy developed, the Commission exhibited a significant degree of autonomy from the Member States, and a real capacity to behave in a deliberate way in relation to other actors. This is evident both from the legal ascription of competence and in actual practice, which has on occasion moved well beyond the 'letter of the law'. The legal foundation is provided by the exclusive competence in trade granted to the Community in the Common Commercial Policy established by Article 133 of the TEC. This 'most frequently used Treaty provision in the exercise of the European Community's powers in the field of external relations' (Macleod *et al.* 1996: 266) transfers the making and implementation of trade policy to the Community level, and requires a common policy on tariff rates, international negotiations, liberalization, exports and trade protection measures; all based on uniform principles. On this basis the Union now has in excess of 10,000 separate tariff lines and a very extensive corpus of Community trade rules and policy instruments.

In the Common Commercial Policy the Commission has the exclusive right to initiate policy and to propose negotiations, while the Council has the right to approve or disapprove, acting by Qualified Majority Vote (QMV). It is in the field of merchandise trade relations that the Union exhibits the highest degree of actor capability through a daily requirement to identify policy priorities and to formulate policy as a single unit. The need to protect the Single Market and to negotiate externally on a Common External Tariff removes the flexibility and limits the inconsistency that may be evident in other areas of economic policy. This is reflected in the use of QMV by the Council. Yet on occasion, where the national commercial interests of large Member States are severely at risk, a *de facto* consensus may be politically necessary.

In a negotiation the Commission will propose and the Council approve a mandate which provides the brief from which the Commission will actually conduct the talks. Even when representatives of the Member States are physically present (as, for example, at WTO meetings) they will remain silent while the Commission articulates the Union's position. At the end of the negotiation the Commission will propose to the Council the conclusion of any agreement that has been reached.

The Commission, for the purposes of the Common Commercial Policy, is DG Trade – a potent force in Brussels politics and usually associated with an essentially liberal and market oriented approach under the leadership of formidable Commissioners including Sir Leon Brittan, Pascal Lamy and Peter Mandelson. Before the 1999 reorganization of the Commission, 'external relations' was essentially defined as trade. Post 1999, DG Trade exists alongside DG Relex which was given a coordinating role across the range of the Community's external relations. As with any government, bureaucratic and functional incoherence will always be present, but it need not diminish actor capability. There have been difficulties between DGs Trade and Relex described by one official in terms of 'permanent friction' (Interview, DG Trade, July 2001). One source has been the divorce of country desks, located in Relex, from Trade. But 'as 90 per cent of external relations is trade' (ibid.) there has been a need to create equivalent geographic desks within DG Trade (Interviews, DG Relex, July, September 2001). The exact division of responsibilities between the DGs varies according to region and issue and resists any set pattern. For example, in the

Union's negotiations with Mercosur, despite the predominance of trade issues, DG Relex has taken the lead. Similar divisions of responsibility have been required for the Commission's external delegations to third countries, whose focus has been described as 'first on trade, second on aid and only third on the CFSP' (Interview, DG Relex, July 2001). The size of delegations appears generally to reflect the scale of trade, but with some important exceptions such as the very large staff located in Sarajevo. This does not necessarily mean that DG Relex personnel will always lead and there are 22 Delegations (including Washington) where 'DG Trade have demanded priority despite the transfer of control to DG Relex' (Interview, DG Relex, July 2001).

Significantly, there is no formal Trade Council composed of national trade ministers within the regular schedule of Community business as there is, for example, an Agricultural or Environment Council. Instead the Council that deals with trade, alongside a great many other issues, is the General Affairs and External Relations Council (GAERC). This meets monthly and holds separate general affairs and external relations meetings. The scope of external relations includes all the Union's overseas activities: the CFSP, ESDP, trade and development. It may, therefore, be attended by several departmental ministers alongside the 25 foreign ministers of the Member States. Its agendas may be wide-ranging indeed, and have extended from the high politics of the Middle East to such recondite matters as anti-dumping measures against imports of Korean manufactured zip-fasteners. While such a forum may have the benefit of bringing greater co-ordination and coherence to the Union's widespread external actions it cannot have the tightly focused sectoral interest in merchandise trade issues that, say, the Agricultural Council will have with regard to the farming industry.

The function of the Council in trade negotiations is to authorize the Commission to negotiate by approving a mandate and then to ratify the results. Ensuring the enforcement of an agreement once ratified is the exclusive responsibility of the Commission, as is the actual representation of the EU at the WTO and elsewhere. Trade ministers do convene as a Council within the context of WTO meetings, allowing them to adjust the Commission's negotiating mandate 'on the spot'.

In the Common Commercial Policy, as in other areas, there has always been a degree of tension, not to say distrust, between the Member States and the Commission. Sir Roy Denman, then a British trade official, observed one of the early forays of the European actor into trade diplomacy: 'a Commission representative would sometimes turn up for negotiations, flanked by French and German officials who appeared to have him under a kind of house arrest' (quoted in Buchan 1993: 13). This was in the very early 1960s, during the transition period. By the end of the decade a more institutionalized means whereby Member States could monitor the external negotiating activities of the Commission was established. This had a treaty basis in Article 133, where the Commission was charged with the conduct of negotiations 'in consultation with a special committee appointed by the Council to assist the Commission in this task ...'.

The Article 133 Committee has been a significant body in the conduct of the Union's trade diplomacy ever since, in many ways obviating the need for a formal Trade Council. It meets in two formations: monthly at the level of 'full members', who are senior national trade officials assisted by their advisors, partly home and partly Brussels based, and more regularly at the level of deputies, who cope with the technical detail. The Commission is similarly represented at the meetings, and at the more specialized *ad hoc* working groups that the 133 Committee spawns. Working relationships become close and informal and a 'club like atmosphere' pertains (Hayes-Renshaw and Wallace 1997: 90). Although the original function of the Article 133 Committee was to monitor the Commission it has become a close policy collaborator, relating the views of Member State governments to the Commission on a day-to-day basis.

The European Parliament has not been allowed to play a major role in the negotiation or conclusion of trade agreements under Article 133. Despite extending the scope of parliamentary powers elsewhere, the Maastricht Treaty maintained the rule that, although the Council was required to consult the Parliament where other international agreements (including association agreements with significant trade elements) were being made, this should not be the case for the Common Commercial Policy.[7] An extensive set of informal practices have, however, grown up involving consultation with the relevant parliamentary committees during trade negotiations.[8] Co-decision powers for the Parliament would have been introduced by the entry into force of the Constitutional Treaty. There has also been a campaign by the Commission to involve 'civil society' in a dialogue on trade policy, largely in response to popular concerns about globalization and antipathy to the WTO reflected in the collapse of its Millennium Round in Seattle at the end of 1999 (Commission 2004k: 26; WTO 2002a: 15).

Beyond trade in manufactures

While in 1958 the substance of what constituted trade was relatively well understood, by the time of the Uruguay Round, with the potentialities of liberalized trade in goods largely played out and with vast alterations in an increasingly globalized economy under way, this was no longer the case. First of all, however, the Uruguay Round served to place the question of agricultural subsidies at the heart of the trade agenda – a position that it has retained ever since.

The Common Agricultural Policy

As one official rather wearily put it, 'The EU is always at war with somebody over agriculture' (Interview, DG Trade, July 2001). The historic counterpart of the creation of the Common Market was the Common Agricultural Policy (CAP). The basic mechanism of this policy, which sought to increase food production and raise farming incomes, ensured that there would also be external consequences. Artificially high prices within the EC were maintained by the imposition of a 'variable levy' on imports, which served to adjust their price up to the high level set for European produce. The receipts went into the Agricultural Guidance and Guarantee Fund, which was used to intervene in the market to maintain high prices, thereby guaranteeing farm incomes.

Although the CAP soon became a budgetary nightmare (swallowing at one point around 75 per cent of the EC's financial resources), it achieved runaway success in encouraging ever higher levels of food production – way beyond that which could be absorbed by the domestic market. Obligated under the CAP to intervene and purchase the surpluses, the Community sought alternatives to expensive stockpiling in the infamous 'wine lakes' and 'butter mountains'. The economic answer was to subsidize the export of the surpluses through export restitution payments, which made it possible to sell high priced European food on world markets.

The EC soon moved from being largely a food importer to the status of a major exporter. For example, its share of the world wheat flour market increased from 24 per cent in 1963/4 to 62 per cent in 1980/1, while the corresponding US share fell from 40 per cent to 18 per cent (Paemen and Bensch 1995: 24). Not the least dimension of the EU's presence in the global system, and certainly the most objectionable for third parties, has thus been its position in world agricultural markets. This was a function, not of externally orientated policy, but a series of internal developments and actions to cope with the burgeoning CAP, which essentially served to offload some of its problems on to outsiders. The United States, faced with the economic damage done to its agricultural exports, proceeded to retaliate with its own system of farm subsidies, further driving down world prices and worsening the terms of trade of those countries most dependent upon agricultural exports. The worst affected countries were those, like Argentina and Brazil, reliant upon the export of temperate products – cereals, beef, citrus fruits – falling within the remit of the CAP. The EC had, of course, no interest in interfering with trade in tropical products, which have duty free access to the European market.

Once agriculture had been added to the world trade regime's agenda, EC officials found themselves having to negotiate on and justify their farm subsidies. Driven by this, and by the realization of the financial consequences of enlargement for the CAP, reform involving direct income support for farmers rather than production subsidies has been underway since the early 1990s. Progress has, however, been slow. The level of EU agricultural protection remains high, with an average tariff rate four times that applied to industrial goods and a continuing resort to quotas (WTO 2002a: x). Similarly, in 2000, the EU remained the largest subsidizer of agriculture amongst the OECD countries (ibid.: 72), a position that was challenged during 2002 when the US Senate passed its Farm Subsidy Act raising payments to US farmers by 63 per cent (Jawara and Kwa 2004: 139).

The presence of the Single Market

The original Common Market, despite the removal of all internal tariff barriers by mid-1967, never yielded the expected benefits in terms of internal cross-frontier economic activity. In order to remove the remaining non-tariff obstacles to trade and revitalize the European economy, the '1992' project for the completion of the internal market was put in train. Implicit in this project was an understanding that far-reaching measures were required if Europe was to compete effectively with the United States and Japan. This had major external implications. In the EFTA countries it gave rise to the calculation that most of them could no longer prosper outside the Community and, in a process permitted by the ending of the Cold War, led to the accession of Austria, Sweden and Finland.

Presence is as much a matter of external perception as economic statistics, and in the United States the reaction to the completion of the Single Market, which was frequently dubbed 'fortress Europe', was both excessive and politically significant. It helped to stimulate a new US approach to the EU which increasingly focused upon the provisions of the 1992 project and its significant and largely unintended impacts within the US and elsewhere. Liberalization of the services sector and the active role of the Commission in setting technical and other standards across the Single Market had a number of powerful implications. One example is provided by the single GSM standard for mobile phones, which allowed the phenomenal growth of the mobile networks across Europe. Adoption of product standards has extended well beyond the Single Market to such matters as the metrication of US drink containers. In the words of one American commentator, the EU has become the 'world's regulatory superpower':

> ...because of the sheer size of its market and because the Europeans are more philosophically inclined to regulate than their counterparts in Washington and Tokyo for a vast panoply of agricultural, industrial and financial products. In the twenty-first century the rules that run the global economy are largely Brussels' rules.
>
> (Reid 2004: 232)

Market presence had attracted very large in-flows of foreign direct investment (FDI).[9] European firms of 'American parentage', as they are tactfully described, would include within their number most major US corporations. Within the single market, foreign owned corporations are subject to EU competition policy, where the Commission takes anti-trust action, regulates corporate mergers and polices state aids to industry. These actions are internally directed but have external ramifications. Thus, there have been a number of high-profile merger decisions by the Commission that have reverberated across the Atlantic. A good example is provided by the proposed merger of two American owned firms, Honeywell and General Electric in 2001; although approved by US regulators, it was blocked by the Commission. The Commission has also successfully prosecuted Microsoft for its monopolistic practices in software development.

We may generally describe the effects of competition policy in terms of presence but there is also evidence of the growth of actorness. In 1997 the merger between aircraft manufacturers Boeing and McDonnell was challenged by the Commission, even though their operations were entirely conducted within US jurisdiction.[10] For one analyst, competition policy came to represent 'a new instrument of the EU's foreign economic policy' which significantly increased the EU's role in the international political economy and its identity as an international actor (Damro 2001: 208).

The process of 'perfecting' the Single Market has continued with the 2000 Lisbon Agenda, which sought to make the EU the most competitive and dynamic knowledge-based economy in the world, capable of sustainable economic growth and more and better jobs. Sluggish growth in the major European economies since then has made these aims appear utopian but the difficult quest for the full liberalization of telecommunications, energy, transport and services across the Single Market continues. There are parallel and controversial ambitions to reduce labour market 'rigidities' and to stimulate education, research and e-commerce. Behind the Lisbon Strategy was an implicit fear that the sluggish growth rates of many EU national economies were being outpaced by the dynamism of the main competitor – the United States (Wallace 2004: 102). This is not the least of the ways in which the US serves as the most significant comparator in the construction of the Union.[11]

Trade in services

The Single Market, in common with other developed economies under conditions of globalization, has been increasingly dominated by the tertiary sector and invisible trade across frontiers. Services have been well described as 'things which can be bought and sold but which you cannot drop on your foot' (*Economist*, 12 October 1985), but more precise definition has been problematic provoking major questions as to the extent of Community competence. With manufacturing activity increasingly located in the developing world, it was important for the major developed economies, including the Union, to obtain market access for their service industries and to bring the latter within the disciplines of the world trade regime. Thus the Uruguay Round was not only marked by the inclusion of agriculture but new agreements on trade in services (GATS), intellectual property (TRIPS) and investment (TRIMS) were proposed. If any or all the latter were to be defined as part of the Common Commercial Policy then they would be subject to exclusive Community competence, something that a number of Member States were unwilling to countenance, and indeed regarded as the 'thin end of the wedge' in terms of a loss of national sovereignty.[12] During the Uruguay Round negotiating efficiency dictated that the Commission be allowed to exercise a *de facto* competence, but the issue re-surfaced in a European Court of Justice case between the Commission and the Council at the end of the Round. The result was an unsatisfactory compromise judgement (Opinion 1/94ECJ) of the European Court and persistent confusion and complexity in this area, which was alleviated by revisions made at Nice.[13] While, for insiders, the failure to achieve full competence in the new areas of trade in services clearly diminished the capability of the EU as a single economic actor, other WTO members had already assumed that the unitary representation of the EU's interests would continue – that it would constitute a single and comprehensive trade actor – for the ECJ appeared to deny to the EU 'a competence that the rest of the world already took for granted' (Meunier and Nicolaïdis 1999: 490–1).

Economic and Monetary Union

From the beginning the Member States of the Union have been charged with the coordination of their macroeconomic policies and the ECOFIN formation of the Council of Ministers provides the necessary forum. Yet, for most of its existence, the Union has exhibited a peculiarly unbalanced economic presence, where a coherent trade bloc and investment market contrasted starkly with a fragmented fiscal and monetary order. This represented a missed opportunity to enjoy the power and status that is associated with ownership of one of the principal international currencies.

The main motivation for the creation of the euro was, however, not primarily '… the empowerment of Europe on the international stage and the raising of its stature in global economic diplomacy' (McNamara and Meunier 2002: 849). Rather, Economic and Monetary Union was sought in order to complete the Single Market and to protect its operation from damaging exchange rate fluctuations. These efforts came to substantial fruition with the adoption of a single currency in 1999 and the circulation of notes and coinage throughout the eurozone at the beginning of 2002. The result was incomplete in at least two ways. First, not all EU Member States have adopted the euro. The United Kingdom and Sweden have remained outside the single currency, while Denmark does not use the euro but remains a member of the exchange rate mechanism. Similarly, the ten new Member States will only adopt the euro after an extended transition period. Second, while the EU has a centralized monetary policy for the eurozone members it retains a de-centralized set of 25 national budgetary and fiscal policies, those within the eurozone being imperfectly restrained by the controversial Stability Pact.

Despite these provisos the introduction of the euro had an immediate impact upon the rest of the world and was extensively hailed as providing an alternative reserve and international currency to the dollar. Expectations about currencies are of particular significance because they bear upon confidence and exchange values. There were profound implications for the United States, where the privileged position of the dollar, particularly as the currency in which oil was denominated (after a 1973 agreement with Saudi Arabia and OPEC), had enabled it to sustain huge deficits with the rest of the world. Some external analysts prophesied conflict between the two global currencies (Feldstein 1997) while others, even after its launch, saw only the euro's degeneration (Ferguson and Kolitikoff 2000).

The euro, having recovered from its early weakness against the dollar, is clearly a presence to be reckoned with, something which is acknowledged by its adoption as a reserve asset alongside the dollar by a large number of countries including China. Critics also noted that members of President Bush's 'axis of evil' Iran and Iraq were united by their flirtation with the pricing of their oil in euros and that the third member, North Korea, had adopted the euro as a reserve currency.[14] Although there is some evidence that the Union has included provisions on the use of the euro as a reserve asset in its partnership and association agreements with third parties, there has not been an ambition to establish the currency as a clear competitor to the dollar. Rather, concerns have been expressed as to the dangers of reserve currency status for the stability of the new currency. Nor, apart from the coordinated action that was taken after the destruction of the World Trade Centre in September 2001, has there been an indication of eurozone willingness to intervene in external financial crises (Bretherton 2004: 17). In summary, despite the evident and growing presence of the euro, many expectations and a number of significant opportunities related to the problems of the US dollar, the Union has not yet become a monetary actor.

The most evident reason for this is the lack of full participation by the Member States and the way in which this precludes the type of arrangements and external

Community competence that exist for the Common Commercial Policy. The situation is complicated by the existence of another player alongside the Eurogroup of the ECOFIN Council and the Commission – the European Central Bank (ECB). Obligated to be independent it has day-to-day responsibility for maintaining the value of the euro, but the Council, in association with the Commission, has powers in relation to the 'general orientation' of exchange rate policy. Article 111 of the TEC, negotiated at Maastricht, provides for the external representation of the euro by the Council, but the situation remains confused and unsatisfactory.[15] Expectations of actorness remain unfulfilled while:

> The mismatch of the EU's model of 'single currency, many states' and the assumptions of international financial institutions of a one-to-one relation between states and currencies critically limits the EU's ability to project its power internationally in the two key arenas of the monetary realm: the IMF and the G7.
>
> (McNamara and Meunier 2002: 857)

Although the EC is not a member of the IMF, the larger Member States are amongst the major shareholders and ECOFIN meets 'in the margin' of IMF meetings in order to coordinate a European position. The ECB has been granted observer status but the Commission is absent and the Union's representation is fragmented across five separate executive directors, a situation which may not be unwelcome to some EU Member States.[16]

Recognition of the significance of the EC as an economic entity for the purposes of global macroeconomic coordination has been evident since 1980, when the President of the Commission was first invited to attend G7 summit meetings. The G7 is a very different body from the formal quota-based IMF, being essentially a self-appointed club of rich nations. Thus only some eurozone Member States are represented, Germany, Italy and France, while Britain, outside the zone with its own currency, is also a member. Once again there is fragmentation that emphasizes the failure of the Union to build actor capability upon the basis of the presence of the euro.[17]

Capabilities and instruments

We have described the availability of policy instruments as a key aspect of actor capability. The EU's approach has been characterized, in a rather unfair adaptation of Theodore Roosevelt, as 'speak softly and carry a big carrot'. Certainly, the interruption of trade and the political use of aid continue to be the essential instruments available to the Union.

In 'trade defence' there are a goodly number of 'sticks' available alongside the inducements. Trade instruments, permitted by the WTO, are employed directly by the Commission in support of the Common Commercial Policy and to protect the Single Market and specific European industries. These include the use of countervailing duties (GATT Article VI), emergency protection of industries through quantitative restrictions on imports (GATT Article XIX) and anti-dumping measures. The latter remain the preferred instrument for the Commission's defence of the European market against 'unfair' competition.

In 2001 the EU had 175 product categories in which anti-dumping measures were in force – a total only exceeded by the United States (WTO 2002b: 49). However, measured in terms of investigations initiated and definitive anti-dumping measures in the period 1995–2003, the EU ranked third behind India and the US (Commission 2004k: Annex 4, p. 56).[18] Other trade instruments include the enforcement of rules of origin and regulatory action to prevent imports of goods hazardous to health or the environment and trade defence 'safeguard measures' allowing the imposition of retaliatory duties to protect an industry. It is worth pointing out that the EU has only deployed industrial special safeguard measures once since 1992; in response to the effective closing of the US steel market in 2002 (WTO 2002a: 11).

The use of trade defence instruments is closely connected to the extensive activities of the EU as litigant in the WTO's reformed disputes procedure, introduced as part of the Uruguay Round, involving independent adjudication, which can ultimately lead to WTO sanctioned retaliation. In the period 2000 to 2005 the EU was involved in some 40 disputes. Some of them were well publicized, such as the case of US safeguard action over steel imports and its Foreign Sales Corporation subsidies, where the EU was allowed to threaten the imposition of $4 billion in retaliation. The EU has 'continuously been more on the offensive than the defensive' and has generally been a successful litigant winning 13 and losing only 4 completed cases in the period of the Prodi Commission (Commission 2004k: 10, Annex 3).

For years, trade and aid provided the only hard instruments available to the CFSP and they are still pre-eminent. Trade inducements and penalties are available through the manipulation of agreements, quotas and preferential arrangements, and sanctions are deployable under Article 301 of the TEC.[19] Sanctions, mandated by the UN Security Council, have been imposed in respect of imports from the Former Republic of Yugoslavia (terminated in 2000), Saddam Hussein's Iraq (although there was little or no trade to interrupt) and Liberia (under Security Council Resolution 1343 which prohibits trade in conflict diamonds). In less coercive contexts the granting or withholding of trade relations (alongside aid and other benefits) continue to provide the backbone of the Union's relations with most third parties, as discussed below in relation to association and preference agreements. There are also instances where trade measures have had very specific political objectives. For instance, in the immediate aftermath of the terrorist attacks of 11 September 2001, trade instruments, in the form of a Third Generation Cooperation Agreement including enhanced access for Pakistani textile exports, were deployed to encourage the Pakistani government in its alignment with the US and its allies (WTO 2002a: 20). The Union has also attempted to manipulate its extensive trading relationship with Israel for political ends.[20]

Gatekeeper of the Single Market

The everyday economic role of the Community in the world system, and the role in which most countries have direct experience of the Union as an actor, is as gatekeeper of the Single Market and regulator of trade relations. It also now aspires to a more offensive role, as opener of overseas markets, under the Commission's Market Access Strategy.[21]

Trade, market access and aid provide the core business of the more than 140 Brussels missions accredited to the European Community and the essential reason for their existence. For countries as varied as Russia, New Zealand and Israel, the EU is the major trading partner. The composition of missions will reflect this, although there has been some change as the scope of the Union's external activities has expanded. For example, the New Zealand mission was staffed in 2002 by five foreign ministry officials, four of whom were mainly concerned with agricultural trade issues. The fifth post was created in 2000 to cover 'everything other than trade' (Interview, Brussels mission, October 2002).

The first line of defence at the borders of the Union is through the use of tariffs, which have been progressively reduced – at least on industrial goods. There are also quantitative restrictions or quotas, which, although contrary to the principles of the WTO regime, are often imposed upon textiles and agriculture products. As previously discussed, the Commission also defends European producers through the use of 'safeguard measures' and anti-dumping action. More positively, it can also extend preferential access to the Single Market and it is this that provides the underlying structure of relations with all but a few of the Union's trading partners.

Association and preference

In acting out its role as gatekeeper, the Community benefits from its position at the centre of a complicated web of institutionalized bilateral links, as set out in Figure 3.4.[22] The common element in all these agreements is trade and, usually, some form of discrimination or preference. They are also increasingly 'trade-plus' agreements comprising a great deal more than an agreed removal or realignment of tariffs. Association agreements, for example, include Association Councils, annual meetings at ministerial level plus Association Committees of senior civil servants, and there may even be a parliamentary element.

From the earliest arrangements with Greece and Turkey the number and scope of agreements has increased markedly, especially since the 1980s, and renegotiated 'second and third generation' agreements have further broadened the range of items covered. These now include elements of human rights and political conditionality, cultural and technical/scientific cooperation plus security related measures. They are, therefore, 'mixed' agreements in the sense that both the Community and Member States will be parties and parliamentary assent will be required. Furthermore, items within the agreement will not only be beyond exclusive Community competence, but may, as in the case of political dialogue clauses, be beyond Community competence altogether (Macleod *et al.* 1996: 372).[23] Association and cooperation agreements are now so extensive that the majority of states comprising the contemporary international system beyond the Union itself are now in some form of institutionalized relationship with the Union. At the last count the EC had preferential (non-MFN) agreements with no less than 99 states (Commission 2004j). Those excluded are the Union's principal interlocutors and main trading

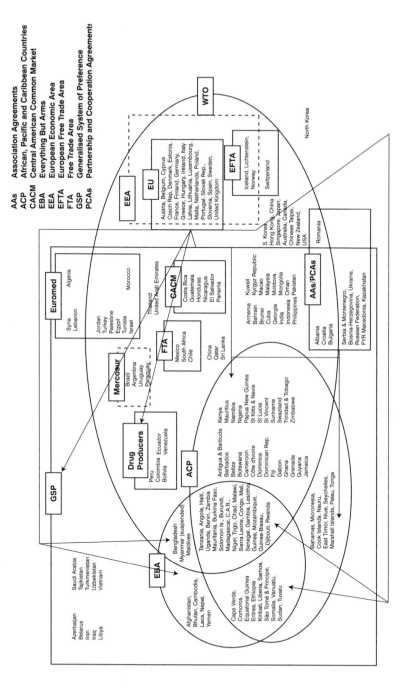

Figure 3.4 EU trade regime 2004

Source: Overseas Development Institute (ODI) 2004c: 3.

partners within the WTO, the ironically styled *most favoured nations*: the United States, Japan, Australia and New Zealand.

The arrangements are legitimized either as Free Trade Areas (FTAs) or customs unions, which are permitted under GATT Article XXIV.[24] This has allowed the Union to attach large areas of the globe, and especially Europe's neighbours in the Mediterranean and the old Soviet bloc countries, to itself. For critics, bilateral FTA agreements between a central customs union and various individual economies have a 'hub and spoke' character in which specific exclusions of 'sensitive' sectors and the use of safeguard clauses can be utilized by import competing industrial lobbies to fend off effective trade liberalization (Hoekman and Kostecki 1995: 226–7). However, the process of accession and the development of trade relations have led to a situation that diverges from such a simple model (see Chapters 5 and 6). The EU's Generalized System of Preferences (GSP) benefits all developing countries, including China, while the Everything But Arms (EBA) initiative of 2001 provides extensive market access for the 49 least developed countries.[25] In addition the Union relates collectively to ACP countries (see Chapter 5) and has tried to develop a Mediterranean regional FTA; opened in 1999 region-to-region talks with Mercosur; and attempted to build upon its links with the Association of South East Asian Nations (ASEAN). These inter-regional exercises have exhibited variable levels of success, but common to all is the propagation of the Union's model of itself and, indeed, an element of mutual identity construction. One explanation of the Union's regional trade strategy reflects a constructivist insight that 'only through self-conscious interaction with comparable "others" does the conception of "self" take shape' (Aggarwal and Fogarty 2004: 15).

Bilateralism, actorness and power

Despite its commitment to WTO multilateralism and to new forms of inter-regional cooperation, the Union continues to rely heavily on bilateral dealings. This has implications for actor capability and for the way in which many states experience it. The 'hub and spoke' arrangement of the EU's preferential arrangements, in particular, bestows a great deal of structural power on the centre in relation to the periphery. The Union is potentially able to dominate a divided set of supplicants and trade partners. For most of the participants in these bilateral arrangements the Union is frequently a domineering actor whose external face is the Commission.

When interviewed, members of the missions in Brussels, professionally concerned with the management of 'trade plus' issues, were in little doubt as to the EU's 'actorness'. It is, said one, 'undoubtedly a coherent actor on trade – almost a trade superpower', and in the words of another 'they are real players' (Interviews, Brussels Missions, October 2002–January 2003). The Union is, of course, inordinately more complex than a state and, as one ambassador put it, the move from negotiating with a government in a national capital to negotiating with the EC in Brussels 'is like changing from playing draughts to playing chess' (Interview, Brussels Mission, June 1996). For others the EU lacked the warmth and cultural tradition experienced in a posting to a normal state. An oft-repeated view, expressed by another trade diplomat, was that the Commission would frequently not be open to negotiation at all, but would simply 'agree a position and push it down our throats … sometimes we say no, but only occasionally'. 'The typical Commission position is "we've cooked up a deal [with the Member States], take it or leave it".' Commission officials will sometimes say 'if you want one word different we will have to go back to the Council' (Interview, Brussels Mission, January 1996).

Behind this lies not only the difficult internal arrangements of the Union, but more brutally, the immense structural economic power of the hub, represented by the Commission, as opposed to even quite substantial trading nations located at the ends of the 'spokes'. For a Trade Counsellor of one such nation it was simply the case that his country was not an equal partner and lacked the muscle to engage in 'aggressive reciprocity' on trade issues; another diplomat's view was 'that ministers had to go to Brussels wearing trousers with reinforced knees' (Interviews, Brussels Missions, June 1996).

The Commission does not solely rely upon an obduracy founded on the difficulty of persuading 25 Member States to agree. In trade matters DG Trade has long experience and competence in every sense of the word, and is quite capable of successfully pursuing its own view even if individual Member States may be uncomfortable. It was a common view amongst the personnel of the Brussels Missions that the Commission could, indeed, behave in an unaccountable way especially in the implementation of external policy. According to the representative of a European neighbour involved in an exasperating dispute over enlargement and the application of anti-dumping duties:

> It is such a complicated machinery and nobody is responsible. When you compare what is said at the highest levels [where support for his country was voiced, especially by individual Member States] and at the technical level the EU is two different actors. At the political level there is encouragement but this is not legally binding; at the substantive, technical level matters are absolutely blocked.
>
> (Interview, Brussels Mission, January 2003)

References to the difficulty of finding out where blockages had occurred in the EU system, and to the influence of individual Commission officials who could single-handedly impose major costs on outsiders dealing with the EC, were made quite frequently by mission trade diplomats. Difficulties frequently occur in the realm of technical detail and the implementation of the Common Commercial Policy, for which the Commission is exclusively responsible. It is, thus, important for the representatives of third countries to know their way around the Commission, the Council Secretariat as well, and increasingly the European Parliament. There was a consensus amongst members of the Brussels Missions interviewed that a critical difference between dealing with the EU and dealing with a state, as far as bilateral trade policy was concerned, was the absence of clear lines of accountability. In other capitals it had usually been possible to resolve technical problems by seeking a political decision from the relevant minister, but in Brussels this was not possible.[26] The EU is different because ultimate decision-making authority in the Union's external economic policy rests with the Member States in Council and with their permanent representatives in the 133 Committee and COREPER. The latter was seen by outsiders as particularly opaque – 'a dark animal'.[27]

Decisions at COREPER, the 133 Committee, and ultimately in the Council, are bedevilled by what trade theorists have called the 'restaurant bill-problem' (Winters 1994). This uses the analogy of a group of depressingly self-interested diners who know that they will have to share a single restaurant bill and, therefore, have an incentive to maximize their own gastronomic pleasure by ordering the most expensive dishes on the menu. In a customs union all members bear the welfare costs of protection but there are individual incentives to obtain protection for the particular products in which a country specializes. Under QMV rules in the Council there is space for a degree of bargaining and reciprocity which, while they may satisfy the immediate political requirements of Member States, will lead to outcomes which are protectionist and, in the view of bilateral trade partners, mean-spirited. Portugal, for example, will not benefit from the restrictions on imported vehicles backed by the French and Italian governments with auto industries to sustain but can set against this measures to protect its own textile sector. For their part, French, Italians and consumers right across the Single Market will be paying higher prices for clothing as well as cars. In bilateral relations it will often be difficult for a partner, who does not have access to the intergovernmental horse-trading that lies at the heart of the EU system, to understand the reasons for discrimination:

> In negotiating with the EU one has to find out which country is obstructing progress and there is a problem of pinpointing which Member [for example Portugal and textiles] is opposing and work on them. Also Member States blame each other. Sometimes it is difficult to pinpoint what is blocking agreement – countries may, for example, veto an issue as a bargaining chip related to some other concern. A deal that you reach is blocked somewhere else for extraneous reasons.
>
> (Interview, Brussels Mission, January 1996)

Diplomats in Brussels are therefore careful to cultivate friendly Member States and their Permanent Representatives, talk, according to one interviewee, 'as much to the *Perm Reps* as to the Commission' (Interview, Brussels Mission, October 2002).

The EU as 'Big Power'

The EU has been portrayed as 'positioned between East and West in the new trilateralism of the early twenty-first century' (M. Smith 2004: 255). One point of this triangular economic configuration was formed by the creation of NAFTA, involving the US, Canada and Mexico, with a further likely extension into Latin America to form the Free Trade Area of the Americas. The situation in the Asia Pacific lacks formal definition and is more 'an emerging notion of economic Asia' (Gilson 2004: 65), where Japanese technological dominance is now matched by a Chinese economy growing at an awe-inspiring rate. The EU has been involved since 1996 in the construction of an Asian bloc (including China, Japan, South Korea and

ASEAN) with which to negotiate in the biannual ASEM meetings. For one observer ASEM allows the Union 'to project onto its embryonic counterpart an ideal-type regional institution' (ibid.: 87). The third, most coherent and equally expansionist point of the triangle is, of course, the EU itself. Despite these formations, the critical relations remain bilateral.

China and Japan

Chinese accession to the WTO at the end of 2001 was '... arguably one of the most momentous events in recent history whose importance far transcends the realms of international trade' (Commission 2004k: 15). As if to reinforce the point, in the subsequent year, China overtook Japan as the Union's principal trading partner after the United States (ibid.: 16). For many years Japan had been regarded as something of an economic superpower with the strength of its exports in manufacture and the impenetrability of its domestic markets a particular problem for the Europeans.[28] Attempts by the Commission to manage these problems in the context of differing attempts at import control by Member States led to what it later described as 'a particularly anguished' trade relationship (Commission 2004k: 7).[29] Until the 1990s this remained the, almost exclusive, focus of the relationship and it was significant that the head of the EC Delegation in Tokyo was not granted the usual full ambassadorial status and accreditation to the Emperor.[30] Attempts have been made to develop a relationship that goes beyond arguments about voluntary export restraints, market access and dumping, based on the 1991 EC–Japan Declaration and involving the creation of an institutionalized political dialogue with annual summit meetings.

According to Buchan (1993: 139), 1991 marked an important turning point for the Japanese who, unlike the US, had no geopolitical interest in the European Union and had previously preferred to deal indirectly through Member State governments. Commission President Delors 'was received by the Emperor, conferring on him virtual head of state status'. Little, however, has resulted and, despite continuing improvements in economic dialogue between the two parties, there remains a sense of mutual indifference. For whatever cultural, historical or geopolitical reasons relations have failed to expand into recognition of the political and strategic significance of either party. The view that here were 'two fledgling superpowers' both 'at a similar stage in taking up their responsibilities on the world stage' (Buchan 1993: 139), now appears far more applicable to the relationship with China.

The Chinese economy has demonstrated extraordinary dynamism with annual GDP growth, in the opening years of the twenty-first century, of the order of 9 per cent. The Chinese themselves expect the EU 'to become China's largest trading and investment partner' (PRC Ministry of Foreign Affairs 2003: 4). Strong trade growth coupled with WTO membership has spawned a rapidly widening political and economic interaction at official level which, by 2005, had produced around 20 separate sectoral dialogues alongside an annual summit meeting. There are many specific problems to be resolved. As a developing country China remains the major beneficiary of the EU's GSP system and its trade relationship with the Union is seriously unbalanced. In 2003 the EU ran its largest bilateral trade deficit with China amounting to no less than €55 billion of a total trade valued at €135 billion (Commission 2004l).

Both sides of the EU–China dialogue entertain geostrategic aspirations that are in some ways mutually contingent. In noting the new maturity of the relationship the key Commission Policy paper asserts that:

> ... the world community expects the EU to play a role which is commensurate with its size and importance not only in the economic area but also on issues of global security and other global concerns. These expectations will grow further as the EU enlarges and streamlines its constitutional structures.
>
> (Commission 2003b: 6)

The Chinese response makes it plain that the 'EU is a major force in the world' and that, 'Despite its difficulties and the challenges ahead, the European integration process is irreversible and the EU will play an increasingly important role in both regional and international affairs' (PRC Ministry of Foreign Affairs 2003: 1). As well as possessing 'highly complementary' economies, both the EU and China 'stand for democracy in international relations and an enhanced role for the UN' (ibid.: 2). This pointed reference to mutual differences with the United States is backed up by the expectation of some future military collaboration and by extensive Chinese involvement in the EU's Galileo programme for a global satellite navigation system.

The developing relationship remains controversial, not least because of long-running concerns over the Chinese human rights record, the enthusiastic and widespread use of the death penalty and the lingering memory of the Tiananmen Square massacre of 1989. The latter was the occasion of a Union arms embargo, but the sheer economic significance of the Chinese relationship has tended to prevent anything other than a polite dialogue on human rights. China policy is also beset by the independent pursuit of the national investment and export interests of some highly competitive Member States, which have exerted pressure to lift the arms embargo. Inconsistency has been endemic in China policy and it is recognized in Brussels that '... it will be important to coordinate Member States' policies towards China to the maximum extent possible, so that the *EU speaks with a single voice* on all key issues ...' (Commission 2003b: 7, emphasis in original). The Chinese government is aware of all this, which makes it all the more significant that it has chosen to place such stress on its emerging geopolitical as well as economic relationship with the Union.

The United States

The multidimensional transatlantic relationship has been studied and agonized over since the days of Henry Kissinger's (1966) *Troubled Partnership*. At the onset of the Cold War the United States was instrumental in the foundation of the European enterprise and its representatives, from Kennedy onwards, have expressed a desire to do business with a European partner on a basis of equality. The only sense in which such an opportunity existed, in an otherwise subordinate and fragmented set of relationships, was economic. In contrast to relationships with Asia, transatlantic economic interaction remains remarkably balanced and interdependent. Both the EU and US have economies of similar size and are each other's most significant trading partner. Around one-quarter of EU–US trade is actually *intra-trade* within transnational corporations, which provides one indicator of the extent of mutual direct investment. This is even more impressive than the trade statistics, with the EU providing 52 per cent of all inward FDI to the US, while the equivalent share of FDI in the Single Market, sourced from the US, was 62 per cent.[31]

Since 1961 the United States has been obliged to deal with a single European trading entity of which the embodiment was the Commission. A symmetrical and in many ways symbiotic relationship has developed over the years, in which the primary interface has been between the European Trade Commissioner and the United States Trade Representative (USTR). This relationship is often viewed by other members as cooperative and apparently collusive, but it is also conflictual. The two continue to dominate the WTO agenda in ways that lead commentators to assume a parity between the US Presidency and the Commission, thus: 'Nothing significant is likely to happen [in the Doha Round] for six months as a result of the US presidential election and the arrival of a new European Commission' (Elliott 2004: 23). Making a further comparison, policy analysts have also argued that the Union has enjoyed a much more defined policy and coherent decision-making system, less open to manipulation by special interests, than its US partner (Heidensohn 1995: 127; Peterson 1996: 111).

The history of US–EU bilateral trade relations is marked by specific conflicts within a broad consensus on the nature of the regime. The pattern was initiated by the celebrated 'chicken war' of 1963–4, in which the US side invoked GATT compensation rules for the loss of markets for poultry exports attendant upon the erection of the Customs Union. Since then the record of GATT and the WTO disputes panels has contained many, often bitterly contested, cases over tuna, subsidized steel exports, wheat, canned fruit, oilseed, bananas, bovine growth hormones and the US Foreign Sales Corporation Act. The US and EU have both been enthusiastic users of the reformed WTO disputes procedure – most often against each other![32]

The military analogies sometimes used to describe US–EU bilateral trade conflicts are essentially misplaced, because they occur within a complex multidimensional relationship which, in the last analysis, has always ensured that even the most acrimonious disputes have been settled. As we have seen, these also included the transatlantic effects of EU policies, in 'beyond the border' areas such as financial regulation and technical standard-setting, which had real implications for US competitiveness emanating from the presence of the UN. This posed what Hocking and Smith (1997: 56) have described as a 'challenge of conceptualisation':

> … was the EC to be treated as proto-state, as a complex set of functional networks or as a type of federal system in which the member states were analogous to the American states?

The answer to this question was an attempt at wide-ranging engagement with the EU on a range of policy dimensions that went well beyond the Community's external trade competence. American objectives were not simply to negotiate with the relevant parts of the European entity but actively to set agendas and to be closely involved with the formulation of policy. The 1990 Transatlantic Declaration sought to institutionalize an impressive range of bilateral meetings and consultative procedures from presidential down to 'technical' levels. For example there were, by 2002, 22 meetings at assistant secretary level between EU and US officials scheduled during each six-month presidency. The activities of the large US Mission in Brussels increasingly shadowed those of the Union itself and US business in Europe developed its own impressive representational arm in AMCHAM.[33]

The transatlantic economic partnership, despite an impressive range of acronyms, initiatives and dialogues, some of them re-launched, has, nonetheless, failed to deliver anything approaching a full transatlantic marketplace. There have been multiple opportunities for discussion but very little substantive achievement to match either the underlying interdependence of the economies or the rhetoric of the various declarations. In the early years of the twenty-first century DG Trade's approach was to foreswear grand initiatives, when 'such initiatives have not prospered in the past', in favour of more limited and concrete regulatory cooperation (Commission 2004k: 13).[34]

The extent to which US recognition has moved beyond trade will be examined in subsequent chapters. There have been conflicts over the Kyoto Protocol and the International Criminal Court where Washington has been obliged to deal with the EU as its principal antagonist. In other circumstances, notably the Iraq invasion of 2003, it has sought to exploit divisions between the Member States, or in defence matters to prefer NATO to the emergent ESDP. Yet the functional basis of the transatlantic partnership remains in the growing interdependence of the EU and US which, although the high hopes of the late 1990s for a fully fledged transatlantic marketplace may have been disappointed, remains real enough to compel both sides to engage deeply with each other. Despite the conflicts and setbacks there has been an expanding US conceptualization of the capabilities of the European entity reflected in the organization of its diplomatic effort, which in the mid-1990s shifted posts from embassies in Member State capitals to the Brussels Mission (Interview, US Mission, Brussels, January 1997). It was undoubtedly symbolic that in February 2005 George Bush, much vilified for his insensitivity to European concerns, became the first serving US President to officially visit the Council and Commission of the European Union.

The Union as multilateral trade negotiator

Observers of the GATT and WTO and the shifting structure of their protracted negotiations are at one in stressing the central importance of the Union and its relationship to the US – whom Jacques Delors called the 'two elephants on the world market' (Buchan 1993: 9). During the Uruguay Round (which ran on from 1986 to 1994) a key group in determining the outcome was the 'Quad'. 'Quad' meetings involved the USTR, EC External Relations Commissioner and trade ministers of Japan and Canada (and on occasion Australia) or their chief negotiators or officials.

While the 'Quad' represented four major developed world players in international trade, the ultimate fate of the negotiations turned upon an intense bilateral confrontation between the two largest participants – including the famous or infamous 1992 Blair House agreement that dealt with the agricultural differences that had held up the conclusion of the round.[35]

Since the conclusion of the Uruguay Round a number of developments have made it more difficult for the EU, US and other large developed powers to dominate the trade regime. In a process which deeply involved the EU, the organization was expanded to around 150 members including China, but also Cambodia, Nepal, Jordan and Moldavia. A substantial developing world majority was now also required to accept and implement the outcomes of negotiating rounds rather than being able to retire to the sidelines. With new popular concern about the manifold implications of globalization, the WTO acquired an unaccustomed political salience and became the target both of NGOs and organized protest. In consequence, the attempt to launch a new Millennium Round at the end of 1999, at the Seattle WTO ministerial meeting, collapsed amidst North–South disagreement within the meeting and violent protests outside it.

A lack of concern with development issues and Southern resistance to the inclusion of 'social' clauses lay at the heart of the failure to agree a new round and it was with this in mind that the Union led attempts to remedy the situation with the launch of the 2001 Doha Development Round (DDR). These efforts revealed how complicated the WTO negotiating situation had become. The EU, which was generally given the credit for bringing the DDR to life (WTO 2002a: ix; Young 2004: 215), engaged in extensive diplomacy within a new context, both before and after another setback at the Cancún Ministerial of 2003. This meeting also saw the emergence of a new grouping of developing economies, the G20 led by China, India and Brazil.

The old developed world dominance of the 'Quad' was replaced by 'a flexible feast of mini and micro Ministerials, ad hoc groupings, always with the EU, US, Brazil and India at the core ...' (Commission 2004k: 7).[36]

Agriculture constitutes the key impediment to the advancement of the EU's other objectives in the trade regime. This has been so ever since the launch of the Uruguay Round with its objective of making agricultural trade and subsidies subject to GATT disciplines. Trade negotiations have served to stimulate reform of the CAP away from production subsidies, a process that has been slowly taking place since the 1992 McSharry reforms.[37] Achieving agreement with the US on agricultural subsidies remained fundamental to progress in the Doha Round, but even when there was progress on this issue, prior to Cancún, the results were rejected by the G20 as insufficient to remedy the damage done to their agricultural producers. They were also insufficient to warrant the kind of concessions that were required by the EU on the 'Singapore issues'.

These 'issues' (so named because they first appeared on the agenda at the 1996 Singapore Ministerial) comprise investment, competition policy, trade facilitation, public procurement and labour standards. The first four reflect sectors in which the EU has extensive and growing presence extending beyond the Single Market. It is in such areas, along with trade in services, that the EU, having opened its market to merchandise imports and liberalized its agriculture, might be expected to enjoy a comparative advantage if closed foreign markets can be unlocked. Such objectives may be regarded as the external counterpart of the liberalization and integration proposals for the internal market set out in the 2000 Lisbon Agenda. The EU's insistence on the 'Singapore issues' precipitated the failure of the Cancún Ministerial in 2003 and they have since disappeared from the agenda of the DDR. Instead the EU has pressed forward with an offer on a further opening up of trade in services, alongside an initiative to ensure that new commitments arising from the round will not be onerous for developing countries – the 'Round for Free' proposal (Commission 2004k: 8).

As a counterpart to these liberalizing moves, EU policy at the WTO has also reflected a concern with labour standards and the links between trade and environmental degradation. The demand that trade liberalization be linked to certain minimum standards for workers was highly controversial at Seattle, where it received backing from a US Democratic administration and trade union demonstrators. Since then it has lost impetus in the WTO. The EU's concern with trade and environment has continued to be significant and is dealt with in Chapter 4. Both issues are regarded with scepticism and hostility by the majority of developing countries as a form of disguised protectionism for the markets of rich countries.

Trade negotiations make exacting demands upon actor capability. The Uruguay Round, for example, involved the detailed negotiation of the 26,000 pages of text that constituted the output of a negotiation conducted at 'expert' level by officials operating within the 15 working groups. In some respects the undisputed centrality of the EU in the trade regime served to highlight the negotiating inadequacies arising from its ambivalent position as an actor – even in the area of trade policy – where it might be expected to be at its most consistent and coherent. This view was commonly and effectively deployed by the US side to blame the internal disagreements of the Community on agriculture for various *impasses* in the long Uruguay process. Those on the European side were more than aware of the vulnerability of 12 states operating by EC rules, with mandates and conclusions dependent on qualified majorities, subject, always, to the threat of national veto under the Luxembourg compromise.

Uruguay was conducted by a Community of twelve Member States; contemporary negotiations will involve 25 or more. A Union delegation will be involved in a continuous two-level negotiation involving the 133 Committee operating in parallel to the formal and informal exchanges of the WTO itself. Mandates and the conclusions of the negotiations will also have to be ratified by the Council. We have in part defined actor capability in terms of the effective formulation of common policy – something that will always raise problems of inconsistency given the varying interests of Member States. A continuing theme has, for example, been the resistance of France and other Member States to the dismantling of the CAP, but there were others too. Greece, Italy and Portugal, for example, protected their national industries by opposing the phasing out of textile quotas under the Multi-Fibre Agreement by allowing the Commission minimal negotiating flexibility (Paemen and Bensch 1995: 136). GATT and WTO negotiations have thus been punctuated by well-publicized deadlocks in the Council. Awareness of the differences between Member States will ensure that Commission negotiators find themselves 'ducking and weaving in multilateral discussions simply in order to avoid a split in the Community ranks' (Paemen and Bensch 1995: 157).

There can be no doubt that the EU's character and decision-making system introduce both complexity and inflexibility into its conduct of negotiations. However, just as it is unfair to assume that the EU is unique in its agricultural protectionism (in some respects it is exceeded by the US and Japan), it is wrong to assume that its policy is uniquely hidebound by its decision-making structure. The internal politics of trade and the power of special interests in Congress, particularly in a presidential election year, can also render United States policy immobile. In fact the record of the Doha Round indicates that it is the EU, despite its internal deficiencies, that has been able, more than any other member, to take the initiative in agenda-setting. At the same time, the history of the foregoing Uruguay Round indicates that despite the delay introduced by the evident inconsistency between Member State trading interests these were ultimately resolved and progress achieved.

Exclusive Community competence for trade certainly helps to explain the relative effectiveness of the Union at the WTO, particularly in terms of the arcane detail of a trade negotiation. Here, Woolcock and Hodges (1996) make a useful distinction between the 'technocratic' and 'political' control of policy. Generally, the Commission has to be given the latitude to negotiate in collaboration with the 133 Committee, and the Council merely 'rubber stamps' the results. The alternative mode of proceeding attracts publicity but applies to only a few high-profile areas, like agriculture or audiovisual services, where there is active 'political' involvement and open controversy.

There is also evidence that the Commission is adept at the deployment of various forms of pressure on other WTO members. In the campaign to build support for the DDR, 'The EC approached the issue of arm-twisting in a more subtle manner than the USA … making sure that negotiators were aware of the EC's expectations' by the Trade Commissioner's 'endless trips to developing countries' and the way in which the latter were 'gently reminded … of the importance of the various preferential economic and trade arrangements their countries enjoyed with the EC' (Jawara and Kwa 2004: 162).

Operating in 'technocratic' mode, the Commission can be an effective, coherent and frequently innovative negotiator. According to one commentator: 'it was possible to reach an agreement [on the Uruguay Round] largely because the European Union negotiated as a unit and showed itself willing and able to take on a global leadership role' (Leonard 1997: 18). In the words of Peter Sutherland, GATT Director General at the end of the Round, and admittedly also a former European Commissioner, 'We wouldn't have a WTO if the European Union did not have a common commercial policy and did not negotiate with one voice' (*New Statesman and Society*, 18 October 1996: 21). Similar comments would not be out of place in describing the role of the Union as the driving force behind the Doha Round.

Conclusion

The growing economic presence of the European Union has ensured that, in many respects, it can be regarded as a great power, rivalling and even exercising a form of trade duopoly with the United States. Initial Community competence for the Common Commercial Policy has ensured that, in the field of trade relations, the Union has developed an equivalent capacity to act. For the many states with which it maintains preferential trade relations it can be a dominating and sometimes inscrutable actor. Its exclusionary practices in this respect, and its aggressive pursuit of market opening, are incompatible with constructions of the Union as a value-based actor. Nevertheless the EU also uses its economic instruments to pursue objectives in the area of human rights and poverty alleviation. The EBA initiative and attempts by the Commission to open up a civil society dialogue on trade policy suggest a more inclusive identity.

Although the EU increasingly appears to outsiders as a single economic entity, its external representation and capacity to act still varies by issue. Changes in the global economy, and the growth of the Union's economic presence in areas such as services and investment, have exerted pressure for the EU to find some way of representing itself externally. While this is being achieved in respect of trade in services there are problems elsewhere which render the Union an incomplete economic actor. Pre-eminent here are the expectations and potential associated with the development of the Single Currency.

This chapter precedes the other substantive considerations of the Union as an actor for a reason. The economic presence of the Union, its construction as a single entity by outsiders and the progressive development of actor capability from its basis in merchandise trade continue to provide the essential base of and roles in the global system. The Union necessarily utilizes its trading strength to underpin what might be described as its broader foreign policy objectives, which are the subject of subsequent chapters. Trade policy has provided the foundation of the Union's relations with outsiders and many of the key instruments available to its emergent foreign policy. It also provides a yardstick for the assessment of actorness in other domains.

4 Environmental policy
The Union as global leader

In contrast with its role as a world trading power, the Union's rise to prominence in global environmental politics was unforeseen. This chapter considers how this came about and how the Union, despite the special difficulties associated with mixed competence in this area, became a leading actor in both regional and global environmental governance. Its roles extend beyond participation in particular negotiations to encompass the propagation of environmental norms, the pursuit of sustainable development and, perhaps most important of all, leadership of attempts to curb the menace of climate change. As elsewhere, presence provides the foundation.

By any standards the countries of the European Union cast a long ecological shadow. Such presence is commensurate with the scale of industry, transport, energy consumption and agriculture within an economy second only in scale to that of the United States. Inevitably the EU will be amongst the largest polluters and resource exploiters on earth. One measure of the burden imposed by the EU on the earth's resources has been calculated in terms of annual 'total material requirement' – the volume of material, excluding air and water, that flows through an economy, about 80 per cent of which is released back into the environment within one year. The figure calculated for the EU, at the end of the twentieth century, was around 19 billion tonnes or approximately 50 tonnes per capita (the US equivalent was 84 tonnes), 'indicating continuous pressure on the global environment due to resource extraction for the EU economy' (Bringezu and Schütz 2001: 12, 16). Significantly, 40 per cent of the material involved was extracted beyond the borders of the EU (ibid.: 31).

In many other areas the countries of the EU exploit a substantial slice of the earth's resources. The scale of the European fishing 'effort' provides an obvious example, as EU-based trawlers range far beyond those depleted waters subject to the Common Fisheries Policy.[1] Apart from the sustainability implications of the Common Agricultural and Fisheries Policies (CAP and CFP) the EU's environmental presence is most directly experienced by the Union's immediate neighbours in Eastern Europe and the Mediterranean, but there has been an increasing realization that an economy the size of the EU's has major responsibilities on a global scale: for stratospheric ozone depletion, climate change, desertification and species loss.

In the beginning the Treaty of Rome was silent upon environmental matters which were, accordingly, almost entirely absent from considerations of Europe's role in the world system.[2] Just as there were no common environmental policies, the salience of environmental questions for international politics was not yet widely apparent. The process whereby the natural environment became the subject of international and even 'high' politics merits study in its own right (Vogler 2002a). It was, in large part, a reaction to scientific understanding and public awareness of the gravity of transboundary environmental impacts (for example 'acid rain' deposition in Europe) and, during the 1980s, the result of a burgeoning concern with change and degradation on a global scale that coincided with the ending of the Cold War. This set the stage for the landmark 1992 Rio Earth Summit (UNCED) which agreed *Agenda 21* – a blueprint for sustainable development – and provided the stage for the signing of the Framework Convention on Climate Change (FCCC) and the Convention on Biodiversity. It also provided a significant opportunity for the development of a European environmental identity and the growth of related capabilities as an actor in the new environmental diplomacy. Participation in 'international environmental discourse' (Lenschow 2004) provided stimuli to domestic action and helped to embed sustainability concepts in the Union's view of itself and its mission.[3]

The initial thrust of environmental policy was to remove trade distortions arising from different national standards and policies, although measures were also introduced with the sole purpose of promoting the conservation of the environment. The Single European Act of 1987 strengthened the latter by according explicit treaty status to the Community's environmental objectives: to preserve, protect and improve the quality of the environment, to contribute towards human health and to ensure a prudent and rational utilization of resources (TEC Article 174). Also embodied in this article were the principles of prevention and that 'the polluter should pay'. Preventive policy has been further developed by adoption of the 'precautionary principle' that dispenses with the requirement that policy must always be based on full scientific evidence that harm to the environment has occurred.[4] As we shall see, this has had significant and controversial implications at the international level.

Since the Single Act there has been a cascade of legislation, making the environment the area in which there was the greatest increase in Community activity; and in which national policies were increasingly determined at the European level (Sbragia 1996: 243).[5] The paradox is that, despite this unprecedented legislative development, environmental concerns are still acute especially over climate change, energy consumption and waste disposal (European Environment Agency 2004: 6). Part of the explanation is to be found in the equally unprecedented number of cases at the ECJ relating to the enforcement of the environmental *acquis* (Knill and Lenschow 2002: 4).

Environmental policy has a markedly expansive quality that goes well beyond the strict responsibilities of the Commission's DG Environment. This, coupled with the inter-sectoral character of much environmental policy, can make 'internal' deliberations quite extensive and often difficult (Sbragia 1996: 244–6). They will involve trade, agriculture, industry, taxation, energy, transport, aid and scientific research. Since the SEA, treaty revisions have reflected this by indicating that environmental protection 'shall be a component of the Community's other policies' (TEC Article 6).

The promotion of policy coherence in the area of trade, agriculture development, fisheries and the environment involves a range of relevant Commission DGs and inter-service consultation procedures and may even require a decision to be taken at the level of the College of Commissioners. DG Environment, responsible for much, but by no means all, environmental policy, is surprisingly small in size compared with national ministries and other Commission DGs. DG Trade and DG Environment both have their own units specializing in the nexus between their two areas of responsibility. The DG Environment trade unit will operate in Geneva and attend meetings of the WTO's Trade and Environment Committee. Good working relations also exist on the overlapping agendas of DG Development and DG Environment (Interview, DG Development, 2001), but serious problems appear to occur with DG Agriculture who 'feel they are attacked from all sides' and insist on relating to other DGs through the formal system (ibid.). Issues will also be determined by the position of the various DGs and the constituencies whose interests they reflect in the Brussels 'pecking order'. Thus Trade, Agriculture and Fisheries are strong DGs with powerful Commissioners, a status not always enjoyed by the 'second division' Environment and Development DGs with 'junior' Commissioners.

Environmental policy has also been beset with problems of consistency between Member States. This is hardly surprising given their differing locations, degree of modernization and varying administrative traditions. However, it is also possible for large industrialized Member States at similar levels of development to have fundamental policy differences over such issues as pollution control and the regulation of the chemical industry. The situation is further complicated by the variety of Community decision-making procedures and shared competences to which environmental policy is subject. This may be seen, in part, as a consequence of the slow and somewhat *ad hoc* development of environmental policy – in comparison, for instance, with the initial establishment of Community competence for trade. Complexity also results from various bargained compromises between a range of interests eager, on the one hand, to restrain the expansion of the Community's competence and, on the other, to advance green legislation while ensuring that common policies do not provide a brake on progressive national developments. Thus, not only does environmental policy touch virtually the entire scope of the Community's policy competences, it can also be subject to almost the whole range of the EU's variegated decision-making procedures. This can be of some importance for the Union's performance as an actor in international environmental politics; not least as a source of bewilderment for third parties.

Externalization of the EC's environmental policies

The same dynamics that have driven the production of environmental policies at Union level also served to internationalize them. There are three main drivers at work here. First, the pressure to respond to transboundary pollution and, increasingly, to global scale environmental changes in areas where the European Community was necessarily involved because of its legislative competence. Second, what may be broadly regarded as the trade implications of environmental policy. Third, and on occasion in contradiction to trade policy, the increasingly articulate demands of European publics and pressure groups for action on issues including animal welfare, climate change and genetically modified food.

The need to respond to transboundary threats provided the impetus for the earliest major international negotiations in which the EC was engaged, that is the negotiation of the Long Range Transboundary Air Pollution (LRTAP) Convention of 1979 and its subsequent protocols relating to transboundary fluxes of nitrous and sulphuric oxides. The opportunity for Community participation in these negotiations, involving over 30 North American and European states, arose in large part from the period of détente in Europe that marked the interval between the first and second Cold Wars. There was a clear link to Community policy on acidification (and so called 'acid rain') which had resulted in a stream of directives from 1970 onwards intended to regulate harmful emissions.[6] An essentially similar point can be made about increasing involvement in marine pollution control, which physically must include both Member States and third parties in the North Sea and the Mediterranean. The Union has also participated in negotiations relating to the sustainability of shared 'common pool' resources. Here, the international dimension of fisheries policy has meant that the Community, with competence in this area, has long been a significant actor. In 2004 it operated some 22 bilateral fisheries agreements, 15 of which involved paying financial compensation to African coastal states in return for access to their waters for EU vessels.[7] The EC is also a signatory, in its own right alongside the Member States, of the 1982 United Nations Convention on the Law of the Sea.

Direct interest in the global change phenomena that achieved such prominence in the 1980s is, perhaps, less immediately evident. In the case of stratospheric ozone depletion, the EC was slow to respond initially and beset by internal competence problems and the special interests of its national chemical industries. However, European publics soon became aware that the dangers of UV-B induced skin cancers and genetic mutations were not confined to the high latitudes of the Southern Hemisphere and the EC had, by the end of the 1980s, assumed a much more proactive stance. More recently there have been widespread concerns about GMOs and strong animal rights lobbies, both of which have significantly influenced EU policy interventions.

Climate change issues associated with the enhanced greenhouse effect dominated the international environmental agenda during the early 1990s. The EU was not amongst those most obviously at risk, although low-lying coastal areas (Netherlands and East Anglia) would be subject to inundation and there has been a dawning realization that climate change is associated with the abnormal weather experienced in Europe. Given the responsibilities of developed countries for the problem of global warming, it would have been unthinkable that the Union should not have been involved from the beginning with the negotiation and development of the 1992 Framework Convention on Climate Change, and in providing financial and other support for the Intergovernmental Panel on Climate Change. The EU has also become a leading participant in the other 'global change' Conventions such as those for biodiversity and desertification.

Apart from the salience of this new global environmental diplomacy, coincident with the ending of the Cold War, another source of opportunity was soon to emerge which led outsiders to construct the Union as an environmental leader – a mantle which, by the late 1990s, was being enthusiastically worn by EU spokespersons. The source was the wholesale abdication of leadership in global environmental policy by the United States. Evident under the Clinton administration it was raised to a point of principle by its successor in the 2001 denunciation of the Kyoto Protocol on climate change. It was a pattern evident elsewhere in biodiversity, hazardous waste, GMOs and across the whole gamut of multilateral endeavour.

The second source of internationalization derives from the fact that implementation of measures to counter environmental threats, or promote good practice at national (or at EU) level, will inevitably impact upon trade, investment and other flows across national boundaries. This provided much of the motivation for the initial inclusion of environmental concerns in the EC's policy-making, and the need to ensure a 'level playing field' remains an incentive for the Community to negotiate with third parties on environmental issues.

The link between trade and environment has become increasingly salient and disputed. It has provided much potential for policy incoherence and indeed for well-publicized contradictions between the Union's role as trader and its aspirations to environmental leadership (Bretherton and Vogler 2000). Such contradictions were evident during the infamous Tuna-Dolphin case in which the EC joined Mexico in challenging the right of the United States to use trade instruments to enforce 'dolphin friendly' fishing practices.[8] They were present, too, in the long-running dispute over 'leghold traps', which set the various Community institutions at loggerheads over the rival demands of free trade and animal welfare.[9] However, antipathy between trade and environmental objectives is hardly the norm and, as we shall see, the Union has gone some way to integrate environmental concerns into its policies at the WTO.

In consequence of all this activity, and much that has not been mentioned, the Community (apart from or alongside the Member States) is now a signatory to, and participates in more than sixty major multilateral environmental agreements, as detailed in Table 4.1. The precise way in which participation occurs is subject to considerable variation and the question of EU actorness is altogether more complex in the area of international environmental politics than it is in the field of trade. The familiar Article 133 type procedures do occur where exclusive community competence has been established; as, for example, in negotiations about the conservation of fish stocks or where matters under discussion fall within the Common Commercial Policy or the Common Agricultural Policy. At the other extreme, there may be exclusive Member State competence equivalent to the Common Foreign and Security Policy within Pillar II. This will involve unanimity voting in the Council, giving each of the Member States an effective veto. The Commission will have a subordinate and implementing role, while the duties of spokesperson and leader of the EU will be assumed by the representative of the Member State that currently holds the Presidency.

Because of the way in which EU environmental policy has evolved, and because of the 'cross cutting' nature of the subject matter of this relatively new area of diplomacy, most negotiations will not align neatly with either exclusive Community or Member State competence. Instead, competence is often 'shared'; Member States and the Community having 'concurrent' powers. The exact mixture, which has major implications for the extent of EU actorness, will depend upon the location of internal competence and the granting of external recognition.

Table 4.1 EC participation in multilateral environmental agreements

ATMOSPHERE

C. on long-range transboundary air pollution GENEVA 1979 and Protocols 1984, 1988, 1991, 1994, 1998, 1999.

C. for the protection of the Ozone Layer VIENNA 1985 and Protocol 1987 MONTREAL and Amendments 1990, 1992, 1997, 1999.

TRANSBOUNDARY IMPACTS

C. on Environmental Impact Assessment in a transboundary context ESPOO 1991.

C. on transboundary effects of industrial accidents HELSINKI 1992.

ANIMALS AND HABITATS

C. on the conservation of migratory species of wild animals BONN 1979.

C. on the conservation of European wildlife and natural habitats BERN 1979.

European C. for the protection of vertebrate animals used for experimental and other scientific purposes STRASBOURG 1985.

C. on the protection of the Alps SALZBURG 1991 and 3 Protocols 1994.

A. on the conservation of African-Eurasian waterbirds the HAGUE 1995.

INFORMATION

C. on access to environmental information AARHUS 1998.

MARINE POLLUTION

C. for the prevention of marine pollution from land based sources PARIS 1974 & Protocol 1986.

C. for the protection of the Mediterranean Sea against pollution BARCELONA 1976 and Protocols 1976, 1976, 1980, 1982, 1995, 2002.

C. on the Law of the Sea MONTEGO BAY 1982.

C. for the protection and development of the marine environment of the wider Caribbean region CARTEGENA DE INDIAS 1983 and Protocol 1983.

A. for co-operation in dealing with pollution of the North Sea by oil and other harmful substances BONN 1983.

C. for the protection, management, and development of the marine and coastal environment of the East African region. NAIROBI 1985 and Protocols 1985, 1986.

Co-operation A. for the protection of the coasts and waters of the North East Atlantic against accidental pollution LISBON 1990.

C. for the protection of the marine environment of the Baltic Sea area. HELSINKI 1992.

C. for the protection of the marine environment of the Baltic Sea area HELSINKI 1972. (EC accession pending)

C. for the protection of the marine environment of the North East Atlantic PARIS 1992.

WATERCOURSES

C. for the protection of the Rhine against chemical pollution BONN 1976.

C. on the protection of the Rhine BERN 1999

C. on the International Commission for the protection of the Elbe MAGDEBURG 1980 and Protocol 1991.

C. on the protection and use of trans-boundary watercourses and international lakes 1992.

C. on the co-operation for the protection and sustainable use of the Danube SOFIA 1994.

C. on the International Commission for the Protection of the Oder WROCLAW 1996.

WASTES AND POLLUTANTS

C. on the control of transboundary movements of hazardous wastes and their disposal BASEL 1989.

C. on PIC procedure for hazardous chemicals and pesticides ROTTERDAM 1998.

C. on Persistent Organic Pollutants STOCKHOLM 2001.

DESERTS

UN C. on Desertification PARIS 1994.

CLIMATE CHANGE

UN Framework C. on Climate Change NEW YORK 1992 and Protocol KYOTO 1997.

BIODIVERSITY AND FORESTS

UN C. on Biological Diversity RIO 1992 & Protocol on Biosafety CARTAGENA 2000.

A. on International Tropical Timber GENEVA 1994.

MARINE LIVING RESOURCES

C. on future multilateral co-operation in fisheries in the North West Atlantic 1978.

C. on future multilateral co-operation in North East Atlantic fisheries 1980.

C. on conservation of Antarctic marine living resources CANBERRA 1980.

C. for the conservation of Salmon in the North Atlantic area 1982.

C. on fishing and conservation of the living resources in the Baltic Sea and Belts 1973. (EC Accession 1992)

UN A. on the conservation of small cetaceans of the Baltic and North Seas NEW YORK 1992.

UN A. on the conservation and management of straddling fish stocks NEW YORK 1995.

The EC is a signatory to all the agreements listed. Source DG Environment website, MEAs, 17/08/04.

Internal and external competence

Initially, as we have seen, exclusive Community competence was limited to the areas where it was expressly provided in the Treaty establishing the European Communities (TEC). However, as the Community's policies developed, conflicts began to emerge between internal legislation and the external agreements made by Member States. In an important 'leading case', the ERTA judgement of 1970, the ECJ went well beyond the provisions of the TEC by establishing the doctrine of 'parallelism', that is to say when the Community acquires internal competence over a subject it also acquires external competence.[10] This had implications for the conduct of external environmental policy which did not have a treaty basis.[11] The ERTA case and subsequent judgements and practice thus provided a means whereby the Commission could assert its right to be involved in the conduct of international environmental negotiations.[12]

Unfortunately, competences cannot be precisely listed and a new negotiation will raise the question of determining competence, which can prove a controversial matter for Member State governments.[13] If the questions under consideration relate entirely to trade or to fisheries, then there is exclusive Community competence and Article 133 type procedures apply. Thus, at the UN Conference on Straddling Stocks and Highly Migratory Fish Stocks, concluded in August 1995, the EC had exclusive competence and the Commission negotiated for the Community on a Council mandate. When the European Community accession to the Convention on the Conservation of Antarctic Marine Living Resources (CCAMLR) was proposed, Member States objected to exclusive Community competence on the following grounds. The CCAMLR is an advanced type of resource agreement because it involves a total ecosystem approach to marine conservation. Its purpose is manifestly not just to preserve fish stocks (a Community competence) but also to protect other forms of life dependent upon them – notably penguins. Penguins are, of course, birds. However, Community competence for the preservation of birds under its Bird Directive only extends to Europe, not the Southern Ocean (Macrory and Hession 1996: 132).

Most environmental issues involve mixed agreements and concurrent competence, where representation is legally shared between the Presidency and the Commission. For example, trade and air pollution issues in the stratospheric ozone negotiations fell within Community competence, while other matters were reserved to Member States.[14] Another example is provided by the Basel Convention on hazardous waste. It has trade aspects (where there is full Community competence), scientific aspects (where there is Member State competence), and environmental aspects – where shared competence prevails. The Biodiversity Convention negotiations were also marked by divided competences, with a strong Community position on trade and intellectual property, but Member State competence in other areas. At the beginning of the process of negotiating the Climate Change Convention there was little Community competence and the Commission was not a formal participant in the Intergovernmental Negotiating Committee (INC). Subsequent to this the EC signed the Climate Change Treaty alongside the Member States and EU delegations have always included the Commission, but competence can raise problems when nationally sensitive taxation and energy policy issues arise.

Finally, there are instances where, although clear Community competence is established, external actors will not afford recognition and participation rights to the EC as opposed to its Member States. A continuing example is provided by the Convention on Trade in Endangered Species (CITES) where the subject matter is clearly within Community competence but where the EC does not have status. Under these circumstances it is understood that Article 10 of the TEC imposes a 'duty of solidarity' on Member States to pursue a common position. This serves to highlight the importance of external conceptions of the European entity and the willingness that exists to recognize and treat with it. While competence issues may complicate the way in which the EU acts they are compounded by problems of external recognition.

External recognition

The European Community, unlike the Union, is provided with a legal personality by the TEC, along with the right to conclude international agreements in areas of its exclusive competence. Thus, the European Community appears, alongside the Member States, as a signatory of various multilateral environmental agreements; the Montreal Protocol; the Framework Convention on Climate Change and the Convention on Biodiversity.

An important step towards external recognition was taken during the negotiations for the 1979 LRTAP Convention. The Commission was necessarily involved alongside Member States because it had acquired competence in matters of atmospheric pollution. It was agreed to allow the EC to participate alongside the Member States as a Regional Economic Integration Organization (REIO).[15] The EC remains the only extant example of an REIO, but the formula has determined its participation in subsequent global environmental conventions.[16]

Having REIO status has come to mean that the EC can be party to a convention without any of its Member States being a party. However, when one or more of the latter are also parties 'the organization and its Member States shall decide on their respective responsibilities for the performance of their obligations under the convention or protocol' (Vienna Convention 1985: Article 13(2)). Voting rights are accorded equivalent to the number of states that are parties, subject to the proviso that the organization shall not exercise its right at the same time as any Member State and *vice versa* (Vienna Convention Article 15). As one diplomat put it, 'We don't mind what they do as long as they all don't want to vote at the same time' (Interview, Brussels Mission, January 1996).

In cases not covered by the REIO formula, participation rights have been negotiated on a case-by-case basis; and have, on occasion, been contested by Member States. In practice the EC currently has full member status in only three international organizations (as opposed to treaty based organizations such as UNCTAD or various 'Conferences of the Parties' in which the EC operates as an REIO). They are the Food and Agriculture Organization (FAO), the European Bank for Reconstruction and Development (EBRD) and the World Trade Organization.[17] In other significant organizations, such as the International Council for the Exploration of the Seas (ICES),

UNEP, the World Bank and the International Maritime Organization (IMO) the EC only enjoys, at best, observer status although it does have rights to participate in the Environmental Policy Committee (EPOC) of the OECD.

Much important environmental diplomacy is conducted under the auspices of the UN General Assembly. Membership is for states alone and the normal pattern is for the Presidency to represent the Union. The Community was restricted to participation in conferences and the deliberations of the Economic and Social Committee and Specialised Agencies, with observer rights at the General Assembly.[18] Prior to the Rio 'Earth Summit' (UNCED) in 1992, after much effort by the Commission, the EC was granted 'full participant status' at the conference.[19] This meant that the EC temporarily acquired rights equivalent to those of participating states, except for voting and the submission of procedural motions. A permanent memorial (indeed a construction) is to be found on the first page of *Agenda 21*, which contains the footnote:

> When the term Governments is used, it will be deemed to include the European Economic Community within its areas of competence.

In relation to *Agenda 21* these areas of competence are, indeed, extensive – ranging across a great deal of the ground covered by that huge document. The same formula was used for EC participation in subsequent UN conferences on Habitat, Health and Environment and the Food Summit of 1996. At the 2002 Johannesburg World Summit on Sustainable Development (WSSD) the EC was the only one of over 3,000 recognized organizations to be treated as a participating state (UN 2002: 74) and the Commission President addressed the plenary session alongside the other heads of government.[20]

Shared competence and environmental negotiations

Because multilateral negotiations are at the heart of global environmental governance, it is worth considering how the Union manages to act under shared competence. The procedure for opening a negotiation where Community competence pertains allows the Commission to take the initiative and seek a mandate from the Council (Article 300 TEC). However, it is sometimes the case that the Community will not have extensive competence and the Commission may be relatively inactive. Without Community competence there is reliance upon a 'lead country approach', involving inputs from key Member States which have particular interests and expertise (Interview, Council Secretariat, July 1997).[21] In practice less than half the Member States are usually active and three or four positions are likely to emerge, rather than 25. Where there can be no Commission proposal for a mandate, the formal responsibility falls upon the Member State holding the Council Presidency. Hence, for example, the March 1997 Council decision on the EU position for the Kyoto climate change conference was engineered by the Dutch Presidency. If a small Member State, such as Luxembourg, holds the Presidency, as it did for the Kyoto negotiations in the autumn of 1997, it may only be able to employ two or three of its officials to specialize in environmental matters and there will necessarily be a greater reliance upon other Member States and upon the General Secretariat of the Council. The Commission will also tend to be involved for, even if it does not enjoy the formal right of initiative, Member States are often reliant upon its resources and expertise if the business of negotiation is to be efficiently carried forward.

The negotiating mandate agreed by the Council is a confidential document. Under the revised terms of Article 300 (TEC) it will be adopted by different decision-making procedures depending upon the issues under consideration. The mandate will establish competences for a 'mixed' negotiation, provide a set of binding directives and give greater or lesser freedom of manoeuvre to the Commission in the conduct of negotiations (Macrory and Hession 1996: 135–6).

The manifestation of the Union that other parties to an international environmental negotiation see across the table will also be determined by the Council acting with reference to Article 300. If Community competence is exclusive, the Commission will negotiate but the delegation will include at least one Member State representative, and there may even be a full Article 133 type committee dealing with the Commission in much the same way as in a trade negotiation. Otherwise, in a 'mixed' negotiation, there will be separate Commission and Member State delegations who will divide up responsibilities according to their competence.[22] Normally, when there is a common position which is not covered by exclusive Community competence, the Presidency will speak for all. This is especially important in cases where the EC does not have full rights of participation and the Presidency will speak using the formula, 'On behalf of the Community and its Member States'.

When there are problems in a 'mixed negotiation' it may be possible for a direct link to be established between the EU delegation and the Council or COREPER, especially when negotiations extend over a long period.[23] But generally this will not be possible and issues will have to be resolved in coordination meetings between officials attending the negotiations. Coordination meetings cover the day-to-day planning of negotiating strategy. They are held every morning during a negotiation but sometimes at midday and in the evening too. This can be onerous for Member State representatives who may find themselves rising at 6 am and being forced to hold national delegation meetings late at night (Interview, UK Department of Environment, September 1997). Much depends upon the leadership role of whichever Member holds the Presidency. If the Presidency is not strong the Commission sees its role as 'doing the work for them' and also acting as a 'sheepdog' to round up straying Member State representatives (Interview, DG Environment, June 1996). On the other hand even a 'strong' Presidency will, on occasion, see the need to delegate responsibility for making first drafts of EC positions to Member State representatives who either volunteer or are requested to 'take the lead'. In such circumstances Member State representatives assist the Presidency but do not supplant it as formal negotiator.

How do all these complexities affect the performance of the Union as an actor? Difficulties in coping with the demands of a 'mixed' negotiation were evident in the performance of the European side in the talks leading to the 1987 Montreal Protocol on stratospheric ozone depletion. This important piece of international policy-making created a regime which continues to address the phasing out of chemicals, such as chlorofluorocarbons and halons, which had been shown to destroy the earth's protective stratospheric ozone layer. The United States, with domestic legislation banning some uses of the offending chemicals already in place, encountered resistance from European chemical industries. There were accusations, at the time, that the EC was condemned by its internal arrangements to move 'at the speed of the slowest ship in the convoy' and that constitutional wrangling between Member States and the Commission spilled over to affect the negotiations.[24] However, the voting changes brought about by the Single European Act helped to resolve these problems. The final comprehensive package involving production and consumption cuts, and subsequently a CFC phase out, owed much to the Europeans, and produced a more extensive and effective agreement than had initially been on offer (Haigh 1996: 246). The Union has since been a proactive participant in the international stratospheric ozone regime. In general, both Member State and Commission sources have attested to the improvement in Community/Member State coordination at negotiations and the way in which participants have learned to negotiate as the European Union, although there are still difficulties in areas such as forestry. The Union is at its strongest as a single actor when operating under exclusive Community competence, but it is not necessarily the case that a mixed competence delegation led by the Presidency will be ineffective. As we will see in the discussion of climate change below, there can be confusion and adverse tactical consequences when negotiating at 16 (and now 26). Nonetheless, this has not precluded the Union from extensive and significant participation in virtually all of the major environmental negotiations held since the 1980s.

Instruments and implementation

In this, as in other areas, capabilities are a key component of 'actorness'. They are potentially available to the Union through its presence, its expertise and its extensive network of economic dependencies plus the bilateral diplomatic links of the Member States. The latter have attempted to coordinate their international activities through an EU climate change network that links national specialists in this area and, more recently, in a green diplomacy network. There is evidence of an increasing willingness to employ policy instruments in the direct support of external environmental objectives. A prominent example is provided by the coordinated diplomatic campaign in support of Kyoto ratification alongside the deployment of trade inducements.

A special characteristic of environmental politics is its necessary reliance upon scientific knowledge. The creation of the European Environment Agency was designed to provide a unified facility in this area and there has also been a realization of the critical importance of an independent earth observation capability for effective participation in global environmental governance. Since 2000 the Union has developed a space policy through the coordination of national efforts and working in partnership with the European Space Agency. The significant outcome for environmental policy is the Global Monitoring for Environment and Security (GMES) project. GMES, which will be fully implemented in 2008, provides an information infrastructure coordinating disparate European remote sensing resources in ways that support EU decision-making and participation in multilateral agreements. In the words of the

Commission's space 'white paper', 'GMES ensures Europe's interest to be [sic] an actor at the global level, relying on independent means for gathering data and information' (Commission 2003f : 15).

A further dimension of capability is the capacity to implement agreements once they have been made. This will bear, not only upon their effectiveness but upon the credibility of the Union, and there have been accusations that the Union cannot be relied upon to carry through its undertakings in the same way as might be expected of a sovereign state. The 'implementation deficit' in respect to environmental legislation has been much discussed (Knill and Lenschow 2002). The EU is engaged in a two level, or often three level, process, where Directives and Regulations agreed at Union level have to be made effective in concrete ways through the enforcement and monitoring of rules at national and local levels. As the 'completion' of the Single Market demonstrated, this is never easy. Although the EU procedures for monitoring and enforcing the compliance of its Member States are considerably in advance of those to be found in most international organizations, this is not the standard against which the EU will be judged. In fact there are advantages in implementing international environmental agreements through the EU, where procedures require that the necessary legislation shall be prepared at the time of ratification by the Member States and the Community, and where the possibility exists that a common external commitment can be based upon differentiated contributions between Member States at different levels of economic development (see Table 4.2).

External environmental roles

It is a pattern, observable elsewhere in the Union's external relations, that it exercises its most powerful sway over its immediate neighbours. Regional environmental policy is no exception. As we have seen, it was in attempting to solve transboundary atmospheric problems that the Community 'cut its teeth' as an international environmental actor. In attempts to manage regional seas, rivers and other shared ecosystems there

Table 4.2 The EU burden sharing agreement, June 1998

Country	%	Country	%
Austria	−13.0	Italy	−6.5
Belgium	−7.5	Luxembourg	−28.0
Denmark	−21.0	Netherlands	−6.0
Finland	0	Portugal	27.0
France	0	Spain	15.0
Germany	−21.0	Sweden	4.0
Greece	25.0	United Kingdom	−12.5
Ireland	13.0		
European Union overall reduction in CO_2 emissions for EU 15			−8%

Source: Council Conclusions, Meeting No. 2106, 16.6.98.

has been a similar pattern. The Union has been obligated by its presence, by its close ecological interdependence with neighbouring states and, indeed, by the expectations and requirements of their governments, to develop an active regional role.

What is more intriguing and problematic, is the clear aspiration of the Commission and certain Member State governments to move well beyond such essentially regional concerns and to adopt a global leadership and 'agenda setting' role. This has been evident across the whole raft of 'global' environmental issues – stratospheric ozone, climate change, desertification and biodiversity – that have emerged over the last two decades. Even though the scale of the Single Market ensures that the EU will be a necessary participant in global negotiations, there is not the kind of direct link between presence and actorness that exists in the regional context. Given its internal disparities, and the problems of mixed competence, the aspiration to leadership might well be regarded as perverse. Yet the opportunity provided by the retreat of the United States from its previous role as environmental policy innovator and global leader has been seized with alacrity in Brussels.

The EU as regional environmental actor

Just as the presence of the Single Market exerts enormous influence over its immediate neighbours, so the related environmental policies and standards of the Union will be very influential. Access to the market requires the attainment of certain environmental standards (phytosanitary regulations or product or emission standards). As well as the exercise of its gatekeeping role, the Union can also deploy a range of other instruments in support of its environmental policy objectives in relation to its neighbours. Access to scientific advice and information is significant but the critical instrument has been the provision of financial aid.

Union environmental policy operates at several regional levels. The EC is a signatory to large-scale international agreements directly affecting the territories of its Member States – the 1979 LRTAP and its associated protocols creating a regional air quality regime have already been mentioned. At a sub-regional level are agreements relating to the management of seas; notably the 1976 Barcelona Convention for the Protection of the Mediterranean Sea against Pollution and the 1983 Bonn Agreement, which provides a framework for international cooperation in tackling oil and other pollution of the North Sea.

The most potent manifestation of the Union as a regional environmental policy actor is, however, in its largely bilateral dealings with neighbours. This is evident in the Union's dealings with the countries of the old Soviet bloc. At the same time, and in some ways counterbalancing the new Eastern policy, there exists a continuing environmental relationship with the countries of North Africa and the Eastern Mediterranean. Both Eastern Europe and the Mediterranean are of some significance for the Union on a number of policy dimensions, and form the subject of Chapter 6. What follows extracts just one of these dimensions.

During the Soviet era, Eastern Europe and the USSR itself were renowned for their profligacy with natural resources and their neglect of good environmental housekeeping. This had the most dramatic and direct impact upon the countries of the Community in 1986, when the explosion of a nuclear reactor at Chernobyl in the Ukraine caused radioactive debris to be blown on the wind as far as the most westerly parts of the EC. Unsurprisingly, the major part (56 per cent in financial terms) of the Union's immediate post-Cold War environmental policy towards its Eastern neighbours has involved financial and technical assistance with improving the safety of nuclear installations and, indeed, with the closure of the Chernobyl complex itself.[25]

Other aspects of Union policy towards the East developed from 1991 in the context of the 'Dobris Assessment' of the state of the European environment, which launched a process of consultations and biannual Ministerial meetings in which the Union has played a leading role. The Environment Programme for Europe (agreed at the Sofia Ministerial Meeting of 1995) was not, as some in Eastern Europe had hoped, an 'environmental Marshall Plan' (Liberatore 1997: 201). Instead, the Community contribution was initially, between 1991 and 1995, to fund a specific series of projects and activities within the Phare (Poland–Hungary: Aid for Reconstruction of the Economy) programme and the Tacis (Technical Assistance to the Commonwealth of Independent States) programme for the countries of the former Soviet Union.

In the next decade the relationship of the Union towards the candidate countries of Eastern Europe was transformed by preparations for accession. This required that the environmental *acquis* of the Community, the whole body of law built up since the early 1970s (some 300 legal acts) be 'transposed' into the national legislation of the new members. The necessary changes in environmental policy and performance were extensive and costly and the extent to which they will transform the environment of Eastern Europe policy is not yet clear (Carmin and Vandeveer 2004). According to the Commission, enlargement 'may in fact be the biggest single contribution to global sustainable development that the EU can make', allowing new members to 'leapfrog development upgrading environmental protection, social development and economic growth' (Commission 2001d: 13).[26]

Those countries not favoured with candidate status are subject to the EU's Neighbourhood Policy. Under the sustainable development strategy any bilateral and multilateral agreements concluded with them will be required to contain an environmental dimension, although this was usually the case with existing undertakings. Here the most important relationship is with Russia. She suffers from very high levels of environmental degradation and pollution – one salutary indicator is that an amount of oil greater than that released into the environment in the *Exxon Valdez* disaster is spilled every day in that country (Commission 2001g: 6). Yet Russia is also a store of vast natural resources including forests and fresh water and a source of both threat and great economic opportunity for the European Union – not least in realizing the gains from energy efficiency. The EU engages in environmental dialogue with the Russian Government with a view to the harmonization of environmental standards and monitoring procedures, promoting nuclear safety and opening up the market for environmental investment.

A similar pattern of dialogue, technical collaboration and the funding of specific projects describes the other important and long-standing set of environmental policy relationships with the non-member countries of the Mediterranean. The ecology of the Mediterranean is particularly fragile and southern Member States have a direct concern with its conservation. Environmental cooperation is part of the larger Barcelona Process and Mediterranean Partnership that aims to establish a Free Trade Area by 2010. A significant environmental dimension is provided by the Short and Medium Term Action Programme for the Mediterranean (SMAP). It covers five priority fields of action: integrated water and waste management, dealing with 'hot spot' areas of heavy pollution and threat to biodiversity, integrated coastal zone management and countering desertification. The programme involves the Union and its Mediterranean neighbours in a continuing consultative network that will not only 'promote the transfer of Community experience in the field of financing techniques, legislation and environmental monitoring and integration of environmental concerns in all policies' but also provide financial incentives via the MEDA instrument and European Investment Bank (Commission 1998: 21).

The EU as global leader?

In the politics of global environmental change, the Union's representatives were by the 1990s quite self-consciously claiming leadership. The concept of leadership has a number of relevant meanings. It is associated with rule and dominance and with the Union's presence and negotiating strength in multilateral environmental regimes. Yet it can also mean, to guide, to go ahead or even to inspire. Each of these aspects of leadership are present to some degree in four roles to which the Union may lay claim. First, there is the role of architect of sustainable development. Very closely related, and at points indistinguishable, is a normative actor role in the dissemination of environmental principles and practices that may inspire, influence or show the way ahead. Much of this chapter has been concerned with another active role, as participant in global governance regimes. Finally, all are combined in a fourth role that deserves more extensive treatment and for which the Union has perhaps become best known. This is the EU's leadership role in the politics of climate change.

The concept of sustainable development was coined in 1987 by the Brundtland Commission, as 'development which meets the needs of the present without compromising the ability of future generations to meet their own needs'(WCED 1987: 8). It emerged in anticipation of the Rio Earth Summit of 1992 and the political requirement to engage the environmental concerns of the developed North with the pressing development needs of the South. Since then the idea of sustainability has been enlarged and refined such that it encompasses not only the protection and maintenance of the natural environment but also of the economic and social systems with which it is critically interlocked. The range of the EU's policy concerns – the internal market, trade, agriculture, fisheries, environment, transport, overseas development – indicates the relevance of sustainability thinking, even if many of them had originally been designed with very unsustainable production objectives in mind. Thus attempts have been made, since the Cardiff Council in 1998, to integrate environmental considerations across the range of the Union's policies and more specifically in the strategy drawn up in advance of the 2002 WSSD 'to make sustainable development an objective in bilateral development cooperation and in all international organisations and specialised agencies' (Council Conclusions, Göteborg 2001: 26).

Thus, the ambitions of the 2000 Lisbon Agenda have a counterpart in the 2001 Göteborg Council's strategy for the establishment of a new approach to policy-making.[27]

It is easy to be cynical about such high-level promotion of sustainability – the 1999 Helsinki Council even called for a 'net reduction in the use of natural resources in order to bring economic growth in line with the Earth's carrying capacity' (Bringezu and Schütz 2001: 6). Nonetheless, it forms part of the identity that the Union is constructing for itself and has already had some real external policy implications which are more than declaratory.

The world trade, agricultural and fisheries regimes are arenas in which the EU is at its most capable as an actor and provide the acid test of its commitment to sustainable development. Thus, when Union spokespersons enunciate green policies in the WTO and elsewhere their critics will inevitably refer, not only to the continuing sustainability implications of an unreformed CAP, but also to the Common Fisheries Policy (CFP). Operated under Community competence the CFP brings the Union into contact with significant numbers of states and international organizations.[28] Continuous over-fishing and the desperate need to conserve stocks both within and beyond EU waters has meant that fisheries policy is essentially becoming sustainability policy.[29] The pursuit of sustainable development objectives appears to have had some influence here with DG Fisheries and Maritime Affairs, who have been persuaded to modify their bilateral fisheries agreements with developing countries to incorporate impact assessment, funding to promote sustainable fisheries and 'capacity building'.

At the WTO during the Doha Round the Union has single-handedly attempted to place the trade-environment relationship on the negotiating agenda. There is some evidence that sustainability commitments have allowed environmental and even animal rights provisions to be inserted into the preparation of trade negotiations and actions – a process enabled by significant backing from some Member States and from 'civil society' groups (Interview, DG Environment, 2001). There have also been less obvious actions such as the re-definition of harm in anti-dumping action. Previously there had been an exclusive focus on injury to producers, but 'Community interest' has been re-defined to include environmental harm.

In April 2001 the Council instructed the Commission to undertake sustainability impact assessments (SIAs) on all its trade agreements – this to include the DDA and all regional and bilateral FTAs. At the WTO it has called for action to consolidate the status of multilateral environmental agreements (MEAs) in relation to WTO rules, such that they are mutually supportive rather than subordinate, and for the creation of a transparent and participative relationship between the various secretariats. It has also called for the removal of trade barriers to environmental goods and services and for the adoption of eco-labelling to surmount the difficulties posed by WTO rules that forbid discrimination against goods on the grounds that their 'process and production methods' may be environmentally damaging. Accounts of WTO negotiations indicate that, although not all these objectives have been achieved, EU representatives took them seriously and were prepared to use the Union's formidable trade muscle in support of them (Jawara and Kwa 2004: 62).

In considering the EU as an economic power it was observed that the Union had, on the basis of its presence, become the pre-eminent global regulator and standard setter. In environmental policy this was a role traditionally played by the United States, where State authorities invented many of the concepts and instruments that are commonplace today, including emissions trading. There are some signs that the Union has begun to disseminate its practices in a similar way, becoming 'a policy *shaper* rather than a policy *taker* in international environmental affairs, generating rather than simply responding to policy imperatives' (Lenschow 2004: 143). Notable examples are provided by pioneer work on 'eco-labelling' and the 'precautionary principle', which has begun to be adopted outside the EU and was an important contribution to the development of the Biosafety regime. The EU's support for precaution is significant because it contradicts a fundamental principle of the WTO trade regime that disallows discrimination against products without clear evidence of harm (Bail *et al.* 2002: 410–22). As will be discussed below, the creation of a large-scale international trading system for carbon emissions will, if successful, constitute the Union's most compelling policy innovation to date.

The most evident indication of EU leadership has been in its growing role within multilateral environmental regimes – whether in strengthening the Montreal Protocol, creating the Intergovernmental Panel on Forests, or promoting the Basel Convention on hazardous waste (Commission 1997c). Claims to environmental policy leadership are credible in areas where Community competence has been long established and which are a natural extension of the Union's role as pre-eminent trade actor. In 1992 the Community was the first to adopt legislation on the export and import of certain dangerous chemicals and has been in the forefront of negotiations to establish a binding prior informed consent procedure (PIC) for the movement of hazardous chemicals such as asbestos and pesticides across frontiers. It has also pressed other signatories of the Basel Convention on the matter of a total ban on the export of hazardous wastes from OECD to non-OECD countries.

Responding in part to European public unease about developments in the genetic modification of food, the EU was also at the forefront of attempts to provide an international regulatory framework for GMOs. It can claim some credit for facilitating the negotiation of the 2000 Cartagena Protocol on biosafety. Here, as elsewhere, comparison can be made with an inactive Japan and an obstructive United States.[30] Its paramount claim to environmental leadership, however, is in the rescue of the Kyoto Protocol to the United Nations Framework Convention on Climate Change.

Climate change

Although often compared to the problem of stratospheric ozone, climate change has an all-encompassing character and is still subject to a degree of scientific uncertainty and contestation. Attempts to control those human activities that are increasingly believed to cause the enhanced greenhouse effect have dominated international environmental diplomacy for over a decade, from the signature of the United Nations Framework Convention on Climate Change in 1992 to the ratification of its landmark Kyoto Protocol in 2004. During this period the attitudes of US governments, presiding over an economy responsible for some 25 per cent of global carbon dioxide emissions, have ranged from constructive abstention under Clinton to denunciation of the Kyoto Protocol and active obstruction under the Bush administration. This has provided an historic opportunity, even an obligation, for the EU to lead and sustain the emergent climate regime.

In these circumstances climate change has acquired a political salience well beyond the humdrum and technical treatment of other environmental issues. It has become a principal agenda item at G8 summits and European Council meetings and the stuff of conversation between heads of government.

The main focus of efforts to construct a global climate regime has been on the need to control emissions of the three principal 'greenhouse gases' – carbon dioxide, methane and nitrous oxide (there are three other industrial gases, hydrofluorocarbons, perfluorocarbons and sulphur hexafluoride). Carbon dioxide is seen as the principal culprit – responsible for some 80 per cent of global warming potential – but there is no simple answer equivalent to that available for the ozone regime, where the offending chemicals could simply be banned. Neither are there 'end of pipe' solutions of the type found in the long range transboundary air pollution regime, where the chemicals responsible for acidification can be removed at source. Instead there is a need to reduce the use of those fossil fuels which provide the essential bases of industrial society. The 1997 Kyoto Protocol, championed by the EU, provides for a 5.2 per cent reduction in developed world greenhouse gas emissions with an EU 15 commitment to an 8 per cent reduction (from a 1990 base) by 2012. Beyond this the EU's sixth Environmental Action Plan acknowledges that effective control of climate change will ultimately require reductions of the order of 70 per cent (*OJ* L242, 10.9.2002: 1).

The problem of achieving such reductions is compounded by the fact that the scientific basis of the enhanced greenhouse effect continues to be disputed, despite the increasing certainty of successive IPCC assessments of the trend of global mean temperatures and more immediate evidence of unusual and turbulent weather. Further very difficult dimensions of the problem arise once the developing countries and their likely contribution to global warming over the coming years are brought into consideration. A related and equally controversial matter is the need to conserve forests – due, in part, to their role as 'sinks' for carbon dioxide. Thus the ramifications of climate change potentially go far beyond the current concern with reducing gas emissions, and call into question the sustainability of the world trade and monetary regimes – by implication, involving many of the external roles of the EU alongside its internal tax, energy and transport policies. An abiding concern must be the potential costs and competitiveness implications of climate policy for an already sluggish EU economy and, indeed, the principal justification for US rejection of Kyoto has been economic. By forging on alone the EU has abandoned its previous stipulation that all industrialized countries must be engaged in making emission reductions and ensured that, in the first phase at least, the costs of the climate regime will be mainly borne by its Member States. There are also, of course, potential benefits in terms of energy efficiency and the gains from emissions trading.

The EU has been a major participant in the attempt to create an international climate change regime since its inception in the late 1980s. This was despite the fact that climate change policy remains an area in which the main competencies rest with the Member States. This is not the place to examine the long-drawn-out and complex negotiations involved in setting up the climate regime or, indeed, the difficult internal disputes that attended them. What is clear from the accounts of this period, however, is that the EU was routinely regarded as an entity with the capability to act.[31]

As a climate change negotiator the Union was, however, beset by a number of difficulties. In an area largely beyond exclusive Community competence, the rotating presidency (held by Luxembourg during the Kyoto talks) did not encourage efficient and settled representation. Processes of policy formulation were largely inter-governmental and although QMV generally obtained, 'the close relationship with national energy policies' (where Article 175 TEC specifies unanimity) produced a 'tendency to work at the level of the lowest common denominator' (van Schaik and Egenhofer 2003: 4). Inconsistencies between Member State approaches led, on occasion, to what Grubb and Yamin (2001: 285) described as a 'Herculean' task of coordination. This is compounded by the differing external orientation of Member States, particularly towards the US, and the temptation to circumvent the Presidency through bilateral talks.

The difficulties of mixed competence and diverse national energy interests should not obscure the fact that at a strategic level the Union was able to set objectives and lay serious claim to have been a leader in climate change policy – in comparison with the passivity or opposition of the other major developed countries. Prior to the signature of the FCCC the common European position was for binding commitments to emission targets. However, US opposition, in an election year, led to the negotiation of a much weaker Article 4 of the FCCC, which merely expressed the 'aim [for Western industrialized countries] of returning individually or jointly to their 1990 levels of … anthropogenic emissions of carbon dioxide and other greenhouse gases'. The 1995 Berlin Conference of the Parties formally judged this to be unsatisfactory and set itself the target of producing new commitments by December 1997 at the Conference of the Parties scheduled for Kyoto (CoP 3). At this meeting, in the view of one observer, 'the EU countries remained the most proactive with the EU as a group … seeking specific commitments in emission reductions below 1990 levels on specific "targets and timetables" '(Grubb 1995: 3).

Actually delivering the ambitious declaratory targets for greenhouse gas emissions set by the Union in advance of Kyoto was bound to present problems, but a common stance was achieved through the mechanism of the 'burden sharing agreement' or 'bubble' (see Table 4.2). This has served to aggregate the interests of 15 states and to reconcile differences between economies at different levels of development through differential contributions to a common target for emission reductions.[32] It was on this basis that the EU entered the final Kyoto negotiations with a proposed target of 15 per cent reductions in emissions for the developed countries. The question of emissions targets had the highest visibility, but there were other issues including the responsibilities of developing countries, the relationship between sinks and sources of emissions, the review of national inventories and commitments and the introduction of the so-called 'flexibility mechanisms'. These involve emissions trading along with Joint Implementation (JI) and the Clean Development Mechanism (CDM). JI and CDM allow industrialized countries to offset some of their national emission reduction commitments by funding energy saving measures in transitional or developing countries. Flexibility was at the heart of the US position at Kyoto along with a commitment merely to return emission levels to 1990 levels by the period 2008–12, and a controversial demand from the Senate that any agreement be dependent upon commitments to emission reductions by developing countries.[33]

The Protocol negotiated at Kyoto in 1997 was inevitably a compromise, which reflects, only in part, the objectives of the EU. The industrialized countries agreed to an average 5.2 per cent cut in emissions for a basket of six greenhouse gases by 2008–12. The parties committed themselves to different targets – the US, 7 per cent, Japan 6 per cent and the EU 8 per cent overall. The price of achieving these limited targets was the inclusion of the 'flexibility' mechanisms. It is, perhaps, the great irony of the Kyoto process that by 2001 the EU was to find itself committed to the defence of policy mechanisms that ran quite contrary to its own regulatory tradition, against their original US authors! From another perspective this may be seen as a policy transfer, accelerating existing moves from a 'command and control' approach towards the use of new market-based policy instruments (Damro and Méndez 2003).

The post-Kyoto phase of negotiations involved the laborious task (outlined in the Buenos Aires CoP of 1998) of fleshing out the detail and implementation of the 'heads of agreement' agreed in 1997. The process was scheduled to end at the 2000 Hague CoP 6 in the dying days of the US Clinton administration. This bad-tempered and ill-organized meeting became bogged down in the discussion of the compensatory role of forest sinks but it was already clear that, in the words of the CoP President, Jan Pronk, as far as preserving Kyoto was concerned 'the EU had become the only game in town' (*Earth Negotiations Bulletin (ENB)*, July 2001: 34).

The arrival in office of the administration of George W. Bush finally put paid to attempts to placate the United States and somehow induce its ratification of Kyoto. Indeed, in March 2001 the US formally denounced its signature of the Protocol. The Union was now faced with the dilemma of whether to proceed on its own. Its momentous decision to do so was affirmed at the Göteborg European Council of June 2001 and the heads of government further expressed the determination that the renewed CoP 6 *bis* to be held in Bonn in the subsequent month 'must be a success' (Göteborg European Council Presidency Conclusions 2001: 28). This hope was realized at a political level and the subsequent CoP 7 held at Marrakech provided the technical detail necessary for a ratifiable legal instrument.

Success at Bonn had been preceded by an intense diplomatic effort to persuade waverers and to break the unity of the 'umbrella group' that united the US with other sceptics. EU diplomatic missions were undertaken to Australia, Canada, Japan, the Russian Federation and Iran while the UK, Germany and France applied coordinated bilateral pressure on key governments, notably that of Japan. There now began the process of ensuring the widest possible participation of industrialized countries to ensure the entry into force of the Protocol by 2002.

Because this involved not only 55 ratifications but that they should also account for no less than 55 per cent of developed world carbon dioxide emissions, further intense diplomatic effort was required, particularly towards Russia whose ratification became critical to surmounting the 55 per cent emissions hurdle. The negotiations that extended through 2003 and 2004 involved two high level summits in November 2003 and May 2004 assisted by Troika visits. The outcome reveals the EU as an actor capable of coordinating a range of instruments and inducements. The key was Russian ambition to join the WTO. The EU side demanded the raising of low Russian gas prices and the deregulation of the natural gas industry as the price of its support. The eventual deal, finalized at the May 2004 EU–Russia summit in Moscow, changed the terms of EU support for WTO admission to an increase in prices by 2010 and, critically, Russian agreement to ratify Kyoto. This was finally achieved in the latter part of 2004.[34] On 16 February 2005 the Protocol entered into force.

Even achieving the 8 per cent emissions reduction target required by the Kyoto Protocol poses difficulties, that only serve to accentuate the profound challenges that lie beyond the 2008–12 'first commitment period'. The EU approach to implementation, upon which its credibility as a climate leader ultimately depends, has been twofold. First, the Commission has developed the European Climate Change Programme (ECCP) which is comprehensive in identifying in excess of 40 potential sources of emissions reductions and which serves as a framework for specific directives to be brought forward over a ten year period. To reverse what appears to be a rising trend of carbon emissions, Member States will have to implement policies in the spheres of energy, transport and construction which are likely to be 'visibly unpopular in nature' (European Parliament 2002: 10). The Commission's proposals for the first phase of the ECCP certainly address such issues, requiring, *inter alia*, 'a modal shift from road and air' to cleaner transport via railways and waterways (Commission 2001h: 14).

Most critical to the effective implementation of Kyoto is the EU's other policy approach that takes up the 'flexibility mechanisms' through instituting the world's first large-scale transnational carbon emissions trading scheme.[35] Operational at the beginning of 2005, the scheme covers power generation and other large installations responsible for some 45 per cent of total EU carbon dioxide emissions. Under its terms Member States issue an allocated number of permits to emit which under this 'cap and trade' system will be progressively reduced on an annual basis. Permits are tradable across the European Economic Area (and ultimately beyond it) such that firms have the choice of either cutting their emissions and profiting from the sale of excess permits or continuing to emit higher levels of carbon dioxide while bearing the financial penalty of purchasing additional permits. This new market in rights to pollute is designed to allow firms flexibility in their energy use, coupled with incentives for efficient and reduced use of hydrocarbons, while ensuring that aggregate emissions will fall. As well as providing a direct response to the long-running question of how the EU will back up its aspirations to climate leadership with credible implementation of its commitments, the scheme is also designed to be extendable beyond the EEA. There are embryonic attempts at emissions trading elsewhere and within individual US states. By elaborating its own dominant scheme the EU may well become the international standard-setter and 'find itself in control of the most important international regulatory effort to limit greenhouse gases' (Legg and Egenhofer 2001: 4). If this were to occur it will be a powerful demonstration of the Union's presence.

Conclusion

The European Union has developed a wide-ranging set of environmental policies to deal with questions of air and water pollution, waste management and the conservation of nature. The external aspects of these competences meant that, by the end of the 1970s, the Community had begun to establish itself as an international environmental actor – and the first, and indeed only, recognized REIO.

Unlike the Common Commercial Policy, competence is normally shared between Community and Member States and agreements and negotiations are 'mixed'. This can raise particular, and on occasion niggling, coordination difficulties in the conduct of environmental diplomacy and provides scope for divergence between Member States, laying Union policy open to charges of immobility and reduction to the lowest common denominator. However, the Union has over the years managed to fulfil our criteria for actorness and to define policies across the whole gamut of sustainability issues. This inevitably involves trade, agriculture and fisheries questions which yield both opportunities and coherence problems.

A significant regional environmental role, arising from the environmental presence of the Union and its close and increasing interdependence with its neighbours, has been evident for some time. The accession process that necessitated the adoption of EU environmental standards by applicants, and the incorporation of environmental objectives and funding into the agreements that the Union concluded with its neighbours has created a dimension of green regional actorness. However, as we have seen, the EU's policy aspirations have since the 1980s had a global dimension. This development provides an excellent example of the interaction of presence, opportunity and external expectations in the construction of actorness.

Opportunity was afforded by the rise of global environmental diplomacy in the wake of the ending of the Cold War. Centred upon the UNCED process it provided the Union with a new stage. During the 1990s the abdication of responsibility by the US and the central role that Union delegations had assumed in various MEAs generated growing demands for European leadership, contrasting with previously grudging acceptance of the Community as a participant in its own right. This has helped to build a green identity for the EU. Its inspiration owes much to European societies and governments in Scandinavia, Germany, the Netherlands and Austria. They brought to the EU a strong commitment to environmental causes and green politics which has now been externalized (Andersen and Liefferink 1997).

By the millennium there were huge expectations amongst environmentalists that the EU would act to 'save' the Kyoto Protocol. Important as it has been elsewhere in, for example, propagating the precautionary principle, EU environmental policy was raised to an entirely different level of political significance by the struggle over the climate change regime. It appeared at times as if the credibility of the Union was as much, if not more, dependent upon the success of the Kyoto Protocol as it was on the fate of the CFSP or the new European Security and Defence Policy.

5   The EU as development and humanitarian actor

In the distinct, yet overlapping, policy areas of development cooperation and humanitarian assistance, Union activity is truly global in scope. It is also significant: the EU (that is the Community together with the Member States) is the world's largest donor of both development and humanitarian assistance, accounting for 51 per cent of the global total in 2002 (Overseas Development Institute (ODI) 2004a: 2). Moreover the Community itself had, by the mid-1990s, become the world's fifth largest aid donor (Cox and Koning 1997).

The Union has not only acquired a role as an aid donor. The years since the EC was created have seen the evolution of increasingly complex relationships with developing countries in all parts of the world, denoting an important role in North/ South relations. Nevertheless, the EU has yet to develop a coherent, overarching approach to development policy. Indeed the Union's engagement with the countries and regions of the South has been described as 'a policy patchwork' characterized by considerable variations in focus and intensity (Holland 2002: 1). These variations have arisen, not primarily from the differing circumstances and needs of the Union's 'development partners', but from a range of internal and external factors which have combined to construct the opportunity structure, and hence shape the direction, of EU development policy.

Below we briefly consider the contextual factors that have shaped EU practices as a prelude to discussion of the Union's roles as a development actor in three areas – its long-standing, highly structured relationship with (sub-Saharan) African, Caribbean and Pacific (ACP) states; its relatively new and more traditional relations with Asian and Latin American (ALA) states; and the role of the European Community Humanitarian Office (ECHO). Relations with former colonies in North Africa, other Mediterranean non-EU members and members of the former Eastern bloc evolved differently again, and are discussed in Chapter 6. Due to its greater longevity and distinctive nature, the EU–ACP relationship will receive particular attention below.

The policy context: presence and opportunity

Most significant among the internal factors that have influenced the Union's development practices and priorities has been the historical legacy of European imperialism. Both the Union's presence in North/South relations, as the political and cultural 'metropolis'

at the centre of a network of asymmetrical relationships, and its associated role as patron/
mentor, were prefigured in the late colonial era. Thus, from its creation, the Community
was involved with the colonies and former colonies of the founding Member States,
perpetuating, in particular, French and Belgian interests in sub-Saharan Africa. The
accession of the UK, Spain and Portugal widened the geographical scope of EC
responsibilities towards its members' former colonies, but did not substantially disturb
the Community's existing highly structured relationship with sub-Saharan Africa – to
which former colonies in the Caribbean and Pacific were added, to form the ACP
Group in 1975. Outside this Group, relations with the new Member States' former
colonies in Asia and Latin America developed very differently.

While the geographical scope and differing levels of intensity characteristic of EU
development policy were initially a consequence of the imperial legacy, the evolution
of a specifically *Community* development policy, alongside and distinct from the
policies of the Member States, is attributable to the character of the EU itself; and its
emerging identity as a singular actor. Significant, too, have been key aspects of its
economic presence – the Common Agricultural Policy and the Single Market.

Introduction of the Common Agricultural Policy established, from 1967, an
important Community involvement in food aid, particularly as implementation of
the CAP led increasingly to surplus production.[1] The CAP also had the effect, through
use of trade protectionist measures, of driving down world prices of temperate food
products, thereby reducing the export earnings of countries such as Argentina and
Brazil. Of significance, too, has been the impact of the CAP upon developing countries'
exports of rice, sugar and bananas. This has necessitated a range of policy responses
from the EU in relation to these 'sensitive' products.

More generally, the economic presence of the Union, in terms of the attraction of
its market, has been central to policies seeking to promote 'development' through
economic diversification. This has involved use of trade incentives to encourage the
export sectors of developing countries. Trade policy instruments, of course, lie within
Community competence, thus necessitating active EU involvement in trade related
aspects of development policy. Today, bilateral and multilateral agreements between
the Union and third parties, in all regions of the South, typically include a range of
differentiated and highly complex trade provisions. Moreover, from 1971, the
Community's Generalized System of Preferences (GSP) accorded to all developing
countries non-reciprocal, preferential access to EU markets for industrial products
and a range of processed foods. This was supplemented, from 2001, by the 'Everything
but Arms' initiative which extends, to least developed countries, duty and quota free
access for all products except arms and ammunition. This applies even to the 'sensitive'
agricultural products excluded from the GSP.[2]

Finally, the character of the EU, as a singular polity – a non-state, having no direct
experience of imperialism – has been conducive to the evolution of a distinctive
approach to development cooperation. So, too, have been constructions of EU identity
as a value-based community. These have been associated with increasingly proactive
attempts to promote internal values externally – through a range of conditionalities
applying both to trade and aid.[3] Thus, by 1982, the Community's role had evolved to
the extent that the Commission was to claim:

Development policy is a cornerstone of European integration ... The policy is an important one because of the institutional, financial, technical and trade resources it deploys; because of the number of countries it reaches; because of the novel forms of international cooperation it has pioneered. Today it is a manifestation of Europe's identity in the world at large and a major plank in the Community's external policies generally ...

(Commission 1982: 8)

The proactive role today played by the Union in development matters has also been shaped by the shifting structures of opportunity and constraint that have formed the external context of EU action. Here, the role of ideas and beliefs in shaping understandings of historical events has been of particular significance. Four distinct yet overlapping phases can be identified in the evolution of EU development policy, with a fifth phase becoming increasingly apparent:

- The late colonial period, when the ideology and practices of 'associationism', which have strongly influenced subsequent EU–ACP relations, were constructed.
- The period of Third World anti-imperialist political activism in the early 1970s, when the context was relatively favourable to the South and the first EU–ACP Lomé Convention was negotiated.
- The dominance of neo-liberalism in the 1980s, strengthened by the end of the Cold War, when democratization and market liberalization became EU priorities and the practices of associationism were challenged and diluted.
- The post-millennium focus on poverty alleviation in least developed countries – in response to the failure of previous approaches to development cooperation.
- A reprioritization of issues in the post-9/11 environment, which threatens to subordinate development priorities to security concerns.

The legacy of the early phases of development cooperation remains discernible today. While these phases were characterized by a distinctive approach to development 'partnership', the new context provided by the ending of the Cold War weakened the position of the South. This permitted increased politicization of development policy, in that the Union's aims and ambitions became increasingly dominant. Here the TEU clearly indicated the intention to act more proactively in world affairs – both in the general sense of the Union's aspiration to 'assert its identity on the international scene' (Article 2), and because the TEU, for the first time, explicitly provided for an EU policy on development cooperation.[4]

The accordance of Treaty status to this policy area reinforced the Union's role as patron/mentor in relation to ACP 'partners' weakened by the sudden shift in EU attention from the South to Eastern Europe. At the same time, the post-Cold War relaxation of US influence in Latin America permitted the EU to 'rediscover' that region (Holland 2002: 56). The post-Cold War context, too, saw the development of new priorities for the EU, in terms of short-term emergency humanitarian assistance – hence the creation of ECHO in 1992.

While the 1990s saw increased emphasis upon neo-liberal, market oriented approaches to development, by the end of the decade their inappropriateness to least developed countries (LDC) had become evident. Many of the poorest countries experienced negative growth throughout the decade, and the resulting, increased inequalities between developing countries could no longer be ignored. In response to the 2000 United Nations 'Millennium Declaration' of Development Goals,[5] the Commission and Council issued a joint statement declaring the alleviation of poverty, and its eventual eradication, to be the primary objective of EU development policy (Commission 2000a: 7).

Of the 78 current members of the ACP Group, 41 are classified by the UN as LDCs, while a further nine LDCs remain outside the ACP Group.[6] In order to pursue its poverty alleviation agenda the Union thus needed both to differentiate between ACP members, by according special privileges to the LDCs among them, and to extend these privileges to non-members. The 2001 'Everything but Arms' (EBA) initiative reflects this new focus on LDCs. In the context of EU development policy it accords, for the first time, a higher level of preference to non-ACP states than to many ACP members. Inevitably this is a divisive issue for the ACP Group and non-LDCs among them have lobbied (discreetly) concerning their relative loss of privileges. There is awareness, however, that this 'shows us in a bad light … you're not on the moral high ground and appear selfish' (Interview, ACP Mission, January 2003).

The renewed commitment to poverty eradication at the Millennium was closely followed, and in part over-shadowed, by the events of 9/11. Thus an Extraordinary European Council (21 September 2001) agreed, *inter alia*, to develop 'a coordinated and inter-disciplinary approach embracing all Union policies'. The potential for political direction of development policy was subsequently increased by the incorporation of the Development Council into the General Affairs and External Relations Council in June 2002.

Of particular significance for the relationship between development priorities and security concerns is the 2003 *European Security Strategy*. Stating that 'Security is the first condition for development', this document explicitly refers to coordination of EU instruments, including the European Development Fund. 'All of these can have an impact on *our security* and on that of third countries' (European Council 2003: 13, emphasis added). While this new focus upon the relationship between security and development is associated with a great deal of rhetoric, its influence can be discerned in policy choices, as we shall see.

Clearly, from the early 1990s, many factors in the policy context have combined to facilitate the extension of scope and diversification of EU development policy – to the detriment of the established EU–ACP relationship. Nevertheless, we maintain below a focus upon this relationship. This is merited because it is here that the Union's presence has been most apparent. ACP trade is overwhelmingly oriented towards the Single Market;[7] the EU provides more than 30 per cent of all aid to sub-Saharan Africa and the countries of the Pacific and Caribbean are highly dependent upon ACP membership for representation in Europe. More particularly, it is in relation to the ACP that a distinctive EU approach to development cooperation has been most apparent. It is here, too, that the institutional framework of 'cooperation partnership' is most fully developed with, *inter alia*, a Directorate-General of the Commission – DG Development – focusing exclusively on the EU–ACP relationship (see Table 0.1).

Associationism and 'partnership': EU–ACP relations

EU involvement in North/South relations originated from the need to accommodate the remaining colonial interests of Member States, in particular French colonies in Africa.[8] It was thus inevitable that the ideological preferences and policy priorities of French officials, representing both the dominant partner during the early stages of integration and the major colonial power, would shape the Community's initial approach to development policy. Thus, despite opposition from the Dutch and German governments, which would have preferred a broader, more traditional approach, the principles of associationism formed the original basis of Community development cooperation. These principles, which established a separate political identity for remaining colonies and afforded a degree of guided autonomy to indigenous elites, found formal expression in the TEC, where Articles 182–7 provide for 'association of non-European countries and territories with which Member States have special relations'.[9]

From these essentially colonial provisions the practices of post-colonial association evolved – that is a structured system of 'cooperation partnership' and a range of trade and aid instruments. Despite numerous complicated refinements, and considerable dilution of the concept of partnership, these three elements have remained the basis of EU–ACP relations, persisting through three generations of formal agreements – Yaoundé, Lomé and Cotonou – that have structured EU relations with African, and subsequently Pacific and Caribbean, countries.

Evolution of a partnership: the Yaoundé, Lomé and Cotonou Conventions

In order that the (expanding) geographical scope of EU development cooperation with the 'associates' can be appreciated, Table 5.1 charts the evolution of the Yaoundé relationship and its successor Lomé and Cotonou Conventions. The current ACP membership is set out in Table 5.2, which also shows the 1995 and 2004 United Nations Development Programme (UNDP) *Human Development Index* ranking of the ACP countries. This indicates the considerable differences in level of development among the ACP countries. Figure 5.1, which shows the geographical scope of the ACP, also illustrates the diversity of a Group originally created by the EU in order to facilitate the conduct of relations with selected groups of former colonies. Since the central elements of the EU–ACP relationship have endured, to a greater or lesser extent, throughout the various Conventions, they are briefly outlined below.

The concept of partnership has been of great importance to EU–ACP development cooperation. It indicates formal recognition of the political independence of the ACP states and the right, at least in principle, to manage their own affairs without interference from their European 'partner'. Hence, the terms of the Conventions are the subject of negotiation between the parties rather than imposition by the EU. To facilitate the processes of negotiation, and the administration of the Conventions, joint institutions were established, including an Association Council and a

Table 5.1 EU–ACP Conventions and Agreements

Convention or Agreement	Date	EU	ACP
Yaoundé Convention I	July 1964	6	18
Yaoundé Convention II	January 1971	6	19
Lomé Convention I	April 1976	9	46
Lomé Convention II	January 1981	10	57
Lomé Convention III	May 1986	12	66
Lomé Convention IV	March 1990	12	69
Lomé Convention IV *bis* (review)	November 1995	15	70
Cotonou Partnership Agreement	June 2000* (entry into force April 2003)	15**	78***

Notes

* The Cotonou Agreement is of 20 years duration, expiring in 2020.

** EU membership increased to 25 on 1 May 2004.

*** South Africa is a member of the ACP Group but is not a signatory of the Cotonou Agreement (nor of its predecessor) but relates to the EU in economic terms via a bilateral free trade agreement.

Table 5.2 Current ACP membership and Human Development Index (HDI) ranking[1] – by region (asterisks denote LDC status[2])

Country[3]	HDI ranking	
	1995	2004
Africa (47 countries)		
Angola	164	166 *
Benin	155	161 *
Botswana	74	128
Burkina Faso	169	175 *
Burundi	165	173 *
Cameroon	127	141
Cape Verde		105 *
Central African Republic	149	169 *
Chad	162	167 *
Comoros	139	136 *
Congo	122	144
Congo (Democratic Republic of)	143	168 *
Côte d'Ivoire	145	163
Djibouti	154	154 *
Equatorial Guinea	142	109 *
Eritrea		156 *
Ethiopia	171	170 *
Gabon	114	122
Gambia	161	155 *
Ghana	129	131
Guinea	168	160 *
Guinea Bissau	163	172 *
Kenya	130	148
Lesotho	131	145 *
Liberia	159	*
Madagascar	135	150 *
Malawi	157	165 *
Mali	172	174 *

Country[3]	HDI ranking	
	1995	2004
Mauritania	150	152 *
Mauritius	60	64
Mozambique	167	171 *
Namibia	108	126
Niger	174	176 *
Nigeria	141	151
Rwanda	156	159 *
São Tomé and Príncipe	133	123 *
Senegal	152	157 *
Sierra Leone		177 *
Somalia	166	*
South Africa	95	119
Sudan	144	139 *
Swaziland	124	137
Tanzania	147	162 *
Togo	140	143 *
Uganda	158	146 *
Zambia	136	164 *
Zimbabwe	136	147
Caribbean (15 countries)		
Antigua and Barbuda	55	55
Bahamas	26	51
Barbados	25	29
Belize	29	99
Dominica	69	95
Dominican Republic	96	98
Grenada	67	93
Guyana	105	104
Haiti	148	153 *
Jamaica	88	79
St Kitts and Nevis	37	39
St Lucia	84	71
St Vincent	79	87
Suriname	77	67
Trinidad and Tobago	39	54
Pacific/Indian Ocean (16 countries)		
Cook Islands		
East Timor		158 *
Federal States of Micronesia		
Fiji	46	81
Kiribati		*
Marshall Islands		
Nauru		
Niue		
Palau		
Papua New Guinea	126	133
Seychelles		
Solomon Islands	125	124 *

continued…

Table 5.2 continued

Country[3]	HDI ranking	
	1995	2004
Tonga		63
Tuvalu		*
Vanuatu	119	129 *
Western Samoa	102	75 *

Notes
1 The HDI ranking is taken from the United Nations Development Programme (1995 and 2004) *Human Development Report*, Oxford: Oxford University Press. The HDI is based on three criteria – gross domestic product *per capita*, adjusted to take account of purchasing power; life expectancy at birth, and level of education.
2 In categorizing Least Developed Countries the Economic and Social Council of the UN uses three criteria – low income, human resource weakness and vulnerability. All must be present. The third category gives priority to landlocked and small island states and states susceptible to natural disasters.
3 Number of countries listed was 174 in 1995; 177 in 2004. Gaps indicate data not available.

parliamentary assembly composed of ACP representatives and Members of the European Parliament.

Financial assistance to ACP countries is provided through a fund established specifically for this purpose – the European Development Fund (EDF). Other arrangements pertain for assistance to ALA countries and disbursements by ECHO. In recognition of differing levels of Member State commitment to the ACP relationship, the EDF has derived from national funding rather than the Community budget. However, it is probable that this practice will change in the 2007–13 budgetary period, when the EDF will be incorporated in the overall EU budget (Commission 2004b: 27). Each EDF has been of five years duration. Following agreement of the global amount by the Member States, the EDF is managed at the policy level by DG Development, which deals exclusively with the ACP. Since 2001 the EuropeAid Cooperation Office has been responsible for disbursement of all EU financial assistance, with the exception of the humanitarian relief funding disbursed directly by ECHO.

Finally, in relation to trade, the associated countries were given privileged access to EC markets, which placed them above all other developing countries in the Community's system of preferences. This system discriminated against the exports of non-associated developing countries and was greatly resented by ALA governments. However, ACP trade privileges have been gradually eroded as a consequence of the general tariff reductions agreed within the GATT framework and by measures introduced by the EU itself, in particular the 2001 EBA initiative. In extending tariff free access only to LDCs, this initiative has created divisions within the ACP – further contributing to the 'patchwork' of EU policies.

Yaoundé

The two Yaoundé Conventions (1964 and 1971) set important precedents for the future. Linking the six Member States of the EC and eighteen Associated African States and Madagascar (AASM), they were negotiated between the parties and

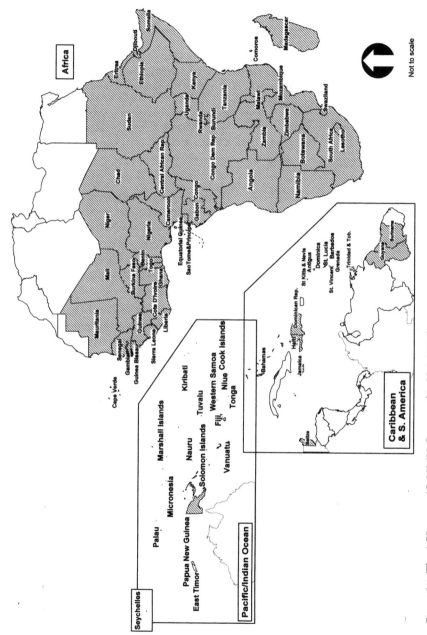

Figure 5.1 The ACP group (© LJMU Cartographic Unit 2005)

contractual in nature. These arrangements created conditions under which a complex, bilateral relationship could develop between the EC and the AASM, providing a forum for AASM countries to coordinate and articulate their demands. They also facilitated AASM contributions to broader demands – by the increasingly assertive Third World lobby operating as the Group of 77 (G77) within the United Nations system – for a New International Economic Order (NIEO). This was to be based, *inter alia*, on radically altered terms of trade, which would ensure both more generous and more stable receipts for primary product exports.

Strengthened by the significant increase in oil prices imposed by the Organization of Petroleum Exporting Countries (OPEC) in 1973, Southern demands for a more equitable North/South balance considerably influenced the renegotiation of Yaoundé necessitated by UK accession to the EC.[10] This ensured that the Yaoundé formula was comprehensively upgraded.

Lomé

The first five-year Lomé Convention (1975) linked the EC with 46 associates from Africa, the Caribbean and the Pacific (ACP).[11] Reflecting aspects of the NIEO programme, the new Convention was hailed as:

> … a new model for relations between developed and developing States, compatible with the aspirations of the international community towards a more just and more balanced economic order …
>
> (Preamble, Lomé I Convention)

In economic terms, the existing formula of EDF assistance and trade concessions was enhanced. In relation to trade, two changes partially reflected NIEO demands. First the requirement for reciprocity in trade concessions was abandoned; in future Community concessions to ACP states would be unilateral. Since this breached GATT rules the Lomé arrangements became the subject of a special GATT waiver. Second, measures were introduced to ameliorate the impact of price fluctuations on export earnings.[12] For a number of products considered 'sensitive' because they compete with Community products, but having particular significance for specific groups of ACP countries, additional Protocols were negotiated over the years. These introduced special arrangements for sugar, rum, beef, veal and bananas. Politically, the Protocols proved useful to ACP negotiators, as they facilitated discussion between Commission officials and sub-groups of the ACP having a common interest (Interview, ACP Secretariat, June 1996).

In acknowledgement of the robust stance of the ACP negotiators, the new model accorded greater importance to the notion of partnership – the rhetoric surrounding the launch of Lomé I proclaiming the establishment of '… a relationship very much based on equal terms between the two partners' (*The Courier* 1975: 3). The partnership institutions were strengthened accordingly; an innovation being establishment of the ACP Committee of Ambassadors, which is responsible for detailed negotiation with Commission representatives.

The context of the negotiations for Lomé I proved to be propitious for the ACP Group. Subsequently the OPEC model did not prove transferable to other commodities and the effects of oil price rises on the economies of Third World oil importers, which included the majority of ACP, were disastrous – causing chronic balance of payments difficulties and deepening debt.[13] The Lomé provisions were to prove hopelessly inadequate to meet these challenges. Moreover, the ideological climate of the 1980s was very different from that of the 1970s. The newly dominant neo-liberal approach emphasized market liberalization and foreign direct investment as the most appropriate route to economic development – '*La pensée unique*', as one Commission official observed (Interview, DG Development, June 1996). In this climate the ACP 'equal partners' of Lomé I were anxious to maintain the concessions gained in 1975. There were, in consequence, few innovations in Lomé II (1980) and III (1985).[14]

While its essential elements remained intact, the Lomé relationship lost much of its impetus.[15] The context of negotiations for Lomé IV, during 1988/9, was particularly unfavourable to the ACP. The momentous changes in Europe, culminating in the symbolic breaching of the Berlin Wall on 9 November, inevitably overshadowed the negotiations. At the signing ceremony (in December 1989) Togolese President, Gnasingbe Eyadema, called upon the Community:

... not to abandon their friends of the South for the benefit of their brothers of the East, whose opening to the Community market will basically change the fundamental element of North–South cooperation.

(Quoted in *The Courier* 1990: 4)

In the event, while the three central elements of the EU–ACP relationship were maintained, Lomé IV saw a significant shift away from the principle of 'equal' partnership. This was reinforced in the 1995 review of the Convention.[16] For the first time, explicit political conditionality was introduced to the EU–ACP relationship, in the form of a human rights clause (Article 5) which was in 1995 expanded to include '... application of democratic principles, the consolidation of the rule of law and good governance ... good governance shall be a particular aim of cooperation operations'. As with the human rights provisions, non-observance of these conditions could lead to suspension of assistance.

These provisions encroach substantially upon the principle of equal partnership and their inclusion, which had been strongly resisted by ACP governments in the past, demonstrates their weakness in the new negotiating context of the 1990s. This reflected not only the evident shift of EU commitment to Eastern Europe but also a more general sense that the Lomé relationship was an increasingly irrelevant remnant of Europe's colonial past. Hence, by the mid-1990s, there was considerable speculation about the continuation of the Lomé system beyond 2000. The ACP Group, however, expressed strong commitment to continuation of the Lomé arrangements.[17] Our interviews at this time (in February and June 1996) with staff of ACP missions revealed much concern about the future, particularly among Caribbean representatives. Francophone African representatives were more optimistic, however – 'the French government will not let Lomé die', it was claimed (Interview, ACP Mission, February 1996).

Cotonou

In the event, the Cotonou Partnership Agreement, which entered into force in April 2003 and will expire in 2020, represents an uneasy compromise that maintains, yet also potentially undermines, the central features of the EU–ACP relationship. The principal innovations undoubtedly reflect the priorities of the EU. They include comprehensive provision for 'political dialogue'; measures to promote regionalization of the ACP Group; and an emphasis upon trade liberalization and integration of the ACP into the global economy.

In relation to the political dimension, the concept of 'partnership', as previously, is given great prominence, indeed it is reflected in the Agreement's title and constitutes its first 'fundamental principle' (Article 2). Nevertheless, the rhetorical nature of the Article 2 commitment to equal partnership and respect for ACP sovereignty is revealed by the inclusion of 'essential elements' which must be respected by ACP governments (Article 9). These expand upon the Lomé provisions on human rights, democracy and good governance and include an additional focus on corruption. Failure in these respects on the part of ACP governments can lead to suspension of the Agreement, although – in a departure from Lomé practice – provisions in this respect have been given a contractual basis that permits recourse to external arbitration.[18] In addition there is provision for 'political dialogue' on peace building and conflict prevention (Article 11) and migration (Article 13).[19]

A further innovation in the political *acquis* of Cotonou, and the second fundamental principle of the partnership, is a strong emphasis upon participatory development. This envisages involvement of non-state, and in particular civil society, actors in the ACP-EU context – 'in order to encourage the integration of all sections of society' (Article 2).[20] While involvement of civil society organizations is regarded by EU representatives as an essential element in building democracy within ACP states, it is resented by ACP governments. 'They are very clever – this is interference in our affairs, but interference in ways which are difficult to object to' (Interview, ACP Mission, January 2003). In practice, while involvement of ACP civil society actors is considered to be 'difficult but not impossible' (Interview, EuroStep, January 2003), its extent and quality varies considerably between ACP countries (ODI 2004b: 3).

The final 'fundamental principle' of the partnership is of great significance, in that it relates to 'differentiation and regionalization'. Differentiation means that, for the first time, ACP countries will be accorded different treatment according to their level of development (with special treatment for LDCs), needs and 'performance'. The concept of performance would appear to afford additional scope for EU influence upon the internal practices of ACP members. While this new differentiation is intended to further the Union's aims in relation to poverty reduction, it is potentially undermining to the ACP Group.

Even more significant in this respect is the 'particular emphasis' placed upon the regionalization of the Group (Article 2). In a major departure from the Lomé approach, which simply gave encouragement to regional initiatives, the Cotonou Agreement requires that six regional groupings of the ACP negotiate distinctive Economic Partnership Agreements (EPA) with the Union.[21] As ACP ambassadors point out, dividing the Group in this way gives 'structural advantage to Commission negotiators in addition to their traditional advantage in terms of the expertise and experience of their personnel' (Interview, ACP Mission, January 2003). Here it should be noted that EPA negotiations are conducted by DG Trade, a less familiar environment for the ACP than DG Development. Officials of DG Development, however, 'help us to temper [DG] Trade's belief in absolutes' (ibid.).

While the ACP Group is attempting to coordinate the various sets of negotiations in order to maintain 'ACP unity and solidarity' (ACP General Secretariat 2002: 1), ACP ambassadors believe that, ultimately, the Group will be undermined as some regions gain strength and coherence while others fail to flourish (Interviews, ACP Missions, January 2003).[22] Potentially, also, other sources of allegiance may serve to undermine the ACP, in particular the African Union (AU), which replaced the Organization for African Unity in 2002. The EU has supported the African Union, for example through creation of its Peace Facility for Africa (comprising €250 million diverted from the EDF) to support the AU's conflict prevention mechanism.[23]

The regionalization provisions of Cotonou directly link the political and economic dimensions of the EU–ACP partnership. Thus, financial assistance is available to support the institutions and practices of regional cooperation, including special support to foster the participation of LDCs. Central to the EPA concept is the phased establishment of WTO compatible Free Trade Areas between the EU and the various regions. This will follow a transition period (to 2008) during which Lomé non-reciprocal preferences will be maintained. While it is expected that full trade liberalization by the ACP participants will take at least a further decade (ODI 2004c), these provisions accord with a central objective of the Cotonou Agreement – the 'gradual integration of the ACP countries into the world economy' (Article 1).

Establishment of coherent and effective regional EPAs faces a number of challenges. ACP governments are, in general, sceptical about the supposed benefits of market opening. And for the poorest ACP members, the prospect of reciprocal free trade in the context of a regional EPA would appear to be both unrealistic and unattractive – both because they have little to export and because they already enjoy non-reciprocal access to the EU market under the EBA initiative. Nevertheless, in 2003 two regions having a high proportion of LDC members – West Africa and Central Africa – opened negotiations with the EU for establishment of EPAs.[24] Politically, this is believed to undermine the possibility of non-cooperation with the EPA initiative in cases where no benefits are perceived (Interview, ACP Mission, January 2003). In response to criticism from ACP governments and NGOs, reforms were introduced to the EPA negotiating process, including a 'monitoring mechanism' intended to ensure that EPAs are consistent with development goals (Commission 2005b).

In relation to the third element of the partnership, development assistance, the changes in Cotonou reflect, primarily, the perceived need to simplify and streamline EDF disbursement procedures. It is hoped that this will reduce the administrative burden in general, and upon recipients in particular; and that it will accelerate disbursement – thus reducing the backlogs that have been a persistent feature of the EU–ACP relationship.[25] Disbursement delays have also been addressed through institutional reforms within the EU, centrally with the creation of the EuropeAid Cooperation Office, and at local level through strengthening of the Commission delegations to facilitate 'deconcentration' (devolved management) of programmes. In interviews in January 2003, however, ACP representatives reported having noticed 'no difference so far'.[26]

The ninth EDF, which funds the first five years of the Cotonou Agreement, was set at €15.2 billion. As previously, identifying the objectives and priorities of national indicative programmes is the responsibility of ACP governments. These are, nevertheless, subject to various overall objectives of the Agreement, the first of which is commitment to 'reducing and eventually eradicating poverty' (Article 1). Funding will also be available to support the objectives referred to above – regional cooperation, participation of civil society and economic liberalization. The Agreement also identifies three 'thematic and cross-cutting issues' that must be integrated in all aspects of the partnership. These comprise standard EU references to gender issues (including special measures to promote the participation of women) (Article 31),[27] environmental protection and sustainable use of natural resources (Article 32).[28] In addition, considerable attention is given to 'Institutional development and capacity building', which are also to be integrated across all aspects of the partnership (Article 33).

Taken together, the various objectives and themes incorporated into the Agreement, and the range of conditionalities inserted, represent an attempt by the EU to exert stronger overall direction of the Partnership than has been the case previously. Before examining the rather different EU approach to ALA countries, we briefly assess the record of EU–ACP relations; and their future prospects in the context of the 2005 review of the Cotonou Agreement.

EU–ACP relations: record and prospects

The Lomé system was heralded, at its launch, as a revolutionary approach to North/ South relations. The years since 1975, however, have witnessed a progressive weakening of the ACP position. A cursory glance at Figure 5.2 demonstrates that, in the majority of cases, the fundamental aim of assisting the political, social and economic development of ACP states has not been realized – having enjoyed more than forty years of 'development cooperation', many ACP countries remain among the poorest in the world. In seeking explanations for this failure, we briefly examine the impact of each of the three elements of cooperation.

With regard to trade, ACP preferential access to Community markets undoubtedly privileged these countries' products over all others. Nevertheless, ACP exports have not fared well in relation to exports from non-preferred competitors in Latin America and Asia.[29] The poor performance of ACP exports reflects lack of expertise, technology and investment, which tend both to impede efforts to enhance the competitiveness of traditional exports and to preclude economic diversification. Neo-liberals have long argued that trade preferences confer only minimal advantages, and that

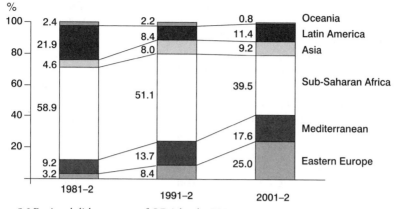

Figure 5.2 Regional disbursement of ODA by the EU

Source: ODI 2004a: 4.

discontinuation of preferences would advantage the ACP in the long run by obliging them to be more competitive (Davenport 1992). The new emphasis, in Cotonou, on trade liberalization appears to reflect this view.

For the poorest ACP Member States, trade preferences have been largely irrelevant; these countries are only marginally involved in export activities. Consequently in many cases financial assistance has been the core of the EU–ACP relationship. Here, while the overall amount of the EDF has increased at each five year renewal, it has not expanded in relation to the enlargement of the EU, nor the extension of ACP membership; nor has it kept pace with demographic growth in ACP countries.[30] Moreover, as Figure 5.2 indicates, assistance to the ACP Group has declined as a proportion of the overall EU aid effort. This largely reflects the Union's post-Cold War political shift in priorities towards Central and Eastern Europe.

The failure of EDF assistance to promote the economic development of ACP countries is only in part a function of its inadequacy. Many of the problems besetting ACP States stem from changes in the international environment since the mid-1970s, and from the failure of policy-makers, both within the EU and the ACP, to respond effectively to these changes. The failure to anticipate or ameliorate the problem of ACP debt is central here.

A final issue in relation to the EDF has been the tendency, in recent years, for the EU to divert EDF funding to, for example, the UN AIDS fund and the African Peace Facility. This practice, which permits the EU to support new initiatives without providing new funding, raises sensitive and potentially divisive issues in that, despite their departure from the established purposes of the EDF, it is difficult for ACP governments to oppose such initiatives.

Partnership has arguably been the most distinctive aspect of the EU–ACP relationship. The Community created the ACP to facilitate its interaction with a diverse group of economically weak former colonies. Thus the Lomé system encapsulated, from the outset, an inherently asymmetrical relationship. In recent years this asymmetry has increased markedly. ACP membership has, in consequence, brought benefits. Without the support of the ACP Secretariat, and the potential to maximize the expertise of individual Missions through the Committee of Ambassadors, few ACP countries would be in a position to maintain an effective relationship with the EU. As one ACP Ambassador commented, 'the Community is a world power and it helps to have a mechanism to deal with it' (Interview, ACP Mission, June 1996).[31]

An indication of 'success' may be that the ACP has endured. No members have left the Group; indeed membership has grown considerably, as Figure 5.1 shows. In some respects, too, the EU–ACP relationship has been characterized by remarkable continuity. Despite the maintenance of the multi-faceted institutional relationship, however, by the mid-1990s 'partnership' had ceased to mean that ACP political arrangements and development strategies remained the responsibility of their own governments. Increasingly the EU has concerned itself with the promotion of democratic governance and economic liberalization among its associates.

The changes introduced at Cotonou are of great significance in this respect. EU priorities are clearly evident throughout the Agreement – from the increase in political dialogue, and political conditionality, to the requirement for regional groupings to negotiate EPAs based on free trade. Our interviews with ACP representatives in 2003 revealed little optimism that the new arrangements would prove successful. There was a sense of disillusionment – 'We send our best educated and most talented people to Brussels to beg' – and perceptions of 'a shift in the Commission away from its development focus' in order to prioritize more immediate political and security issues (Interview, ACP Mission, January 2003).

At the time of our interviews in 2003, perceptions of ACP marginalization had been exacerbated by the loss of responsibilities, and staff, from DG Development to EuropeAid. Indeed, at that time there was a strong belief that DG Development would not survive into the 2004 Commission. This proved unfounded, however. A further matter causing concern was the incorporation of the Development Council into the newly named General Affairs and External Relations Council in 2002. This was seen, by ACP and NGO representatives, as indicative of the subordination of development to political and security issues.

It was in this context that the preparatory phase of the first Cotonou five year review began in 2004. Perhaps predictably, controversy centred upon the Commission's proposal to expand the 'essential elements' of the Agreement to include clauses reflecting the Union's post-9/11 political priorities – combating terrorism, non-proliferation of weapons of mass destruction (WMD) and commitment to the International Criminal Court. While it is the intention that such clauses will be inserted into all future agreements negotiated on behalf of the Union, the ACP countries are strongly opposed to the inclusion of new elements that distract attention from the poverty reduction focus of the Agreement (Interview, DG Development, October 2004).

A further source of controversy has been the Commission's desire to introduce additional flexibility into the EDF disbursement process, in order that funds can be made available to meet exceptional needs in crisis situations. This diversion of support from development priorities was heralded by use of EDF funds for the African Peace Facility. Subsequently the Development Commissioner has advocated use of EDF funding to train militaries in post-conflict situations.[32] Such proposals provide further evidence of the subordination of long term development commitments to more immediate political and security priorities.[33]

Undoubtedly the Cotonou Agreement represents a turning point in EU–ACP relations. There has been increased emphasis upon EU political priorities and a diminution in ACP special privileges, while the new focus upon differentiation and regionalization may well mark the beginning of the end of this highly institutionalized relationship. EU enlargement to the East will doubtless also reinforce the Union's already perceptible shift of attention from former colonies of old members to relations with neighbours of new members.

In the short term, however, the preservation of DG Development in the Barroso Commission, and the appointment of Louis Michel (a former Belgian Foreign Minister with a strong commitment to development) as Development and Humanitarian Affairs Commissioner, ensures that there will continue to be advocacy for an EU 'development focus'. Moreover the severe problems suffered by much of sub-Saharan Africa ensure that EU development policy will continue to prioritize that region (Interview, Council Secretariat, October 2004). Ultimately, when considered alongside EU policy towards ALA countries, the Cotonou provisions do not yet signify 'normalization' of EU–ACP relations (Holland 2004).

Beyond the associates: EU–ALA relations and humanitarian assistance

In ALA countries (and especially in Latin America) there has long been resentment of the Union's discriminatory practices in favour of the ACP.[34] UK accession in 1973 did not immediately disturb the focus of development cooperation; however it reinforced pressure for a broader approach. Consequently, in 1976, a series of bilateral agreements was negotiated with ALA countries. These did not include the 'partnership' dimension of Lomé and were less advantageous than Lomé arrangements in other ways – for example financial assistance was provided on an annual basis rather than through a multi-annual programme.[35] In relation to trade, the position of non-associated developing countries was recognized initially, and to a limited extent, by the 1971 GSP. It was not until 2001, however, that the EBA initiative extended equal privileges to non-associated LDCs (see note 5).

From the mid-1980s changes in the internal and external policy context – including the Union's Southern enlargement and the relaxation of Cold War tensions – provided both impetus and opportunity for EU initiatives. These included moves to strengthen relations with ALA countries and the creation in 1992 of a new agency, the European Community Humanitarian Office, which provides emergency assistance to victims of natural disasters or armed conflict. We deal separately below with EU relations with Asia and Latin America and with the work of ECHO.

Relations with Latin America

EU relations with Latin America have strengthened considerably since the mid-1980s. This was a consequence of the accession of Portugal and Spain to the Union in 1986, and a broader desire to support the processes of democratization and economic reform occurring in much of Latin America during the 1980s. The relaxation of Cold War tensions was also significant, since it enabled the EU to pursue a more proactive role in a region traditionally seen as the preserve of US foreign policy.

From the outset, EU relations with Latin America were highly politicized, an early priority having been the desire to develop a role distinctive from that of the USA and, indeed, to compete with the USA for influence (and for markets). Thus the EU was to contribute to conflict resolution in Central America through the San José process, launched in 1984 and involving political dialogue supported by development assistance. Of particular significance, in terms of establishing a distinctive EU approach to the region, was the Commission's insistence (despite strenuous opposition from the US government) upon including Nicaragua in this programme.[36] The Union's willingness to encroach upon areas sensitive to US foreign policy is also evidenced by establishment of relations with Cuba during the 1990s.

In contrast with the ACP relationship, the EU has not developed a single, overarching approach to Latin American countries. However, following the success of the (sub-regional) San José process, the EU has supported various regional and sub-regional groupings, engaging in dialogue on economic and political issues across a broad range of topics. These include issues of particular concern within the EU, such as the illicit trade in drugs and, more broadly, the Union's Security Strategy. In addition the Union has bilateral relations with individual Latin American countries and has concluded multi-faceted agreements with Mexico (2001) and Chile (2002).

At the regional level, the Union's dialogue is with the Rio Group, which developed in 1986 from the San José process and now includes all Latin American countries. Inevitably, however, dialogue at this level has been somewhat formulaic. Moreover attempts at the 2002 Madrid Summit to develop a 'strategic partnership' between the regions foundered due to EU insistence upon prioritizing political and security issues over the development issues favoured by the Rio Group (Allen and Smith 2003: 110).

The most important aspect of EU relations with Latin America has been at the sub-regional level, where the Union has strongly supported processes of cooperation and integration, both through funding common institutions and through insistence that their interlocutors negotiate as a bloc (Interview, DG External Relations, September 2001). The principal groupings with which the EU interacts are the Andean Community (Bolivia, Colombia, Ecuador, Peru and Venezuela) and Mercosur (Mercado Común del Sur), comprising Argentina, Brazil, Paraguay and Uruguay.

While, in both cases, inter-regional Framework Cooperation Agreements were concluded with the EU in the mid-1990s, the EU–Mercosur relationship has been given higher priority by the EU. This reflects the significance of inter-regional trade and investment flows (by the mid-1990s the EU had supplanted the USA as Mercosur's principal trading partner) and the political pre-eminence of Brazil within the region (Klom 2003).[37] A further factor impelling EU ambitions to create a Free Trade Area with Mercosur has been the US initiative for a Free Trade Area of the Americas, which, if successful, would impact negatively upon EU trade. Despite the priority accorded to Mercosur, however, progress in negotiations (commenced in 2000) to build upon the 1995 Framework Agreement has been gradual at best.[38]

In EU–Latin America relations, as elsewhere, priority has been given to inter-regional initiatives. There has, in consequence, been a failure to develop a coherent strategy towards the region. Thus, EU relations with Latin America remain patchy, lacking in direction and slow to develop. Similar problems have affected the Union's relations with Asia.

Relations with Asia

Despite its significance in terms of the colonial past of several Member States, Asia has historically been the region most neglected by the Union. Factors that account for this include the early focus upon Africa and a sense that the UK was excessively influential in Asia. Following UK accession in 1973, the decision to exclude Asian Commonwealth members from the Lomé Convention ensured that Asia remained a low priority in the Union's relations with the South.

A compounding factor, here, was the considerable and increasing diversity within Asia, which elicited a range of responses from the EU. Thus Asian LDCs were included in the GSP from 1971 and financial assistance was extended to South Asian countries, notably India. However, the rapidly growing, newly industrializing countries (NIC) of South-East Asia (Hong Kong, Singapore, South Korea and Taiwan) were regarded as a serious threat to European producers and, from the mid-1970s, an overtly hostile trade policy was operated towards them. This involved, *inter alia*, frequent use of anti-dumping measures.

In terms of region-to-region cooperation, the preferred approach of the Union, relations with the Western-oriented Association of South-East Asian Nations (ASEAN) were established following its creation in 1967.[39] These were formalized, from 1980, through the EC–ASEAN Cooperation Agreement. This provided the framework for economic relations and political dialogue with a strategically important region during the Cold War. Opportunity, here, was provided by the withdrawal of the USA from Vietnam in 1975. Despite this, the EC–ASEAN relationship lacked dynamism from the outset. The EU was very much preoccupied with internal matters during the 1980s (enlargement and the Single Market process), while a number of issues divided the two regional bodies, including the Commission's criticism of ASEAN's 'open regionalism' approach to integration.[40] Moreover, in this context the ending of the Cold War did not bring new opportunities, indeed the strategic importance of ASEAN diminished.[41] At the same time the strengthening of the Union's agenda on human rights and democracy promotion brought new tensions to the relationship, particularly after the accession of Myanmar (Burma) to ASEAN in 1997.[42]

The growing economic significance of Asia had nevertheless long been evident by the mid-1990s when, somewhat belatedly, the Commission became 'seized with the importance of Asia' (Interview, External Mission, January 1996). In consequence, given the inability to reinvigorate the EU–ASEAN relationship, a new and parallel process, known as the Asia–Europe Meeting (ASEM) was launched in 1996. This originally comprised the EU members plus ten rather diverse Asian states (Brunei, China, Indonesia Japan, South Korea, Malaysia, the Philippines, Singapore, Thailand and Vietnam) and is a multi-level process (from heads of government to NGO level) comprising political, economic and cultural elements. While innovative in terms of its informality and wide-ranging agenda, ASEM has tended to avoid tackling sensitive issues such as China's human rights record. Moreover the expansion of the Asian membership (in response to the Union's enlargement to 25) has now introduced into this forum the difficult issue of Myanmar, whose representatives attended an ASEM summit for the first time in October 2004.[43] It thus seems likely that ASEM will suffer similar problems to the EU–ASEAN relationship. Moreover it is not clear that ASEM, which excludes important countries such as India, is the most appropriate forum for conduct of EU relations with Asia; nor, more specifically, with Japan and China. Indeed, given the diversity of the region, it may be that inter-regional relations are not a feasible option.

While the ending of the Cold War did not provide a stimulus for EU–Asia relations, the events of 9/11 heralded an intensification of EU relations with Asia that has been manifested, primarily, in strengthened bilateral relations with key countries. The aftermath of 9/11 saw intense EU diplomacy across the region. Relevant, here, are the EU–Pakistan Cooperation Agreement of November 2001 and the inclusion of non-proliferation and anti-terrorism topics in the annual EU–India summit the following month. Of great importance, too, has been the Union's dialogue with Iran (see Chapter 7). The Union subsequently concluded comprehensive 'Strategic Partnership' agreements with Japan, China and India, which provide for economic and cultural cooperation and political dialogue on a range of issues, including conflict prevention, combating terrorism and non-proliferation of WMD.[44]

Given its economic dynamism and political potential, relations with China will doubtless prove to be of great importance in the future. Since 9/11 and the invasion of Iraq, the Chinese government has shown great interest in improving relations with the EU in order, in part, to provide a counterbalance to US dominance. There nevertheless remain several impediments to this strategy, not least China's record on human rights and democratic governance, which continue to influence EU–China relations despite efforts to downplay these issues in recent years.

Perhaps most significant, in terms of EU activity in Asia post-9/11, has been the commitment to post-war reconstruction in Afghanistan. This has included appointment of an EU Special Representative and an important role in the management of development assistance, with the Union itself pledging aid of a billion euros for the period 2002–6. Clearly, however, policy towards Afghanistan cannot be viewed solely from the perspective of development cooperation. Here the overarching political and security aspects demonstrate very clearly the way in which post-9/11 priorities, incorporated in the Union's Security Strategy, intrude upon and potentially override other policy priorities. Policy towards Afghanistan also overlaps with humanitarian assistance and the work of ECHO, to which we now turn.

The European Community Humanitarian Office

ECHO, which operates essentially as a Directorate-General of the Commission, was established in 1992. While the EU had been involved since the 1960s with provision of emergency assistance to non-members on an *ad hoc* basis, the ending of the Cold

War brought new opportunities and increased demand. Thus media-led concern over humanitarian crises in the aftermath of the 1991 Gulf War, and attendant upon the dissolution of Yugoslavia, combined with the Union's 'ambition to promote itself externally', to provide the impetus for a better coordinated, higher profile approach to humanitarian assistance (Interview, ECHO, September 2001). The work of ECHO has thus been subject to political pressures from the outset.

ECHO's task is to provide emergency assistance, on the basis of need, to victims of natural or man-made disasters. Funding derives primarily from the Community budget, although a small proportion of the EDF (€14.1 million in 2003) is used for emergency assistance purposes. ECHO does not itself carry out field operations, these are sub-contracted to more than 180 organizations which have signed a Partnership Contract with the Commission, including UN agencies, the Red Cross/Crescent and numerous NGOs. Due to the need for speedy transmission of funds, disbursements are made directly to the contracted partners without recourse to EuropeAid. While funding levels vary each year according to assessments of need, ECHO typically provides more than 25 per cent of all humanitarian assistance, with Member States' combined efforts contributing a further 25 per cent. The Union as a whole thus provides more than half the world's emergency aid.

Allocation of funding can be a sensitive issue and there is inevitably political pressure from Member States for prioritization of high profile crises, particularly those in close proximity to the Union. The case of Kosovo (in 1999) is an example here. Politically there was a demand for a 'huge' ECHO input but little budget remained. This problem was resolved through allocation of Community budget reserves totalling €346 million. For ECHO staff this was 'a difficult situation' and there was a desire to 'avoid such political involvement in the future' (Interview, ECHO, September 2001).

Since 1999 there has been increasing emphasis upon 'neutrality, impartiality and independence' in determining ECHO's priorities (Commission 2004c: 9). Currently, two principal criteria are employed, of which the 'global needs assessment' (a ranking across 130 developing countries) is the most important.[45] In 2003, 64 per cent of ECHO's funding was spent in areas of highest need. Also of importance, indeed an area upon which great emphasis is placed, is ECHO's commitment to 'forgotten crises' (in, for example, Western Sahara, Nepal, Thailand and Northern Uganda) where media attention is absent and the Union 'is almost the only donor'. For ECHO staff it is this commitment that makes ECHO 'special', particularly when compared with Member State humanitarian efforts, where there is a tendency to focus upon high profile emergencies and 'compete for publicity' (Interview, ECHO, September 2001). Twenty per cent of ECHO funding was devoted to 'forgotten needs' in 2003 (Commission 2004c: 3).[46]

As a complement to its geographical commitments, ECHO has identified four cross-cutting themes for prioritization – child related activities, water, disaster preparedness and linking relief, rehabilitation and development (LRRD). This last has been a matter of enduring concern. As an agency responding to humanitarian crises, it is anticipated that ECHO involvement will normally last a maximum of six months (areas of 'forgotten need' are an exception here). Subsequently, in principle, there should either be no further need for assistance or ECHO's involvement should be phased out as longer term development strategies are introduced. In practice LRRD procedures have been subject to difficulties and delays, particularly in areas, such as Tajikistan, where the Union's development instruments are 'very limited'. In such circumstances, ECHO simply informs DG External Relations that it is leaving in the hope that development assistance will follow (Interview, ECHO, September 2001).[47] Since establishment in 2003 of a Commission Inter-Service Group on LRRD, 'significant progress' in coordination has recently been claimed (Commission 2004c: 6).

While the performance of ECHO is widely acknowledged to have improved considerably since the late 1990s, important concerns remain. In particular there is criticism that ECHO's work addresses the symptoms of development failure while, at the same time, diverting attention and resources from the painstaking work which would prevent crises from occurring (van Reisen 1997). There is also concern about circumstances where ECHO is obliged to act as a 'gap filler' – when development assistance has been interrupted by political conditionality or economic sanctions have been imposed (Interview, ECHO, September 2001). Myanmar provides a current example here. Similar concerns centre upon ECHO operations to meet post-conflict humanitarian needs in areas such as Afghanistan and Iraq, where EU Member States have participated in the military actions contributing to the humanitarian crisis. In such circumstances there is a danger that the independence and impartiality of ECHO's humanitarian role will be jeopardized.

Undoubtedly there have been enduring concerns about politicization of ECHO's work; indeed, in the post-9/11 security context, such concerns have increased. In this climate, where 'certain political forces tend to regard humanitarian aid as an instrument of foreign policy or crisis management' the Commission continues to stress the importance of 'strict adherence' to the fundamental values and principles of humanitarianism (Commission 2003c: 9; 2004c: 17).

EU actorness: towards a strategy for development?

The 'patchwork' nature of EU development policy is apparent from the discussion above. In addition to the Union's very different approaches to the ALA and ACP groupings, there is increasingly differentiation between countries or groups of countries within each region. There is also potential for tension between the aims of development cooperation and the work of ECHO.

Since the end of the Cold War, as part of the broader aim of enhancing the international profile of the Union, there has undoubtedly been a desire both to provide overall political direction for EU external policy generally and to intensify the focus of development policy. Here we can identify three approaches to provision of strategic direction. Partially overlapping and partially competing, these approaches reflect the most recent phases in the evolution of development cooperation referred to above.

The first approach reflects the Union's value-based identity, which features prominently among the political objectives of the Union as elaborated in the TEU – that is, promotion of the Union's core values of democracy and the rule of law, and respect for human rights and fundamental freedoms.[48] Promotion of regional integration may also be considered to reflect the Union's values. Our overview of EU development policy demonstrates that these principles have indeed guided practice. Political conditionality clauses (relating to human rights and democracy) are routinely included in agreements with third parties, and suspension of assistance has followed violations of this conditionality. Similarly, we have seen evidence of EU commitment to regionalization. Nevertheless, enhanced relations with Pakistan and China since 2001 are indicative of the limits to a value-based approach to development cooperation.

A second approach involves the emphasis, since 2000, upon poverty reduction as the principal aim of development policy. This would, if systematically implemented, provide a credible strategy. Again, we have seen attempts to implement such a strategy – through the EBA initiative, the elements of differentiation introduced into the Cotonou Agreement and development of ECHO's 'global needs assessment'. Despite this, a recent report concluded that EU development assistance remained insufficiently focused on poverty reduction (van Reisen 2004).[49] In the context of the ongoing Cotonou review process, however, the Commission is proposing that stronger prioritization of poverty eradication, and achievement of the Millennium Development Goals, be inserted in the Agreement. This prioritization also appears in the Commission's 2007–13 policy perspectives (Commission 2004b: 24).[50]

Third, the Union's Security Strategy, developed in the post-9/11 context, potentially provides an alternative framework for development cooperation. This document identifies, and links, four 'key threats' to the Union's security – terrorism, proliferation of WMD, regional conflicts and state failure. It concludes that 'the first line of defence will often be abroad' (European Council 2003: 7). Development policy, including use of EDF funds for such 'defence', is explicitly referred to. The inclusion of clauses on combating terrorism and non-proliferation in recent agreements with third parties, diversion of EDF funds to the African Peace Facility and ECHO's controversial involvement in conflict situations are indicative of a security focus to development policy. While this is not necessarily incompatible with value-based and poverty reduction approaches, there are fears that development needs will be subordinated to security priorities. ACP resistance to inclusion of the new security clauses in the Cotonou Agreement reflects such fears.

Of the three approaches to development policy we have identified, all can be seen to influence policy, none to predominate. Moreover, despite the fears expressed in interviews with ACP and NGO representatives, a major shift in focus towards a security-based strategy will, we believe, meet resistance. This reminds us that, while failure to implement an overarching approach to development can be attributed, in part, to the enduring influence of historical precedent and to the diversity evident in the South, it also reflects the problems of consistency and coherence that afflict, to varying degrees, all aspects of EU external policy.

Issues of consistency affect this policy area in two ways. First, in determining overall development priorities for the EU. And, second, because the Member States operate parallel, bilateral development and humanitarian assistance policies, the priorities of which are not necessarily compatible with those of the EU.[51] This undermines the claim that the Union (comprising Community and Member States' combined efforts) is the world's largest aid donor.

Consistency problems can be found in all aspects of EU development policy. Thus Member States are divided over the extent to which the security agenda should influence development cooperation. Differing levels of Member State commitment to relations with ACP and LA countries are also evident. However, it is in the context of Asia that consistency problems have been most severe; indeed they have impeded development of a credible approach to the region. This has been manifested through high profile disagreements in the ASEM context – over relations with North Korea and inclusion of Myanmar, for example. Perhaps most significant have been the divisions between Member State governments over relations with China, which centre upon the extent to which concerns over human rights issues should be subordinated to economic and geo-strategic interests.

The parallel operation of EU and Member State policies is a distinctive feature of the Union as an actor *sui generis*.[52] It is a key issue because the co-existence of EU and Member State policies impinges negatively upon the overall impact of development policy. The TEC addresses this issue through the provision that:

> The Community and the Member States shall coordinate their policies on development cooperation and shall consult each other on their aid programmes, including in international organizations and during international conferences.
>
> (Article 180)

This provision is potentially very important. Effectively coordinated development assistance emanating from combined EU and Member State sources would have considerable impact. In practice, however, success in achieving the necessary coordination of development programmes has been modest. There have been attempts, for example, to ensure that both the EU and Member States are not 'covering health' in a particular country, and there is evidence of increased consistency in specified areas such as policy on HIV/AIDS (Interview, Council Secretariat, Director General E (DGE), July 1997). However, uncoordinated efforts are frequent. They result in situations where up to ten Member States and the EU are operating aid programmes simultaneously. In such situations, staff in the Commission Delegations attempt to assist with coordination on the ground. However, this cannot remove the pressure on the administration of a very poor country obliged to interact with eleven different donors (ibid.). Since his appointment in 2004, Development Commissioner Louis Michel has been vociferous in his demands for improved coordination of EU and Member State development efforts.

In relation to humanitarian assistance, coordination of EU and Member State efforts has been more successful. Contacts between Member State and ECHO officials are frequent and a '14 point' fax system is in operation whereby Member States and ECHO exchange information about all decisions on humanitarian assistance.[53]

While consistency is central to the overall effectiveness of Union policies, in development policy as elsewhere, issues of coherence also pertain. As we have seen, responsibility for development policy is divided between DG External Relations, which deals with ALA countries, DG Development, which deals with ACP countries, and ECHO, which deals with emergency assistance. In addition, since 2001, the

EuropeAid Cooperation Office has been responsible for implementation of all development programmes. This reform, which was intended to increase the efficiency of aid disbursement, has resulted in an uncertain division of labour between policy-making and implementation. This causes tensions at Desk Officer level, with staff in DG Development expressing particular concern (Interview, DG Development, July 2001). Tensions also arise between DGs having geographical responsibility for development and those responsible for horizontal issues, such as fisheries and, in particular, agriculture. Similarly relations between DGs Trade and Development can be difficult. Despite efforts to promote internal coherence through a range of high level Inter-Service Groups, some disagreements have to be resolved at the College of Commissioners level. Here DG Development is perceived to be weak in relation to Trade and Agriculture (Interview, DG Development, July 2001).

Despite the problems that undoubtedly arise, lack of coherence is not the most significant impediment to EU actorness in this policy area. Rather it is failures of consistency, which prevent the emergence of an overarching development strategy and impede the close coordination of Member State and EU policies that is necessary to realize the Union's potential as a development actor.

Conclusion

The past 45 years have seen the evolution of relationships between the EU and developing countries in all regions of the world, many of them former colonies of the Member States. At the centre of these relationships has been a multi-faceted and highly institutionalized system of development cooperation involving a significant number (currently 78) of the world's poorest countries, collectively known as the ACP.

This chapter has focused disproportionately upon the ACP–EU relationship. This emphasis is justified, we believe, because it is here that a distinctive approach to development policy is most apparent. Moreover creation of the ACP, and the subsequent growth in size of that grouping, is itself an indication both of EU actorness and of its significant presence. A further manifestation of actorness lies in the increasingly prescriptive nature of the EU–ACP relationship since the mid-1990s. Continually expanding political conditionalities, and penalties for failure to meet EU prescriptions, have become a significant aspect of development cooperation. The attempt to impose upon the ACP the Union's agenda on regionalization, and the priorities identified in its Security Strategy, are the most recent examples of this trend.

Since initiating the EU–ACP relationship, the Union has developed relations with many countries and regions in Asia and Latin America. While lacking the highly institutionalized character of the ACP Convention system, relations with ALA countries have become increasingly broad in focus, incorporating a range of political and other conditionalities. Relations with Asian countries, in particular, have increasingly reflected the priorities of the Union's security agenda. This is exemplified by the Strategic Partnership agreements concluded with Japan, India and China, which provide for dialogue on a range of security issues including proliferation of WMD and combating terrorism. However, while relations with Asia (and to a lesser extent Latin America) are increasingly important for the Union, for ALA countries the relationship with the EU does not have the centrality of the EU–ACP relationship – for many ALA countries the EU is a relatively minor player.

Alongside the Union's geographically expanding development role, there has been an increased emphasis, since the creation of ECHO in 1992, upon provision of emergency humanitarian assistance. Here, aid provided by the Union exceeds the total of Member State efforts and there is relatively effective coordination of programmes. While tensions between the principles of emergency relief and development cooperation have not been fully resolved, the high profile achieved by ECHO in recent years has undoubtedly enhanced the reputation of the Union as a global actor.

In relation to development cooperation, EU programmes have evolved alongside, and in addition to, the development policies of Member States. Indeed their bilateral arrangements have remained the major focus of Member State policies; they have neither been subsumed within EU policy nor effectively coordinated at the Union level. This continuing significance of Member States' policies serves to divert resources, and distract attention, from EU efforts. The full potential for EU actorness in this policy area could be realized only if greater consistency was achieved between EU and Member State policies.

Lack of consistency has also impeded efforts to provide overall strategic direction for development policy (and to a lesser extent humanitarian assistance). Here the TEU introduced broad, value-based principles intended to guide EU external action, which have subsequently been complemented by identification of poverty reduction and achievement of the UN Millennium Development Goals as the central objectives of EU policy. Adherence to these objectives, however, has been impeded by divisions between Member States over the extent to which historical precedents and economic interests should influence policy priorities. The more recent emphasis upon security issues is likely to reinforce these divisions.

Despite these difficulties, the EU has developed a distinctive approach to development policy that has been important in establishing the Union's role as a relatively benign 'patron/mentor' in relation to the South. It has attempted, however imperfectly, to develop models of partnership and cooperation; and has avoided the practice of tying aid to commercial interests. Our interviews demonstrated that, in the South, the European Commission is regarded as a relatively unbiased interlocutor, in that it is distanced from the colonial ties of individual Member States. It would thus be unfortunate if the principles of EU development cooperation were subordinated to market oriented approaches, as suggested by the new focus of the Cotonou Agreement; or subsumed within an increasingly insistent security discourse.

Ultimately, the Union's significant presence in North/South relations, and the responsibilities thereby entailed, preclude the option of abandoning Southern 'partners'. Nevertheless, the increasingly prescriptive approach adopted by the Union, together with the intrusion of political and security priorities into development policy, may so erode the principles of partnership, and hence the distinctive character of Union policy, that relations with the EU will prove less attractive to Southern partners in the future.

6 Candidates and neighbours

The Union as a regional actor

It is through its relations with candidates and neighbours, more than in any other area of its external activity, that the collective identity of the EU will be constructed. For it is here that the Union's value and interest-based personae, and its exclusive and inclusive practices, are most evidently at odds. Here, too, the EU faces some of the key political issues of our times. The ability to successfully manage its relations with Turkey, Russia and Ukraine, and with the countries of the Western Balkans and the Southern Mediterranean, will be an important test of the Union's Common Foreign and Security Policy (see Chapter 7) and of its actor capability more generally. Thus, the conduct of regional relations, over the next decade, will have profound implications for the fundamental character of the Union, its physical borders and its reputation as an actor.

Following the end of the Cold War, when the need arose to relate to 'new' neighbours to the East, opportunity and the Union's presence combined to promote potent displays of EU actorness. However, this has been evident primarily in circumstances where it has been possible to use the prospect of EU membership as a policy instrument. Thus candidate members among the Union's Eastern and Southern neighbours have been required to undergo protracted periods of 'apprenticeship', as they strive to approximate their institutions, policies and values to those of the Union. But where membership is an unlikely or distant prospect, or candidate status has been denied, the Union's ability to exert influence over neighbours is diminished.

In contrast with the declining importance, for the EU, of cooperation with its ACP 'partners' (the subject of the preceding chapter), the significance of the Union's relations with its two peripheries – to the East and the South – has increased since the end of the Cold War. This is particularly so in the case of the Union's Eastern neighbours, both because of the limited nature of relations with Eastern Europe during the Cold War, and the perceived need to respond urgently to the dramatic events which characterized its end. Thus, the Commission observed in 1990:

> The peaceful revolution which swept Eastern Europe in 1989 is probably the most significant event in global terms of the past 45 years. It is happening on the very doorstep of the European Community. It represents a challenge and an opportunity to which the EC has given an immediate response.
>
> (Commission 1990b: 5)

While less momentous than the events in the East, a number of contextual factors, both external and internal, ensured that EU relations with Mediterranean non-member countries (MNC) also increased in salience from the late 1980s. First, the accession of Greece in 1981 and of Spain and Portugal in 1986 increased the Mediterranean focus of the EU itself. Subsequently the generally poor economic performance of the region, and associated increases in migratory flows into the Union, led Southern Member States to press for strengthened relations with MNC.[1] In addition, since the 1990–1 Gulf conflict, when anti-Western sentiment became evident across much of the Arab world, EU concerns about its Southern periphery have been increasingly security-related. Indeed the region was prioritized as an early focus of CFSP activity in 1992.[2]

In this context, concerns about the relative neglect of the Southern neighbours, despite their long association with the Union, prompted attempts to introduce an element of parallelism to relations with the two peripheries, notably through the launch of the Euro-Mediterranean Partnership (EMP) in 1995. Despite these efforts, the Union's relations with Eastern and Southern neighbours have become increasingly differentiated since the end of the decade. While several Eastern neighbours attained candidate status and moved towards accession, the Euro-Mediterranean process failed to gain momentum, in part as a consequence of the deteriorating security situation in the Middle East. In the context of the post-9/11 security environment, this failure is a source of concern.

In addition to these overall patterns of differentiation between the Eastern and Southern peripheries, divisions have also been created, within each region, as a consequence of the Union's decisions on eligibility for membership. The 2004 enlargement, to include eight Central and East European Countries (CEEC), brought into greater proximity, both geographically and politically, neighbours on the Union's Eastern periphery. While it is envisaged that the Balkan countries will accede to membership, Ukraine, Moldova and the countries of the South Caucasus, which have aspirations for membership, are excluded – as are Russia and Belarus. In contrast the 2004 enlargement, which included only Malta and Cyprus (but excluded Northern Cyprus[3]), did not impact so directly upon relations with Southern neighbours.

Undoubtedly the 2004 enlargement represented a success for EU external policy. Nevertheless it raised a number of challenges – not least that of managing relations with neighbouring countries to the East and South in a manner that will avoid creating destabilizing processes of inclusion and exclusion. This will necessitate development of mutually satisfactory relations with neighbours temporarily or permanently excluded from candidacy. Here, the launch of the European Neighbourhood Policy (ENP) in 2003 is an attempt to provide an overarching framework for EU relations with Southern and Eastern 'non-candidate' neighbours. The nature and potential of the ENP, and EU relations with countries encompassed by it, are considered below. First, since the Union's distinctive model of EU-neighbour relations was initially developed in the context of the 2004 Eastern enlargement, we provide a brief overview of that process. We then examine relations with various groups of candidates and potential candidates, divided according to the Union's prioritization for accession/candidacy – Romania, Bulgaria, Turkey and the countries of the Western Balkans.

Relations with candidates

While our principal concern is with the Union's relations with outstanding candidates, an overview of EU–CEEC relations in the pre-accession period is instructive. Here, the Union's ability to capitalize upon its significant presence permitted the development of a novel form of association, characterized by intense bilateral relations – through which the EU adopted a patron/mentor role in relation to CEEC transformation – and a system of multilateral political dialogue. Here, too, the formal 'Copenhagen Criteria' for membership were established, at the June 1993 European Council. These criteria, which apply to all subsequent candidates, are:

- Possession of stable institutions guaranteeing democracy, the rule of law, human rights and protection of minorities.
- The existence of a functioning market economy and the capacity to cope with competitive pressures within the EU.
- The ability to adopt in full the *acquis communautaire*, including adherence to the aims of political, economic and monetary union.[4]

This last, in particular, makes clear the Member States' intention that the ongoing process of integration internally should not be jeopardized by future enlargements. Effectively, candidate countries face a moving target; and the Union is provided with unparalleled leverage in its role as mentor during the pre-accession period.

EU–CEEC relations prior to accession

During the Cold War, relations between the EU and the CEEC were minimal. In consequence, understandings about the EU formed in CEEC during that period were partial and distorted, but strongly positive – based primarily upon acute awareness of the Union's relative economic strength. A compelling combination of opportunity and the Union's presence ensured that early EU membership became a central policy priority of the new CEEC governments post-1989. This led the Commission to conclude (1990b: 31) that, for CEEC, 'The European Community has what might be termed a mystical attraction'.[5]

The challenges facing the EU following the 1989 'velvet revolutions' were both daunting and unique. In response, a number of decisions were taken that had considerable implications for EU actorness. At the April 1989 European Council the Member States decided to coordinate their policies towards CEEC through the Union. Shortly afterwards the Group of 7 (G7) industrialized countries decided that the European Commission should be responsible for coordinating financial assistance to the CEEC provided by the Group of 24 Western donors, thus giving unprecedented recognition to the EU as an actor in international affairs. The December 1989 European Council requested the Commission to produce proposals for a new type of association agreement which would be appropriate to the developing EU–CEEC relationship. The bilateral Europe Agreements[6] subsequently negotiated with the CEEC were wide-ranging and included provision for 'approximating' legislation – that is bringing CEEC legislation into conformity with that of the EU. However, they contained no formal commitment to CEEC accession, thus failing to meet the central demand of CEEC governments. It was not until the June 1993 European Council that the principle of CEEC membership was formally endorsed and the Copenhagen Criteria for membership established.[7]

Subsequently, the Commission was charged with devising a pre-accession strategy for the CEEC, which involved two major tasks – assessing the readiness of candidates for accession;[8] and assessing the potential impact of enlargement upon the EU itself. The results of this effort were presented, in June 1997, as *Agenda 2000* (Commission 1997a).[9] In this document the Commission recommended adoption of reinforced pre-accession strategies in respect of all ten CEEC candidates. This involved creation of a new EU instrument, the Accession Partnership, which focused exclusively on the Union's priorities for accession. The Partnerships provided for a continuous dialogue, or screening process, between individual CEEC and the Commission, which enabled the Commission to identify priority areas for attention by CEEC governments. The screening process was a new procedure for the EU – 'never before have all the accession priorities been identified and then applied in this manner' (Interview, [then] DGIA, February 1998). Provision was also made for Regular Reports, by the Commission, on CEEC progress in meeting the membership criteria. These provisions created the framework for detailed accession negotiations, chapter by chapter, on all 31 chapters of the *acquis communautaire*.

Operating alongside the bilateral processes that dominated EU–CEEC relations were two sets of multilateral processes that aimed to promote harmonious relations between CEEC. The first of these, the Stability Pact, required CEEC to resolve various outstanding border and minorities issues.[10] The second, a multilevel 'structured dialogue', was intended to foster, between CEEC, the habits and levels of cooperation required of Member States.

The culmination of these arduous processes was the decision of the December 2002 European Council that the Czech Republic, Estonia, Hungary, Latvia, Lithuania, Poland, Slovenia and Slovakia (together with Cyprus and Malta) would be ready to accede to the Union in May 2004. The Commission meanwhile undertook to continue monitoring candidates' progress in transposing and implementing the *acquis* up to and following accession (Commission 2002c: 20).[11]

The remaining CEEC candidates, Romania and Bulgaria, were not scheduled for accession in 2004. However, their aim to accede in 2007 was accepted by the 2002 European Council, provided that progress in implementing the *acquis* was maintained. These countries were thus subjected to a further period of close scrutiny and supervision.

The candidacy of Bulgaria and Romania

The Commission Opinions on Bulgaria and Romania attached to the 1997 *Agenda 2000* confirmed that both countries had fulfilled the basic political criteria for membership (relating to democracy and the rule of law) and had made substantial progress in transforming their economies. Since then, democratic processes have been further consolidated and the Commission's Regular Reports on each country have recorded steady progress in the areas of concern noted in 1997. It is clear, nevertheless, that the internal reforms required for transposition of the *acquis* – in the areas of administrative and judicial capacity, for example – have been more effective in Bulgaria than in Romania.

The Commission's 2004 Regular Reports confirmed that, with continued effort on the part of Bulgaria, and 'vigorous implementation' on the part of Romania, both should be ready to accede in 2007 (Commission 2004d: 3).[12] Here it is instructive to note the comprehensive nature of the pre-accession strategies developed by the Union. These extend beyond the (already very extensive) *acquis* and its implementation to matters such as central/local government relations, the penal system, treatment of mentally disabled persons, and adoption of infants. In all these areas the Commission closely monitors, and reports upon, progress by the candidates.

Subsequent to the 2004 Regular Report, Accession Treaties for Bulgaria and Romania were signed in 2005. Provision was made that, should Bulgaria or Romania fail to make sufficient progress, the accession of either would be delayed by one year. This clearly reflects concerns about the preparedness of Romania.[13] Doubtless, however, the reform processes will be strengthened by the 'enhanced monitoring' to be undertaken by the Commission in all areas of concern highlighted in the 2004 Regular Report (Commission 2004d: 8). As the Commission has noted (ibid.: 2), 'the transformation process in both countries has been accelerated by the prospect of enlargement'.

Relations with Turkey

The decision of the December 1999 European Council formally to accord candidate status to Turkey marked a turning point in EU–Turkey relations. The ensuing period of rapid and radical change in Turkey demonstrates, again, the significant influence that can be exerted by the EU when the prospect of accession is available as a policy instrument. An interim opinion in 2002 gave further impetus to the internal reform process in Turkey and, at the December 2004 European Council, it was finally decided that accession negotiations with Turkey would begin in 2005. To appreciate the significance of these decisions a brief review of EU–Turkey relations is instructive.

Turkey's orientation towards the institutions of the West dates from the creation of the Turkish Republic in 1923. Since then, commitment to Westernization and modernization have been central themes of Turkey's state ideology. Turkey has sought membership of all the key Western international organizations, becoming a member of the Council of Europe and of the North Atlantic Treaty Organization (NATO) in 1952. In 1959 Turkey applied for associate membership of the (then) EEC and an Association Agreement (known as the Ankara Agreement) entered into force in 1964. This provided for Turkey's staged progression, through a Customs Union, to accession to the EU – when Turkey was deemed ready to take on the obligations of membership.

For a variety of reasons, implementation of the Ankara Agreement was not energetically pursued by either party. In relation to the economy, Turkish governments were unenthusiastic about liberalization, preferring to pursue import-substitution strategies behind tariff barriers. And on the EU side, 'sensitive' products (agriculture, textiles) remained sensitive. However, the most significant impediments to progress in EU–Turkey relations have been political. Tensions over Cyprus have been a complicating factor since Turkey's military intervention in 1974, but were greatly exacerbated by the accession of Greece to the EC in 1981. The internal political situation in Turkey also proved an impediment to closer EU–Turkey relations, with the EU on numerous occasions drawing attention to human rights abuses and the unacceptable treatment of the Kurdish minority. Of even greater significance has been the fragility of democratic processes, evidenced by the close involvement of the military in Turkish politics. Since signature of the Ankara Agreement the military has on three occasions intervened in the political system – in 1971 forcing the resignation of the government; in 1980 taking over the government and maintaining military rule until 1983; and in 1997 forcing from office the pro-Islamist minority government of the Welfare Party.[14]

In 1987 the Turkish government submitted a formal application for EU membership. The decision to seek membership, originally taken by the 1980–3 military regime, can be seen as a response to Greek accession in 1981 (following the restoration of democracy in that country) and in the light of Turkey's strong economic growth at that time. The restitution of civilian rule reflected the decision to apply for EU membership. It brought into office a strongly Western oriented government, which embarked upon a programme of economic liberalization in preparation for Turkey's formal membership application. This was rejected on the grounds that the EU was not in a position to consider further enlargement until after the completion of the Single Market in 1992. The Commission's (1989) Opinion on Turkey's application also referred to numerous obstacles to Turkish accession, including concerns over the consolidation of democracy, human rights issues and the dispute with Greece over Cyprus. Turkish opinion was inevitably offended by the political nature of the Commission's comments:

> … which did not feature in earlier Opinions in connection with the applications of the last three members, Greece, Spain and Portugal, themselves hardly paragons of democracy before they joined the Community.
>
> (Töre 1990: 10)

This rejection signalled that Turkey's membership aspirations would be treated with less enthusiasm, within the EU, than those of other potential members. As an alternative to Turkish accession, the Commission recommended that the long delayed Customs Union with Turkey be speedily completed. This was achieved and the Customs Union entered into force in December 1995. While indicating progress in EU–Turkey relations, the Customs Union provides in practice a highly asymmetrical relationship, both politically and economically.[15] From the perspective of Turkey, this was no substitute for membership.

Publication of *Agenda 2000* in 1997 marked a low point in EU–Turkey relations. This document, despite reiteration of Turkey's eligibility for EU membership, did not accord candidate status to Turkey, hence giving priority to all ten CEEC candidates (in addition to Cyprus). Given Turkey's importance as a Western ally throughout the Cold War, this prioritization of former adversaries caused outrage in Turkey. In response, the Turkish government partially suspended relations with the Union. The 1999 decision that Turkey should be considered a candidate for EU membership reflected lobbying by some Member State governments (notably the UK) and a broader recognition of the need to repair relations with a country that had long been considered a 'strategic partner' (but not necessarily a part) of Europe.[16]

The prospects for Turkey's accession

For important sections of the Turkish political elite, accession to the EU has significance far beyond its potential to provide economic well-being and political stability. Indeed EU membership has become:

> ... no less than the symbol for the successful completion of the long-term Ataturk revolution, involving the most basic and vital points of identity and orientation for Turkey.
>
> (Rubin 2003: 1)

Despite a broad orientation towards EU membership, however, internal differences remain concerning the extent to which Turkey should comply with EU demands on issues considered sensitive, such as minority rights and relations with Cyprus.[17] In this context the 1999 decision to grant candidate status to Turkey provided a strong incentive to pro-EU groups eager to push forward the reforms necessary to meet the Copenhagen political criteria. Since 1999 there has been an unprecedented programme of institutional and legislative reform, involving more than thirty amendments to the Constitution. Measures have been taken to strengthen civilian control over the military, to secure the independence of the judiciary, to abolish the death penalty and to give additional (but still inadequate, in the view of the Commission) rights to minorities (Önis 2003; Commission 2004e). Here it is important to note that the reform process accelerated following the election in late 2002 of the Justice and Development Party, a party with Islamist roots but committed to maintaining the secular Republic. Able to form a majority government for the first time since 1991, the Justice and Development Party has been ably led by Prime Minister Recep Tayyip Erdogan.

As a consequence of the significant reforms achieved since 1999, the decision to open negotiations was made by the European Council in December 2004. This decision, however, was controversial. Reluctant Member State governments (including those of Austria, France and Germany) sought to ensure that the decision was hedged with various caveats. These include a statement that the negotiation will comprise 'an open-ended process whose outcome cannot be guaranteed' (Commission 2004e: 2); together with a clear understanding that the process will be protracted. Even following a minimum of ten years in negotiation, it is possible that long transition periods or 'permanent safeguards' (in relation to movement of labour) may be considered necessary (ibid.: 5).[18]

These provisions reinforce Turkish suspicions that EU–Turkey relations have become 'an endless game' in which the governments of some Member States entertain the hope that Turkey will fail to comply with EU conditions (Interview, Turkish official, January 2003). Undoubtedly they indicate continuing ambivalence towards Turkish membership. Thus, while CEEC accession has been conceptualized within a discourse of 'return to Europe', relations with Turkey have been characterized by a very different discourse of 'strategic partnership'.[19] This has been evident since the inception of EU–Turkey relations, which reflected Cold War strategic priorities. In the post-Cold War environment Turkey remained strategically important to Western governments; indeed there were expectations that Turkey would make an important contribution to stability in Central Asia, the Caucasus and the Balkans (Craig Nation 1996). Since 9/11 Turkey's role as a 'buffer against everything' (Interview, Turkish official, June 1996) has been reinforced. Turkey is now expected to serve as:

> ... an important model of a country with a majority Muslim population adhering to such fundamental principles as liberty, democracy, respect for human rights, and the rule of law.
>
> (Commission 2004e: 4)

This raises the central problem affecting EU–Turkish relations. Turkey, as a Western oriented, secular, predominantly Muslim country, is expected to play a role in protecting European interests; but has yet to receive in return unqualified acceptance that Turkey is part of Europe.

Candidates and potential candidates in the Western Balkans

Here our concern is with EU relations with the former Yugoslav Republics of Bosnia and Herzegovina, Croatia, Macedonia,[20] and Serbia and Montenegro (including Kosovo[21]), and with Albania. As Figure 6.1 indicates, the geographical location of these countries (between three Member States and Eastern Balkan candidates Bulgaria and Romania) ensures that these countries have great significance for the Union; indeed they constitute the highest priority of the CFSP. There are several reasons for this, including the potential that renewed conflict in the region may threaten the stability of existing or prospective Member States, the prevalence of illegal trafficking in people, drugs and arms, and the possibility that 'international terrorists' may find a safe haven in the region (European Council 2003; Greco 2004: 63).

In its approach to the Western Balkans the Union has attempted to adapt the model developed for CEEC, creating networks of bilateral and multilateral relations through a process of Stabilization and Association. Thus the EU is employing its traditional policy instruments of aid, trade concessions and the 'golden carrot' of potential membership (Missiroli 2004: 19), with associated use of conditionality, to promote domestic stabilization and EU-compatible reform, and to encourage intra-regional cooperation. In this region the Union is also employing its new ESDP instruments – as we shall see in Chapter 8.

Following the end of the Cold War, the bitter inter-ethnic conflicts that attended the disintegration of Yugoslavia provided the EU with opportunities and challenges for which it was demonstrably unprepared. The failure of the Union's attempts at conflict prevention and management in the early 1990s revealed the inadequacy of

Figure 6.1 The Western Balkans in context (© LJMU Cartographic Unit 2005).

the nascent CFSP, and ensured that the Union's role remained subordinate to that of the UN and USA. It was only after the 1995 US-brokered 'General Framework Agreement for Peace' in Bosnia and Herzegovina, and NATO intervention in 1999 to end inter-ethnic conflict in Kosovo, that a comprehensive and proactive EU approach to the region was initiated.

The Union's contemporary, multi-faceted policy began with the launch, in 1999, of the Stability Pact for South East Europe. This broadly based, EU-led Pact combines a range of regional stabilization initiatives with, crucially, the prospect of eventual membership of the EU and NATO.[22] Alongside this multilateral approach, the Union launched a complementary, bilateral Stabilization and Association process (SAP), at the centre of which lies a novel form of association instrument, the Stabilization and Association Agreement (SAA). These agreements, together with the preparatory phases to their negotiation, are intended to provide a framework for the progression of each of the five West Balkan states through stabilization to eventual accession. They contain numerous conditionalities, many of which featured in the Europe Agreements with CEEC. Others are specific to the region, including participation in regional initiatives,[23] facilitating the return of refugees and full cooperation with the International Criminal Tribunal for Yugoslavia (ICTY).[24] The principal financial support for the SAP derives from the Community Assistance for Reconstruction, Development and Stabilization (CARDS) programme, which had a budget of approximately €5 billion for the period 2000–6. In addition, 'exceptional trade measures' extended to the West Balkan countries since 2000 provide free access to the Single Market for most goods.[25]

In June 2003, at the first EU–Western Balkans Summit in Thessaloniki, renewed commitment was made to the membership perspective of the West Balkans five. The Thessaloniki Agenda provided for strengthening of the SAP, including creation of European Partnerships, which set out reform priorities for each of the associates. Also introduced were measures which proved effective in the CEEC pre-accession process, such as 'twinning' (secondment of Member State officials to counterpart authorities in the region) and participation in EU programmes and agencies in order to gain fuller understanding of the Union's operation (Commission 2004f: 11).

In contrast with the regionally-focused Stability Pact, the bilateral SAP has facilitated considerable differentiation in the relationships between the EU and the West Balkan countries. Croatia and (to a lesser extent) Macedonia have made significant progress. In both cases SAAs have entered into force (in 2005 and 2004 respectively) and both countries have formally applied for EU membership.

Following a favourable Opinion from the Commission, membership negotiations with Croatia were due to open in February 2005. In the event, however, it was decided by the EU to postpone negotiations pending fuller cooperation by the Croatian government with the ICTY.[26] This decision was intended to signal to all the West Balkan countries the importance the EU attaches to compliance with the Tribunal.[27]

In the case of Macedonia, there has been considerable use by the Union of its CFSP and ESDP instruments, as we shall see in the chapters that follow. Here, the prospect of future EU membership was used to good effect, in 2001, in persuading all parties to accept the terms of the Ohrid Framework Agreement, which ended a brief period of inter-ethnic conflict.[28] As a consequence of cooperation with the Ohrid terms, SAA negotiations were expedited and the Macedonian government submitted a formal application for EU membership in March 2004. Accession is viewed in Macedonia as a remedy for the country's economic difficulties and political divisions.[29] Thus Macedonia's Foreign Minister has spoken of accession as 'An issue that unites and inspires everybody in Macedonia – the Government, all political parties and all our citizens' (Mitreva 2004: 1). Clearly there is a need for sensitivity in handling Macedonia's application. While concerns over the potential for renewed conflict may suggest that a cautious approach is advisable, excessive delay in opening negotiations could destabilize the fragile, post-Ohrid political settlement.

Although not part of Former Yugoslavia, Albania was included in the SAP due to its proximity and as a consequence of the 1999 conflict in Kosovo, which caused a significant number of Kosovan Albanians to seek temporary refuge in Albania. In addition Albania has itself been undergoing a difficult post-Communist transition, and in 1997 suffered a serious political crisis, involving the collapse of civil authority.[30] Following a period of relative political stability, negotiations for an SAA opened in January 2003. Since then, however, progress in implementing reform has been impeded by intense, ideologically based conflict between and within Albania's principal political parties. Despite this, the Albanian government has played a positive role in regional cooperation processes and continues to stress that negotiation of the SAA remains its foremost priority. However, the potential for the Union to exert influence remains contingent upon the Albanian administration's capacity and willingness to implement reform.

The remaining Western Balkan countries – Bosnia and Herzegovina and Serbia and Montenegro (plus Kosovo) – are not yet in a position to enter SAA negotiations. Although in receipt of financial support in the context of the SAP, their relations with the EU remain at the stabilization rather than the association phase.

In the case of Bosnia and Herzegovina, a Feasibility Study on opening SAA negotiations was carried out in 2003 and sixteen priorities for reform were identified. Since then progress in key areas such as inter-communal relations and cooperation with the ICTY has been minimal. Here, in the absence of internal political commitment, the utility of association and accession as policy instruments is limited.

The situation in Serbia and Montenegro (formerly the Federal Republic of Yugoslavia) is similarly unstable. Following the adoption of a new Constitution in 2003, which created a loose Serbian-Montenegrin federation, the climate appeared to be conducive to progress in relations with the EU.[31] However the fragility of the new arrangements, and the associated failure fully to implement the provisions of the new Constitution, subsequently impeded progress. However in April 2005, following improved cooperation by the Serbian authorities with the ICTY, the Commission recommended that SAA negotiations with Serbia-Montenegro should begin later that year.

A further complicating factor in the Union's relations with Serbia has been the situation in Kosovo, where inter-ethnic tensions between minority Serbs and Albanians remain high, as was evidenced by renewed violence in March 2004. While the final status of the province remains to be determined, EU ambitions in the region are evidenced by the declaration (in February 2005 prior to final status negotiations) that Kosovo will not return to its pre-1999 status as a province of Serbia. Rather Kosovo's future will be secured through making 'the European perspective for Kosovo real and tangible' (Enlargement Commissioner Olli Rehn quoted in *European Voice* 24 February–2 March 2005: 3).[32]

Clearly the Union's role in the Western Balkans has increased significantly since the mid-1990s and the EU is now undoubtedly the most important external actor in the region. The ability of the Union to exert influence, however, is dependent, not only upon the incentives it can offer, but also upon the extent to which generalized domestic political commitment to future EU membership can be translated, in the context of deeply divided societies, into specific commitments to implement the reforms required for progress in the SAP. Failure to comply, particularly as the process moves forward, will be penalized – as evidenced by the case of Croatia.

Relations with neighbours

Our use of the term 'neighbours' in relation to the non-candidate countries located on the Union's Southern and Eastern peripheries reflects a discourse of 'neighbourhood' which accompanied the 2004 enlargement. While intended to convey a desire for close and cordial relations – 'to create a ring of friends' around the borders of the enlarged EU (Commission 2003d: 9) – the concept of neighbourhood is also exclusionary. It implies a denial of candidate status. Indeed, following the launch of the European Neighbourhood Policy (Commission 2003d), the Commission found it necessary to make explicit this denial:

> Since this policy was launched, the EU has emphasised that it offers a means to reinforce relations between the EU and partner countries, which is distinct from the possibilities available to European countries under Article 49 of the Treaty on European Union.[33]
>
> (Commission 2004a: 3)

The apparent denial of 'European' status to countries such as Ukraine is both resented and contested; and may be subject to reversal in the future.[34] Meanwhile the ENP is designed to accommodate considerable differentiation in relations between the EU and its neighbours. Thus, Ukraine was one of seven countries initially prioritized for action in 2004 – together with Moldova, Morocco, Tunisia, Jordan, Israel and the Palestinian Authority. It is envisaged that the Union's existing relations with these countries will be progressively strengthened, in the context of the ENP, via Action Plans negotiated between the EU and individual neighbours.[35]

The Action Plans are guided by a number of 'common principles'. Foremost among these, and a determinant of progress in other areas, is effective commitment to shared values (that is values espoused by the Union). These range from commitment to democracy and the rule of law, through rights of minorities, trade union rights and gender equality, to combating terrorism and the proliferation of WMD (Commission 2004a: 13).[36] Other priorities include economic and social development, trade and border management. Promotion of regional cooperation, as in the case of the Western Balkans, will also be a priority, and specific regional initiatives are proposed in the areas of energy supply (several countries in both peripheries are important sources of, or transit routes for, oil and gas), transport and the environment.

Differentiation between neighbours will doubtless reflect progress in implementing Action Plan commitments. Here, in a process reminiscent of pre-accession strategies, progress will be 'carefully monitored' and subject to regular reports (Commission 2004a: 7). Inevitably, however, questions arise concerning the ability of the EU to use its established, highly intrusive, pre-accession procedures to influence the policy preferences of neighbours denied the 'golden carrot' of a membership perspective. The incentives offered by the ENP include increased financial assistance, with the prospect of additional assistance, from 2007, through a new European Neighbourhood Instrument. Technical assistance (including access to 'twinning' procedures) is also offered. Most significant is the prospect, depending upon progress, of moving beyond cooperation to integration – in relation to the Single Market and other EU policies and programmes. These provisions will be covered by new contractual arrangements, in the form of European Neighbourhood Agreements. Thus the ENP could lead to a relationship extending to 'everything but the institutions'.[37] Potentially this could provide the Union with an important source of influence – a 'silver carrot'. Nevertheless, significant progress in the context of ENP priorities is a distant goal for many of the neighbours; moreover the Union's record, particularly in its relations with the Mediterranean countries, has been unimpressive, as we shall see. First, however, we consider relations with Eastern neighbours.

Eastern neighbours

Today, the priority accorded to EU relations with Eastern neighbours is second only to that accorded to the Western Balkans. The 2004 enlargement brought into close proximity countries troubled by a series of unresolved conflicts, poor consolidation of democracy and a range of economic and social problems. 'Spillover effects' for the Union could, it is argued, range from narcotics trafficking to proliferation of WMD (van Oudenaren 2004: 256).[38] In addition, several states in the region have importance for the Union as suppliers of oil and gas.

The Commission-led ENP, with its presumption of progressively closer, but differentiated relations, has become the principal instrument for achieving the Union's aim 'to promote a ring of well governed countries to the East' (European Council 2003: 8). Given their importance for the region, we consider separately below EU relations with Russia and Ukraine. First, however, we review the history of EU involvement in the region.

Following the end of the Cold War, the Union's relations with countries to the East followed two very different paths. For CEEC the well-funded Phare programme and the comprehensive Europe Agreements facilitated the path toward accession.[39] Subsequently, as we have seen, the countries of the Western Balkans have been afforded similar treatment. But for the successor states to the Soviet Union, collectively referred to as the New Independent States (NIS), the Tacis funding programme, which provides technical assistance,[40] and negotiation of Partnership and Cooperation Agreements (PCA), involved less intense relationships and relatively modest levels of support.[41] As elsewhere, the EU has imposed various conditionalities, and funding and cooperation have been interrupted as a consequence of failure to meet standards of democratic governance and rule of law demanded by the Union. This applies in particular to Belarus and Turkmenistan.

From the outset, EU–NIS relations underwent a process of differentiation. This began with the transfer of the three Baltic Republics (Estonia, Latvia and Lithuania), following the dissolution of the Soviet Union, from 'neighbour' to candidate status. Prioritization of relations with Russia (and to a lesser extent Ukraine) from the mid-1990s has been a further source of differentiation (Commission 1997d).

More recently, the launch of the ENP embraced differentiation as a principle of EU–NIS relations. It also introduced a *formal* division between NIS, in that the countries of Central Asia – Kazakhstan, Kyrgyzstan, Tajikistan, Turkmenistan and Uzbekistan – are excluded from the programme. For these 'non-neighbour' countries, all of which suffer serious political and economic problems, the PCA process remains the central element of relations with the EU. These countries have significance for the EU for several reasons, not least as suppliers of energy and as potential sources of insecurity.[42] Moreover there is desire for closer relations with the EU and a sense that Central Asia has been neglected – 'We are far away but we are closer than the Mediterranean countries' (Interview, Tajik official, January 2003). Nevertheless, the Union's influence in the region is limited. Economically, while the Single Market will be important for Central Asian countries when their economies are more diversified, the present concentration of exports in the energy sector provides the energy-dependent EU with little leverage. Politically, too, the Union's frequently reiterated commitment to democracy promotion has inhibited the development of relations with the authoritarian governments of the region. Finally, of course, it has been decided to prioritize relations with more proximate Eastern neighbours.

Among the neighbours encompassed by the ENP, considerable differentiation is already evident. The Eastern countries originally included in the programme were Belarus, the Russian Federation and Ukraine, which directly border the EU, and Moldova, which will border the Union following the accession of Romania (see Figure 6.2). Of the four original Eastern ENP partners, Ukraine and Moldova were the first to conclude ENP Action Plans in 2004. Relations with Belarus, however, have long been impeded by the failure of that country to undertake democratic reform; indeed regime change is needed before Belarus can fully participate in the ENP process. Finally, in the case of the Russian Federation, ENP processes and funding are regarded as complementary to other initiatives rather than the centrepiece of EU–Russia relations (Commission 2004a: 6).

In 2004 the scope of the ENP was extended to include the countries of the Southern Caucasus – Georgia, Armenia and Azerbaijan. Action Plan negotiations with all three commenced in 2005. While all have PCAs in force, and there is a general aspiration for closer association/integration with the EU, the inclusion of these troubled countries reflects to a considerable extent the priority given to the Southern Caucasus by the Union's Security Strategy (European Council 2003: 8; Commission 2004a: 10).[43] The belated inclusion of these countries, and its explicit justification on security grounds, represents a further division within the ENP. Nevertheless, promotion of stability and security is a priority of the ENP generally. Here, success depends, to a considerable extent, upon the progress of EU relations with the two largest Eastern neighbours, Russia and Ukraine.

Relations with Russia

While Russia has been included in the ENP alongside other Eastern and Southern neighbours, the special character of EU–Russia relations is emphasized, within the EU, through a discourse of 'strategic partnership'.[44] This acknowledges Russia's importance in international affairs (as a permanent member of the UN Security Council) and, more particularly, its continuing influence in the NIS (Commission 2004g: 1). Development of a mutually satisfactory relationship with Russia is thus a condition for success of the ENP.

Figure 6.2 Eastern members of the ENP (© LJMU Cartographic Unit 2005).

The process of creating the 'strategic partnership' began at the EU–Russia Summit in May 2003. It involves strengthening the (already dense) network of joint PCA bodies, in particular through creation of a Permanent Partnership Council.[45] Central to the partnership is the phased development of four 'common spaces'. These are a common economic space (which includes energy and environment), a common space of freedom, security and justice, a common space of cooperation in the field of external security and a common space of research, education and culture. While this implies that Russia will ultimately share with the EU 'everything but the institutions', progress in filling the common spaces has, in practice, been slow. EU–Russia relations 'are often high on rhetoric but light on substance … wide but thin' (Lynch 2004: 36).

There are many reasons for this limited progress. The Union had been preoccupied, for some years, by preparations for the 2004 enlargement and, from 2002, by the launch of the euro and the Constitutional Convention. Thus initiation of the strategic partnership concept (and indeed of the ENP) in 2003 represented a tardy recognition of the broader implications of enlargement to the East. It has yet to develop into a coherent, sustained strategy.

From the Russian perspective, the EU is said to be 'taken very seriously' (Interview, Russian official, January 2003). Undoubtedly this reflects the Union's economic presence as Russia's principal trading partner. Indeed, following the 2004 enlargement, the EU market became the destination for more than 50 per cent of Russian exports, the bulk of which (almost 70 per cent) comprise fuel products. The EU is also Russia's most important source of financial assistance and foreign direct investment. While, given EU energy dependence, it is possible to speak of 'positive interdependence' between the EU and Russia (Commission 2004g: 1), the structural backwardness and low level of diversification of the Russian economy ensures that, in practice, the economic relationship is highly skewed in favour of the EU.[46]

The economic leverage enjoyed by the Union has undoubtedly induced the Russian government to cooperate, and indeed compromise, on key issues such as energy market liberalization and ratification of the Kyoto Protocol to the Climate Change Convention (see Chapter 4). There has also been compromise on sensitive matters such as the position of Kaliningrad. This Russian enclave has, since accession of Lithuania and Poland, been encircled by EU Member States (see Figure 6.2). Following difficult negotiations, it was agreed that Russian citizens travelling to and from Kaliningrad would be issued with EU funded 'Facilitated Travel Documents' (visas in all but name) by the Lithuanian government. Since it had vehemently opposed imposition of a visa regime, this represented a 'significant defeat' for the Russian government (Shemiatenkov 2002: 5). EU economic assistance to Kaliningrad was increased for the period 2004–6.

Despite this evidence of EU ability to capitalize upon its economic presence, a number of sensitive and intractable issues continue to generate tension in EU-Russia relations. These include Russia's military presence in Moldova and Armenia, and close interest in the separatist Georgian province of South Ossetia, all of which are impediments to the ENP process.[47] While frequent reference is made, within the strategic partnership discourse, to shared responsibility towards shared neighbours, it is not evident that the Russian government is keen to share responsibility for its 'near abroad'. Rather there is a tendency to view relations with shared neighbours as a zero-sum game, in which increased EU influence can be achieved only 'at Russia's expense' (Haukkala 2004: 46).

Attempts to strengthen EU–Russia relations have also been complicated by developments within Russia, including human rights issues in the context of the Chechen conflict and the centralization of authority during the Putin Presidencies, which 'raises questions about Russia's commitment to pursue democratic reforms' (Commission 2004g: 2). Such criticisms reflect the Union's assumption of 'the main responsibility for providing the standards of peaceful development and socio-economic progress' for the region (Aalto 2004: 1). They are not well received in

Russia, however, and have tended to be followed by a temporary cooling of EU–Russia relations.[48]

The record of EU–Russia relations is thus mixed, with evidence of EU influence primarily in relation to economic matters. On sensitive issues relating to Russia's internal political system and relations with close neighbours, the 'benign docility' which is said to characterize the Russian government's relations with the EU (Shemiatenkov 2002: 1) is less evident.[49]

Relations with Ukraine

In some respects EU relations with Ukraine have paralleled those with Russia. PCA processes and institutions are in operation, albeit subject to slow progress in implementation, Tacis assistance is in place, despite difficulties with disbursement, and Ukraine is included in the ENP. A key difference, however, has been the significant divergence between EU and Ukrainian ambitions for their relationship.

From the EU side, the 'strategic partnership' discourse has been muted and Ukraine has been treated similarly to other NIS. For the Ukrainian government, full EU membership has been a central aim since 1998 when a 'Decree on the Strategy of Integration into the European Union was issued' (Burakovsky *et al.* 2000: 17). This reflected a belief that Ukraine is 'at the centre of Europe' – and awareness of the preferential treatment accorded to neighbouring Poland as a consequence of candidate status (Interview, Ukrainian official, January 2003).

Repeated Ukrainian assertions of its 'European vocation' have been largely rhetorical, however. The processes of reform required by the PCA process have been uncertain – the political system remains highly centralized and opaque, corruption is widespread and state control of large enterprises is common. Moreover Ukraine's exports continue to be heavily oriented towards the NIS (77 per cent in 2002) with only 20 per cent to the EU (Commission 2004h: 18). This orientation is reflected in Ukraine's participation – with Russia, Kazakhstan and Belarus – in a Single Economic Space agreement, which was ratified by the Ukrainian parliament in 2004. Should the aim of creating a customs union be achieved, this would impede not only Ukraine's EU membership but also closer economic integration in the context of the ENP.[50]

In late 2004 Ukraine underwent a period of political turbulence which, following two sets of Presidential elections, culminated in the election of a Western oriented President, Victor Yushchenko.[51] The considerable interest and sympathy generated within the EU by these events gave greater prominence to Ukraine's membership aspirations, which have political support within Poland and Lithuania. While there has been little enthusiasm, elsewhere, for Ukrainian membership, the External Relations Commissioner found it necessary to state that membership of the ENP 'does not close any doors to European countries that may at some future point wish to apply for membership' (Ferrero-Waldner 2004: 1).

Undoubtedly the turbulent presidential elections in 2004 achieved a key Ukrainian aim 'to increase Europeans' knowledge of Ukraine' (Burakovsky *et al.* 2000: 23). This may herald the emergence of a discourse of 'responsibility' towards Ukraine and, ultimately, accordance of candidate status. Much will depend, however, upon progress with implementation of PCA and ENP Action Plan measures, upon the future direction of Ukraine's relations with Russia and upon factors internal to the Union – not least acceptance by existing Member States of the principle of further enlargement. Member States are divided on this matter, as they are on relations with Southern neighbours, to which we now turn.

Relations with Southern neighbours

As in the case of Eastern neighbours, relations with Mediterranean Non-member Countries (MNC)[52] are a high priority for the Union's foreign and security policy – for similar reasons. Characterized by 'economic stagnation, social unrest and unresolved conflicts' they are believed to pose risks to European security, ranging from terrorism to illegal trafficking in people (European Council 2003: 8). Several of these countries, too, are suppliers of energy to the EU.[53]

Despite these similarities, there are important differences between EU–MNC relations and those with Eastern neighbours. Foremost among these has been the often difficult colonial legacy, which has contributed to the failure to develop an effective overall strategy towards the region.[54] In consequence, EU–MNC relations have been characterized by periods of neglect punctuated by a series of (ultimately disappointing) EU initiatives – in response both to external contextual factors and internal pressures, primarily from Southern Member States.

First of these was the attempt, in the early 1970s, to construct a Global Mediterranean Policy (GMP) – in the context of worsening conflict in the Middle East and fears about the security of oil supplies. Two decades later, the ending of the Cold War, and the subsequent shift of attention from the South to the East, brought demands from MNC and Southern Member States for parallel treatment of the two peripheries. These resulted, in 1995, in the launch of the Euro–Mediterranean Partnership (EMP). Inclusion of the MNC in the Union's Neighbourhood Policy, in the context of the 2004 enlargement, is the most recent manifestation of this approach. Here, however, the parallelism is no longer with the Union's closest Eastern neighbours, but with the more distant 'new' neighbours of the ENP. To understand this continuing relative marginalization of the Southern neighbours a brief overview of EU–MNC relations is required.

At the time of the European Community's creation an aspect of the colonial legacy was heavy MNC trade dependence upon European markets. This has persisted, with the Single Market providing the most important destination for MNC exports and poor development of intra-regional trade.[55] Although a Declaration of Intent annexed to the Rome Treaty promised special treatment for exports of MNC products (citrus fruits, vegetables and olive oil), these were in direct competition with French and Italian produce. Consequently the MNC were not accorded treatment commensurate with that of ACP states (see Chapter 5), whose exports of tropical products are not in competition with EU production. Thus, from the outset, there has been unequal treatment of MNC.

By 1972, the EC had negotiated some form of economic agreement with the majority of MNC. However, the uncoordinated and *ad hoc* development of these agreements was considered to be inadequate in the changed context of the 1970s. Consequently, in 1972, the GMP was announced. This proved disappointing to all parties. The Commission had hoped to apply to MNC the Lomé Convention model negotiated with ACP countries. MNC governments rejected the collective clientelism of the Lomé model, however, and EC–MNC relations remained strictly bilateral.[56] At the same time the trade privileges accorded to MNC continued to fall short of Lomé preferences. In 1979 they were subject to considerable erosion following tariff reductions agreed by the EC during the GATT Tokyo Round. Accession to the EC of Greece, Spain and Portugal during the 1980s was even more damaging to MNC preferences, due to the greatly increased production of Mediterranean products within the Union. In consequence, from the mid-1980s, in the context of economic decline across much of the region, MNC governments 'were left with the prospect that the GMP would soon be giving them a preferential share of nothing' (Pomfret 1992: 79).[57] Shortly afterwards events in Eastern Europe threatened remaining MNC privileges, as CEE countries began to negotiate preferential trade agreements with the EU.

The ending of the Cold War necessitated reconsideration, by the EU, of relations with its Eastern and Southern peripheries. Following unsuccessful attempts to develop a 'Redirected Mediterranean Policy' (Commission 1990c), demands for parity of treatment with CEEC increased. Indeed governments of Southern Member States made support for Eastern enlargement conditional upon strengthened EU–MNC relations. It is in this context that the Union's Euro–Mediterranean Partnership (EMP) was launched.

From EMP to ENP

By the mid-1990s several factors had combined to suggest that it might be possible to replace the bilateralism of past EU–MNC relations with an overarching approach to the region. First, entry into force of the TEU provided impetus for an explicitly political dimension to the Union's 'partnerships' generally. Second, the Union's experience with CEEC since 1989 suggested that 'a similar all-encompassing strategy' would be appropriate for the Mediterranean region (Piening 1997: 80). Finally, and perhaps most importantly in the Mediterranean context, progress in the Middle East Peace Process at that time permitted adoption of a comprehensive approach.[58] Thus, it was hoped that the new 'Partnership' would not only engender more satisfactory EU-MNC relations but would also provide a framework through which the Union could play a more prominent role in the Peace Process.

In terms of scope, the Partnership included Algeria, Morocco, Tunisia, Egypt, Jordan, Lebanon, Syria, the Palestinian Authority and Israel, together with (originally) Cyprus, Malta and Turkey. Figure 6.3 shows the current MNC membership of the EMP. In terms of content, the three elements of the Partnership – financial assistance, bilateral association and multilateral dialogue – mirrored the pre-accession relationship with CEEC and, more recently, with the Western Balkans.

The first two elements of the Partnership represented yet another attempt to strengthen the existing EU approach. 'Old wine in new bottles', as Gomez has argued (2003: 61). Financial assistance, substantially increased relative to previous funding,

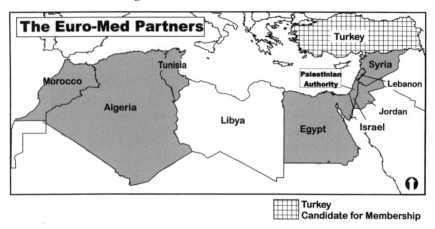

Figure 6.3 The Euro–Med Partners (© LJMU Cartographic Unit 2005).

is provided through a single MEDA budget line.[59] While for the first time in the EU–MNC context, political conditionality was introduced (in the form of democracy and human rights provisions), the Union's priorities are evident from the provision that funding will 'first and foremost benefit MNC embarking on modernizing and reforming their economies to culminate in free trade' (Commission 1995a: 33). The second element of the Partnership comprises upgraded bilateral agreements known as Euro-Mediterranean Association Agreements. At the core of these Agreements is economic cooperation, with a major emphasis upon movement towards free trade in industrial goods and services.

The final element of the Partnership denotes a potentially important departure from past practice. Based on the 1995 Barcelona Declaration and known as the Barcelona Process, this provides for multilateral dialogue using a 'three-basket' formula reminiscent of the CSCE process.[60] The Declaration thus contains three chapters – political and security;[61] economic and financial (including establishment of a Free Trade Area by 2010); social, cultural and human affairs.[62] The agenda comprised by these chapters is pursued through multilateral meetings operating at various levels.[63] Particularly productive have been meetings between technical experts, who discuss a wide range of issues from conservation of wetlands to use of the Internet (Interview, [then] DGIB, February 1998). Thus the Barcelona Process has provided a framework, however fragile, for meetings involving representatives of countries, not least Israel and Syria, who rarely interact in other fora.

Despite the optimism with which it was launched in 1995, the EMP (like its predecessor GMP) proved disappointing. In the traditional, economic sphere of the relationship a number of problems arose. Disbursement of funding under the MEDA I programme was subject to delays and inefficiencies, although substantial improvements are claimed in relation to MEDA II.[64] Nevertheless funding levels remain inadequate to compensate for the negative impacts, for MNC, of trade liberalization.[65] In consequence the programme has had little impact upon the problems of high unemployment and acute poverty that afflict the region.

From the outset, 'The prospect of creating a free trade zone was met with modified rapture across the region' (Marks 1996: 14). The concerns of MNC governments were reinforced, during negotiation of bilateral Euro-Med Association Agreements, by the continued refusal of the EU fully to include agricultural products in the 'free trade' provisions.[66] It is thus an indication of the Union's economic presence that such Agreements have been concluded with all MNC except Syria, where negotiations continue. Progress in trade liberalization by MNC, and development of trading relations between them, has nevertheless been slow (Commission 2000c).

Beyond the economic sphere, the Union's ability to exert influence has been limited. This is illustrated by the failure to pursue the political (democracy and human rights) components of the EMP. In this region, it is considered, to take action on such issues would be 'an extremely grave step' (Interview, [then] DGIB, February 1998). This reticence, which contrasts with the treatment of ACP and NIS members, undoubtedly reflects the sensitive nature of EU–MNC relations. A further complicating factor has been the ability of MNC governments to justify their actions, post-9/11, in the context of the 'war against terrorism'. In consequence, political conditionalities have yet to be invoked.

While the bilateral component of the EMP proved less dynamic than had been hoped, it was in relation to the multilateral Barcelona Process that disappointment was greatest. Efforts to disassociate the EMP dialogues from the vicissitudes of the Middle East Peace Process proved impossible in the context of unfolding events. An early setback was the election (in mid-1966) of the hardline Israeli Prime Minister, Binyamin Netanyahu, which caused the Lebanese and Syrian governments largely to confine their participation to the technical level. Inevitably the Barcelona Process was further impeded, after 2000, by the events associated with the Second Palestinian Intifada. Nevertheless, low-level multilateral dialogue has continued, despite these setbacks, and the EMP remains the only context in which MNC representatives interact. Sustained revival of the Middle East Peace Process could thus contribute to its reinvigoration. Nevertheless, previous attempts to reinvigorate EU–MNC relations have proved ineffective.[67]

Their inclusion in the ENP is the Union's most recent attempt to deepen relations with MNC. The ENP will replace the bilateral element of the EMP – hence it will be complementary to the multilateral Barcelona Process. It will permit greater differentiation in bilateral EU–MNC relations and, from 2007, MEDA will be replaced by the new Neighbourhood Instrument. The ENP is claimed to have 'aroused considerable interest in the Mediterranean region' and (yet again) to be 'reinvigorating the Barcelona Process' (Ferrero-Waldner 2004). Certainly the early agreement of ENP Action Plans (in 2004) with Morocco, Jordan, Tunisia, Israel and the Palestinian Authority (with Lebanon and Egypt to follow) indicates, in principle, the willingness of these countries to make substantial progress in adopting the Union's values and approximating EU legislation. Thus Tunisia 'has committed itself to important reforms concerning human rights' (ibid.) while, for Israel, the 'everything but institutions' concept has considerable advantages that can be realized only following satisfactory progress in the Peace Process (*European Voice*, 16 December 2004–12 January 2005).

Despite these optimistic signs, MNC inclusion in the new discourse of 'neighbourhood' should be viewed in the context of previous attempts to engage and influence them, which have been similarly launched with much enthusiasm and rhetoric but have proved to contain insufficient substance. Since the 'golden carrot' of a membership perspective is denied, and at present only Israel is sufficiently strong economically to take full advantage of the ENP proposals, it is unclear that ENP incentives will be adequate to provide the Union with the influence it clearly seeks in the region.

EU actorness in relation to candidates and neighbours

The 2004 enlargement of the EU has great significance for relations with candidates and neighbours – for two reasons. First, the successful management of the 2004 enlargement process provided a template that could be applied elsewhere. The 'golden carrot' of a membership perspective, and associated processes of monitoring, reporting and rewarding progress, has thus been applied to the Western Balkans. And, second, the Eastern enlargement extended the Union's borders, bringing into close proximity NIS countries that are of importance to the new Member States but had previously been neglected by the EU. In relation to these countries, and the Mediterranean non-member countries whose long-term relations with the EU have failed to prosper, the Union's Neighbourhood Policy is intended to offer a 'silver carrot' – that is, progressive integration into most areas of Union policy, with associated processes of monitoring and reporting, but excluding membership of the common institutions. It is envisaged that the degree of integration achieved will vary according to the needs and capacity of each neighbour.

In principle, this dual approach to candidates and neighbours constitutes an overarching strategy for the Union's conduct as a regional actor. In practice, however, the Union's ability to capitalize upon its undoubted economic presence is likely to vary significantly – in accordance with the structures of constraint and opportunity provided by the external context of ideas and events, and the internal context of the EU policy environment. Here, as elsewhere, consistency between Member States is a particular issue. In relation to coherence, however, the fragmentation of effort noted in the case of development cooperation is less evident. Coordination of policy towards candidates and neighbours was greatly enhanced by changes introduced in 2000 by the Prodi Commission, which have been maintained. Creation of DG Enlargement proved a particularly effective reform, while DG External Relations, with its responsibility for relations with both Southern and Eastern peripheries and for the Commission's input into CFSP, has provided a focus for inter and intra-pillar cooperation that was previously lacking.[68] Moreover, in relation to the ENP, a Task Force has been created comprising officials from both the External Relations and Enlargement Directorates-General. The Task Force is headed by the Deputy Director-General of DG External Relations but the principal policy input will come from DG Enlargement, thus combining political direction with DG Enlargement's experience of the pre-accession procedures to be applied, in modified form, to Eastern and Southern neighbours.

Candidates and potential candidates face protracted and, in some cases, potentially inconclusive pre-accession processes. As we have seen in the case of Romania and Bulgaria, and to some extent also Turkey, it is when accession seems (relatively) attainable that EU influence is strongest. Here the decision in February 2005 to delay accession negotiations with Croatia has demonstrated that candidate countries are expected to make strenuous efforts to comply with the conditions imposed. Ultimately, it is evident that many factors may impede the accession of Turkey and the Western Balkan countries – and hence impact negatively upon EU actorness.

In the case of Turkey, while there may be resistance to EU influence in relation to issues deemed central to Turkey's national sovereignty, the very evident reservations about Turkish accession in some Member States suggest that lack of consistency may prove a greater impediment to EU actorness.[69] The case of the Western Balkans is somewhat different, in that there is a strong geographical logic to their inclusion and consensus among Member States concerning the Union's overall strategy. Nevertheless differences are evident concerning, for example, Croatia's candidacy.[70] Should negotiations with Croatia falter, this will send a negative signal to the remaining countries of the region, where, with the possible exception of Macedonia, formal candidacy is a distant prospect. However, while setbacks are inevitable, in the Western Balkans the Union is committed to a long-term strategy that has made it the most important external actor in the region.

In its relations with neighbours, EU actorness is problematic. For Eastern neighbours, the presence of the EU is significant, in some cases mirroring the 'mystical attraction' evident among CEEC in the early years. It is thus not clear that the incentives offered by the ENP will prove adequate to achieve the Union's aim of ensuring the economic and political stability of the Eastern neighbours. Moreover, the Union is involving itself in a highly volatile region, which is regarded by the Russian government as its special responsibility. The need to exercise caution in the face of Russian sensitivities may prove a major impediment to EU actorness. Here issues of EU inconsistency arise once again, with the French and German governments adopting a placatory stance towards Russia, and the Polish and several other Eastern Member State governments urging that relations with Ukraine be prioritized.

While the ENP represents a new, enhanced approach to Eastern neighbours, in the case of Southern neighbours it can be seen as yet another attempt to reinvigorate a long and difficult relationship. Nevertheless, in a region where membership is neither offered nor desired (except by Morocco) and economic dependence is high, it may be that ENP incentives will prove effective in some cases. Too often, however, EU actorness in the Mediterranean has been impeded by problems of consistency. These reflect, in part, a broad North/South divide between Member States over prioritization of the Eastern and Southern neighbours, which is likely to be exacerbated by the 2004 enlargement. More important, however, has been the enduring colonial legacy and the related importance, for individual Member States, of their established bilateral relations with various MNC. In consequence, the Commission has urged that, 'In the implementation of the ENP it is of the utmost importance that the Institutions and Member States act in a consistent and coherent way' (Commission 2004a: 6). A further impediment to EU actorness in the Mediterranean region is the involvement of other interested external actors. In the Middle East, in particular, the Union's considerable economic presence has not been translated into political influence; here the United States remains the most important external actor.

Conclusion

The end of the Cold War fundamentally changed the external context of EU action, bringing unprecedented opportunities but also daunting challenges, many of which remain. Within the EU, the 1989 decision by the Member States to coordinate their response to 'new' Eastern neighbours through the EU initiated the processes through which the Union has become the leading actor in the region.

In the context of high expectations from CEEC, the traditional EU instruments of financial assistance, trade concessions and loose association, employed (albeit without great effect) in relation to MNC, proved hopelessly inadequate. After some hesitation, the offer of a membership perspective to selected CEEC, subject to various conditions, provided the Union with its most powerful and effective policy instrument. It also increased expectations of the EU among MNC and excluded Eastern neighbours. The 2004 enlargement thus marks only the first, and least difficult, phase of the Union's construction as a regional actor.

Today, success in developing mutually satisfactory relations with neighbours and (potential) candidates is of paramount importance to the enlarged Union. Both the Eastern and Southern peripheries are characterized by economic and political instability and bitter, unresolved conflicts. In consequence, both are identified in the Union's Security Strategy as potential sources of risk to European security. Both, too, are important in the supply or transit of energy to the EU. While the Security Strategy makes clear the Union's interest in surrounding itself with a 'ring of well governed countries' (European Council 2003: 8), the principal discourses employed within the Union have not been of security and interest but of inclusion and neighbourhood. Rhetorically, at least, the central aim of the Union is to extend to the East and the South its values and practices, and hence its stability and prosperity. This is to be achieved either through incorporation (the Western Balkans and Turkey) or 'neighbourhood' (NIS and MNC). In practice, the Union's response has been to differentially employ its policy instruments, including the prospect of enlargement, in ways that reflect the various facets of its identity – both inclusive and exclusive and value and interest-based.

Policy towards the Balkans approximates most closely to conceptions of the EU as inclusive and value-based. Thus a membership perspective has been offered and a wide range of political conditionalities imposed. Some of these, including cooperation with the ICTY, may temporarily impede EU actorness. Here, too, in accordance with the Union's own practice, incentives have been provided for regional cooperation in economic and other spheres. These measures denote a substantial, long-term commitment and high levels of Member State consensus. Should they succeed, in the face of continuing inter-ethnic tension across the region, they will contribute significantly to the Union's reputation as a regional actor. In the case of Turkey, however, the long delayed and grudging accordance of a membership perspective sends mixed messages. Ultimately, the juxtaposition of exclusionary discourses of Turkish 'otherness' (prevalent in several Member States) with a value-based approach to human rights issues in Turkey, may suggest a level of hypocrisy that impedes EU actorness.

Extension of a membership perspective beyond Turkey and the Balkans is at present precluded. However, the dynamic of inclusion and exclusion implied by the distinction that has been made between candidates and neighbours is divisive and, given the high expectations of Ukraine in particular, may be unsustainable. Nevertheless, the ENP is potentially ambitious. In relation to Eastern neighbours, where EU presence is strong and governments of countries in transition relatively open to external advice, it implies a new level of engagement and a more sustained effort to encourage the adoption of EU values. Much will depend, however, upon the commitment and consistency shown by Member States and the Union's ability to manage its difficult relationship with Russia.

In the case of Southern neighbours, the ENP denotes little that is new. There is a long and undistinguished record of EU involvement in the Mediterranean region, during which Member State sensitivities and the intransigence of entrenched MNC elites have prevented the Union from pursuing a value-based agenda. Here, economic interests and security concerns have predominated. Nevertheless the Barcelona Process represents an ambitious, long-term strategy that aims to encourage cooperation between MNC; indeed it attempts to apply the Union model of functional cooperation to the construction of peaceful relations in the region. In consequence there is an aspiration for the Union to become, in the event of resolution of the Israeli-Palestinian conflict, 'a deciding factor in the post-conflict process' (European Council 2000: 1).

In its relations with candidates and neighbours, the Union is undoubtedly developing an ambitious, long-term strategy. The extent to which the discourses of inclusion and neighbourhood will result in shared understandings and commitments depends upon a number of factors, however. Many of these, such as Russian acceptance of an enhanced EU role in the NIS and US commitment to the Middle East Peace Process, are located in the external environment. Others relate to the Union's capacity to exploit opportunities and capitalize on economic presence. Foremost, here, are issues of Member State consistency in the enlarged EU. Should significant divisions arise between Member States over prioritization of relations with particular candidates or neighbours, this would impede the Union's effectiveness as a regional actor. Nevertheless, in 1989 the Member States accorded to the Union responsibilities in the region and there is an expectation on the part of third parties that it will discharge them. Ultimately, for many countries in the region, the EU has become 'the only game in town' (Dannreuther 2004: 158).

7 Common foreign and security policy

A political framework for EU external action?

> It is my belief that in this global age a Union of our size, with our interests, history and values, has an obligation to assume its share of responsibilities ... The question, therefore, is not *whether* we play a global role, but *how* we play that role.
>
> (Solana 2002: 3, emphasis in original)

These words of Javier Solana, High Representative of the CFSP, reflect a discourse of responsibility associated with recent, dramatic changes in the external context of EU action. The opportunities provided by the ending of the Cold War, and the challenges presented by the post-9/11 security environment, have brought increased demands, both from within the EU and beyond, that the Union should play an enhanced role in international affairs. In order to assume its responsibilities, however, the EU must develop effective political/strategic coordination of its external activities – whether these are in the field of economic policy, environmental negotiations, development cooperation or relations with neighbours. If the potential of its significant presence is to be realized, the economic power of the Union must be articulated to a stronger sense of collective political purpose.

Following the end of the Cold War, introduction of the CFSP (by the TEU in 1993) represented an attempt to provide overall strategic direction for external policy. The 2003 European Security Strategy – *A Secure Europe in a Better World* – has a similar aim; its potential is discussed below. To date, however, achievement of strategic direction has proved elusive. This reflects the singular character of the Union, whose Member States are jealous of their role in the politically sensitive areas of traditional foreign and security policy. In consequence, the inconsistency problems that have been identified as impediments to EU policy-making in previous chapters are particularly acute in relation to CFSP.

Differences in Member State foreign policy priorities reflect a variety of factors, including pre-existing bilateral ties (or antipathies), geographical location and extent of support for a policy stance distinct from that of the USA. Successive enlargements of the EU have tended to exacerbate these differences. Divisions have also long persisted over approaches to decision-making, with (broadly speaking) large Member States preferring intergovernmental methods and smaller Member States advocating a more 'Community' approach. Here, a still unresolved central issue has been the extent to which the European Commission, with its responsibility for the economic instruments of policy, should be actively involved in decision-making.

Problems of consistency were, of course, starkly revealed by Member State divisions over the 2003 invasion of Iraq. While it is important to note that 'business as usual' continued across all the Union's external policy areas (including CFSP/ESDP) during this period,[1] such highly public disputes over important policy decisions, and the resulting failure to decide, inevitably impinge upon the Union's presence in foreign policy. They also remind us that, despite its title, CFSP cannot be regarded as a common policy in a sense analogous to the Common Commercial Policy; rather it is a highly institutionalized and complex process of consultation and cooperation between Member State governments. Nevertheless, where there is consensus among Member States, effective common action can ensue.

In the CFSP context, problems of coherence are also endemic. Regarded as a specialized and quintessentially political policy area – frequently referred to as 'high politics' – foreign and security policy has traditionally been considered as entirely distinct from the mundane 'low politics' of external economic relations. In practice, of course, this distinction has always been blurred. It is increasingly so today, given the significance of the economic instruments of statecraft and of 'soft', non-military security, where, despite recent developments in the field of ESDP, the Union's principal strengths continue to lie. The evident overlap between the economic and political dimensions of external policy has not, however, been reflected in the creation of institutions that facilitate their coordination. Instead, the evolution of the EC/EU has seen the entrenchment of a division between external economic policy and 'political' foreign policy that has been formally enshrined in the Treaties and reflected in the parallel development, within the Commission and the Council Secretariat, of two separate, externally oriented and potentially competing bureaucracies.

Despite the problems of consistency and coherence so evident in this policy area, there has been a gradual strengthening, over the past two decades, of commitment to and capacity for foreign policy cooperation – to an extent that has 'surprised its participants and critics alike' (Smith, M.E. 2004: 2).[2] While the principal concern of this chapter is with the contemporary operation of CFSP, and its potential to provide strategic direction to external policy, awareness of the distinctive fashion in which this policy area developed is essential to an understanding of contemporary issues. Consequently we provide an overview of the evolution of foreign policy cooperation from its inception to the present (see Table 7.1 for a schematic representation) as a prelude to discussion of contemporary organizational issues and policy instruments. Reference is also made to proposals to strengthen the CFSP, which were prominent in discussions surrounding the Constitutional Treaty. Finally, an assessment is made, in the context of its 'fit' with current policy, of the potential for the European Security Strategy to provide an overarching political framework for the Union's external activities.

The early years: absence of 'foreign policy'

The creation of the European Communities following the end of the Second World War, and in the context of increasing Cold War tensions, reflected both the desirability

Table 7.1 CFSP: antecedents and development

1970	Luxembourg Report: established European Political Cooperation (EPC), as an intergovernmental process with no institutional base. Aimed to provide mechanism for foreign policy cooperation/coordination to give political direction to the EC's external relations.
1987	Single European Act: provided treaty basis for EPC, which remained an intergovernmental process between High Contracting Parties. Dedicated EPC Secretariat established in Brussels but not a Community institution — staffed by seconded Member State officials.
1993	Treaty on European Union: CFSP established as intergovernmental pillar of the Union (Pillar II). Provision for Joint Actions and Common Positions. CFSP Secretariat incorporated into Council Secretariat. Commitment of Union to ensure overall consistency of 'external activities'.
1999	Treaty of Amsterdam: Introduced 'Common Strategies' to be determined by European Council. Provided for appointment of High Representative for the CFSP. Policy Planning and Early Warning Unit established in Council Secretariat.
2003	Treaty of Nice: Codified developments in security sphere introduced at 1999 Cologne Council. Established Political and Security Committee comprising Brussels-based national diplomats meeting twice weekly to monitor the development and implementation of CFSP.
2004	Draft Constitutional Treaty signed by all Member States. Provision made for: Foreign Minister to take roles of High Representative and Commissioner for External Relations; creation of External Action Service comprising officials from Council Secretariat, Commission and Member States; elected President, for two and a half year term, renewable once.

of cooperating in the construction of a peaceful and prosperous Western Europe and of seeking, collectively, to recover some of the international influence lost by West European states individually. For much of its history European integration focused upon economic and social matters.

The Treaty of Rome made no reference to orthodox foreign policy issues. Nevertheless the necessity for what became known as EC 'external relations' was acknowledged. The Community was accorded formal legal personality and a further provision of the Rome Treaty empowered the EC to enter into association agreements with third parties. As we have seen in previous chapters, these provisions formed the basis for the Community's evolution as an international actor of some significance – despite the absence of a formal foreign policy role.

By the early 1960s the need to balance the EC's growing significance in external economic relations with an explicit foreign policy dimension became a subject of often contentious discussion. At the centre of this controversy was the extent to which the Commission should be involved in the formulation of foreign policy, with intergovernmentalists, led by French Gaullists, strongly opposed to any Commission involvement.[3] The issue was (temporarily) resolved with the adoption of the 1969 Luxembourg Report, which recommended establishment of a system of foreign policy cooperation on an intergovernmental basis, operating entirely outside the EC framework. No new institutional structure was proposed and the ensuing system of

European Political Cooperation (EPC) initially lacked even a dedicated secretariat. Since many of the problems arising from the operation of EPC remain evident today, it is worth examining its development.

European political cooperation

EPC aimed to increase understanding between Member States on foreign policy issues through regularly informing and consulting partners, and to strengthen solidarity through harmonization of views, coordination of policy positions and, where possible or desirable, joint action. Thus EPC involved regular consultation and formal quarterly meetings between national Foreign Ministers, supported by a Political Committee, comprising Political Directors (senior Foreign Ministry officials) representing each Member State, and a range of specialist Working Groups composed of Foreign Ministry officials. Cooperation between Member State missions in third countries was also encouraged. Formal external representation was provided by the Presidency, supported, from the mid-1970s when the onerousness of the responsibility became apparent, by the immediate past and future Presidencies, in what became known as the Troika.[4] Thus EPC comprised highly formalized, multi-level, intergovernmental cooperation.

Administrative support was provided by the country holding the Presidency and, in order to emphasize the distinctiveness of this policy area, all meetings took place in the capital of the Presidency country. This placed a heavy burden on national officials and also caused problems of continuity arising from the inability to establish a collective, institutional memory. Consequently, by the late 1970s, the practice had evolved of seconding national officials to assist successive Presidencies. While this afforded useful experience in working cooperatively, on a daily basis, with counterparts from other Member States, the peripatetic nature of the EPC process remained an impediment to its effectiveness. As Simon Nuttall observes (1992: 20): 'The fact that EPC archives had to be carried halfway across Europe in a suitcase every six months gave rise to particularly unfavourable comment'. A secretariat for the EPC was established in Brussels only following entry into force of the SEA.

Despite the formal separation between the EC and EPC, which the SEA maintained, the practical development of policy had, from the outset, impinged upon EC competences – necessitating liaison between EPC personnel and the Commission. Indeed it is difficult to identify a policy area discussed in EPC which did not impinge upon EC matters. The very first EPC Ministerial Meeting, in November 1970, had as agenda items East/West relations and the Middle East. Policy in both these areas impinged upon EC competences and, ultimately, Commission involvement was significant. At this first meeting, however, the Commission delegation was, with reluctance, admitted to the last hour of the day-long meeting.

The EPC/EC relationship was a source of considerable tension in the early years, with Member State diplomats '… at best inclined to treat the Commission with the high courtesy of condescension' (Nuttall 1996: 130). Following a decade of *ad hoc* arrangements to accommodate Commission involvement in those frequent circumstances where EC and EPC matters overlapped, and where EC instruments were essential to policy implementation, it was agreed, in 1981, that the Commission should be 'fully associated' with EPC at all levels. This formula, which has persisted, permitted attendance of Commission representatives at all EPC meetings. Moreover, in 1983, in recognition of its role in external policy, the Commission's participation in the Troika was agreed by Member States. There was, thus, a gradual evolution of the EPC/Commission relationship after its inauspicious beginning.

More generally, in the fifteen years which separated the Luxembourg Report and the SEA, the EPC process became established and largely accepted practice. Consultation between Foreign Office ministers and officials of the Member States became routine at all levels, the Coreu telex system which directly linked EC Foreign Ministries facilitating instantaneous communication.[5] While this level of interaction fostered habits of cooperation, the more ambitious aims of policy coordination and joint action produced a mixed record.

The EPC process proved successful as a source of declaratory statements deploring/ welcoming developments upon which Member States were agreed, but initiatives that progressed beyond the routine and declaratory were relatively rare. Nevertheless, some successes can be identified, particularly in the context of the Conference on Security and Cooperation in Europe (CSCE).[6] This process of East/West consultation, which commenced in 1973, provided an opportunity to test the new EPC mechanisms. From the outset the Member States presented joint positions and played a proactive role in the ongoing construction of East/West dialogue. In relation to the Middle East conflict, too, a distinctive posture was adopted. Thus, through its 1980 Venice Declaration, the Community argued for the creation of a Palestinian state alongside the state of Israel. This first articulation of the now accepted 'two state solution' was initially greeted with outrage by both the US and Israeli governments. The EC/EU has subsequently shown remarkable consistency in its position on the Israeli– Palestinian conflict (Asseburg 2003: 183).

Thus EPC gradually developed into an institutionalized system of foreign policy cooperation that functioned best when dealing with routine matters. At times of crisis, however, there was a tendency to disarray. The end of the Cold War heralded a series of crises that highlighted the shortcomings of EPC. It also initiated a policy environment dramatically different from that in which EPC had operated. Thus, in circumstances where US commitment to the Atlantic Alliance was in question, and amidst fears of political instability in Eastern Europe and the Balkans, expectations were growing that the EC would in future play a central role in maintaining peace and stability in Europe as a whole.[7]

It was in this context that an Intergovernmental Conference (IGC) on Political Union was established, in 1990, charged with transforming EPC into a foreign policy system capable of meeting post-Cold War challenges. Throughout its year-long deliberations the urgency of the IGC's task was constantly demonstrated, whether in the need to forge new relationships with CEE countries, respond to the (August 1990) invasion of Kuwait by Iraq or manage the outbreak of armed conflict in (then) Yugoslavia. These two latter crises, despite rapid and coherent EC responses in their initial stages, very quickly demonstrated the inadequacies of the EPC format – both in terms of Member State unity and access to policy instruments.[8] The conflict in Yugoslavia was of particular importance since there was widespread acceptance that, in this European conflict, the EC should play the role of mediator. However, EC officials proved to be inexperienced mediators, while the usefulness (and safety) of EC unarmed monitors was called into question as the conflict escalated. By early 1992 EC monitors were relieved to be joined by UN peacekeepers.

CFSP: the TEU and its subsequent amendments

The events of 1990–1 fuelled expectations that the IGC's conclusions, enshrined in the TEU (signed in 1991 and in force in 1993) would create the conditions for proactive foreign policy-making – that is, provision of strategic direction, greater overall policy coherence and assured access to policy instruments.

In practice the TEU proved disappointing. While provision was made for two new policy instruments – Joint Actions and Common Positions[9] – in terms of strategic direction the objectives of CFSP were very broadly stated (in TEU Title V):

> to safeguard the common values, fundamental interests, independence and integrity of the Union in conformity with the principles of the United Nations Charter,
>
> to strengthen the security of the Union in all ways,
>
> to preserve peace and strengthen international security …
>
> to promote international cooperation,
>
> to develop and consolidate democracy and the rule of law, and respect for human rights and fundamental freedoms.

These objectives reflect the implicit guiding principles of EPC – a common desire, through sharing of information, to protect the Union from negative external influences, and to develop, where appropriate, a foreign policy posture distinct from that of the USA. They also reflect enduring themes that have contributed to constructions of the Union as a value-based actor – commitment to multilateralism, in particular through the United Nations, and promotion externally of the values purportedly embraced internally.

While these broad objectives fall short of providing strategic direction, there is no doubt that they have been pursued, in a general sense, in the course of the Union's external activities. Thus, for example, all Cooperation and Association Agreements concluded since entry into force of the TEU contain 'political conditionality' clauses, which provide for suspension of all or part of the agreement in the event of non-fulfilment of 'good governance', human rights and other obligations.[10]

Within the framework of the TEU's overarching objectives, the European Council was accorded responsibility for providing the 'general political guidelines' of the Union. The European Council accordingly identified five initial priority areas for CFSP action – relations with CEEC, support for the Middle East peace process, conflict resolution and humanitarian relief efforts in former Yugoslavia, and support for democratic processes in South Africa and Russia.[11] Subsequently the scope of

Joint Actions has expanded considerably, with early additions including arms control, nuclear non-proliferation and response to conflict in the Great Lakes region of Africa.[12] However, the absence of an overarching strategy ensured that, as in the past, CFSP remained largely reactive to external events. Moreover, beyond the understandable prioritization of relations with the Eastern and Southern peripheries, policy choices continued to be influenced by historical ties with former colonies, particularly in Africa.

From the outset it was evident that furtherance of the political aims of CFSP would rely, to a considerable extent, upon economic presence and Community policy instruments. Despite this, the TEU did not address the problem of coherence; indeed it further consolidated the structural division between CFSP and other aspects of external policy. Thus, the Union's 'pillar' structure ensured that only Pillar I (the EC) was subject to the Community method of decision-making. The two new pillars, CFSP (Pillar II) and Justice and Home Affairs (Pillar III) were strictly intergovernmental and subject to unanimity in the Council. Nevertheless, the importance of ensuring effective cross-pillar coordination of external activities was recognized in the TEU, and the Council and Commission were accorded joint responsibility in this respect.[13] While this may appear to provide an enhanced role for the Commission in CFSP, in practice the EPC formula that the Commission is 'fully associated' was maintained. Commission representatives may make policy proposals, although they rarely choose to do so, but have no special right of initiative. In the event, the ability to use economic policy instruments has reflected growing habits of cooperation – *despite* the bifurcated institutional structure created by the TEU.[14]

In relation to policy instruments, the policy environment of the period was reflected in the TEU's only significant innovation, which aimed to provide the Union with access to military capability. While reference to military security in the TEU represented an important departure from the exclusively civilian character of the European Community, and the essentially political nature of EPC, the TEU was silent on the many complex and sensitive issues that needed to be addressed in order to put the proposals into effect. These matters are the subject of Chapter 8.

Making the CFSP work? The Amsterdam and Nice amendments

As was the case with EPC, the CFSP provisions of the TEU have been subject to evolution through practice and subsequent Treaty amendment. After only two years of the CFSP's operation both the Council and the Commission published reports expressing disappointment at the failure to progress towards a more proactive and coherent external policy (Council 1995; Commission 1995b). Clearly CFSP did not represent the major change from EPC anticipated by its proponents.

The Treaty of Amsterdam (signed 1997, in force 1999) introduced important reforms intended to provide political direction and to increase the effectiveness and visibility of CFSP, while the Nice Treaty (signed 2000, in force 2003) codified developments since 1999, primarily in relation to matters of security. The CFSP provisions of both Treaties had the effect of amending the TEU. While these changes reflected experience in operating the CFSP since 1993, and frustration at the inability of the

Union to respond effectively to the 1999 Kosovo crisis, they did not address problems of cross-pillar coherence.

Innovations at Amsterdam

In an attempt to provide political direction at the highest level, the Amsterdam Treaty gave the European Council an explicit strategic role – to 'decide on common strategies to be implemented by the Union in areas where the Member States have important interests in common' (TEU Article 13). Common Strategies are explicitly cross-pillar in orientation. They bring together all the policy instruments available to the Union and (potentially) provide a framework for subsequent action. However, they have been used, primarily, as a means of combining and codifying existing commitments in order to symbolize the importance the Union attaches to relations with key neighbouring countries and regions – Russia, Ukraine, the Mediterranean and the Western Balkans. In short, they have significance as political statements rather than guides to action.

To encourage a more proactive approach to CFSP matters, it was envisaged that measures to implement a unanimously agreed Common Strategy would be subject to qualified majority voting. In practice, however, Member State sensitivities over foreign policy matters have precluded use of QMV.[15] Introduction of a 'constructive abstention' procedure was also intended to remove impediments to proactive policy development, but again this provision has not been used.[16] Clearly Member State commitment, in principle, to enhancing the effectiveness of CFSP decision-making was not translated into practice.

In terms of effectiveness, and visibility, the most important innovation of the Amsterdam Treaty was the creation of a new post – Secretary-General of the Council/ High Representative for the CFSP.[17] The functions of the High Representative were defined in the Treaty in very general terms and much depended upon the ability of the first incumbent to develop this role.[18] Here, the appointment of Javier Solana, who was previously Foreign Minister of Spain and at the time was Secretary-General of NATO,[19] demonstrated increased commitment to strengthen the CFSP. 'The Member States consciously chose a senior politician rather than a senior diplomat for the role of High Representative' (Interview, Council Secretariat, July 2001).

Javier Solana brought to his new role considerable experience, political acumen and (from his incumbency at NATO) excellent connections with key politicians in Member States and the USA. Said to have 'a brain the size of the planet' (Interview, Permanent Representation, October 2002), he also brought a political style based upon ease in building personal relationships, a related preference for informal contacts and impatience with bureaucracy. While these qualities have proved a necessary antidote to the excessive bureaucratization of CFSP processes, he was initially impeded by lack of knowledge of their operation and the reluctance of Member State governments (particularly in the context of the Presidency) to allow their high-profile appointee to act independently. After almost two years in office, when he had begun to achieve diplomatic success in the Balkans, he was likened to 'a dog on the end of a lead, over time the lead has been let out but it is still there and could be pulled up at any time' (Interview, Council Secretariat, July 2001).

The establishment of the post of High Representative was coupled with reform of the Troika arrangements for formal diplomatic representation of the Union (originally involving present, past and future Presidencies). Thus the Amsterdam Treaty provided for a 'Troika' comprising up to four members – the Presidency, the future Presidency, the High Representative and a representative of the Commission.[20]

A further innovation at Amsterdam was the creation of a Policy Planning and Early Warning Unit (PPEWU) within the General Secretariat of the Council. Neither the tasks nor the composition of the unit were made clear, however. After some deliberation it was decided that it would comprise one seconded diplomat from each Member State, four members of the Council Secretariat and a single Commission representative. In terms of the Unit's role, however, there was little guidance from the Member States – 'there was an obsession with whether each Member State would get someone on it rather than what it might do' (Interview, Council Secretariat, July 2001). The result was that the PPEWU became 'Solana's tool' – used by him as an 'extended cabinet' to provide 'day-to-day briefings' rather than fulfil the more strategic policy role that its title would imply (ibid.). In consequence there was said to be 'disappointment and dissatisfaction' among some members of the Unit (Interview, PPEWU, July 2001).

The principal outcomes of the Amsterdam reforms were development of a strong role for the High Representative and an enhanced role for the Council Secretariat – thus ensuring further consolidation of the intergovernmental character of CFSP. No substantive change was made to the role of the Commission and financing for CFSP was the only cross-pillar issue to be addressed by the Amsterdam Treaty (TEU Article 28).[21] The purpose of this provision, however, was to speed disbursement of funds from the Community budget for essentially intergovernmental CFSP operations (excluding those having military implications, as we shall see in Chapter 8). Previously, funding decisions had been made on a case-by-case basis and the resulting delays had proved inconvenient and embarrassing. Thus, for example, Special Representatives appointed by the Council had, on occasion, been obliged personally to bear the cost of travelling to take up their appointments (Interview, Council Secretariat DGE, July 1997).

The Nice Treaty

CFSP matters were not a central concern of the Nice Treaty. Nevertheless the opportunity was taken to codify provisions initially launched at the 1999 Cologne Council. These were primarily in the field of ESDP and will be discussed in Chapter 8. An important innovation that spans CFSP and ESDP matters, however, was the creation of a new intergovernmental structure, the Political and Security Committee (PSC).

The PSC effectively replaced the Political Committee, which had operated since the early days of EPC and comprised national Political Directors meeting monthly. While the PSC meets biannually at Political Director level, its normal operation is at the level of Brussels-based Ambassadors or Political Counsellors.[22] Meetings are chaired by the Presidency representative and occur at least twice-weekly. Their purpose is to monitor the development and implementation of CFSP/ESDP. When necessary, additional meetings can be called at short notice.[23]

CFSP: Operational structures

To give effect to the CFSP, changes were required both in Council structures in Pillar II and in the Community Pillar. Below we provide an overview of the current institutional framework of CFSP and the associated problems of consistency and coherence. Finally, in this section, we consider outstanding problem areas and the potential for further reform.

Pillar II structures and procedures

In creating the Union's Pillar structure the TEU further institutionalized the intergovernmental character of foreign and security policy. This had the effect of entrenching the roles of the Presidency, the Council and related bodies at the apex of the CFSP system.

At the highest level, the Presidency, through its role in preparing the agenda for and chairing the European Council, is central to policy prioritization and initiation. The Presidency also chairs all intergovernmental CFSP/ESDP bodies, with the exception of the Military Committee.[24] Despite the structural advantages of this role, in practice the ability of Presidencies to influence policy varies considerably. This can reflect limited resources and/or foreign policy ambitions in the case of small Member States such as Luxembourg, or the eruption of a major crisis that diverts attention away from the Presidency's agenda during its six month term of office. Nevertheless, in the context of ongoing policy commitments, Presidencies can and do prioritize regions or issues in which they have a particular interest. Thus Southern Member States tend to emphasize the Mediterranean region, Finland has successfully prioritized relations with Russia, and Sweden, equally successfully, prioritized civilian aspects of crisis management.[25] Such prioritization, however, can only be achieved if consensus is reached between the Member States. The ability to gather support for its agenda is central to a successful Presidency.

The European Council, which normally meets twice during each Presidency, is subject to unanimity in exercising its 'guiding role' – thus ensuring that the operation of CFSP/ESDP is restricted to issues and regions where Member State positions are consistent. This is reflected in the current priorities of CFSP. These are, in terms of regions, the Western Balkans, relations with 'Neighbours' and the Middle East Peace Process; and, in terms of issues, conflict prevention, the fight against terrorism, weapons proliferation and human rights issues, in particular support for the International Criminal Court (Council of the EU 2003).

In the context of 'guiding principles' established by the European Council, the General Affairs and External Relations Council (GAERC) constitutes the next, more operational, level of CFSP decision-making. This formation of the Council was adapted (from its single, General Affairs format) in 2002 to accommodate separate External Relations meetings, with the aim of enhancing the efficiency of decision-making and the coherence of policy. Despite the reluctance of Member States to use the title 'Foreign Affairs Council', creation of the GAERC represents a further step in the evolution of EU foreign policy-making. In its External Relations format the Council deals with CFSP, ESDP, external trade and development cooperation, and can involve Member State Foreign Ministers and/or Ministers of Defence, Development or Trade, depending upon the items on the agenda.[26] While GAERC decisions on implementing measures, such as appointment of Special Representatives, may be taken by QMV, Member States prefer to decide all CFSP matters by consensus.

Below the level of the Council, an array of bodies is involved with the CFSP policy process. Foremost among these is the Political and Security Committee, comprising Brussels-based Member State diplomats. The PSC has day-to-day responsibility for monitoring the operation of CFSP/ESDP and has become the 'hub around which CFSP revolves' (Cameron 2003: 3). While the PSC submits reports to the Council, these must formally be transmitted through the Committee of Permanent Representatives (COREPER), comprising Member State Ambassadors to the EU. COREPER itself deals with Pillar I matters, but is responsible for all material discussed by the Council. This can be a source of tension. COREPER Ambassadors are resentful of the growing importance of the PSC, which is 'thought to deal with more interesting issues – *not* anti-dumping' (Interview, UK Permanent Representation, October 2004). Potentially, tensions between the PSC and COREPER can impede effective communication between the PSC and the Council.[27] Nevertheless the PSC brought a new sense of dynamism to the CFSP.

The minutiae of CFSP policy are discussed at the level of Council Working Groups, which report to the PSC. While the numerous Working Groups are staffed by specialist Member State officials based in capitals, the increased frequency of Working Group meetings following the introduction of CFSP obliged participants to spend more time in Brussels (Interview, Permanent Representation, July 2001).[28] In the past, Working Group reports tended to be excessively long and lacking in substance (a practice established in EPC days).[29] However, as it became established, the PSC was able to give firmer guidance to Working Groups, hence encouraging them to produce more focused analysis (ibid.).

All of these intergovernmental bodies, from the Presidency to the Working Groups, are serviced by DGE (Directorate-General External Relations) of the Council General Secretariat. The character of DGE has changed very considerably since the creation of CFSP. In 1994 the existing EPC Secretariat was incorporated into DGE, bringing together CFSP officials (both temporarily seconded Member State representatives and permanent Secretariat staff) with officials responsible for external economic relations.[30] DGE has subsequently been augmented by a third element, the EU Military Staff. The activities of those dealing with CFSP/ESDP are divided between three broad areas – policy, operations and 'other instruments', that is civil aspects of crisis management and economic sanctions. Since the complexities of the organizational structures are apparent only when ESDP is included, these matters are considered more fully in Chapter 8.

The appointment of the Secretary-General/High Representative and creation of the Policy Planning and Early Warning Unit, in 1999, considerably strengthened the policy orientation of the Council Secretariat. However, it also brought new tensions, with DGE staff, the PPU and Solana's cabinet all having overlapping and insufficiently defined responsibilities for furnishing the High Representative with information and advice. Amidst the admiration for Solana expressed by all our interviewees, a single (frequently voiced) criticism concerned his reluctance to address these matters, and hence to realize the potential of Council Secretariat staff. While tensions within the Secretariat have abated over time, a consequence has been that DGE staff tend to focus upon servicing the Council, while the PPU works for Solana. Since Solana's own role is to 'assist the Council' in CFSP matters, this is hardly an efficient way of dividing responsibilities among Secretariat staff.

Even if these 'turf' issues were fully resolved, the resources available within the Council Secretariat, in terms of personnel and information, are meagre when compared with those of the foreign ministries of many Member States. Hence there continues to be reliance upon information provided by national ministries, through seconded diplomats and the Coreu system. The quality of information supplied by Member States is variable, however, and there is a general reluctance to share information considered sensitive. Information is also received from the Commission delegations, but again this is of variable quality. Delegation staff are technical experts rather than diplomats and the political content of their reporting is 'very weak'. The focus is 'first on trade, second on aid and only third on CFSP' (Interview, DG External Relations, July 2001).

Despite the inadequacies of the support available to him, Javier Solana, as we have seen, has been successful in developing his role as High Representative. An important aspect of this role, given the ephemeral nature of the rotating Presidency, is to provide the Union with continuity of representation and sustained diplomacy. In this respect, the High Representative strengthens the ability of the Council Secretariat to provide CFSP with the continuity and institutional memory that were lacking under EPC.

CFSP in the Community Pillar

The creation of CFSP also instigated structural change in the Commission, initially through the creation of a new Directorate-General IA (DGIA), which was given responsibility for CFSP, relations with Eastern Europe and the NIS, and management of the Commission delegations. At this time the Community's external relations effort was fragmented geographically, and policy coherence difficult to achieve (see Table 0.1).

The Prodi Commission (1999–2004) initiated far-reaching reforms, which were retained by its successor. Central to these reforms was the creation of DG External Relations, which was given responsibility both for CFSP and for coordination of relations with third countries. This role is challenged, however, by the continuing importance of DG Trade, which has established country desks to rival those of DG External Relations. Moreover, some geographical fragmentation remains, with DG Development having responsibility for the ACP (but not developing countries in Asia and Latin America) and DG Enlargement having responsibility for candidate countries, which are thus separated from countries covered by the European

Neighbourhood Policy.[31] While the coherence problems caused by these divisions are of great importance to EC policy areas such as development cooperation, they also have significance for CFSP, for example in efforts to 'mainstream' conflict prevention measures across all areas of the Commission's external activity (Interview, Commission, DG External Relations, July 2001). In relation to policy implementation more broadly, whether in the administration of aid or the imposition of economic sanctions, the policy instruments employed in furtherance of CFSP fall within Community competence. Effective implementation requires institutional coherence. However, despite the expectation that coherence would be enhanced by the creation of DG External Relations, it was evident from our interviews that tensions between DGs remain; and that staff morale in externally oriented DGs was not high. While this was primarily a consequence of frequent, poorly managed reorganization, among staff involved with CFSP it was associated also with concerns about the growing marginalization of the Commission as Council structures increased in importance (ibid.).

Issues of consistency and cross-pillar coherence

Due to the sensitive nature of CFSP, problems of consistency and coherence are particularly acute. Most Member State governments are determined to retain their independence in matters of foreign and security policy, and to ensure that the more supranational Community institutions, in particular the Commission, are distanced from CFSP processes.

Consistency

The intergovernmental nature of CFSP, and the failure of Member States to utilize the provisions for QMV or constructive abstention, ensures that consistency is a key issue. While many differences of emphasis can be observed,[32] of greatest importance are long established divisions between Atlanticist Member States such as the UK, the Netherlands and Portugal and those, led by France, which advocate an independent EU posture. Important, too, are divisions about the relative importance of civilian and military instruments of policy, with the neutral Member States determined that the former shall not be neglected in favour of the latter.

A further source of tension concerns the relative influence of large and small Member States. The practice has grown for groupings of large member states to meet outside the formal CFSP procedures (and also in the context of Pillar III matters) to discuss and on occasion to implement policy initiatives. The groupings vary, but typically comprise 'the G3' (France, Germany and the UK), 'G4', with Italy in addition, and 'G5' including Spain. Such groupings comprised exclusively of EU Member States are more or less tolerated by those excluded.[33] Meetings including non-members have been looked upon less favourably, however. In particular the operation of an informal *directoire*, known as 'the Quint', comprising the four largest Member States and the USA, was greatly resented by smaller Member States. The Quint developed from the establishment, in 1994, of the Contact Group for former Yugoslavia (comprising the USA, Russia, France, Germany, Italy and the UK) and continued, with the exclusion of Russia, to discuss CFSP matters informally outside the EU framework (Gegout 2002). While it may be inevitable that larger Member States will play important roles in CFSP and ESDP matters, it is noteworthy that the group formed in 2000 in relation to the Middle East Peace Process (known as the Quartet) comprises Russia, the USA, the UN and the EU. In contrast with the Contact Group arrangements, this marks an important external acknowledgement of the role of the Union in international affairs.

Since, in principle, unanimity is more difficult to achieve as the number and diversity of participants expands, it is possible that the 2004 enlargement will increase the consistency problems already evident in relation to CFSP. It should be noted, however, that during the pre-accession period candidates were invited to align themselves with CFSP decisions and actions, and did so progressively from 1994. Thus habits of cooperation were established prior to accession (Regelsberger 2003).

It is evident, nevertheless, that CEEC Member States bring to CFSP concerns that could impact, in particular, upon relations with neighbours – notably scepticism of the Union's attempt to build a 'strategic partnership' with Russia, support for enhanced relations with Ukraine and a strong preference for prioritizing Eastern over Southern neighbours. However, the first priority of CFSP – stabilization of the Western Balkans – is strongly supported by CEEC governments, with Slovenia said to be making a 'very positive contribution … they have good intelligence and are sharing it' (Interview, Council Secretariat, September 2004). CEEC governments, on balance, also bring a preference for intergovernmentalism and close relations with the USA. However, this latter is not fully shared by CEEC publics (Commission 2003a) and may be tempered, over time, by the socialization effects of CFSP participation.

Cyprus and Malta also have a distinctive stance on some issues. Thus, as members of the Non-Aligned Movement, they have a commitment to development cooperation and strongly support decolonization and self-determination of peoples. On security issues they are likely to adopt a posture similar to that of the neutral Member States (Johansson-Nogués 2004). In addition, accession of (Greek) Cyprus while the island remains divided is a source of problems in specific areas, such as relations with Turkey and with Northern Cyprus.[34]

Coherence

In the context of CFSP, coherence problems are greatly exacerbated by the need for cross-pillar coordination – which is essential if the Community's policy instruments, and Community funding, are to be used to further the political aims of CFSP.

The formula that the Commission is 'fully associated' with CFSP ensures that it is represented at meetings of CFSP institutions at all levels, from the European Council to the Working Groups. Thus the Commission President attends the European Council and the Commissioner for External Relations attends the GAERC. Commission attendance (by the Director of the CFSP Unit in DG External Relations) at the twice-weekly meetings of the PSC is said to facilitate coordination between CFSP initiatives and matters falling within Community competence, such as delivery of humanitarian assistance and support for the development of civil society. It is also considered helpful to have 'at the table' representatives of the Community, as the principal source of funding (Interview, Commission, DG External Relations, July 2001). Nevertheless, the Commission had amassed more than thirty years' experience of conducting external economic relations prior to the inauguration of CFSP, and lingering jealousy of its prerogatives in this field is understandable.

In CFSP matters the Commission does not enjoy the exclusive right of initiative that pertains in Pillar I, although it has the right, alongside the Member States, to put forward policy initiatives. In practice, despite the importance of the policy instruments it controls, the Commission has chosen, 'to the regret of many', not to use this right (Cameron 2003: 3).[35] The Commission's reticence in this respect reflects both awareness of Member State sensitivities and resentment at its relative marginalization in the context of CFSP.

A further area of potential cross-pillar tension involves the role of High Representative for the CFSP, which appears to overlap with that of the new Commissioner for External Relations. In practice, however, the first incumbents (Javier Solana and Chris Patten) established a good working relationship, based on a mutual desire to 'get things to work' (Interview, Council Secretariat DGE, July 2001). The practices that have evolved since 2000 are considered likely to continue now that Chris Patten has been succeeded as Commissioner by Benita Ferrero-Waldner (Interview, Council Secretariat, March 2005). Cooperation between Solana and Patten undoubtedly assisted CFSP implementation, for example in the Macedonian crisis in 2001, where Solana's diplomatic efforts were closely supported by Chris Patten and financial assistance was made available through the Community's Rapid Reaction Mechanism (RRM) adopted early in 2001.[36]

While high-level cooperation is inadequate to ensure fully effective policy implementation, it was evident from our interviews that habits of cross-pillar cooperation have developed between officials at all levels, frequently based on networks of informal contacts. This is indicative of cultural and generational change, as practices evolve and shared understandings are constructed. Not only are these understandings evident from everyday practice, they are also reflected in legal provisions dealing with cross-pillar issues such as economic sanctions and the sale of dual-use goods (Koutrakos 2001).

In new areas of policy, where practices and understandings have yet to be constructed, cross-pillar tensions continue to arise. A problem area has been the Union's response to civil emergencies, where the Commission has long established responsibilities. The European Neighbourhood Policy provides a further example of cross-pillar tensions in a new policy area. While formal responsibility for the ENP lies with the Commission, it links economic development with security concerns, cross-border crime, democratization and human rights. In March 2005 the appointment of a CFSP Special Representative to Moldova, primarily in the context of conflict over the disputed region of Transdniester, was met with Commission insistence that the person appointed should not be involved in implementation of Moldova's recently agreed ENP Action Plan. The issue was resolved through negotiation of a compromise mandate, which states that the Special

Representative will deal only with 'relevant aspects' of the ENP (*European Voice*, 10–16 March 2005).

It is evident that, despite insitutionalization of cross-pillar cooperation in some areas, the aims of CFSP cannot be realized in the absence of assured, well functioning links between the making of policy and its implementation. If the CFSP is to provide more effective political direction, there is a need for further reform.

Future reform?

As we have seen, the Union's capacity for foreign policy-making has evolved and strengthened over time. Nevertheless, a number of problems remain. Principal among these are impediments to policy coherence (in particular cross-pillar coordination) and insufficient continuity, in terms of strategic direction, as a consequence, *inter alia*, of the six-monthly rotating Presidency. These matters were among those addressed by the Convention on the future of Europe, and the provisions contained in the draft Constitutional Treaty, which was approved by the Member State governments in June 2004, provide a starting point for debate about future reform.

To enhance continuity, the Constitution provided for an elected President of the European Council (Article I-22).[37] Two provisions of the Treaty would (partially) address problems of policy coherence. First, removal of the pillar structure, with a single Title covering most aspects of the Union's 'External Action' – that is CFSP, ESDP, international trade, development cooperation, and other forms of economic and humanitarian assistance (Title V).[38] It should be noted, however, that voting procedures in the Council would, as at present, vary by policy area, with unanimity still required for CFSP/ESDP matters. Second, the post of CFSP High Representative is replaced by that of Union Minister for Foreign Affairs. The incumbent would also be a Vice-President of the Commission, and would be responsible for ensuring the consistency and coherence of the Union's external action (Article I.40–1).[39] A European External Action Service (effectively a foreign ministry), comprising officials from the Council Secretariat and the Commission, together with seconded staff from Member State diplomatic services, would support the Foreign Minister. The external delegations, which are currently an exclusive responsibility of the Commission, were also to become part of the External Action Service.

As with previous treaties, the Constitutional Treaty provides little detail concerning the practical operation of the proposed arrangements for CFSP. Experience suggests, however, that changes of the magnitude proposed would be likely, initially, to exacerbate existing inter-institutional tensions. Anxiety among Commission and Council Secretariat staff was evident from our interviews, particularly in relation to the composition and location of the External Action Service.[40] The dual role of the Foreign Minister/Commission Vice-President was also a matter of concern – 'He will be double-hatted, how will he tilt?'. Commission officials fear that his approach will be 'foreign policy led' – that he will 'represent the Council and ensure that Commission resources are available' (Interview, Council Secretariat DGE, October 2004).[41] Javier Solana himself was originally opposed to the idea of a dual role but was subsequently said to be enthusiastic about the opportunities provided (Interview, Council Secretariat, September 2004).

A further area of potential tension concerns the relative functions of the President and the Foreign Minister, where again the Treaty gives little guidance. As previously, much would depend upon the commitment, good will and personal qualities of the incumbents and, more broadly, those responsible for the operation of the new institutions and procedures.

The reforms proposed in the draft Constitutional Treaty are the subject of continuing debate. Ultimately, further strengthening of the CFSP is contingent upon the commitment of Member State governments, not only to amending the treaties but also to fully utilizing the procedures and institutions thus provided.

CFSP: policy instruments

The singular character of the CFSP is reflected in the elaboration of treaty-based policy instruments that are intended to provide a framework for coordination of Member States' foreign policies. The TEU (Articles 13–15) provides for:

> Common Strategies, determined by the European Council and intended to provide an overall, cross-pillar approach towards a country or region.

> Joint Actions, used to 'address specific situations where operational action by the Union is deemed to be required', such as imposition of economic sanctions or appointment of a Special Representative.

> Common Positions, intended to 'define the approach of the Union to a particular matter of a geographical or thematic nature' and used to promote consistency between Member State policies.[42]

Within the framework provided by these (sometimes indistinct and overlapping) legal instruments, the Union employs the traditional tools of foreign policy – that is, diplomacy, economic measures (incentives or sanctions) and use of military means. Since Chapter 8 deals specifically with military and policing matters, we discuss here only diplomatic and economic instruments of policy.

Diplomacy

Diplomatic instruments employed by the Union include Declarations welcoming or deploring developments in international affairs, which are produced almost daily,[43] formal démarches by Troika representatives, conduct of political dialogue and appointment of Special Representatives and election monitors.

In 2002 numerous démarches (489) were undertaken, of which almost half concerned human rights issues, in particular to protest at uses of the death penalty and to encourage support for the International Criminal Court (Council of the EU 2003).[44] EU démarches were used to good effect following the terrorist attacks of 9/11 when, in October 2001, visits were made to Washington, Moscow, Iran, Saudi Arabia, Egypt and Syria to coordinate support for measures to combat terrorism.

While it is difficult to assess the impact of this considerable activity, Javier Solana is said to find the formal, and formulaic, activities of the Troika frustrating. 'He genuinely believes that the product of formal visits is less than he can achieve informally on his own' (Interview, Council Secretariat, July 2001). Certainly Solana's involvement has been decisive on several occasions in the Balkans, most notably in negotiating the 2001 Ohrid Framework Agreement that ended armed conflict in Macedonia, and the 2002 Belgrade Agreement that provided for new constitutional arrangements between Serbia and Montenegro. Subsequently, in Ukraine, Solana played an important role in defusing the crisis that followed flawed Presidential elections in late 2004.

'Political dialogue' is a further aspect of EU diplomacy that can be somewhat formulaic. The insertion of provisions for political dialogue in the Union's association or partnership agreements with third countries (see Chapters 5 and 6) enables issues prioritized by CFSP, from human rights to weapons proliferation, to be discussed at regular meetings, at levels ranging from head of state/government to technical expert. Political dialogue is also conducted with non-associated countries and regions where the Union has established special relations – including, amongst others, the USA, Canada, Japan, China, Australia, Iran, ASEM, the Andean Community and the Gulf Cooperation Council. The frequency and intensity of political dialogue varies considerably.[45] According to one participant who has experienced the confusion sometimes caused by the Union's four-member 'Troika', there can be 'more negotiation with the host country over seats for the EU delegation than over the substance of the agenda' (Cameron 2002: 7).

In order to facilitate policy implementation on the ground, the practice has become established of deploying EU Special Representatives (EUSR) to areas of concern to the EU. The EUSR's presence symbolizes the Union's commitment, while facilitating sustained diplomacy in support of conflict resolution and transmission of locally gained information to policy planners in Brussels.[46] The responsibilities of EUSRs are set out by the GAERC in Joint Actions, which take the form of a mandate. Inevitably, the effectiveness of Special Representatives has varied according to the difficulty of the tasks assigned, the willingness of local elites to engage with the EUSR and the skills of the appointee. Moreover, the operation of EUSRs has, on occasion, been impeded by cross-pillar disputes over provision of funding and other resources.[47] In 2003 revised procedures were introduced for their appointment and financing. While these established that EUSRs would be funded from the Community budget, shortfalls and delays in provision of funding have persisted. In 2005 Special Representatives were operating in relation to the Middle East Peace Process, the Stability Pact for the Western Balkans, the South Caucasus, the Great Lakes region of Africa, Afghanistan, Bosnia-Herzegovina,[48] Macedonia and Moldova.

A further, well-established policy practice has been deployment of missions to assist with the organization and monitoring of elections. These may be deployed either by the Commission, in the context of cooperation or association agreements,[49] or under CFSP provisions. Thus, in 2004, CFSP electoral missions operated in Sri Lanka and Indonesia, while Community monitors were deployed in Mozambique, Malawi, Ukraine and the West Bank and Gaza. This last involved some 170 monitors (forty of them deployed for more than a month) to supervise the presidential elections that followed the death of Yasser Arafat.[50] While cross-pillar tensions can arise in relation to CFSP electoral missions, in Community operations these problems do not arise.

Economic instruments

The economic instruments of policy remain, as we have seen, located within the Community. Measures employed to further CFSP priorities can be positive, in terms of financial assistance or trade concessions, or negative, involving economic sanctions or other restrictive measures.

The Commission has traditionally shown a preference for positive engagement and use of incentives in its relations with third countries. Foreign policy aims in the broadest sense have undoubtedly been served by extension of candidate status to neighbouring countries, and the subsequent imposition of numerous pre-accession conditions and strategies. It remains to be seen whether the 'everything but institutions' formula of the European Neighbourhood Policy will be similarly effective.

In more specific terms, in furtherance of the Union's political aims in relation to third countries, a dedicated funding instrument, the European Initiative for Democracy and Human Rights (EIDHR), was established in 1994. This is used to promote four priority areas in recipient countries[51] – promotion of democracy and the rule of law; abolition of the death penalty; prevention of torture; and support for minority rights (Commission 2001e). While external consultants have reported positively upon the impact of EIDHR funding (Smith 2003: 113–14), it is relatively modest when compared with the development assistance provided from the Community budget and the EDF.

In relation to Community assistance programmes, the Union's political objectives are reflected in the numerous conditionalities routinely inserted into agreements with third countries. These include provisions on human rights, democracy and 'good governance' and, more recently, on proliferation of WMD and measures to combat terrorism. As we saw in Chapter 6, there has been reluctance to invoke these conditionalities in the context of the Union's difficult relations with Mediterranean countries. Nevertheless Karen Smith (2003) lists 32 instances, between 1988 and 2002, where assistance has been reduced or interrupted consequent upon failure to meet EU provisions on human rights and democracy. Of these, 21 relate to ACP countries. Interruption of assistance to these impoverished countries is inevitably controversial, and the 2003 EU–ACP Cotonou Agreement introduced special provisions for consultation with the ACP Group, including recourse to arbitration, in the event of proposals to suspend any part of the Agreement. Suspension of assistance has also been used in relation to Myanmar (on a long-term basis) and China, Russia and Pakistan (amongst others) for short periods.

Decisions concerning imposition of sanctions or restrictive measures are taken in the context of CFSP, usually through a Common Position adopted by the GAERC. Restrictive measures are not confined to economic sanctions (such as trade embargoes or freezing of financial assets), they also include diplomatic sanctions, such as severance of diplomatic relations and suspension of official visits, and the imposition of admission restrictions. In practice, imposition of wide-ranging trade sanctions is avoided in favour of measures designed to target specified individuals or groups. Thus, in the context of the Western Balkans for example, financial sanctions and admission restrictions have been imposed in relation to named individuals wanted for questioning by the International Criminal Court for Yugoslavia. Similar restrictions are in force in relation to individuals considered to be supporters of Al Quaeda or the Taliban.[52] Frequent use is also made of embargoes on arms exports and export of equipment that can be used for internal repression. Such measures were imposed upon eleven countries in 2004. Responsibility for implementation of these measures is shared between the Commission and the Member States, although the Commission is charged with ensuring overall consistency and with tasks such as publication of lists of targeted persons and groups.

A final economic instrument that falls within Commission competence is the Rapid Reaction Mechanism. This was adopted in 2001 and authorized the Commission to make rapid disbursements of funds from a dedicated budget line. The RRM is intended to support conflict prevention measures or assist in maintaining or re-establishing civic structures. Following its first use in Macedonia in 2001, it has been used in Bolivia, Nepal, Georgia, Iraq and Lebanon.

While assessment of the effectiveness of the Union's policy instruments is difficult, recent years have undoubtedly seen a very considerable increase in CFSP activity. There has also been increased external recognition of the Union as a political actor. This is reflected in the broad participation in the EU-led Stability Pact for the Western Balkans (which includes Canada, Japan, Russia and the USA amongst others) and the Union's role in the Middle East Quartet. Further afield, it is instructive to note the assessment of the Chinese government – 'the European Union is a major force in the world' (PRC 2003: 1). As the Union has become more active, and its role is increasingly accorded recognition, provision of overall strategic direction for the Union's external activities is imperative. The European Security Strategy is intended to fulfil that function.

The European Security Strategy: a framework for the future?

Through its analysis of the external context of EU action, in terms both of challenges and opportunities, the Security Strategy seeks to promote a shared vision of the Union's role in the world. This is intended to provide a framework for future action, and for use of the Union's policy instruments.

With the broad aim of procuring 'A Secure Europe in a Better World', the Security Strategy commits the Union to three 'strategic objectives' – addressing 'key threats', building a secure neighbourhood and promoting an 'international order based on effective multilateralism' (European Council 2003). By examining the extent to which the Union's recent activities accord with these objectives, we attempt to assess the potential for the Security Strategy to provide an overarching framework for EU external policy.

Addressing 'threats'

In the post-9/11 environment, the 'key threats' identified by the Security Strategy are unremarkable – terrorism, proliferation of WMD, regional conflicts, state failure and organized crime. While this approach to threat assessment echoes US thinking on these matters, the EU strategy for addressing threats differs considerably from the US preference for (potentially pre-emptive) military action. It reflects the dual 'hard' and 'soft' approach that is implicit in the repetition of references to 'security' in CFSP and ESDP. Thus the Security Strategy emphasizes the importance of long-term, essentially civilian measures to address the root causes of external threat (by, for example, linking security and development), as well as shorter-term responses, including those that utilize ESDP instruments.

Since the third source of threat identified by the Security Strategy – regional conflict, state failure and organized crime – overlaps considerably with neighbourhood issues, and is also dealt with in Chapter 8, we deal in this section only with measures to combat terrorism and the spread of WMD.

Measures to combat terrorism

In the aftermath of the terrorist attacks of 9/11 the EU acted rapidly. Its initial response included an extensive series of ministerial and Troika visits during October 2001 which led to the intensification of political dialogue and economic and financial cooperation with Pakistan, Iran, India, the Central Asian countries and the Gulf Cooperation States.[53] Subsequently, following the overthrow of the Taliban regime in Afghanistan, the Union developed a comprehensive approach to post-conflict reconstruction based on Community funding instruments, despatch of a CFSP Special Representative and promotion of cooperation with neighbouring countries.[54] This initial response to the events of 9/11 thus represented an attempt self-consciously to consider the underlying sources of support for terrorism.

This holistic approach was supplemented, from July 2002, by measures to ensure that 'the fight against terrorism' is incorporated in all aspects of external policy. From this time the Union's approach has been overtly security driven. Thus, in order to guide future EU policy 'threat analyses were developed on a large number of countries and regions' (Council of the EU 2003: 43). On the basis of these analyses, counter-terrorism elements have been included in contractual relations with third countries, and technical assistance has been provided.[55] Counter-terrorism has also become a priority of the Union's political dialogue with third countries (ibid.).

Anti-terrorism initiatives in the context of Justice and Home Affairs and Pillar III (police and judicial cooperation in criminal matters) have been both security-driven and exclusionary in effect. Thus, in relation to JHA matters (immigration and asylum), the Common Position on combating terrorism adopted in December 2001 emphasized the need for strengthening of border controls and increased surveillance, introducing a discourse of exclusion that prioritized security over respect for human rights (Den Boer and Monar 2002: 27). In Pillar III, initiatives included production of a common definition of terrorism, compilation of a list of 'terrorist' organizations (for the purpose of freezing assets and imposing entry restrictions), introduction of the European Arrest Warrant and greatly accelerated procedures for extradition of suspects. While progress in (strictly intergovernmental) Pillar III matters declined somewhat after the early period of activity,[56] the Madrid terrorist attacks of 2004 brought fresh impetus, resulting, *inter alia*, in the appointment of an EU anti-terrorism coordinator.

Measures to prevent proliferation of WMD

The EU has long supported multilateral approaches to arms control and non-proliferation. In addition to coordinating Member State positions, and those of associated countries, in international forums, the Union has actively promoted universal adherence to the various international conventions pertaining to these matters. Of particular significance in this respect was the leadership role played by the Union in relation to the International Code of Conduct on ballistic missile proliferation. Following 125 Troika démarches on this topic in 2002, the Code was launched in November that year with 94 states initially subscribing (Council of the EU 2003: 41).

The Union's active role in multilateral diplomacy has been complemented by bilateral initiatives. Somewhat controversially, new conditionalities on WMD have been inserted into cooperation and partnership agreements with third parties, including the ACP countries, thus prompting accusations that security concerns are being prioritized over development and, in particular, the eradication of poverty. More specifically, the Union provides funding and technical support to assist countries with the disposal of chemical weapons. Russia has been the principal beneficiary of this funding.

Of great importance has been the Union's approach to concerns about potential development of a nuclear weapons programme in Iran. In sharp contrast with the belligerent stance adopted by the US government, the EU (represented in high-level diplomatic initiatives by the G3, France, Germany and the UK) embarked upon a process of 'conditional engagement' with Iran. Thus, the Union has made negotiation of an EU–Iran trade and cooperation agreement, and EU support for Iran's member-ship of the World Trade Organization, conditional upon suspension by Iran of its weapons programme – this to be verified by the International Atomic Energy Authority. Adoption of this distinctive approach to an undeniably 'high politics' issue inevitably provides 'a test case for EU foreign policy' (Everts and Keohane 2003: 179).

Building a secure neighbourhood

Promotion of regional security has been the first priority of CFSP since its inception, and the Security Strategy continues to emphasize the importance of 'a ring of well governed countries' to the East and South (European Council 2003: 8).

As we saw in Chapter 6, considerable effort has been expended in this respect – most particularly in the Western Balkans where the EU manages the broadly-based, multilateral Stability Pact, operates bilateral Stabilization and Association Processes and has in post three Special Representatives. Proactive diplomacy on the part of the CFSP High Representative has also contributed to conflict resolution in the region. Here, too, the Union has deployed its ESDP instruments both in Macedonia and in Bosnia-Herzegovina. It is thus in the Western Balkans that the Union has made most progress in pursuing strategic objectives and in utilizing all available instruments of policy. In this region, the Union is now the principal external actor and its success, as the Security Strategy admits, is crucial to the 'credibility of our foreign policy' (European Council 2003: 8).

In the context of the 2004 enlargement attention has also turned to 'new' Eastern neighbours, including Ukraine, Moldova and the troubled South Caucasus region. Here the European Neighbourhood Policy (launched in 2003) aims to promote stability within and improved relations between these countries through a range of (primarily economic) incentives, accompanied by a range of conditions that must be met by the 'Neighbours'. The ENP is complemented by diplomatic initiatives, including interventions by the High Representative in Ukraine and Moldova,[57] and the appointment of Special Representatives to Moldova and the South Caucasus. In this region, however, the Union's success in building a 'strategic partnership' with Russia remains the key to policy success; and here Russian sensitivities impede use of ESDP instruments.

The Union's long and problematic relations with Mediterranean neighbours are also discussed in Chapter 6. Of particular significance in the CFSP context is the multi-faceted Euro–Med Partnership (EMP). Launched in 1995 and involving the Maghreb and Mashreq countries, together with Israel and the Palestinian Authority, this ambitious project aims not only to strengthen bilateral relations between the EU and participating countries but also to create a multilateral forum for political dialogue between them. As a consequence of worsening relations between Israel and the Palestinian Authority, particularly following the outbreak of the second Intifada in 2000, the EMP has faltered. In 2003, in an attempt to reinvigorate the process, the Mediterranean countries were included in the European Neighbourhood Policy. Ultimately, however, the Union's ability to influence its Southern neighbours depends upon progress in the Middle East Peace Process.

The Union has been concerned with the Middle East conflict from the inception of EPC and has, since 1980, consistently argued for a settlement based on Israel's right to peaceful existence and the right of the Palestinian people to achieve statehood. Until relatively recently, however, the Union has not been actively involved in high level conflict resolution efforts, which have been dominated by the USA. Nor has it realized the potential of its economic presence in the region. Neither in relation to the beneficial trade arrangements enjoyed by Israel, nor the very considerable financial assistance provided to the Palestinian Authority,[58] has there been Member State consensus on the introduction of restrictive measures in response to human rights abuses or use of violence by either party to the conflict. The chief political contribution of the Union was thus the attempt, through the efforts of its Special Representative (appointed in 1996) and dialogue promoted within the multilateral EMP process, to create an environment conducive to the success of peace negotiations conducted by others.

The failure of the EMP to prosper after 2000 prompted the Union to seek more direct involvement in the peace process. A number of localized mediation efforts were undertaken by the Special Representative and Javier Solana, including an intervention that ended a siege by the Israeli military of the Church of the Nativity in

Bethlehem.[59] Inclusion of the Union (with Russia, the UN and the USA) in the Quartet formed in 2002 to coordinate policies towards the region, denotes recognition of the Union's more proactive political role. In the past the attitude of the US government had been 'you may take your bag of gold and leave it on the doorstep' (Interview, External Mission, January 2003). Within the Quartet the Union has played a proactive role, particularly in drafting the 'road map for peace' adopted by the Quartet in 2002 and subsequently published, following EU pressure in the face of US reluctance, in 2003. Despite the subsequent lack of progress in implementing the 'road map', its publication as a basis for working towards a settlement of the conflict represents 'an important success for European diplomacy' (Asseburg 2003: 185). However, despite the enhanced role played by the Union since 2000, the US remains the dominant actor in the region. But if the peace process were to succeed, the Union's aim of becoming 'a deciding factor' in the post-conflict environment might, perhaps, be achieved (European Council 2000: 1).

Promoting effective multilateralism

Commitment to multilateralism is at the core of EU external activities. A reflection of its own character, it expresses both the Union's preferred approach to international affairs and a desire to emphasize its distinctiveness from the unilateralism of the USA. The extent of the Union's commitment is evident from references, throughout this book, to the Union's role in promoting multilateral dialogue (whether in relation to the ACP, Euro-Med, Mercosur or ASEM), and to its proactive participation in multilateral processes and organizations.

In previous chapters we have considered, for example, the Union's role in relation to the World Trade Organization. Here, the EU is not only a major player, it actively promotes the extension of WTO membership to problematic applicants such as Russia and Iran – provided that such countries comply with conditions imposed. The Union also played a key role in promoting the Kyoto Protocol to the Climate Change Convention, including use of its economic power to procure ratification by Russia, thus ensuring entry into force of the Protocol in early 2005. In the present chapter reference has been made to the significant diplomatic effort expended by the EU – particularly to ensure establishment of the International Criminal Court, but also in relation to the International Code of Conduct on proliferation of ballistic missiles.

With the exception of areas, such as trade policy, that fall within exclusive Community competence, the ability of the EU actively to promote its policies in international forums depends upon the unanimous support of the Member States. Consistency is thus vital, not least since the EU itself is a member of few international organizations.[60] In the context of the United Nations, for example, the Union's effectiveness depends upon the ability to coordinate Member State positions, and the willingness of Member State governments to permit the Presidency to speak on their behalf.

Since the inception of EPC the Member States have attempted to coordinate their positions in the UN General Assembly and related UN bodies, with considerable success in recent years (Dedring 2004). Since the EU can muster 25 votes from Member

States (and considerably more when candidates and associates are persuaded to vote with the EU) it is not surprising that the Union is 'recognised among the UN membership as a formidable force' without whose support 'nothing gets accomplished' (Laatikainen 2004: 5). It is in the UN Security Council (UNSC), however, that decisions are taken on key issues pertaining to international security. Here the superior status accorded to France and the UK, due to their permanent UNSC membership, is inevitably a divisive factor. Since introduction of CFSP in 1993, however, the practice has developed of presenting written and verbal statements on behalf of the EU, with both the Presidency and Javier Solana regularly addressing the Security Council (Laatikainen 2004: 6).[61] While these coordination efforts are successful when relatively mundane issues are at stake, the divisions between Member States over the 2003 invasion of Iraq remind us that consistency problems continue to impede EU actorness.

The Security Strategy, in its reference to '*effective*' multilateralism, seeks to promote both Member State consistency and a more robust approach to ensuring that international norms are adhered to. The two are intimately linked, in that the Union's preference for using incentives rather than restrictive measures reflects, in part, the greater difficulty in achieving consensus to employ the latter. Only in relation to Myanmar has the Union imposed a comprehensive set of restrictive measures. While 'conditional engagement' is likely to remain the preferred policy option, those who are unwilling to engage, the Security Strategy warns, 'should understand that there is a price to be paid, including in their relationship with the European Union' (European Council 2003: 10). The extent to which Member States can reach consensus on the application of negative measures remains to be seen.

Conclusion

The aim of this chapter was to assess the potential for CFSP to provide an overarching political framework for the Union's external activities. To achieve this aim we first outlined the evolution of a foreign policy system for the EC/EU since 1970.

In the face of significant divisions between Member States concerning the desirability of common policy in this area, the EPC system was a compromise that facilitated routine consultation and cooperation, but precluded proactive policy formulation. However, from the late 1980s the successful deepening of policy integration internally, combined with the dramatically changed external policy environment of the immediate post-Cold War period, appeared to provide the conditions for significant progress towards a common foreign policy. In the event the CFSP provisions of the TEU, while strengthening the policy-making machinery, proved a disappointment. CFSP remained an intergovernmental process, subject to unanimous voting procedures. Indeed the TEU, in creating the pillar structure of the Union, consolidated the separation between external economic relations and foreign policy.

CFSP nevertheless marked an important stage in the evolution of foreign policy, heralding a perceptible shift towards the basing of decision-making procedures in Brussels rather than in communication between officials in national capitals. The implementation of subsequent Treaty amendments further strengthened the CFSP, notably through the appointment of Javier Solana as its first High Representative. Solana proved an able appointee, who has contributed significantly to the effectiveness and visibility of CFSP. A further important innovation was the establishment of the Political and Security Committee, with its twice-weekly meetings of Brussels-based national diplomats, which has become the hub of the foreign policy-making process.

These positive developments have been reflected in increased CFSP activity. The Union is now undoubtedly an important regional actor, particularly in relation to Eastern neighbours. But political activity has also ranged widely, in terms of content and scope, from proactive support for the International Criminal Court to development of a distinctive, multi-faceted approach to combating terrorism and to relations with Iran. This has been associated with greater recognition by third parties of the Union as a political actor; and a discourse that constructs the EU as a serious protagonist, providing an alternative to US unilateralism and even a potential counter to US hegemony (Keohane 2002; Kupchan 2002; Morascvik 2003).

A number of problems persist, nevertheless. The most significant of these is lack of consensus among Member States concerning the content and direction of policy. This is reflected in the willingness of Member States to agree institutional reforms, or to insert provision for QMV in the Treaties, and their subsequent reluctance to use them effectively, or indeed at all. Coherence, in particular cross-pillar coordination, has also remained an impediment to implementation of CFSP decisions. While the marginalization of the Commission from CFSP processes has been offset by habits of cooperation, through frequent utilization of Community policy instruments by the CFSP, in new policy areas cross-pillar tensions and jealousies continue to arise.

An attempt to address outstanding problem areas, and a further phase in the evolution of the CFSP, was marked by the agreement of Member State governments, in 2004, to the provisions of the Constitutional Treaty. The decision to create the posts of President and Foreign Minister, in particular, indicates growing awareness, even in large Member States, that it is both desirable and necessary to construct a foreign policy actor capable of connecting the economic power of the EC to some form of collective political purpose. Debates about the future development of CFSP/ESDP will undoubtedly be framed by the provisions of the failed Constitutional Treaty.

The external policy environment has also provided impetus to the process of constructing the CFSP, in particular new understandings about the nature of foreign and security policy in the post-Cold War, post-9/11 world. In the context of high profile, damaging divisions between Member States over the 2003 invasion of Iraq, the need to provide strategic direction for EU external action was perceived to be urgent. Production of the European Security Strategy reflects that perception.

The Security Strategy provides a framework that links long-term priorities of the EU – promotion of regional stability and strengthening of multilateral processes and organizations – with renewed (essentially post-9/11) commitment to combat terrorism and prevent the proliferation of WMD. While these new threats have become the first priority of the Union, the Security Strategy, in its introductory section, envisages a comprehensive approach to security. It refers to the challenges associated with poverty and disease in 'much of the developing world' (European Council 2003: 2). It concludes, nevertheless, that 'security is a condition of development' (ibid.). In consequence, while use of development assistance for purposes of security is proposed, poverty eradication, despite its status as an aim of the EU, is not included among the Union's 'strategic objectives'. This omission is a matter of concern to proponents of a comprehensive approach to human security, among them several Member State governments.

To the extent that perceptions of external threat remain a central preoccupation of the Union and the Member States, a security focus to external policy may provide an effective strategy for re-framing CFSP priorities. However, a new security discourse that incorporates, or subordinates, EU development and humanitarian policies is inconsistent with the dominant, value-based identity constructed for the Union. If the European Security Strategy is to provide a framework for uniting Member States in common action, this dissonance must be resolved through development of shared understandings about the meaning of security, and about the appropriate use of the Union's security instruments. We turn to these matters in Chapter 8.

8   The EU as a security community and military actor

> The European Union is a global actor, ready to share responsibility for global security.
>
> (Council of the EU 2004a: 1)

> The EU is in itself a peace project and a supremely successful one ... Through the process of enlargement, through the Common Foreign and Security Policy, through its development co-operation and its external assistance programmes the EU now seeks to project stability also beyond its own borders.
>
> (Commission 2001c: 5)

The evolution of the EU places it at the heart of major contemporary debates, not only about the meanings of security in a post-modern world, but also the time-honoured and defining relationship between sovereignty and the means of violence.[1] The acquisition of military capability by the Union must raise the question as to whether its civilian identity is now fundamentally challenged. In attempting to provide an answer, we consider, in this chapter, the rapid development of ESDP and the alternative constructions of the security identity of the EU which it has stimulated.

In many ways the EU, from its original conception in the form of the European Coal and Steel Community, was always in the business of providing security. This role derived from its presence. However, significant developments from the late 1990s through to the first deployment of forces under the European Security and Defence Policy (ESDP) in 2003 can be regarded as a transformation in which the Union acquired not only an unprecedented military capability but a security strategy to inform its use. A substantial part of this chapter will thus be devoted to examining the expectations and opportunities that led to the formation of military actor capability and the associated decision-making procedures and instruments.

Although, subsequent to the collapse of the European Defence Community (EDC) project in 1954, the European Community was explicitly un-involved in defence matters, this did not prevent expectations and discussions of a potential military role. In the early 1970s, when the EPC system of foreign policy cooperation was initiated, fears were expressed that this would inevitably lead to the development of a predatory, militarized 'European super-state' (Galtung 1973). Alternatively, it was contended, the EC should remain a 'civilian power', playing an important role in the promotion of world peace (Duchêne 1972). In the event, as the previous chapter demonstrated, the achievements of EPC were modest and EC influence, whether benign or malign, failed to meet these early expectations.

Twenty years later, the terms of the renewed debate reflected failures in security policy, not least the inability to provide an effective response to the outbreak, in 1991, of violent conflict in the (then) Yugoslav Federal Republic. The EU was criticized for its inability to act 'in the manner of a conventional superpower' (Buchan 1993: 4). Ultimately, it was contended, '… defence is the key to the development of the Community's place in the world' (Hill 1993: 318). As we saw in Chapter 2, the lack of access to military capabilities was central to discourses on EU identity either for those wishing to disparage or, indeed, to celebrate its pacific nature.

The lack of military instruments to support the policy aims of the Union, even before the humiliating events of the Balkan wars of the 1990s, contributed to pressure for the development of an EU defence dimension. Provision for this was included, as an aspiration for the future, in Article J.14 of the Treaty on European Union. After an indecisive period of experimentation, which kept a European military dimension at arms length through the attempt to infuse new life into the Western European Union (WEU) and the development of a European Security and Defence Identity (ESDI) within NATO, the move to an autonomous EU military capability was clearly evident by 1999 and formally endorsed by the June Meeting of the European Council in Cologne. At the end of the following year, an ambitious 'headline goal' of 60,000 troops deployable by 2003 was agreed at the Helsinki Council. The interim period was also taken up with providing the Union with its own political/military structure and with the difficult task of negotiating the relationship of the new European Security and Defence Policy to NATO. By 2003 the Union had embarked upon its first military ventures and upon the elaboration of a security strategy.

However, there is an alternative perspective informing contemporary debate, its exponents often regarding the appearance of uniforms in the once exclusively civilian Council of Ministers as a distinctly retrograde step. This view focuses upon the EU's presence as an 'island of peace' in Europe, serving as a reference point for its relatively unstable neighbours to the East and South (Tunander 1997; Smith 2000). From this perspective, both the security of the EU itself, and of the region more widely, can best be ensured through extension of the stability and prosperity enjoyed within the EU. Consequently, the key security challenge to the EU is not defence of its territory, which is no longer the issue, but the need to construct a policy towards its neighbours that responds in a sensitive manner to aspirations for inclusion and fears of exclusion. Thus it is important to ensure that access to the communication and support networks provided by the EU is prioritized; and the construction of exclusionary, defensive walls avoided. In the translation of presence into actorness, the 'soft' security provided by development assistance and humanitarian aid is considered to be more efficacious than the 'hard' security of military defence.

This broad approach to security and stability in Europe emphasizes the significance of the EU's 'civilian' or 'soft power' role. In relations with some of the Union's more troubled neighbours, however, its traditional civil instruments may prove inadequate. Here, humanitarian concerns, as well as the broader interests of European security (from which EU security cannot be divorced), may on occasion demand some form of military intervention. There are many lessons to be learned from the tragic conflicts in ex-Yugoslavia during the 1990s, but one must surely be that a more robust approach to conflict management in the early stages would have been preferable to the EU's exclusively civilian efforts.

From the perspective of the first decade of the twenty-first century three active roles for the EU are apparent. First, the essentially civilian provision of stability and security for the wider Europe. Second, an anti-terrorism role, stimulated not only by the events of September 2001 but by the Madrid railway bombings of March 2004 and the 7 July 2005 attacks on London. The character of the threat dictates that responses will have both external and internal dimensions. It is closely associated with efforts to counter the proliferation of weapons of mass destruction. These essentially civilian roles form an important part of the Security Strategy and were considered in the previous chapter. Third is the new interventionary role in external crisis management. Such action is the province of the ESDP but it will also, necessarily, call upon the extensive civil capabilities of the Union. There is a potential fourth role, comprising the classic task of armed forces in the defence of territory. It remains potential, not only on account of the absence of any immediate threat, but also because of the residual strength of the NATO Article V guarantee for many, but not all, Member States.

In important ways, however, all these actor roles are based upon another security function – the development of the EU itself as an 'island of peace'. This underlying dimension of security, which is an aspect of presence rather than purposive action, is central to understanding the wider issues under consideration. Consequently, prior to discussion of the EU's active security roles, we briefly examine the genesis of this fundamental security dimension.

In the aftermath of the Second World War, the desire to maintain peace in Europe was a major concern of policy-makers, providing significant impetus for cooperation and integration between the countries of Western Europe. Agenda 2000 put the matter succinctly:

> Over the last four decades and in line with the basic intentions of Europe's founders, the Member States have developed between them a real Community of security within which it is inconceivable that there would be the slightest threat of recourse to force as a means of settling disputes.
>
> (Commission 1997c: 27)

Today this is a largely taken-for-granted achievement. Nevertheless in the early years this outcome was by no means assured. Despite much rhetoric about the desirability of creating some form of federal Europe it appeared that, as in the past, the construction of defensive walls rather than the forging of integrative links would be the most likely approach to security problems within Western Europe.

The Cold War and the failure of defence integration

The first post-war cooperative ventures between West European countries were rooted in concern to prevent a resurgence of German militarism. Thus the 1947 Treaty of Dunkirk was a mutual defence agreement between the UK and France. This was extended, a year later, to include the Benelux countries, becoming the Brussels Treaty. The members of the Brussels Treaty Organization agreed 'to take such steps as may be held necessary in the event of renewal by Germany of a policy of aggression'. This agreement was reinforced by a generalized collective defence commitment should any of the signatories be 'the object of an armed attack' (Article V).

By mid-1948, however, the Cold War was underway and the protection offered by membership of the Brussels Treaty Organization appeared far from adequate. Consequently, immediately after signature of the Treaty, its members began negotiations with the governments of the USA and Canada for the establishment of a transatlantic collective defence arrangement. The ensuing Washington Treaty, which created the North Atlantic Treaty Organization (NATO) and to which Denmark, Iceland, Italy, Norway and Portugal also acceded as founding members, entered into force in August 1949. NATO participation formally committed the USA and Canada to the defence of Western Europe; and, ultimately, to the maintenance of a formidable military presence in Europe throughout the Cold War period.

While this commitment formed the backbone of the West European security architecture, NATO was an exclusively defensive alliance focused upon potential aggression from the Soviet Union. In consequence it did not resolve the internal security problems of Western Europe, of which the most sensitive was the relationship between France and Germany. Nor did it adequately determine the role to be played by the West Europeans in their own defence.

These issues surfaced only a year after the creation of the Atlantic Alliance, however, when the US's costly involvement in the Korean War convinced American policy-makers that West European states should assume greater responsibility for their own defence. The result was an essentially federalist proposal envisaging a European Defence Community (EDC) with a fully integrated European Army 'tied to political institutions of a united Europe' – including a European Minister of Defence and a European Council of Ministers (Rene Pleven quoted in Weigall and Stirk 1992: 75). The plan had the advantage of firmly linking German rearmament to European political institutions, but the British remained aloof. In August 1954 the French National Assembly rejected the proposal by a substantial majority. The significance of these events cannot be over-estimated, for measures taken to meet the ensuing alliance crisis led directly to the subsequent evolution of the EC as a civilian entity.

In defence terms the difficulties caused by the collapse of the EDC proposals were quickly resolved. On a UK initiative it was agreed that West German rearmament would be achieved, as originally proposed, within the framework of NATO, but via an explicitly European institution, the Western European Union (WEU), created in 1954 by the amended Brussels Treaty, which was extended to include West Germany and Italy. This compromise solution had the effect of entrenching NATO's position as the principal instrument of European defence.[2] The Western European Union established modest headquarters in London and developed an equally modest role – as a discussion forum for European NATO members when the presence of US representatives was considered undesirable. Both NATO and the WEU, however, were strictly intergovernmental organizations. Following the failure of the EDC, attempts to submit security and defence issues to supranational decision-making were abandoned for the foreseeable future, and West European collaborative efforts focused upon less sensitive areas.

The presence of North American security guarantees effectively provided a defensive wall behind which West European governments were able to concentrate upon economic reconstruction, assisted by US financial assistance in the form of Marshall Aid. Further impetus for these efforts was provided by the establishment of the Soviet Bloc as an apparently monolithic enemy espousing a non-capitalist economic system and strongly anti-capitalist rhetoric. In these circumstances the successful regeneration of the West European capitalist economies was not only a matter of increasing prosperity and the ability to meet welfare needs – it was perceived also in terms of ensuring the survival and, indeed, demonstrating the superiority, of the capitalist system itself. In the context of the Cold War, despite the considerable emphasis upon military issues, security essentially involved the survival of competing economic and social systems. In Western Europe this was increasingly perceived in terms of economic integration.

The EDC proposals of the early 1950s were formulated alongside an earlier initiative, which formed the essential foundation stone of Community Europe, and which had been explicitly designed to fulfil a security purpose. Thus the European Coal and Steel Community (ECSC), which was established in 1952, placed the coal and steel production of its members (France, Germany, Italy and the Benelux countries) under the partial control of a supranational High Authority. At its core was the desire to pool the coal and steel resources of France and Germany, hence inextricably linking the economic recovery of these former adversaries – while also facilitating supervision of German industrial production to prevent unauthorized manufacture of armaments. The security function is made explicit in a Memorandum from Jean Monnet, in which he sets out his vision of the ECSC as the starting point of a broader European integration process:[3]

> Wherever we look in the present world situation we see nothing but deadlock – whether it be the increasing acceptance of a war that is thought to be inevitable, the problem of Germany, the continuation of French recovery, the organization of Europe … From such a situation there is only one way of escape: concrete, resolute action on a limited but decisive point, bringing about on this point a fundamental change, and gradually modifying the very terms of all the problems.
> (Jean Monnet 1950, quoted in Vaughan 1976: 51)

These ideas were shared by a number of prominent Western politicians and intellectuals. They underlay establishment of the ECSC, the first of the European Communities, and they clearly reflect the desire to construct, through a process founded initially upon economic integration, a Community of security in Western

Europe. In practice, of course, this construction suffered numerous problems and setbacks. Nevertheless, in the relative stability of the Cold War period, when the major players were evidently the USA and the USSR, West European politicians enjoyed a unique opportunity to construct the EC's 'civilian power' role. There are parallels here with the advocacy of the EU model in regional trade arrangements and in the security implications for outsiders of being drawn into the orbit of the EU's widening presence. For a long time this was prevented by the rigid Cold War division of Europe.

The TEU and its aftermath

The failure of the EDC initiative, and the Cold War reality that territorial defence of Western Europe as a whole was realized through NATO, ensured that for more than two decades defence-related issues were discussed outside the EC context. This was all the more remarkable because the headquarters of the two organizations were after 1966 located in the same city yet, for all the contact that occurred between them, they could have been on opposite sides of the planet. There were, however, continuing expectations of a wider security role for Europe which helped in 1984 to prompt the reactivation of a dormant WEU.

In 1987 the agreement by the USA and USSR to withdraw all intermediate nuclear forces (INF) heralded the end of the Cold War; and inevitably, also, initiated debate about the future of NATO. The rapidly changing international climate of the period suggested both new demands and new opportunities for European defence. Thus, immediately after conclusion of the INF Agreement, proposals were launched for the formation of a joint Franco-German brigade as the first step towards a European military force. Shortly afterwards the WEU adopted a 'Platform on European Security Interests' which declared 'that the construction of an integrated Europe will remain incomplete as long as it does not include security and defence' (Preamble, The Hague Platform 1987).

Thus, in the closing stages of the Cold War, a number of preliminary steps had been taken towards creation of a European defence dimension. Ultimately these were reflected in the provisions of the Treaty on European Union. Thus Article J.17.1 referred, somewhat cautiously, to '... the eventual framing of a common defence policy, which might in time lead to a common defence'. In the interest of achieving this aim, the Western European Union was declared to be '... an integral part of the development of the Union' and was requested 'to elaborate and implement decisions and actions of the Union which have defence implications' (Article J.17.2). In a Declaration attached to the TEU, the role of the WEU was stated to be 'the defence component of the European Union' *and* 'the European pillar of the Atlantic Alliance' (Declaration I). This dual role envisaged for the WEU reflected significant differences among its members over the future European security architecture and a function for the organization as a form of buffer between the Union and NATO.

The complexities surrounding WEU membership reflect the particular sensitivity of this policy area for Member State governments. They reveal three broad positions on European defence and security – the Atlanticists, led by the UK; proponents of an

EU defence dimension, led by France; and the neutral countries plus Denmark, which prefer to de-emphasize military defence in favour of soft security. This disunity, and the associated lack of coincidence between EU and WEU membership, inevitably impeded development of an EU defence dimension. Nevertheless, inclusion of reference to defence was undoubtedly a major innovation of the TEU, potentially heralding a departure from the exclusively civilian nature of the EU.

The 1990s proved to be a decade of uncertainty and ambiguity in which both NATO, the WEU and the Union struggled to re-define themselves in relation to the radically altered security environment of the post-Cold War era. The fundamental change was the sudden absence of a Soviet threat. It meant that NATO's *raison d'être* had evaporated and that the constraints of alliance solidarity that had bound Europeans and the US together for so long were suddenly diminished, opening up a new and more pointed debate between the Atlanticists and those convinced that the time for real European autonomy had arrived. The ending of the Cold War also led to an unanticipated outbreak of conflict within Europe, notably in former Yugoslavia. This was not a generalized, massive but essentially hypothetical threat to be managed through collective defence arrangements, but an immediate problem requiring actual military intervention in the European region. It was not at all evident that the EU Member States, let alone the US, shared a compelling interest in bearing the costs of intervention. Neither were the existing institutional structures or the bulk of Europe's armed forces, static and reliant upon conscript troops, ready for the task. Thus, in retrospect, it is clear that conflict in the Balkans provided the crucible in which an EU security identity and capability began to be forged.

External intervention and the impact of Yugoslavia

In the Cold War context of bloc-to-bloc confrontation there had been no demand, and hence no structured provision, for peacekeeping activities in Europe. Since the existing European security architecture appeared no longer to be relevant, but had yet to be adapted or replaced, Yugoslavia became a testing ground for post-Cold War security arrangements. The subsequent events, which reflected little credit on any of the organizations involved, profoundly influenced the outcome of controversies over the most appropriate arrangements for Europe's security – not least the aspiration that the EU should develop a traditional security role.

The initial phase of the conflict occurred during the currency of the 1990/1 IGC on Political Union, where the issues of security and defence were the subject of ongoing controversy between Member States. Consequently the crisis, which was in part a consequence of failure by the EC to communicate a clear and consistent message to the parties, was perceived as an opportunity to demonstrate the ability to manage crises on its borders. Shortly after Yugoslav Federal forces entered Slovenia, Foreign Minister Jacques Poos made clear the views of the Luxembourg Presidency:

> … if one problem can be solved by the Europeans, it is the Yugoslav problem. This is a European country and it is not up to the Americans. It is not up to anyone else.
>
> (Jacques Poos quoted in Smith 1996: 1)

The first six months of the conflict saw considerable EC diplomatic activity as well as use of economic instruments (Salmon 1992; Buchan 1993). However, proposals for military intervention, under the auspices of the WEU, were abandoned in the face of opposition, in particular from the UK. The EC's extensive involvement in the early stages of the conflict resulted not only from excessive enthusiasm, but also from the absence of alternatives.[4] In the event the presence of unarmed, civilian EC monitors had little effect in preserving the several ceasefires negotiated by the EC Troika during 1991; moreover the monitors themselves were in considerable personal danger. In January 1992 five EC monitors were killed when their clearly marked helicopter was shot down. This tragic incident, perhaps more than any other, highlighted the limitations of an exclusively civilian approach to the conflict; and hence the need for access to peacekeeping and peacemaking capabilities. While deployment of UN peacekeeping forces provided the immediate solution, the need, in the longer term, for a European capability in this sphere was a concern for policy-makers. At the WEU, in consequence, the organization's potential role in external intervention was under consideration. Similar concerns were also preoccupying NATO policy planners.

In June 1992 the WEU, meeting at Petersberg near Bonn, declared its willingness to participate in '… conflict-prevention and crisis-management measures, including peacekeeping activities of the CSCE or the United Nations Security Council' (Petersberg Declaration, I-2, 1992).[5] This was the genesis of the 'Petersberg Tasks' which were to find their way ultimately into the text of the TEU (Article 17.2). NATO adaptations in response to the conflict developed in parallel with those at the WEU, at least in the early stages of their involvement. Thus in June 1992, shortly prior to the WEU's Petersberg Declaration, NATO Foreign Ministers announced the organization's readiness to become involved in peacekeeping operations in support of the CSCE. Effectively ending the Cold War prohibition on NATO operations 'out of area', this announcement was to have major implications for NATO's future role.[6]

The development of NATO's role in ex-Yugoslavia contrasts markedly with that of the WEU. NATO interventions in Bosnia, on the basis of UN Security Council Resolutions, represented not only the first time that the alliance had fired a shot in anger, but also a decisive development of its new role. Under the Dayton Agreement this was subsequently extended into a longer term commitment to peacemaking and the arrest of war criminals through the deployment of a stabilization force (SFOR) in Bosnia-Herzegovina.

During the course of the 1990s the WEU, and indeed the EU, became increasingly marginalized. But this did not result in abandonment of the European security project. Bosnia sowed the seeds for the development of the ESDP in a number of ways, most obviously by its demonstration of EU impotence, necessitating a humiliating reliance upon US action that might not always be forthcoming. It was realized that the circumstances which had united NATO members during the Bosnian operation might not easily be replicated, and that some other mechanisms for the mobilization of European forces would be required. Within NATO this involved extensive discussion of ways in which alliance facilities could be used by a group of European states in crisis interventions not directly involving the US – the European Security and Defence

Identity (ESDI) and the related notion of constructing *ad hoc* Combined Joint Task Forces (CJTF).[7] There was a problem, then and now, with the different orientation of Member States in respect to NATO. The situation that pertains at the point of enlargement of the Union in 2004 is outlined in Table 8.1. There was also the experience of a 1997 intervention in Albania, hastily assembled on the basis of a 'coalition of the willing'.[8] While all these concepts, as we shall see, were to be echoed in the construction of the ESDP, they were really no substitute for it.

Less immediately apparent, but still very significant, was the way in which the Europeans acquired the habit of working together in regional military activities. In July 1994 the German Constitutional Court ruled that German forces could participate in peacekeeping missions abroad in support of UN, NATO or WEU missions, thus enabling German participation in NATO's peace stabilization force in Bosnia-Herzegovina. However, it was a change of British policy, on the election of a new Labour government in May 1997, that initiated decisive progress towards a new European Security and Defence Policy for the EU.

Table 8.1 EU and NATO membership (2005)*

Common members	NATO only	EU only
Belgium	Bulgaria**	Austria
Czech Republic	Canada	Cyprus
Denmark	Iceland	Finland
Estonia	Norway	Ireland
France	Romania**	Malta
Greece	Turkey**	Sweden
Germany	USA	
Hungary		
Italy		
Latvia		
Lithuania		
Luxembourg		
Netherlands		
Poland		
Portugal		
Slovakia		
Slovenia		
Spain		
UK		

Notes

* Three further countries – Albania, Croatia and the former Yugoslav Republic of Macedonia – are formal candidates for NATO membership and subject to NATO's Membership Action Plan. These countries, plus Serbia and Montenegro and Bosnia-Herzegovina, have been promised eventual EU membership. Croatia has been granted candidate status by the EU.

** Candidates for EU membership. Bulgaria and Romania are scheduled for accession in 2007. Turkey is to open negotiations in 2005, but is unlikely to accede for at least a further decade.

St Malo, Kosovo and the birth of the ESDP

Some of the experience of previous years was reflected in the Amsterdam revisions to the TEU. Yet the new text was still ambiguous, giving room for 'coalitions of the willing' and including specific mention of the Petersberg Tasks but still hedged around with the importance, attached by the UK and others, to operation within a NATO framework.[9] In the end it was a convergence of British and French policy at the end of 1998 that was to be of far greater significance than Amsterdam, amounting, according to some commentators, to a 'military revolution' (Andréani *et al.* 2001). Although Franco-British consideration of the need for the EU to develop a capacity for autonomous action had been afoot for some months, it was formalized in a declaration issued following a December 1998 meeting between French President Chirac and UK Prime Minister Blair at St Malo. The declaration stated:

> The European Union must have the capacity for autonomous action, backed up by credible military forces, the means to decide to use them and a readiness to do so, in order to respond to international crises ...
>
> (Cited in Haine 2004a: 143)

This represented a landmark reversal of the long-standing UK position that no such capability could be allowed to exist outside NATO. It was a consequence of a common awareness that there was likely to be a continuing requirement for peace-keeping in Europe; that experience in former Yugoslavia demonstrated that the WEU expedient was inadequate and that US action to provide military cover for European incapacity might not always be available (Deighton 2002; Howorth 2000). This conclusion was to be greatly reinforced, within weeks, by the very negative experience of the US-led NATO campaign over Kosovo in the spring of 1999. There were also a set of specifically British motivations involving the desire of the Blair government to be 'at the heart of Europe' while remaining outside the single currency, and at the same time to ensure the survival of the Atlantic alliance by strengthening its European pillar (Interview, Permanent Representation, 2002).

There was a critical ambiguity here, which although necessary to the launching of the ESDP, has continued to haunt its development. It is exemplified in the second part of the St Malo Declaration which reads:

> In strengthening the solidarity between the Member States of the European Union, in order that Europe can make its voice heard in world affairs, while acting in conformity with our respective obligations in NATO, we are contributing to the vitality of a modernised Atlantic Alliance which is the foundation of the collective defence of its members.
>
> (Cited in Haine 2004a: 143)

French policy has never accepted the British interpretation that the ESDP must always be complementary to NATO. Instead it is regarded as a first step towards counter-balancing US power and providing some real autonomy for Europe. For the UK, ESDP must be concerned with crisis management not collective defence. However, the French Government can continue to refer to the fact that the TEU mentions the possibility of the latter.[10]

Crisis management capability

The Union's military enterprise was formally launched by the 1999 Cologne Council, which, in the midst of NATO's Kosovo intervention, confirmed Javier Solana as the new High Representative for the CFSP and defined the military role of the Union in terms of the Petersberg Tasks. In the December of the same year, the European Council meeting at Helsinki announced its 'headline goal' of 60,000 troops available to the ESDP and initiated its new decision-making structures – the PSC, the EU Military Committee (EUMC) and the EU Military Staff (EUMS).[11] Within only three years of its initiation the ESDP was to undertake its first operations. The installation of the new structures 'proceeded in leaps and bounds and represented an extraordinary commitment by Member States' (Interview, Council Secretariat, July 2001). It was remarkable in a system where institutional change often proceeds at a glacial pace. Remarkable, too, was the character of the new capability, designed to undertake 'crisis management'. In the words of one of the senior officers seconded to the new military structure, 'we are trying to build a global crisis management organization including military and civil assets. Nothing like it exists elsewhere in the world' (Interview, EUMS, July 2001).

Operationalizing the ESDP required the installation of a military and a strategic culture in an organization, the Council Secretariat, which had previously not only been entirely civilian but whose tasks had initially been restricted to the preparation of meetings and minutes.[12] The exclusively intergovernmental character of the ESDP required that it should be run from the Council Secretariat located in the Justus Lipsius Building in Brussels and its new secure military annexe in the Avenue de Cortenbergh. At the same time an institutional means had to be found to enable the Council to take the kind of rapid decision that might be expected in a crisis involving the deployment of forces. Such expedition had not been a notable characteristic of the EU's decision-making, especially operating beyond Community competence and in the expectation of a Union of 25 or more Member States. In addition, the intergovernmental mode meant that dedicated Community funding was unavailable and that cross-pillar obstacles would have to be overcome, if the multifunctional aspirations of the ESDP were to be realized. All this was to be compounded by differences between the Member States to which we have already referred, in terms of size, military tradition and orientation towards the difficult question of autonomy. Critical to the latter debate was the question of the extent to which the ESDP might be seen as independent of NATO. When, somewhat prematurely, it was declared operational at the Laeken Council of December 2001, there were four days of conflict over the wording of the declaration. Eventually a solution was found in linguistic ambiguity. The English text declared the EU 'is now able to conduct *some* crisis management operations'. The French referred to 'des opérations' (Interview, Permanent Representation, October 2002).[13]

A review of the EU's military structure (Figure 8.1) must proceed from the understanding that the ESDP is an integral part of the CFSP, described in the preceding

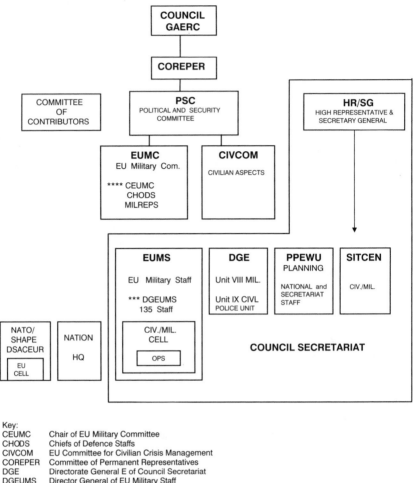

Key:
CEUMC   Chair of EU Military Committee
CHODS   Chiefs of Defence Staffs
CIVCOM   EU Committee for Civilian Crisis Management
COREPER   Committee of Permanent Representatives
DGE   Directorate General E of Council Secretariat
DGEUMS   Director General of EU Military Staff
DSACEUR   Deputy Supreme Allied Commander Europe
GAERC   General Affairs and External Relations Council
MILREPS   Military Representatives (of the Member States)
PPEWU   Policy Planning and Early Warning Unit
SHAPE   Supreme Headquarters Allied Powers Europe
SITCEN   Situation Centre

Figure 8.1 ESDP crisis management structure

chapter, and that therefore its operations are 'joint actions'.[14] The ESDP works to the GAERC formation of the Council. There is no Defence Council but informal meetings are held and defence ministers do attend the GAERC. The PSC provides the 'linchpin' of the ESDP. The Council decision establishing the procedures of the PSC gives it the 'central role in the definition and follow up to the EU's response to a crisis'. It also has the important crisis role of 'political control and strategic direction of the EU's military response' (*OJ* L27, 30.1.2001: 2). What is implied by the term 'crisis management' is Union intervention that assists in the resolution of a foreign conflict. This may also involve the EU in crisis decision-making, that is to say that the EU would have to move from a relatively routine to a crisis mode, involving a raised level of threat and acute time pressure. In such circumstances, which have not yet occurred, the PSC may be chaired by the High Representative, who is also required to keep the Council abreast of developments. A characteristic of the PSC is that being now composed of Brussels-based representatives of the Member States, it meets frequently and could convene within thirty minutes (Interview, Permanent Representation, October 2002).

The PSC directs and is advised by another body created by the Council – the EU Military Committee (EUMC). This body can operate at Chief of Defence Staff level, but normally comprises their national 'milreps'. It is chaired by a 'four star' officer (other Council Committees are chaired by the representative of the President in Office) who enjoys a three-year term of office. The function of the EUMC is modelled on NATO's Military Committee and is designed to be a purveyor of neutral advice with the setting of a 'political direction' left to the Presidency (Interview, Council Secretariat, October 2002).[15]

Subordinate to the EUMC, but regarded as the 'real core of business' in the conduct of military policy, is a dedicated military staff (the EUMS) led by a 'three star' general (Interview, Council Secretariat, October 2004). This has built up to a strength of some 135 national officers as a Council Secretariat Department directly attached to the High Representative. It is 'the source of the EU's military expertise' and functions to provide early warning, situation assessment and strategic planning, plus options available to the EUMC. It also provides the link to operational headquarters (*OJ* L27, 30.1.2001: 8–9).

Unlike NATO, memorably described to us as a 'one trick pony' (Interview, Permanent Representation 2002), the distinctive mission of the EU is to provide a mix of crisis responses whereby policing, re-establishment of the rule of law and other civil protection activities run concurrently with (or are undertaken separately from) the deployment of forces. In order to plan, advise the PSC and coordinate the use of Member States' civil assets, a Civil Committee (CIVCOM) was created by decision of COREPER and a small police unit has also been established within DGE (IX) of the Council Secretariat. The CIVCOM apparatus lacks the status of its military equivalent and continues to rely heavily on the short-term secondment of Member State personnel (European Council 2004a: 13). The seven staff in the police unit contrast with the 135 located in EUMS and the planning capabilities of the civil side of the ESDP bureaucracy are still under-developed and 'amateurish' (Interview, Council Secretariat, October 2004). Although its primary function is advising the PSC on 'Second Pillar and Member States' activities', CIVCOM also has to ensure that duplication of Community activities does not occur.[16]

The collection and assessment of the intelligence upon which an operation may be based is carried out by a dedicated Situation Centre (SITCEN) which works to the High Representative. It will derive from various sources: the Member States, EUMS, the Commission and the Policy Planning and Early Warning Unit. Once the Council has given political approval to the 'crisis management concept' there will be a strategic planning process involving interaction between the PSC and its military and civilian advisory bodies, resulting in the presentation of a recommendation for action to the Council. In the Council there is a requirement for unanimity, allowing only qualified abstention if an operation is to proceed. Clearly, decisions on the use of force will be based on approval at the highest political level in the Member States and are likely to involve direct consultations between the High Representative and the heads of government of contributing states.[17] All the operations undertaken in 2003–5, with the significant exception of *Artemis* in the Congo, have been subject to a lengthy period of advance planning and have not really tested crisis decision-making capability. *Artemis*, however, was planned under conditions of urgency and it took ten days from approval by the Council of the crisis management concept to agreement of the operational plan and actual launch of operations. The intention is to reduce this to five days, leading to the actual appearance of forces on the ground within a further ten days (GAERC Conclusions, 17 May 2004: 1).

The conduct of operations and relations with NATO

So far the ESDP has conducted three types of operation. The most visible are the EU Force (military deployment) (EUFOR) in Macedonia (*Concordia*, March–December 2003), the Democratic Republic of Congo (*Artemis*, June–September 2003) and in Bosnia-Herzegovina (*Althea*, December 2004). Their scale has varied from 350 lightly armed troops in Macedonia; 2,000 in the Congo to a 7,000 strong force in Bosnia. On the civilian side there have been the EU police missions (EUPOL); with 554 personnel in Bosnia (EU Police Mission to Bosnia and Herzegovina (EUPM)) during 2003 and then missions to FYROM (*Proxima*) from December 2003 and a 30-strong mission to Kinshasa (Congo) commencing in 2005. A pattern is immediately apparent, in that police missions have preceded or succeeded military forces in the three countries involved. In the case of operation *Althea* there is a EUPOL unit included within the military deployment. Finally, we have also witnessed the beginning of another type of operation to provide technical assistance in establishing the rule of law and criminal justice systems (EU Justice Mission (EUJUST)), the first of this type being a ten-strong mission to Georgia in 2004 (*Themis*). This was followed by a limited contribution to the stabilization of Iraq (EUJUST *Lex*), launched in the summer of 2005 with a police and judicial training operation located outside the country.[18]

Operations, both police and military, are also marked by the involvement of non-EU Member State personnel. Military participation is organized on the basis of the NATO PfP experience, with oversight of the operation being provided by a 'Committee of Contributors' that involves participating Member States' EUMC representatives sitting alongside their non-EU counterparts.[19]

All ESDP missions have a 'stand alone' character, with a chain of command that reaches ultimately to the High Representative. The operational organization of police missions appears relatively straightforward, with an EU appointed Police Commissioner working alongside a local EU special representative (EUSR) and reporting to the HR.[20] The management of military operations has been anything but straight-forward. Issues have been provoked that go directly to the heart of the Union's autonomy as an actor, the ways in which United States governments have constructed and recognized the EU as a strategic partner, the future of the NATO alliance, and, finally, the European vocation of Turkey.

The launching of a military operation, after due consideration within the ESDP structures outlined above, begins with the approval of an operational plan (OPLAN) and rules of engagement (RoE) by the Council. Execution involves two levels of headquarters and associated military assets, an operational HQ and a force HQ. Political controversy has centred upon the operational headquarters and the extent of their autonomy. As a consequence of previous attempts to create a European identity within the alliance, culminating in the 1996 Berlin agreement, the new ESDP and NATO were already intertwined in many ways. Most of the forces that the EU might call upon are also assigned to NATO; one of Javier Solana's main qualifications for the job of High Representative was his previous role as NATO Secretary General and many of the staff involved in the EUMS have NATO experience, although the importance of non-members of NATO, notably Sweden and Finland, should not be forgotten (as well as the fact that one NATO member, Denmark, maintains an 'opt out' from the ESDP). Finally, the general practice of EU Member States within NATO (apart from France) has been to 'double hat' their NATO military representative to sit on the EUMC as well (see Figure 8.1). At the same time, the Atlanticists within the EU would not have proceeded with ESDP without alliance involvement. Achieving this raised three problems: first, the position of the alliance leader, the United States; second, the existence of non-EU NATO members, notably Turkey; and third, to a lesser extent, the non-NATO EU Member States, Sweden, Finland, Ireland and Austria.

The EU–NATO arrangements that were eventually put in place are known as 'Berlin-plus' because they modify and substantially extend the original 1996 agreement. Initially NATO responded to St Malo, and to the inclusion of the WEU within the Union, by a 1999 Washington Summit Communiqué which, while 'acknowledging the resolve of the European Union to have a capacity for autonomous action', stressed that alliance assets should be 'separable but not separate'.[21] Underlying the Communiqué were the Clinton administration's concerns that, in Secretary Albright's celebrated three 'Ds', there should be no discrimination between allies, no decoupling from the alliance and no duplication of military effort.

Essentially the US regarded the ESDP as being within the alliance, providing NATO, and hence the United States, with the option of first refusal of any proposed operation, and indeed of defining what would be an autonomous European action through engagement in joint advance planning. From an EU, and especially a French, perspective, this was unacceptable. 'The definition of the Union's autonomy cannot belong to another organisation' (Haine 2004a: 138). The Union response which, as ever, represents a compromise between Atlanticists and their opponents, envisaged the possibility of fully autonomous action, without NATO, but employing an existing national headquarters (as would be the case in the *Artemis* operation in 2003).[22] Full agreement on the new NATO–EU relationship was to be delayed until December 2002, with a formal text concluded in March 2003, thus allowing Operation *Concordia* in Macedonia to proceed under 'Berlin-plus'.[23] This involved the command being placed in the hands of NATO's Deputy Supreme Commander (DSACEUR), who is always a European officer, and operational use of NATO's headquarters and other assets.

The delay to agreement on 'Berlin-plus', upon which implementation of the entire ESDP depended, was the consequence of an effective Turkish veto within the NATO Council. Turkish concerns were that, as an outsider, it would be excluded from ESDP deliberations about using NATO assets and even that certain Member States, although Greece was never explicitly mentioned, might use the machinery against Turkish interests. Underlying the specifics was a simmering grievance over the treatment of Turkey's EU application, which was only ameliorated by the agreement to allow Turkish representatives to participate in the Constitutional Convention and by the arrival of the new Erdogan government. While, politically, the un-blocking of 'Berlin-plus' allowed the ESDP to proceed, there remains widespread scepticism that arrangements of such inordinate complexity could ever work in any situation other than that pertaining in Macedonia and Bosnia-Herzegovina, where the ESDP simply assumed ownership of an existing NATO operation. The implication is that future ESDP operations are likely to be independent of NATO.

Having established that two types of HQ and operational planning were available to the ESDP, either via 'Berlin-plus' or through the use of national HQs which would be 'multi-nationalized', the controversy re-appeared with proposals for a third form of operational planning capability. Despite being the ESDP's first year of operation, 2003 proved to be a difficult and divisive year for NATO and the EU, subject as both were to acrimonious divisions over the US-led invasion of Iraq. In a symbolic gesture of European autonomy, the French, Germans, Belgians and Luxemburgers met in Brussels in (the so-called Chocolate or Tervuren Summit of 29 April) to discuss a proposal for an independent EU headquarters. This was anathema to the British, who considered such moves to be an irresponsible threat to NATO. Their concern was underlined by evidence of increasing American disregard for the multilateral alliance, reflecting the new doctrine of the Bush administration that the mission (rather than the existing alliance structure) defines the coalition.[24] Franco-British arguments then ensued over the name, form and function of an independent EU operational planning capability, amounting at one point to Council 'micro-management' of the amount of office space to be devoted to a civil/military cell (Interview, Council Secretariat, September 2004).

These disagreements spoke to questions about the fundamental character and autonomy of the ESDP that had simply been elided by the St Malo agreement. Deliberations between the Germans, British and French finally delivered a compromise, whereby a civilian/military planning cell was created within the EUMS, which would have the capacity to set up an operations centre if called upon to do so in the absence of recourse either to 'Berlin-plus' or a national headquarters. This was justified through the special need to integrate the civil and military aspects of a small-scale operation and balanced by the parallel creation of an EU cell at NATO SHAPE. It 'would not be a standing HQ' (European Council 2004c: 21).[25]

Capabilities

The presumed absence of military capability provides the core assumption behind various, often dismissive, external constructions of the Union and its pacific identity. As is often the case, the comparator is the United States.

While we have measured economic statistics and capabilities and observed that the United States and the EU exercise a relatively balanced duopoly in the world trade regime, the picture is very different in security affairs. The United States is a military hyper-power many times more potent than its potential rivals. In 2003 its defence budget stood at €330 billion in comparison to the EU 25's combined total of €180 billion. It possessed 400,000 deployable ground troops, global power projection capabilities in its carrier battle groups and applied military technology (network centric warfare) so advanced as to raise questions about the continued possibility of combined operations with its allies. This means that the United States has extensive military capability, but it does not imply that the Union's assets are negligible. In 2004 the EU had 1.8 million personnel under arms and its aggregate defence budget was actually equivalent to those of China, Russia, Japan, Saudi Arabia, India and South Korea combined (Biscop 2004b: 7). Furthermore, sometimes unflattering comparisons with NATO neglect to mention that European nations have only one set of forces and that those deployed under the auspices of NATO in Afghanistan, for example, are also those that are being committed to the ESDP.

The EU does not aspire to rival the United States in global power projection but it has, since the announcement of the Helsinki 60,000 strong force 'headline goal' in December 1999, sought to organize forces that could undertake the 'Petersberg Tasks'.[26] The emphasis on a quantitative goal was perhaps beside the point, diverting attention from pressing issues of quality and deployability. Europe has more than adequate numbers of personnel under arms, the problem is in the means to move and support them effectively. Thus the more relevant 'headline goal 2010' envisages rapidly deployable specialized battalion size 'battle groups'. With the first of these formations being organized in 2005, some seven or more will be available by 2007. This is a significant development, not only because it betokened a realistic evaluation of the ESDP's military tasks, clearly based upon the *Artemis* experience in the Congo, but also because it involved practical Franco-British and German cooperation in the spirit of St Malo. The agreement on battle groups also earmarks them specifically for use under a UN mandate.[27]

The problem is one of generating useable forces from the expenditure that already exists, when so much of it continues to be tied down in static territorial defences left over from the Cold War period or in the inefficient duplication of assets on a national basis. As was implicit in the St Malo developments, the British and French possess the main European forces capable of independent expeditionary operations, but even they are subject to severe logistical and other limitations. Since 2000 extensive efforts have been made to catalogue the capabilities potentially available to the Union, and to begin the process of ensuring that they are interoperable, deployable and sustainable. To this end, three European Capability Commitment Conferences have been held by defence ministers. The first in 2001 launched the European Capability Action Plan

(ECAP). ECAP is intended to serve as a 'conscience and catalyst' in identifying short-falls in military capability and attempting to prod Member States into remedying them. This is an avowedly 'bottom up' and voluntaristic intergovernmental process and progress has been inevitably slow, yet it is grappling with problems to which NATO failed to find an effective answer over decades. Attempts have been made to quicken the pace and inject a Union dimension by involving the Military Staff in setting an ECAP 'road map'.[28]

Although the May 2003 Capabilities Commitment Conference judged the ESDP to have operational capability across the range of the 'Petersberg Tasks', major impediments to the aim of 'global deployability' remain, particularly in strategic lift capability, logistics and independent command, control and intelligence facilities.[29] Some of these deficiencies will be partially remedied through the acquisition by Member States of the A400M Airbus military transport and the development of a European satellite capability. The CFSP/ESDP already has a dedicated European Union Satellite Centre for the production and interpretation of 'overhead imagery' at Torrejón in Spain. It works to the political direction of the PSC and under the operational control of the High Representative (*OJ* L200/5, 25.7.2001). The Union as a whole already has distinctive ambitions in space policy, in both earth observation (Global Monitoring for Environment and Security) and in global positioning with the Galileo satellite programme. This is an area in which industrial and environmental policy, the pursuit of the Lisbon Agenda and the ESDP have come to intersect (Vogler 2002b). The Commission has accordingly developed a major stake in a common space policy where 'to be credible and effective, any CFSP and ESDP must be based on autonomous access to reliable global information so as to foster informed decision-taking' (Commission 2003g: 9). The military potential of the Galileo Public Regulated Service, which breaks a US monopoly, proved to be a highly controversial transatlantic issue.

The longer-term development of collective military capability of the Member States is the task of the European Defence Agency, established by Joint Action of the Council in July 2004. With the High Representative as its titular head, the Agency employs seventy-seven temporary staff with a budget of €20 million. The essential problems are, again, ones that NATO has long sought to address in collective military procure-ment and the encouragement of a European military industrial base and research and technology infrastructure. With no public enthusiasm for additional military expenditure, there is a need to spend more wisely. Here the interests of the increasingly concentrated European defence manufacturers are involved but also those of defence ministries, who may well look to provide the best value equipment rather than that which supports European industry. There is also a need for a fundamental shift in attitude towards military specialization:

> Clinging to a 'full toolbox' is useless, as the range of necessarily small scale (and thus inefficient) capabilities would not allow smaller – or medium sized – states to implement autonomous operations, so they are dependent on other states anyway – although not all states have come to realize this.
>
> (Biscop 2004: 11)

The financing of operations is another area affected by the highly intergovernmental character of the ESDP. The TEU (Article28) allows the administrative expenses of the ESDP to be charged to the Community budget along with non-military operating expenditures, which includes police missions. Initially this meant the adoption of *ad hoc* arrangements for military actions that followed the NATO convention that 'costs lie where they fall' amongst contributing states. A sign of the growing maturity of the ESDP was the adoption in 2004 of a longer-term and more systematic funding arrangement in the Athena mechanism.[30] This provides a budget for the common costs (such as barrack facilities) of military operations into which participating nations pay according to a GNP based scale. This can cause problems when applied to non-EU contributing countries with high per capita GNPs.[31]

It is still worth pointing out that the budgets available to the CFSP/ESDP are dwarfed in scale by the financial resources available to the Pillar I operations run by the Commission.

The provision of civilian capabilities, initially in the area of policing and criminal justice, presents some novel problems. There is, for instance, no tradition nor indeed established national capability in expeditionary policing. Unlike the military, police forces are domestic and service in an EU operation is not an accepted part of a police career. The civil sector of the ESDP also directly abuts the very extensive post-conflict and development activities of the Community, with opportunities for coherent action often bedevilled by inter-pillar rivalry. As one observer of the Bosnia-Herzegovina police mission put it, this can lead to a situation where:

> ... declarations highlighting the need for a comprehensive approach and the close coordination of various mission components are matched with so little inter-institutional dialogue and cooperation.
>
> (Hansen 2004: 183)

The problem, as well as the potential 'synergies', is acknowledged at a high political level, and better coordination will need to develop alongside operational experience in this new enterprise (European Council 2004a).

Ambitious civil capability aspirations were expressed at the June 2000 Feira Council, involving a potential force of 5,000 police (with 1,000 deployable at 30 days notice) undertaking a broad spectrum of tasks from support and training to actual executive policing. Although pursued by the subsequent Swedish presidency, progress in capability development has been slow. Few Member States possess deployable police forces, although the Netherlands, France, Italy, Spain and Portugal have begun to cooperate outside the strict Union format in the creation of a multinational Gendarmerie. A headline goal for civil capabilities had not been developed by 2004 and neither was there a catalogue equivalent to that developed for the military (Interview, Council Secretariat, October 2004). Progress was, however, observable in the November 2004 Civil Commitment Conference, where Member States pledged 5,761 police, 631 rule of law, 562 advisory and 4,988 civil protection personnel (European Council 2004b: 1).

Security roles of the EU

The Union has, by its very nature and the intentions of its founders, always been involved in the provision of security, or as the Commission puts it, a 'peace project'. This security dimension of the Union's presence has been reflected most powerfully in the stabilizing effect of the enlargement process. The development of actor capability has provided the Union with the necessary civil instruments for an active security role and, as outlined in Chapter 7, the Common Foreign and Security Policy has attempted to provide an integrated framework for their use. We have treated it separately because it represents such a major departure, with implications for the core identity of the EU, but the ESDP essentially provides an additional set of instruments for the conduct of the CFSP. For the framers of the Security Strategy there was a certain inevitability to the way in which the presence of the Union gave rise to expectations of actor capability and security responsibility:

> As a union of 25 states with over 450 million people producing a quarter of the world's gross national product (GNP) and with a wide range of instruments at its disposal, the European Union is inevitably a global player. Europe should be ready to share the responsibility for global security and in building a better world.
>
> (European Council 2003: 1)

In line with this expectation, rapid steps were taken from 1999 onwards to provide a military edge to the Union's external relations but, as with the other capabilities of the CFSP, some of which had been equally 'events driven', the precise part that the new capability would play remained uncertain. The Security Strategy was devised and approved during 2003 and provides, along with the operations that have already been undertaken, some guidance as to what the active military tasks of the ESDP may come to be.[32] However, questions about the developing security roles of the EU cannot be confined to the circumstances in which force may be employed. It is a distinctive characteristic of the European approach that military instruments should not be disconnected from the EU's more established capabilities and, therefore, that the ESDP comprises one aspect of the broader security roles of the Union – which in turn relate to the perceptions of threat discussed in Chapter 7. These actor roles may be characterized in terms of their scale and geographical scope, their multilateralist intent and operation and, in distinct contrast to NATO, the multifunctionality of their methods.

Limits

The language of the ESDP is not helpful in divining its purposes. The use of the word 'defence' might imply a commitment to the territorial defence of Members. Although there is a tantalizing reference in the Treaty, collective defence of the territory of the Union continues to be covered under Article V of the North Atlantic Treaty and under the same article of the vestigial WEU Treaty. Major armed aggression against its territories is, in any event, seen as 'improbable' (European Council 2003:

3) and the ESDP is clearly not configured for territorial defence. War fighting and global power projection are not the functions of the ESDP, but stabilization and peace enforcement, with the capability to operate beyond Europe are.

The forces available and under development suggest that the scale of operations is likely to remain relatively small. Future planning envisages ESDP forces that are much more rapidly deployable and capable of undertaking concurrent operations.[33] A formal commitment to the 'Petersberg Tasks' remains in the Treaty but considerations of the future role of the ESDP, in the Security Strategy and elsewhere, reveal the emergence of a broader agenda. The Strategy highlights the need to think of a 'wider spectrum of missions' that might include: joint disarmament, support for third countries in combating terror and security sector reform in the context of wider institution building (European Council 2003: 12).[34] The use of force is permissible in cases of state failure 'should it prove necessary, as a last resort' (Council of the EU 2004c: 6). There is also a responsibility for the international community to intervene 'where there is a serious risk of large scale loss of life, ethnic cleansing and acts amounting to genocide' (ibid.).[35]

In conjunction with the other capabilities of the CFSP, there is also the possibility of intervention in the face of terrorist or criminal activity in a third state. Military action may in certain circumstances be justifiable, when a state is 'unwilling or unable to deal with the threat posed by a non-state actor on its territory' (ibid.: 12). Transnational threats of this type, posed by terrorist groups or organized criminal activity, are to be addressed by a range of EU capabilities. The ESDP contribution has been evident in the police missions deployed in Bosnia-Herzegovina and Macedonia which, alongside the provision of support and training to the local authorities, have had an operational role in countering transnational organized crime. Such activities have direct internal implications for the EU in terms of drugs and people trafficking and have been strongly supported by Member State governments uneasy with military interventionism, as being consistent with the EU's civilian tradition (Hansen 2004: 183).

There was intense debate in the Council about the circumstances in which the Union might use its newly acquired capabilities as a security actor (Haine 2004b: 19–20). Highly controversial, and requiring a significant change in the original draft of the Security Strategy, was the question of the need to act before 'countries around us deteriorate' where 'Preventive engagement can avoid more serious problems in the future' (European Council 2003: 11). The original draft presented to the Thessaloniki Council of summer 2003 employed the word 'pre-emptive' rather than 'preventive'.[36] Nonetheless, the final draft still refers to the need to develop a strategic culture that fosters early, rapid and, when necessary, robust intervention (European Council 2003: 11).

In terms of where the EU will exercise an active security role, the Balkans has provided the initial focus and represents a critical test of the credibility of the whole CFSP, including long-standing civilian interventions (European Council 2003: 8). The enlargement process may have enhanced security but it brings the Union 'closer to troubled areas'. The task is, then, 'to promote a ring of well-governed countries in the East of the European Union and on the borders of the Mediterranean with whom we can enjoy close and cooperative relations' (European Council 2003: 8). There is also 'a strong interest in events in the Southern Caucasus' (ibid.). These developments, along with the expressed intention of the Ukrainian and other NIS governments to seek EU membership, have led to a situation in which there is a new and highly significant strategic dimension to the EU–Russia relationship. Having worked to develop a special partnership with NATO, the Russian government is now confronted with a situation in which the European security system is increasingly superintended by the EU (Webber *et al.* 2004; Lynch 2004). Both Russia and the EU are jointly concerned with instability on what has or will become their common borders (for example Moldova in the case of Romanian accession). Such issues will have to be resolved jointly and the Russian government has established a monthly meeting with the PSC. The military instruments of the ESDP would never be deployed in these areas without the support and collaboration of Russia.

Beyond Europe, the Union recognizes the strategic priority of the Arab–Israeli conflict, but its interventions in the Middle East are likely to retain an exclusively civilian character, not least because of the dominant position of the United States in the region. Thus one of a range of limits upon the military potential of the ESDP is that forces would not be used in circumstances where either Russia or the United States was opposed. Both the latter states are permanent members of the Security Council, enjoying the right of veto, and the concern of France and Germany with maintaining good relations with Russia and of the Atlanticist Member States with the US would also come into play.

While the Balkan operations, with a direct and local relationship to the security of the Union, were long-expected and planned, operation *Artemis,* the sudden intervention in the Democratic Republic of Congo in the summer of 2003, was not. Executed at the request of the UN Secretary General to provide a bridging force between two UN deployments in the town of Bunia, it provides a clue to the future military role of the Union. This would focus upon the ACP and the special and continuing relationship of Europe's ex-colonial Member States with Africa in particular. Once again military instruments would complement the other activities of the CFSP in development aid, the promotion of good governance and the protection of human rights. They would also tend to be something of a last resort if a military solution through the funding of African Union forces (on the model of the Sudan conflict 2004) was unavailable.

Multilateralism

'The UN is at the core of the EU's concerted efforts to re-launch multilateralism as a general and widely accepted method to conduct international relations' (Heusgen 2004: 5). To this end all the previous and current ESDP police or military operations have been conducted under the aegis of UN Security Council resolutions and, given the strongly expressed views of a number of Member States and the public position established by the Security Strategy, it is doubtful whether any departure from this rule would be countenanced.[37] Indeed, on the basis of the limited but successful *Artemis* operation, the 'battlegroups' concept was explicitly linked to UN operations.[38] In addition, a number of EU members, Ireland, Sweden, Spain and France, had recent military involvement in UN peacekeeping operations. Finally, such a determination is important to the evolving security relationship with a Russian government that recalls the 'illegal' use of force in Kosovo without a UN Security Council mandate.

On the basis of these commitments, the EU has embarked upon formal collaboration with the UN based upon an initial Joint Declaration on Crisis Management in September 2004. This was followed up by discussions in a 'steering committee' composed of staff from the two secretariats, leading to a full EU–UN agreement of 18 June 2004 (European Council 2004b). Under its terms there are two ways in which the EU may support UN peace operations: either through coordinating individual Member State contributions or through an ESDP operation at the request of the UN. In the latter case, an EU rapid response capability 'would bring a particular added value' and EU forces could be employed in a 'bridging' role to provide time for the UN to mount its own operation or to reorganize an existing operation as exemplified by *Artemis* (ibid.). Alternatively the EU might provide an 'over the horizon reserve' or an 'extraction force' (ibid.).[39] These arrangements indicate that both the EU and UN Secretariat see the Union's role as that of an increasingly close collaborator in peacekeeping operations, something that is evidenced by extensive staff collaboration and the holding, in April 2005, of the first joint exercise between the two organizations.[40]

Finally, the format of actual ESDP operations demonstrates a commitment to multilateral practice, in that outsiders have always been involved. Regular contributors are the applicant countries Bulgaria, Romania and Turkey, but also Canada, which has participated in all the ESDP operations so far including *Artemis*, plus the Swiss, Norwegians and Icelanders.[41] There are continuing negotiations with nine 'strategic partners' for framework participation agreements. Three have been concluded with Iceland, Norway and Romania. Also, Member States are welcome to include elements from third states (non-EU/NATO members and accession states) in their 'battle-groups'.[42]

A multifunctional role

The EU is developing an understanding of its role as a security actor that differs both conceptually and operationally from the conventional model of a great power. While essentially still a civilian power, the role of military instruments is complementary – to provide a more robust approach. It continues to possess substantial assets in terms of existing external policies within Pillar I and its own experience of conflict management and institution building. The Security Strategy's delineation of contemporary threats – terrorism, weapons of mass destruction and failed states – are conventional enough. The difference is to be found in the nature of the response, indicating the need and aspiration to become a truly multifunctional actor. 'With new threats the first line of defence will often be abroad.' They do not have a purely military character 'nor can any be tackled by purely military means'. It follows that a mixture of instruments is required and the EU is 'particularly well-equipped to respond to such multi-faceted situations' (European Council 2003: 7). Furthermore:

In almost every major intervention, military efficiency has been followed by civilian chaos. We need greater capacity to bring all the necessary civilian resources to bear in crisis and post crisis situations.

(ibid.: 12)

These points are exemplified in the Balkans, where all but one of the ESDP's military and police missions have been mounted and where Community instruments have been deployed. These involve extensive conflict prevention activities and action to provide police and judicial support and to counter drug trafficking and organized crime (Commission 2001c). The challenge, at one level, is to establish more coherence between Community instruments and the new interventionary capabilities of the ESDP, when these are located within different Pillars and where institutional turf and budgets are jealously guarded in Brussels. Previous ineffectiveness has been recognized and the objective is to establish the capability 'to conduct concurrent civilian operations at different levels of engagement' and to 'deploy multifunctional civilian crisis management resources in an integrated format' (European Council 2004a: 3). This would be assisted by reform of the pillar structure, but the lesson of previous experience with the CFSP is that, once initial organizational misgivings have subsided, ways will be found to make the system work.

Internal and external aspects of security are indissolubly linked and thus involve not only the ESDP and the Community but also Pillar III, Police and Judicial Cooperation on Criminal Matters. In this respect the Security Strategy makes specific reference to the 'trafficking of heroin (90 per cent from Afghanistan where poppies pay for private armies) and women (200–700,000) most distributed through Balkan criminal networks' (European Council 2003: 5). The attempts to combat transnationally organized terrorist groups encounter a similar situation. The logic of the interconnection is undeniable, but so are the problems of devising a coherent policy. This is, however, not a difficulty unique to the European Union.

Attempts to bring coherence to these developing areas of policy are only in their infancy, but will be important to the future effectiveness of the Union as a multifunctional security actor. Within the Council itself there have been attempts to initiate a dialogue between CIVCOM and CATS (the Article 36 Committee of senior national officials). The latter Committee serves to coordinate national police and judicial cooperation under Pillar III. Member State Chiefs of Police have also been encouraged to 'actively and jointly engage in aspects of civilian crisis management' (European Council 2004a: 6). The need to pull intergovernmental activities together was underlined by the appointment by the High Representative of a counter-terrorism coordinator with a 'brief to coordinate action in terrorism matters inside the Secretariat and between different Council bodies as well as liaising with the Member States' (Nilsson 2004: 13).

Conclusion

The European Union grew up in the shadow of the Cold War and under the protection of NATO. After the collapse of attempts at defence integration in the early 1950s, it effectively became a non-military actor with a civilian identity. The momentous events of 1989 created both opportunity and widespread expectations for change. Much of the ensuing decade was spent in experimenting with the WEU and the creation of a European Security and Defence Identity within NATO, while the Balkan wars focused attention on the need for the Union to augment its civil capabilities with military instruments. The result was the ESDP, which proceeded to conduct its first operations during 2003 and which continues to develop its military and policing capabilities.

The ESDP has a highly intergovernmental character and the new structures for 'crisis management' have thus been developed within the Council Secretariat. In terms of policies and institutions, the ESDP is embedded within the Common Foreign and Security Policy. It provides it with additional instruments while supporting its normative positions and commitment to multilateralism. As we have seen, it is also beset by the problems posed by the separation of the Pillars and the need to articulate military, police and judicial assets contributed by Member States with extensive Community action in the same area. Achieving this, rather than the more visible 'headline goals' of forces committed to the ESDP, will probably be the ultimate determinant of effectiveness.

Do these developments, as some have argued, alter the established civilian identity of the Union in global politics? To the extent that there is now a demonstrated willingness to use force in support of crisis management operations there has been a change. This can be employed to rebut the negative assertions of commentators, such as Kagan (2002), who make unfavourable comparisons between a potent and war-like United States and a pacific and ineffectual European Union. As we observed in Chapter 2, it is very difficult to discuss identity without becoming involved in some form of binary opposition to the United States and much of the recent discourse concerning the Union's security role, and indeed the detailed arguments within the ESDP about such matters as headquarters, are inherently concerned with the extent to which the EU represents an alternative model to US hyper-power.

We conclude that the EU does retain an alternative identity and that its acquisition of limited military instruments does not imply militarization or an attempt to emulate US approaches to security. The EU, unlike NATO, is not a defence organization and does not possess the capacity for large scale war-fighting. Its submission to the UN High Level Panel reads like a critique of US security policy since 2000. Military intervention is only justifiable for the EU if there are no other valid options:

> ... the means should be proportional to the objective, taking into account the need to prevent the recurrence and to ensure the stability necessary for reconciliation and reconstruction; and that it should carefully weigh the consequences of action against the consequences of inaction.
>
> (Council of the EU 2004c: 8)

In contrast to the Coalition's experience in Iraq from 2003, ESDP operations will not be conducted without Security Council authorization and appear to attract participation from a wide range of non-members. The character of the ESDP is exemplified through the position of a Member State like Sweden. On the one hand

Swedish troops, deployed in the *Artemis* operation in the Congo, took robust military action when required. On the other, the presence of Sweden in the Council and the PSC ensures that there can be no resort to aggressive or unlawful conduct. Although the need for consensus in the Council may be portrayed as a restraint upon the possibility of decisive military action, it also has advantages in ensuring that such action will not be precipitate and will reflect the pacific and internationalist traditions of European societies along with the military pragmatism of Member States such as Britain and France.

There is a further set of contrasts between the European and US approach, in terms of the very limited role that force has been allowed to play within European security policy. This continues to emphasize the civil dimensions of EU identity and action that have been elaborated in the preceding chapters of this book, along with the powerful and transformative security implications of the EU's presence. Thus, for example, the Council's submission on UN reform also drew 'the Panel's attention to the importance of the International Criminal Court' (ibid.: 5) and dealt extensively with the consequences of global warming and the need for 'a collective willingness to design and implement the necessary policies and measures' to cope with this threat (ibid.: 3). A multidimensional civil identity continues to be at the core of the EU's external persona. ESDP is designed to support this and will not fundamentally undermine the EU's identity, provided that the habits of cooperation developed elsewhere in the CFSP, relating to the use of economic instruments and inducements, are also applied to this significant additional capability.

Conclusion

The European Union is a political system under construction – a moving target that can frustrate the best efforts of the analyst. This is the result of its own expansionary dynamic, the power of promises made and expectations raised. Since our first edition the EU has enlarged from fifteen to twenty-five countries, further extending its borders with the Russian Federation. It faces new challenges to the East, both in constructing an effective strategic partnership with Russia and in offering, to former Soviet Republics, a form of enhanced relationship that will meet their demands without the prospect of immediate membership. The European Neighbourhood Policy attempts to provide this.

The promise of Turkish membership has hardened into accession negotiations and others, in the Balkans and elsewhere, wait expectantly in the wings. This continuing process of enlargement must provoke anxiety concerning the Union's ability to meet expectations and to fulfil its roles as a global actor. The Constitutional Treaty, agreed by the Member States in 2004, attempted to provide a more efficient structure for an enlarged Union; but has suffered with popular rejection.

We argued, in the first edition, that the Union held up a mirror to the contemporary international system and was in many ways uniquely suited and equipped to cope with its complexities. Since this pre-millennial statement the international situation has changed in ways that both threaten and provide opportunities for the Union. Opportunity provides the external context of actorness, both in terms of ideas and events. The effects of the Al Quaeda terror attacks upon the United States of 11 September 2001 reverberated across the system. The Union, which was to suffer its own terrorist atrocities in Madrid in March 2004 and London in July 2005, became heavily involved in using both its internal and external capabilities to deal with a continuing yet ill-defined terrorist threat. Counter-terrorism became a new and important sphere of action for the CFSP that included commitments to deal with the associated problems of failed states and weapons of mass destruction. These actions, which had a largely civil character, were in marked contrast to the very militarized response of a wounded United States.

When the US administration also took the opportunity to launch a full-scale attack upon Iraq, in the spring of 2003, with the objective of finally removing the Baathist regime of Saddam Hussein, the challenge to the Union was acute. The Member States were almost equally divided upon the legitimacy of the invasion;

some actively participated (Britain, Spain, Italy and Portugal) while others (France and Germany) led opposition at the UN Security Council. Public opinion across the Union was largely opposed, with hostile demonstrations of unprecedented size occurring on the streets of European capitals on 15 February 2003. After inconclusive Council meetings, and embarrassing public dissension between Member States, the Union remained a bystander. With hindsight, this failure to respond may reflect the wisdom of inaction as much as the paralysing inconsistencies of the CFSP. Rather than destroying the ESDP at birth, divisions over Iraq had no discernible effect. Indeed the first three ESDP operations occurred in 2003.

The Iraq war sharpened transatlantic divisions that were already evident across a range of issues. The Kyoto Protocol on climate change, in which the Union had invested so much, was finally rejected by the incoming US administration of George W. Bush – along with a raft of other multilateral projects. The abdication by the US of its previous role as environmental leader, the militarization of its foreign policy, the contempt it expressed for the UN system and its active opposition to a range of human rights and international judicial concerns, accentuated a discourse of EU responsibility. Many now placed a counter-hegemonic duty upon the EU as the only body large enough and principled enough to oppose the United States.

Although bound to cooperate with the United States, particularly at the WTO and in the construction of the ESDP, the Union was still able to meet at least some of the expectations that had been raised and to exploit some of the opportunities offered. The pursuit of Kyoto ratification in outright defiance of US wrecking activities was the most prominent example, but the struggle over the International Criminal Court and the pursuit of a human rights agenda that included opposition to the death penalty provide others. Grasping all of these opportunities required actor capability in the mobilization of international opposition.

These were not the only new opportunities that became available to the Union. In Europe, the challenges of enlargement provided the opportunity for new neighbour-hood policy and the expectation that the Union would act to consolidate and control its borders. The discourse on Turkish accession was coloured by the events of 9/11, to the extent that the EU now had a new destiny to demonstrate that peaceful accommodation between Christian and Muslim societies was possible. Increasingly, the EU was regarded as having the primary responsibility, in the Balkans and elsewhere, for re-shaping the economic and political map of the continent. The disastrous condition of Africa also led to expectations of EU responsibility, founded upon ex-colonial ties and the long-standing ACP relationship. As we have seen, they were reflected in actions in the Congo and in support for the African Union.

In the international economy the collapse of the WTO Millennium Round at the end of 1999 generated expectations that the EU was already equipped to fulfil, in engineering a new Doha Round that attempted to meet the demands of the Group of 20 developing countries. Further intriguing opportunities opened up as China joined the WTO, overtook Japan as an EU trading partner and began to engage in a political relationship with the Union.

All these activities were underpinned by the presence of the Union. The growth in the size and area of the EU, through enlargement in 2004, is central here. A Single

Market containing over 450 million people, with its own currency and internal regulations, exerts continuing attractive effects upon outsiders. There are clear indicators of presence in the increasing dependence of economies around Europe's periphery and between Europe and the ACP Group. Some aspects of presence arise from the largely unintended implications of internal regulations. Thus we have observed how the Union has become a global regulator – in product and environmental standards and in competition policy. This is another way in which the Union has been in successful competition with the United States. Such presence has a structural quality, in that, although no specific external actorness is involved, outcomes will be determined by the dominant position of the Union because of its ability to write the rules by which others operate.

Collective identity mediates between opportunity and action and links the Union's presence, and understandings about its capabilities, in constructing expectations concerning EU practices. We have described the growth of exclusive and inclusive identities. Exclusive identity is reflected in policies to protect the integrity of the Single Market, in the construction of new borders around the enlarged Union and in policies to control immigration and combat transnational organized crime. In an era of increased migration and post-9/11 anxiety, the identity of 'fortress Europe' has moved well beyond its original context, which was the assumed erection of barriers against US economic competition in 1992. Other identities are more value-based and inclusive – as a promoter of human rights and sustainability and as a model of regional integration. The European Neighbourhood Policy struggles to resolve the inclusive/exclusive contradictions, just as trade policy must now attempt to reconcile the identity of self-interested market opener and aggressive economic liberalizer with the value-based identity of champion of sustainable development.

There is also a sense in which identities are a dimension of presence. The EU may represent an attractive vision to outsiders, something that transcends hard calculations of economic and political interest by potential applicants. Most intriguing is the contemporary discourse of the good life. Rifkind (2004), amongst others, has argued that the approach to welfare and quality of life issues now constitutes a 'European dream' with which to identify. It is supposedly supplanting the 'American dream' of unfettered economic freedom, opportunity and individual responsibility. The latter, founded upon the myth of an ever-expanding frontier, no longer has relevance to a more constrained and 'networked' world to which the Europeans are well-adapted.

Clearly presence is central to an understanding of the construction of actorness. Here a generalization would be that presence denotes latent actorness. However, the relationship between presence and actorness is not direct. It is mediated by the patterns of constraint and opportunity afforded by the external environment in which the EU operates; and by the capacity to respond. This last is central to the complex and uncertain relationship between presence and actorness. It denotes the political will to create a European actor capable not only of responding to external expectations but of actively contributing to the construction of understandings and practices which in turn shape the expectations of others.

Actor capability

At the centre of our study is the question of actor capability, or actorness – that is, the extent to which the EU has the capacity to exploit opportunity, to capitalize on its formidable presence, and thus to function effectively as a global actor. We identified, in Chapter 1, a number of requirements for actorness. Of these, the most significant concern the ability to formulate and implement external policy. They can be studied at three distinct levels – shared commitment to a set of overarching values, the ability to provide overall strategic direction for EU external activity, and the everyday requirements of policy-making and implementation, including the availability of policy instruments.

At the highest level, commitment to the Union's values is strongly articulated and frequently reiterated. As we have seen, understandings about values are central to constructions of the Union as a normative actor, and hence to expectations, both within and beyond the EU, that action will be consistent with values proclaimed. Thus, in a very general sense, the Union's identity as a value-based community provides a framework for external action. This identity is, of course, contested. Moreover, it does not provide the strategic direction necessary for policy prioritization and for the formulation of proactive, consistent and coherent policies across the range of issue areas in which the Union acts externally.

In the first edition we argued that lack of overall strategic direction was an impediment to EU actorness. External policy had tended to be *ad hoc* and reactive. Beyond the prioritization of relations with Eastern and Southern neighbours, which has led to the Union's current position as a major regional actor, policies have been shaped by Member States' historical or post-colonial ties. As we saw in Chapter 5, this has resulted in a 'patchwork' pattern of development policies that do not fully accord with the Union's value-based commitment to poverty eradication; nor with interest-based constructions that would suggest that Asia be given higher priority.

The European Security Strategy attempts to remedy the lack of overall direction that has afflicted the Union. It provides an assessment of 'global challenges and key threats', which encompass the full range of the Union's activities, suggesting a comprehensive approach to security (European Council 2003: 3–5). Three 'strategic objectives' are identified – addressing key threats, promoting security in the Union's 'neighbourhood' and supporting 'an international order based on effective multi-lateralism' (European Council 2003: 9). As we saw in Chapter 7, these objectives provide a systematic statement of policies already pursued by the Union, albeit reframed within a security discourse that may be discordant with aspects of the Union's value-based identity.

In order to achieve its objectives, the Security Strategy acknowledges that the Union must be more proactive and more capable if it is to fully exploit its presence – that is, 'to make a contribution that matches our potential' (European Council 2003: 11). Enhanced capability, of course, depends upon the more mundane aspects of actorness – and hence upon the ability to address the problems of consistency (between Member State and EU policies) and coherence (internal coordination within the Commission and between Commission and Council) that we have encountered in previous chapters. It is probable that, as the Union enlarges, problems of consistency will be exacerbated, and that a balance will need to be made between size and effectiveness. Coherence problems, particularly in relation to cross-pillar coordination, also need to be addressed. The Constitutional Treaty attempted to deal with these matters, and its rejection can only be a setback to the aspirations contained in the Strategy.

For a consideration of the Union's ability to formulate consistent and coherent policies, trade must be the starting point. Exclusive Community competence for the Common Commercial Policy has meant that trade policy priorities have been articulated by the Commission, and that inconsistencies between Member State policies have been resolved into a single external policy. In consequence, the distinctive approach of the EU, and especially its predilection for multi-faceted preferential agreements, has become a feature of the international trading system. This is not to disregard the influence of national commercial interests in the Council and 133 Committee, which can give rise to mean-spirited and protectionist outcomes. Agricultural policy remains a central issue in the trade regime. Difficulties in reforming the subsidy regime of the Common Agricultural Policy have continued to complicate the Union's approach to the world trade regime. However, the problem of reconciling entrenched sectional interests with trade liberalization is shared with the other major players, especially the United States. The latter, with the Union, has exercised an effective duopoly over the trade regime that has only recently been challenged by the G20 group of developing nations.

The introduction of the euro represented a huge extension to the economic presence of the Union. It also remains a primary example of the way in which presence will not necessarily promote actorness. For a range of reasons, including the incomplete Member State membership of the eurozone, the absence of a single European seat at the IMF, and disinclination among participating Member States for the euro to assume a major role as an international currency, the EU is not yet an important monetary actor. Nevertheless, the effects of its presence may be profound.

Mixed competence for environmental issues has the potential to cause problems in the formulation of external policy. Yet differences between the Member States have not meant that EU policy has been immobile or reduced to the lowest common denominator. Some incoherence in terms of defining the overall objectives of the Union is inherent because of the intersectoral character of environmental policy. Achieving coherence between environment, trade, agriculture, transport, energy use and development represents the holy grail of sustainability policy. Progress may have been limited, but the Union has attempted to take the lead in making these connections. Despite the negotiating difficulties arising from mixed competence, the EU has established itself as the leading player in global environmental politics. Its successful promotion of the ratification of the Kyoto Protocol was a real demonstration of multi-dimensional actorness.

Development policy is a somewhat different case. Here, the Community has its own long established approach to development cooperation with ACP countries. While the central elements of the EU–ACP relationship – partnership, trade concessions and economic assistance – have persisted over time, the notion of equal partnership has become increasingly debased. A growing range of conditionalities has been imposed upon the ACP 'partners', and action taken to interrupt relations in cases where human rights or democracy provisions have not been met. In recent years the Union's political and security priorities have increasingly intruded upon EU–ACP relations. Here, the attempt to divide the ACP Group into regional Free Trade Areas, through negotiation of Economic Partnership Agreements, reflects the Union's commitment to export its own model of conflict resolution and economic development. Undoubtedly, in EU–ACP relations, the Union is more than ever dominant. Nevertheless, EU development policy operates alongside the, sometimes competing, national policies of Member States, and can result in duplication or inconsistency 'on the ground'. This parallelism, which inevitably undermines the overall effectiveness of EU (Community and Member State) efforts, was prioritized for action by Development Commissioner, Louis Michel, in 2005.

Policy towards Asia and Latin America does not share the distinctive, highly institutionalized character of EU–ACP relations; nor is it dealt with by DG Development. Here, problems of consistency have been evident, not only through the operation of parallel policies, but also in relation to policy prioritization. Relations with Asia have been particularly problematic. Nevertheless, there is evidence that, in the post-9/11 context, the European Security Strategy is providing a framework for policy prioritization. Again this may prove inconsistent with the Union's commitment to poverty eradication.

Humanitarian assistance is a further area where Community and Member State policies operate in parallel. Here, however, there is relatively effective coordination and a strong commitment, within the Commission, that the political neutrality of this policy area must not be compromised. The ability of ECHO to operate relatively independently, particularly in the disbursement of funding, has also avoided internal problems of coherence that can arise as a consequence of the separation of development policy-making from the implementation phase, which is entrusted to the EuropeAid Cooperation Office. In the field of humanitarian assistance, the Union's claim to be the world's pre-eminent actor has credibility.

Relations with candidates and neighbours have been, and remain, among the foremost priorities of the Union. The granting of a membership perspective is the most potent policy instrument available to the Union, and there is no doubt that it is used to some effect. The acceleration of the processes of reform in Turkey, as membership became more evidently attainable, attests to this. In the Western Balkans, too, the decision (in early 2005) to delay accession negotiations with Croatia on the grounds of inadequate compliance with the International Criminal Tribunal for Yugoslavia is instructive. It was followed immediately by enhanced cooperation with the ICTY by a Serbian government anxious to embark upon the road towards EU membership. It is in the Balkans, moreover, that all the policy instruments available to the EU are in use. There is no doubt that the Western Balkans provide a test case for the credibility of the Union as an actor. Here, consistency between Member States is not a major issue, although disagreements can arise on matters of detail. However, ensuring coherence between policies and policy instruments can be an issue, as we saw in Chapter 8, which highlighted the coordination problems between the Commission and the ESDP relating to the civilian and military instruments of crisis management and post-conflict reconstruction.

Policies towards neighbours are more problematic. In the context of the 2004 enlargement, the Union's ambitions towards Eastern neighbours are relatively recent. They also raise issues of great sensitivity for Russia, and here Member State governments are divided between those (notably France and Germany) wishing to placate Russia and those (particularly new Eastern members) eager to prioritize demands for closer association, or EU membership, emanating from Ukraine and other NIS. The longer established relations with Southern neighbours are also troubled by problems of consistency, not least because of the residual effects of colonialism. Nevertheless, the Union's multi-faceted Euro–Med Agreements, and the related Barcelona Process, represented an ambitious and innovative approach to a troubled region that faltered, primarily, as a consequence of deterioration in the situation in the Middle East. Here, the Union has gained unprecedented recognition as a member of the Quartet (alongside Russia, the UN and the US) in supervising the Middle East Peace Process. There is an aspiration that, following progress in the MEPP, the Union will become the principal player in the region. Certainly this would accord with its substantial economic roles as aid donor and trade partner.

In 2003, the Union's approach to Southern and Eastern neighbours was encapsulated in the European Neighbourhood Policy. This represents an attempt to produce major incentives, initially short of a membership perspective, that would provide the Union with more systematic policy prioritization and strengthened policy instruments. Early indications suggest considerable interest in this initiative among Southern and Eastern neighbours.

The EU has struggled for years to achieve a common foreign policy that would articulate the diverse aspects of its external relations and be in some way commensurate with its presence in the world. In no other area have rising expectations so exceeded performance – and this has been reflected in attempts to reform the CFSP at Amsterdam, Nice and at the Constitutional Convention that negotiated the major changes contained in the Constitutional Treaty.

In the previous edition of this book we referred to the CFSP's 'sorry record of inconsistency, from German recognition of Croatia through to the divergent paths taken by Member States over Iraq'. Since then, the difficulties over Iraq have been accentuated. Nevertheless, there have been a number of positive trends. These include a higher volume of CFSP activity, an enlarged scope for political dialogue with significant third parties and a greater propensity for the Member States to act through the EU at the United Nations. The appointment of a High Representative for the CFSP, in 1999, has also contributed significantly to its focus and visibility. In our interviews with Missions we specifically asked if their perspective on the EU had changed since the late 1990s. Without exception they replied that it was increasingly recognized as a foreign policy, as well as a trade and aid, actor. Independent statements by important third party governments such as China, and the level of contact that they maintain with the Union, provide additional confirmation. However, it is not a fully developed actor by any means. There are areas of very extensive activity in the promotion of human rights and other multilateral causes, and in an understandable preoccupation with events in the Balkans. The Middle East has long been a subject for the CFSP as well but, although having some significance, it would be difficult to describe the actions of the Union in this region as proportional to its presence and strategic interests.

The reasons for under-performance, or limited actor capability, can be summarized under the headings of consistency and coherence. It must always be remembered that the CFSP is not a 'common policy' in the same sense as the Common Commercial Policy. The practical necessity for consensus in the Council remains, despite the Amsterdam provisions to the contrary. The variance between Member State foreign policy traditions and conceptions of national interest can only have been increased through enlargement to 25. The CFSP is also burdened by the inefficiencies and uncertainties that attend the six-monthly rotating Presidency. As High Representative, Javier Solana has done a great deal to bring fixity of purpose to the CFSP. Nevertheless, as was agreed, both by the Constitutional Convention and by all the Member States, a permanent foreign minister is required if the CFSP is to further progress.

The CFSP is also affected by problems of coherence, not least in relation to cross-pillar issues. This is important because most of the instruments, finance and, indeed, the dedicated external delegations of the union reside within Pillar I. It is evidently crucial to actor capability that the gap between the pillars is spanned. There have been real attempts, at the level of policy formation, to make the system work more coherently and there is evidence that initial inter-institutional problems have been subordinated to the practical requirements of working together. Nonetheless, the divide between the CFSP and most of its policy instruments remains unsatisfactory, and not the least of the conclusions of the Constitutional Convention was its resolve to demolish the Maastricht pillars.

Critics have long argued that the Union will always be a deficient foreign policy actor if it lacks military capability. The attempt to provide this in the new European Security and Defence Policy represented a critical and controversial step for the Union. It was the culmination of a period of post-Cold War re-evaluation of the European security architecture, involving the WEU and the attempt to create a European Security and Defence Identity within NATO. The structures created between 1999 and 2003 bore the marks of this, particularly in the 'Berlin-plus' arrangements with NATO. The Union acquired and used its new military and police capabilities very rapidly. Much of the inspiration for the ESDP derived from the salutary experience of the wars in Bosnia-Herzegovina and Kosovo during the 1990s, when the Union had been militarily incapable. It was no accident that its first operations were police and military interventions in the Balkans, the largest, *Althea*, being in direct succession to NATO. However, there was a very significant exception in the independent (of NATO) operation *Artemis,* staged in support of the UN in mid-2003. Thus, the decision-making structures and capabilities now exist for the EU to engage in crisis management operations, and the Union has demonstrated its actor capabilities at this level. What is incontrovertible is that, despite very widespread scepticism, the Union has become a military as well as a civil actor.

The ESDP should properly be regarded as an instrument of the CFSP, and shares in its problems. The existence of neutral and non-aligned states on the Council provides a guarantee that the ESDP will not act beyond the constraints of multilateralism or the resolutions of the UN Security Council. The ESDP also aspires to a multifunctional role, and is working to develop its police and civil capabilities. In this new area, with important civilian capabilities located in Pillar I, problems of coherence have arisen between, for example, ESDP and Community police support activities. Coherence thus continues to be a determinant of effective actor capability in countering the threats outlined in the Security Strategy, whether in terms of failed states or terrorism.

Roles in world politics

One is struck immediately by the scope of EU policies. They cover all the significant issue areas of contemporary global politics, including the military dimension of crisis management. This excludes a formal responsibility for territorial defence or any aspiration to large-scale war-fighting, but not wider strategic issues. The Union has adopted CFSP joint actions on non-proliferation, has engaged in attempts to ensure that the Iranian nuclear programme does not lead to weapons capability and has inserted anti-WMD clauses into its agreements with even the most unlikely countries. The Union is a pre-eminent economic power and trade actor. It has established itself at the centre of international environmental politics as well as being, when Community and Member State efforts are combined, the largest funder of development and humanitarian assistance. It has come to dominate its own region. There are no actors with a comparable range of interests, policies and relationships in the contemporary system. On this basis we have attributed to the Union three broad roles – as a model, as a promoter of its proclaimed values, and as an alternative to the USA.

Its role as a model, closely associated with its presence as a security community and a template for the 'good life', is of long standing. The attraction that it exerts has altered the shape of post-Cold War Europe. The role is actively pursued through the EU's insistence on negotiating with regional groupings, whether composed of its Mediterranean neighbours, the Latin American members of Mercosur or the African, Caribbean and Pacific countries.

The Union has translated its value-based identity into normative action, as promoter of human rights and sustainability across the international system. As a development and humanitarian actor the Union is distanced from the imperial legacy of the Member States and has developed a distinctive approach. Nevertheless, the provisions of the European Security Strategy imply the subordination of value-based priorities, such as poverty eradication and environmental protection, to the security of the Union. The Strategy is quite clear that the first line of the Union's defence should be abroad; its interpretation, in future practice, may come to undermine the Union's value-based identity.

Since the collapse of the Soviet Union, the international system has had a unipolar structure. Increasingly ill at ease with US hyper-power, politicians and commentators as diverse as Jacques Derrida and Jeremy Rifkind have cast around for a counter-hegemonic alternative – and found the European Union. For French governments, it is a question of re-balancing the system by ensuring the autonomy of the Union, and for the Chinese a shared interest in 'democratic' international relations. This construction of the Union's role and duty overlays all the particular ways in which the

Union has found itself confronting the United States at WTO disputes panels, environmental conferences and discussions of the development of the international criminal justice system. It has crystallized into an alternative identity and even a rival 'European dream'. Many within the European Union are unhappy with a construction that undermines a long tradition of transatlantic solidarity and might seem to deny the necessity of cooperation with the sole remaining superpower. Yet, whether they approve or not, the enlarging scope of Union presence and actorness, that we have attempted to chart in this book, invests this role with a certain inevitability.

Notes

Introduction

1 At that time the principal challenges facing the Union were conclusion of accession negotiations with the ten candidate states now members of the Union (since May 2004) and introduction of the euro, successfully accomplished in January 2002.
2 Although the TEU provides for use of qualified majority voting in specified areas relating to the implementation of unanimously agreed decisions (Articles 23 and 24) these provisions have not been used in practice.
3 Inevitably, the capacity of the Presidency varies between Member States. In terms of commitment, Member State governments have a range of orientations towards CFSP and, indeed, ESDP, that reflect, *inter alia*, traditions of Atlanticism or of neutrality or non-alignment. These matters are discussed in Chapters 7 and 8.

1 Conceptualizing actors and actorness

1 For a representative sample of this literature see Buzan (1991), Deudney and Matthews (1999) and Vogler (2002b). Environmental security has even been considered as an issue of potential concern to NATO (see Leitzmann and Vest 1999).
2 Here, too, there have been important, recent developments in the literature, in IR generally and (to a lesser extent) with specific reference to the European Union. Overviews of constructivist approaches to IR can be found in Fierke and Jørgensen (2001) and Kubálková (2001). Constructivist approaches to the EU are summarized in Christiansen *et al.* (2001) and Risse (2004).
3 An example of extreme disaggregation of world politics into a myriad of individual and social actors, where states exist merely as barriers to interaction, is to be found in the concept of 'world society' developed by John Burton (1972).
4 For example, Merle has argued that, to be autonomous, international actors must be capable of playing 'a specific role independent of their constituent members'. In consequence he dismissed the EC as an actor on the grounds that the decision-making procedures of the Council of Ministers were, at that time, subject to unanimity. We must assume that the subsequent introduction of qualified majority voting (QMV) means that, for Merle (1987: 296), the EC has become a (disaggregated) actor in those areas where QMV applies.
5 A version of this debate was expounded over thirty years ago by J.D. Singer (1961) in his 'level of analysis problem'. Singer contrasted systems level analyses with what he referred to as the 'nation-as-actor focus'. He concluded that, in explanatory as opposed to descriptive terms, '... there seems little doubt that the subsystemic or actor orientation is considerably more fruitful'. By 1961 the assumption of what came to be known as 'subsystem dominance' was strongly entrenched. Referring to a survey of the texts,

Sondermann (1961: 11) wrote '… almost without exception, the analysis is mainly "actor orientated" '.

6 Alternatively the Member States might seek to maximize their collective status through providing the EU with a credible military capability. An 'emerging united Europe' would thereby attain the status of a powerful state, perhaps then forming one pole of a tri-polar system (Jervis 1991/2: 42). It is difficult to see how this outcome could be predicted, however, on the basis of neo-Realist assumptions of an adversarial, self-help international system.

7 The Lisbon Strategy, agreed in 2000, aimed to build upon progress in completing the Single Market process and, in particular, to promote growth, competitiveness and employment.

8 It is interesting to note that Wallerstein speculated in 1988 (when his 1991 essay was originally published) about the possibilities for and implications of 'European unity' through EC enlargement to the East. This, he concluded, would 'breathe considerable new life into the existing capitalist world-economy' (1991: 63).

9 For a detailed analysis of the evolution of practice in the employment of Pillar I (EC) economic instruments in pursuit of Pillar II (CFSP) objectives, see Koutrakos (2001).

10 The 'structuration theory' of Anthony Giddens (1984) provides a starting point for much constructivist work, although the strategic-relational approach of Bob Jessop (1990) provides a more structurally oriented alternative. For a criticism of constructivist approaches, which rejects the validity of attempts to overcome the agency/structure dichotomy, see Hollis and Smith (1991).

11 Here it is instructive to examine the process by which, for purposes of environmental negotiations, the EC was accorded the status of Regional Economic Integration Organization (REIO), a UN category having a membership of one.

12 In our first series of interviews with representatives of Central and East European countries, in 1996, mentions of betrayal and responsibility were frequent.

13 See Friis and Murphy (2000) for a discussion of the EU's decision to offer membership to Albania, Bosnia-Herzegovina, Croatia, Macedonia, and Serbia.

14 This formula was routinely used by EU officials during interviews in 2003. It also features frequently in speeches by Javier Solana and others.

15 For information on public opinion, see 'Flash Eurobarometer 151: Iraq and Peace in the World' (Commission 2003a).

16 Derogations are periods of delay accorded to Member States unable for various reasons to adopt particular policies. Opt-out can be a more permanent arrangement. It is particularly prominent in relation to Economic and Monetary Union and the Schengen Area but also applies elsewhere. For example Denmark has opted out of EU citizenship.

17 It is noteworthy that the 1999 Treaty of Amsterdam introduced procedures for suspension or partial suspension of Member States which fail to respect the democracy and human rights aspects of the Common Provisions. They also feature prominently in the 1993 'Copenhagen Criteria' which set out the conditions applying to candidates for EU membership.

18 In Article 3, TEU, the Union (through the agency of the Commission and the Council) is charged with 'ensuring the consistency of its external activities as a whole in the context of its external relations, security, economic and development policies'.

19 For an excellent discussion of the concept of enhanced cooperation, and the deliberations which attended its incorporation in the Nice Treaty, see Galloway (2001).

20 The Constitutional Treaty strengthens the provisions for enhanced cooperation (Article I-44). It also provides for 'structured cooperation' in the field of Security and Defence Policy (Article I-41.6). This envisages 'binding commitments' among the most militarily capable Member States with a view to undertaking 'demanding missions'. See Chapter 8 for discussion of this measure.

21 For discussion of the changing structure of the Commission and various proposals for its reform, see Spence (2000); Nugent and Saurugger (2002); Commission (2002a).

22 EuropeAid Cooperation Office is a Directorate-General established in 2000 to manage the implementation of all development assistance to third countries – excluding humanitarian assistance managed by the European Community Humanitarian Office (ECHO).

23 This tendency is very evident in relation to trade/environment disputes. See Bretherton and Vogler (2000) and Ryborg (2002).

24 The Troika is the term given to those formally representing the Union on such occasions – at that time it comprised the Presidency (the Belgian Foreign Minister), the next Presidency (the Spanish Foreign Minister), the High Representative for the CFSP (Javier Solana) and the External Relations Commissioner (Chris Patten).

25 For discussion of the ad hoc arrangements for sanctions that pertained prior to 1993, see Macleod *et al.* (1996).

2 Nature of the beast

1 We do not intend to imply that state identities are fixed or uncontested. See Banchoff (1999) and Zehfuss (2001) for discussion of these issues. Zehfuss also provides a critical assessment of constructivist approaches to identity.

2 Association refers to a range of privileged relationships with the EU, which involve close cooperation on a range of policy areas but stop short of accession. Membership of the European Economic Area, for example, entails involvement in 'everything but the institutions' and the special relationships being developed in the context of the European Neighbourhood Policy are expected to evolve along similar lines, albeit to differing degrees.

3 See Neumann 1996 for a discussion of the processes and implications of othering.

4 Studies investigating the extent of identity change have tended to focus upon national officials interacting within EU institutions. In addition to Checkel's own work, see Egeberg (1999) and Trondal and Veggeland (2003).

5 In a series of interviews between January and July 2001 we talked with permanent Commission officials, seconded and non-seconded officials in the Council Secretariat and FCO officials about the Union's policies towards conflict prevention. While we do not claim to have carried out an exhaustive survey, the differences in perspective and orientation were marked. With the exception of the Commission officials, all those interviewed were British.

6 See, for example, the *Vision of a Responsible Europe* produced by Eurostep, a network of European non-governmental development organizations, which begins with a reiteration of the Union's declared values:

> The European Union is a community, born of a desire for peace and stability, and based upon a commitment to the values of democracy, equality, solidarity, social justice, human rights, tolerance and the international rule of law.
>
> (Eurostep 2004)

7 Is our chosen cover photograph intended to promote understandings of the EU as an ethical actor, engaged in important humanitarian tasks; or as an agent of neo-imperialism, engaged in patronizing behaviour towards African children?

8 Numerous internal and external commentators make such complaints. Particularly prominent have been exhortations from the NGO community in relation to environment and development policy. See, for example, the 2002 Oxfam report 'Rigged Rules and Double Standards – Trade, Globalisation and the Fight against poverty' (http://www.markettradefair.org). This elicited an immediate, pained and lengthy rebuttal from the Commission (http://europa.eu.int/comm/trade/pdf/oxfamreply).

9 For a discussion of the relationship between values and interests in the construction of the Union's external identity see Youngs (2004).

10   The European Neighbourhood Policy offers 'a significant degree of integration', but not membership, to a wide range of non-member states (Commission 2004a: 8). These include Ukraine, Belarus, Moldova, Armenia, Azerbaijan and Georgia to the East, and Algeria, Egypt, Israel, Jordan, Lebanon, Libya, Morocco, Syria, Tunisia and the Palestinian Authority to the South. Russia is included in the ENP but accorded 'special' status. See Chapter 6.

11   Nevertheless the assertion that 'Security is a precondition of development' (European Council 2003: 2) implies a prioritization of security concerns. This is discussed further in Chapters 5 and 7.

12   The controversy over the International Criminal Court provides an excellent example of EU/US differences. While the EU was a strong supporter of the Court, the US government made strenuous efforts to dissuade countries from ratifying the ICC Statute and subsequently launched 'an aggressive diplomatic campaign to undermine the core concepts that underpin the ICC' (Weller 2002: 694). This included unprecedented US pressure upon the (then) candidate countries for accession to the Union, which were 'torn on the rack' by the competing demands of the US and the EU (*The Guardian*, 17 August 2002).

13   Typical comments ranged from 'we must try harder to respect these important rights' to 'they [EU representatives] must understand that we have different values'.

14   The Schengen Agreement on the removal of 'internal' border checks between Member States was originally concluded between Belgium, France, Germany, Luxembourg and the Netherlands but has since been extended to include all Member States except the UK and Ireland. Norway, Iceland and Switzerland subsequently joined the Schengen area. While a Schengen member, Denmark has opted out of parts of the Schengen *acquis*, opt-outs were not made available to the members acceding in 2004.

15   The EP is only consulted on these matters, however, while the role of the ECJ has not been strong. The Court has rarely been called upon to clarify issues in this policy area.

16   This number is subject to increase as states are added to the 'negative list'. Those on this list are primarily developing states and East European non-member countries.

17   Agreements have been concluded with Hong Kong, Macao, Sri Lanka and Albania. Negotiation of these agreements tends to be complex, and hence lengthy, with third countries such as Morocco, Algeria, China and Russia requiring concessions on various unrelated issues as a *quid pro quo* for signature (Interview, DG JHA, September 2003).

18   Both the French Front National and the UK Independence Party, for example, are significantly better represented in the European Parliament than at national level.

19   Morocco's 1987 membership application, and the Union's response, should be seen in the context of decades of relative neglect of the Maghreb region, as we shall see in Chapter 6.

20   It should be noted that Ukraine's declared commitment to reform has yet to be put fully into practice. Many problems remain in relation to economic reform, democratic governance and in the conduct of public administration.

21   Citizens of Norway, Iceland and Liechtenstein also enjoy free movement rights as a consequence of their membership of the EEA (since 1991), which involves full participation in the single market without involvement in the Union's institutions. The Swiss people rejected EEA membership in a popular referendum, but were granted free movement rights in the EC–Swiss Agreement, which entered into force in June 2002.

22   The SIS is a complex, shared database, originally established in 1995, which allows police and other authorities to exchange personal identification data on persons subject to arrest warrants or extradition proceedings, or information concerning objects such as stolen cars or works of art. Following updating it is now known as SIS II.

23   Here the situation of Kaliningrad, the Russian enclave situated between Lithuania and Poland, is of interest. Following protracted negotiations, it has been agreed that Russian citizens travelling to and from Kaliningrad must apply for a 'Facilitated Travel Document'.

The difference between this document and a visa is said to be 'purely linguistic' (Shemiatenkov 2002: 5). This matter is discussed further in Chapter 6.

24 This is elucidated in, for example, *Communication from the Commission on Conflict Prevention*, which maintains that 'The EU, itself an on-going exercise in making peace and prosperity, has a big role to play in global efforts for conflict prevention. For this, it has at its disposal a wide range of instruments for long term or short term action' (Commission 2001c: 4).

3 The EU as an economic power and trade actor

1 Japan and China have GDP figures of 5.2 and 1.6 trillion euros (World Bank Group 2004, data in dollars for 2002 converted to euros). Current EU population levels display a precipitate relative decline since the 1950s, when the Union (pre-2004 Member States) represented 11.8 per cent of world population (and the US 6.1 per cent). Such a demographic trend will continue into the twenty-first century when, by 2025, the two economic giants of the millennium will each comprise no more than around 4 per cent of world population. By that time most estimates agree that, on current rates of growth and assuming that it survives as a single entity, the scale of the Chinese economy will have surpassed that of both the EU and USA.

2 The initial average level of tariff protection for goods, set by the 'six' in 1960 at 8.2 per cent, was actually lower than the average of their existing national tariffs – 9.3 per cent (Swann 1975: 238).

3 In 1958 the trade between EC members was 35 per cent of their overall total, by 1975 it was 49 per cent and by 1992, 59 per cent (Heidensohn 1995: 10). These figures are somewhat misleading because over this period the Community enlarged from six to twelve members – automatically transferring trade from the category of external to internal.

4 Customs unions are permitted if they comply with three conditions: that there is no average rise in trade barriers after integration; that tariffs and other trade barriers within the union are eliminated on 'substantially all' goods within a 'reasonable' period of time; and that fulfilment of these conditions is scrutinized by a working party.

5 The original negotiations for the ITO were based on a much more ambitious definition of the scope of an international trade regime, covering such issues as employment and social conditions but also commodity markets, investment and business practices.

6 A strong Commission presence was established in Geneva, the base of the GATT (and now WTO) Secretariat and Council meetings, where the *Maison de l'Europe* housed both the Commission's delegation and the ambassadors of the Member States to the GATT. The significance of the GATT/WTO for the EU is underlined by the fact that the only external representation of the Council General Secretariat is located in Geneva, where it services meetings of the 133 Committee and coordination meetings before specific WTO sessions. The setting up of the World Trade Organization provided a proper organizational framework for GATT activities and, in the process, regularized the position of the EC by making it a member on the same basis as the original contracting parties (WTO, Article XI, Original Membership).

7 At Maastricht a derogation was added to this general rule, whereby the Parliament was granted powers of assent over agreements establishing a specific institutional framework for organizing cooperation procedures or having important budgetary implications (Article 300(3) TEC).

8 These informal procedures, which include agreements under Article 133, are detailed in Macleod *et al.* (1996: 98–100). They conclude that, 'The practical effect of these various procedures and declarations should not be underestimated. They are observed closely in the day-to-day conduct of the business of the Council and Commission in external relations'.

9   The original creation of the Community led many corporations based in the US, Japan and elsewhere to establish subsidiaries within the tariff wall, in order to avoid the competitive disadvantages of exporting to the Community as opposed to producing within it. Between 1985 and 1990, for example, over five hundred Japanese firms established themselves within the EC market (Commission 1991c: 6). FDI grew fivefold from 1982 to 1990, the EC accounting for 47 per cent of the total (*Financial Times*, 2 June 1992).

10 The justification for this move was that the merger inevitably affected the market in which European Airbus would be the only competitor to the new conglomerate. There were a number of ramifications in terms of threats and counter-threats of trade sanctions and the requirement to negotiate directly with the US (there had already been a prior agreement in 1991) on competition matters.

11 A study in 2005 (carried out for Eurochambres) estimated that, in terms of productivity and R&D investment, the EU economy was at the level achieved by the US in 1987 and that, even if the EU managed to exceed US growth rates by 0.5 per cent per annum, it would still take the EU until 2056 to equal US productivity rates and 2123 to match its R&D (*Financial Times*, 11 March 2005).

12 There was also an acute French sensitivity over the cultural implications of allowing a services agreement that might grant Hollywood unfettered access to national cinemas.

13 The problem of Community competence, the Commission's prerogatives and the new forms of international trade persisted into the Inter-Governmental Conference that negotiated the 1997 Treaty of Amsterdam, with implications not only for the competencies of Member States but also for actor capability. At the Nice IGC, Article 133 was further amended to bring trade in services and the commercial aspects of intellectual property within the ambit of the Common Commercial Policy, but with the proviso that unanimity voting in the Council would be required on agreements covering these new areas if that was required for making internal rules and where the Community had not adopted such rules (Article 133 (5)). Matters were further complicated by a derogation (Article 133 (6)) under which trade agreements in cultural, audiovisual, educational, social and health services were explicitly made subject to the shared competence of the Community and the Member States. The Commission pushed for, and achieved, further clarification in the Constitutional Treaty.

14 For a fuller development of this argument see Gokay (forthcoming):

> With an additional ten member states from May 2004 the EU represents an oil consumer 33 per cent larger than the US. The fact is that following this enlargement 60 per cent of OPEC oil will be imported by the EU. From a purely economic perspective it would make sense for Iraq (and all other OPEC countries) to require payment for oil in euros not dollars. If OPEC were to decide to accept euros for its oil, then American economic dominance would be practically over.

15 The operative article is TEC Article 111 in which the decision-making procedures for establishing the EC as a fully-fledged international monetary actor are provided. These include: (1) the power for the Council acting unanimously to make exchange rate agreements for the single currency in relation to other currencies; (2) acting by QMV to formulate 'general orientations' for exchange rate policy in relation to other currencies; (3) acting by QMV to decide the arrangements for international monetary negotiations and the conclusion of agreements ensuring that the Community expresses a single position and that the 'Commission shall be fully associated with the negotiations'; (4) acting by QMV to decide the 'position' of the Community on international economic and monetary issues and acting unanimously to decide its representation. The right of initiative is given to both the Commission and the ECB for (1) and (2) and to the Commission alone 'after consulting the ECB' for (3) and (4). The European Parliament is only to be consulted in relation to (1).

16 EMU members are represented by five separate executive directors: two representing France and Germany respectively and three who are in other groupings involving non-EMU states. There is an incentive under the IMF rules to retain these arrangements because movement to single representation would involve re-calculation of the quotas on which IMF voting is based and the EU's would be reduced below its current 30 per cent share (McNamara and Meunier 2002: 858).

17 The finance minister who is 'president in office' has a key role in representing the Union at G7 and other meetings. When the presidency is not held by a G7 member, informal arrangements can be made to invite that state's finance minister. While the G7 continues to meet at the level of the finance ministers and central bank governors of the major industrialized countries (USA, Canada, Japan, Italy, France, Germany and UK), it has been expanded for other purposes to become the G8. By the addition of Russia what used to be the G7 annual summit meeting is now a G8 meeting and the arrangement is that, when a G8 member holds the EU presidency, they should also chair and host the summit during their term of office.

18 The relevant GATT Article VI recognizes that 'dumping, by which products from one country are introduced into the commerce of another at less than the normal value, is to be condemned if it causes or threatens material injury to an established industry'. Under these circumstances members are permitted to levy an anti-dumping duty. The controversial element in anti-dumping policy, as executed by a large staff in DG Trade, is that it is very difficult to obtain objective measures establishing that dumping has occurred and that, in the view of critics, numerous fanciful calculations are performed to serve protectionist ends (Hindley 1992).

19 An action by the EC in pursuit of the CFSP 'to interrupt, or to reduce, in part or completely, economic relations with one or more third countries' will involve the Council taking 'necessary urgent measures' and the Council will act by QMV on a proposal from the Commission.

20 In November 2001 the Commission used rules of origin to threaten the ending of preferential treatment of goods imported from the occupied territories but labelled 'made in Israel' in order to register displeasure at policy of the Sharon government (*The Guardian*, 13 November 2001).

21 The basis of the strategy is a large database recording the specific difficulties experienced by EU exporters in accessing third country markets. The data is then used by the Commission and 133 Committee to devise market-opening actions which may involve resort to the WTO disputes procedure, consultations under bilateral preferential trade agreements or, in the case of emerging markets, the setting of conditions for WTO membership.

22 They are provided for by Article 310 of the TEC, whereby the Community may establish 'an association involving reciprocal rights and obligations, common action and special procedures'.

23 A related and politically significant point is that the Council must decide Association Agreements by unanimity and an assenting majority vote in the European Parliament is required (Article 300(3)). The ACP countries were originally associated under separate articles 182–5 of the TEC, which cover the 'association of overseas countries and territories'.

24 As defined in GATT Article XXIV(8), a customs union means the substitution of a single customs territory for two or more customs territories. As with the setting up of the EEC, 'restrictive regulations of commerce' are removed within the union, while 'substantially the same duties and regulations' are applied by each member of the union towards outsiders (as in the Common External Tariff). A Free Trade Area means 'a group of two or more customs territories in which duties and other restrictive regulations of commerce ... are eliminated on substantially all trade between the constituent territories in products originating in such territories'. The Cotonou Agreement, because it is non-reciprocal and cannot be classified as an FTA, enjoys its own WTO waiver. Steps are now being taken to make the agreements with ACP countries WTO compatible.

25   Alongside arms there remain restrictions on the import of bananas and sugar, subject to special Protocols for ACP members, and rice – which should all be removed by 2009.

26   Most of the mission staff interviewed stressed the significance of their contacts in the Commission and the importance of the nationality of individual *fonctionnaires*, and indeed the 'national' characteristics of whole DGs.

27   As one Trade Counsellor put it:

> If you could get to represent your case at COREPER it would be ideal, but you have to rely upon your representatives lobbying Member States. It's like being unable to lobby a ministry when dealing with a national state. You don't cross COREPER and you have more chance of finding out what goes on in Council than in COREPER.
>
> (Interview, Brussels Mission, January 1996)

28   The historic trade problem for both the EU and USA was not only a highly adverse visible balance but also the concentration of Japanese export success in key sectors such as automobiles and consumer electronics. The closed nature of the Japanese home market, protected by a range of non-tariff barriers, some of which are both subtle and culturally specific, alongside very unsubtle agricultural protectionism, has contributed to the unbalanced pattern of EU-Japanese trade and what is regarded as its incomplete integration into the multilateral system. Investment flows were equally unbalanced with the EU during the 1990s.

29   In the face of a patchwork of VERs (voluntary export restraints) negotiated by Member States to restrain imports of Japanese consumer goods the Commission had long been attempting to negotiate on trade issues with Japan and a new Community based trade relationship was agreed in 1991, followed by a 'trade assessment mechanism' and in 1994 a dialogue on deregulation. In 2002 an agreement on the mutual recognition agreement on conformity assessment in a number of product areas entered into force. Such activities have particular importance for the EU because of the long-standing requirement to gain some sort of equivalent access to Japanese markets.

30   A continuing coolness may not have been entirely unconnected to the well publicized remarks about 'a country of workaholics who live in … rabbit hutches' made by one Delegation head (cited in Piening 1997: 152).

31   'In 2003, exports of EU goods to the US amounted to €226 billion (25.8 per cent of total EU exports), while imports from the US amounted to €157.2 billion (16.8 per cent of total EU imports).' The average annual value of EU FDI in the US over the period 1998–2001 was €162.663 million, while the equivalent figure for US investment in the EU over the period 1999–2001 was €72.041 million (Commission 2005a, Bilateral Trade Relations, http: //www.europa/comm./trade/issues/bilateral/countries/usa).

32   Since 1995 'The US is the trading partner most often concerned with the EU's complaints (24 of 57) and most frequently lodges complaints against the EU' (WTO 2002b: 20).

33   AMCHAM is the acronym for the EU Committee of the American Chambers of Commerce in Belgium. It is an extremely good source of information on Union developments and lobbies for the US corporate sector. Symptomatic of the scale of the US diplomatic operation is the six monthly 'torch-passing' procedure whereby personnel meet in the capital of the country assuming the EU Presidency (Interview, US Mission Brussels, January 2003).

34   Following the 1990 Transatlantic Declaration the New Transatlantic Agenda (NTA) was initiated at the end of 1995 and involved attempts to remove trade barriers in the New Transatlantic Marketplace (NTM) and the private sector Transatlantic Business Dialogue (TABD). Objectives were reduced by 1998 to the current framework, which is the Transatlantic Economic Partnership (TEP). The ongoing process had, by 2002, spawned over 20 different transatlantic dialogues involving both government and private sector (*E-Sharp*, November 2002: 15).

35 Blair House is a US Government residence across the street from the White House. The Commission struck this deal without the full formal backing of the Council and in the face of French opposition. It was to be a source of severe internal tension within the EC for the subsequent year, leaving the outcome of the whole round hanging in the balance.

36 According to the Commission the 'Quad' met only once from 1999–2004; 'for precisely twenty minutes ... in the margins of an OECD meeting in Paris in 2001' (Commission 2004k: 7). Others, however, have discerned its continuing influence. One close study interprets the new fragmented diplomacy as an exercise in maintaining the dominance of the 'Quad', and one in which the Union was a primary mover. Once agreement with the US had been obtained the circle of consenting nations was broadened through informal 'green room' and 'mini ministerial' meetings to obtain a tenuous agreement on the Doha agenda (Jawara and Kwa 2004).

37 It remains incomplete and the *Economist* could still portray the Union at Cancún as 'the most egregious farm subsidizer of all' although, doubtless, rivalled by what the EU Agriculture Commissioner described as the 'stone age' farm subsidy policies of the United States' (*Economist*, 20 September 2003: 13).

4 Environmental policy

1 Since 1987 more than 50 per cent of fish consumed within the Single Market have been sourced from beyond European fishing grounds. In 2001 the total catch by EU trawlers was around 6 million tonnes (7 per cent of a probably inflated world total), making it the third largest producer after China and Peru. About 40 per cent of this catch, or 2.7 million tonnes, was caught outside the boundaries of the Common Fisheries Policy (European Commission 2001d: 9).

2 Bailey (1972), for example, reviews the European Community's 'place in the world' in its first decade of existence and, while devoting a whole chapter to the 'world energy problem', makes no mention of environmental degradation.

3 It required the first major UN environmental conference, held in 1972 at Stockholm, to persuade the leaders of the European Communities, meeting in Paris, to take steps towards an environmental policy.

4 This principle, following German practice, was legally recognized in the Maastricht revision of TEC Article 174:

> The precautionary principle covers cases where scientific evidence is considered insufficient, inconclusive or uncertain and preliminary scientific evaluation indicates that there are reasonable grounds for concern that the potentially dangerous effects on the environment, human, animal or plant health may be inconsistent with the level of protection chosen by a particular country.
>
> (Commission 2003b: 21).

5 The current trend is to consolidate existing law into 'framework directives' and to adopt a more integrated and horizontal approach to the maintenance of environmental quality, with increasing reliance upon 'market based' instruments such as eco-labelling, green taxes and emissions trading. An important initiative in this regard is the IPPC or Integrated Pollution and Prevention Control, which provides for a system of controls and impact assessment covering the whole range of pollutants.

6 They included Directive 70/220 on road vehicle emissions, 75/716 on the sulphur content of fuels, 84/360 on industrial plants, 85/203 setting limits to atmospheric concentrations of nitrogen dioxide and 88/609 on reduction of emissions from large combustion plants.

7 Commission 2001d: 14–16, updated from DG Fisheries website. These 'southern' agreements have proved to be controversial and in the past DG Fisheries, in pursuit of commercial objectives, has negotiated unsustainable agreements. Although a proportion

of the compensation paid is now routinely assigned to the monitoring and sustenance of fish stocks, there must be concern over the impact of EU fishing operations on the sustainability of indigenous fishing communities.

8 In this instance the EC followed Mexico in mounting a successful challenge to the United States using the GATT disputes procedure. The Community and Mexico objected that a US ban on importing tuna caught using nets which incidentally snared dolphins was a form of protectionism; and the EC particularly objected to the 'secondary embargo' imposed by US law, whereby European companies dealing in Mexican tuna were also barred. For details see Esty (1994: 268–9).

9 The source of the problem was a 1991 Regulation to ban the import of furs from countries which had not outlawed the use of such traps (Canada, Russia and the USA). These barbaric instruments subject animals to a cruel and often prolonged death. The Environment Council responded to protests by proposing an import ban but DG Trade of the Commission opposed this on trade policy grounds. The European Parliament threatened to take the Commission to the ECJ and the issue was only resolved through agreement with the fur exporting countries in 1998.

10 The relevant case is 1970 ERTA, 22/70 Commission v. Council.

11 The involvement of the Community alongside Member States in external environmental policy was subsequently recognized in TEC Article 174 (4) – 'Within their respective spheres of competence, the Community and the Member States shall cooperate with third countries and international organizations'.

12 For example in the LRTAP negotiations, where there was internal Community competence in relation to atmospheric pollution. The most important of the subsequent rulings involved 'potential competence'. This extended ERTA principles to areas where, although there were no common rules in existence, participation of the Community in an international agreement 'is necessary for the attainment of one of the objectives of the Community' (European Court of Justice 1970, Commission vs. Council, 22/70).

13 The determination of competence will rely, *inter alia*, upon interpretation of the treaties, judicial rulings and, most significantly, on judgements concerning the fulfilment of the purposes of the Treaties (teleology). Although taking judicial form it will also, of course, be an intensely political process given the differing views of Member State governments as to the proper extent of Community powers.

14 As Benedick's (1991) rather hostile account makes clear, the extent of competence was under active dispute within the Community delegation during the negotiation of the Montreal Protocol. These negotiations were, in part, conducted during the formulation of the Single European Act, which reduced the number of areas in which Member States alone could make agreements.

15 Initially the Soviet Union was opposed to any EC participation but was subsequently prepared to agree to a new formulation, that of Regional Economic Integration Organization (REIO), that allowed recognition of the Community. The LRTAP itself was very much part of the Helsinki CSCE process, which attempted to construct bridges across a divided Europe, and the Soviet concession was apparently in the expectation that similar status would be accorded to Comecon – a long-standing ambition (Interview, DG Environment, June 1996).

16 The relevant provisions are Articles 6, 4(2b), 18 and 22 of the *United Nations Framework Convention on Climate Change*, UN Doc.A/AC.237/18 (Part II) Add.1, 15 May 1992. Also, Articles 2, 31 and 35 of the *Convention on Biodiversity*, UNEP, Na.92-7807, 5 June 1992.

17 The FAO has a role in international environmental politics, particularly in relation to the conservation of fish stocks, while the impact of the WTO is potentially enormous, although the activities of its environment committee (the CTE) have to date been confined to a discussion of legal conflicts between the provisions of MEAs and the trade regime.

18 Resolution 3208 (XXIX), 11 October 1974.

19 This was in an amendment to the draft rules of procedure, on the express understanding that this applied only to the forthcoming 'Earth Summit' and not beyond (Brinkhorst 1994: 612; Mensah 1996: 32). It was the result of what a DG Environment official described as a 'huge battle' with Member States arising from the possible implication for the EC's status at the UN (Interview, DG Environment, June 1996).

20 Similar rights were sought in relation to participation in the Commission for Sustainable Development (established as a follow-up to UNCED) and a two-year long argument ensued within ECOSOC, the parent body of the new CSD. To the usual disputes about competence and voting strength was added a new consideration arising from the fact that membership of the CSD was to be limited to fifty-three. This meant that the European Commission was demanding full membership of a body to which only some of the EU's constituent Member States would be elected.

21 The lead states mentioned in terms of climate change were UK, Netherlands, Germany and Denmark. With the very notable exception of the UK, these are the three advanced environmental modernizers often mentioned in the environmental policy literature. See Sbragia (1996: 241).

22 The precise division of competence in any negotiation is a confidential and often difficult matter, but it can sometimes be turned to advantage. As one member of a Union delegation put it: 'Negotiation is a three card game. We don't tell third parties which articles are covered by Community competence and which by Member States. They would never let you say this and it allows us to wash our dirty linen in private' (Interview, DG Environment, July 1997).

23 During the Basel Convention negotiations in Geneva there was a parallel Council meeting in Luxembourg which allowed constant reference back. Another example is provided by the fortnight-long negotiations held in Jakarta in 1995 on the biosafety protocol to the Biodiversity Convention. Here, Member States felt that the Commission was 'going too far' and matters were put on hold, while other delegations were left in ignorance of the EC position. Officials saw positive advantages in the impact that this had in 'producing a favourable outcome' (Interview, Council Secretariat DG I, July 1997).

24 The Member States of the EC were divided. Denmark and Germany pressed for immediate and extensive action while British and French governments, in line with the interests of national chemical industries, responsible for a substantial share of world CFC exports, took a more negative initial attitude.

25 Phare and Tacis funding for environment and nuclear projects between 1991 and 1995 totalled 912.4 million ECUs, while 515 million ECUs of this was devoted to action on nuclear safety. This includes the 62.5 million ECUs specifically devoted to the closure of Chernobyl under an EU/G7 action plan.

26 Before, some 20 per cent of annual pre-accession assistance of €3 billion was devoted to environmental projects. Most of the work of actually raising environmental standards had still to be done, with the costs of actual compliance with the *acquis* for new members being estimated as between €80 and €110 billion (http: //www.europa.int/comm/ enlargement/negotiations/chapters/chapter22/index.htm).

27 This involves knowledge-based decision-making; more stakeholder involvement; more development of framework legislation; more ex-post analyses on effects and effectiveness; more ex-ante (sustainability) impact assessment (EEA 2004: 3).

28 The CFP had a basis in the Treaty of Rome, in that fish were defined as an agricultural product (TEC Article 38). However, it took until the early 1980s, under the stimulus of a worldwide extension of Exclusive Economic Zones to 200 miles from national coasts, to create a common policy for the management and marketing of the fish stocks in EC waters. Almost immediately, the number of fishermen and the tonnage of trawlers subject to the policy more than doubled with the accession of Spain and Portugal to the Community.

29 This is recognized in the Commission's 2001 Green Paper on the reform of the CFP. Progress since then has been slow.

30 For an account by participants of the Cartagena Protocol negotiations see Bail *et al.* (2002) and especially the chapter by Christopher Bail.

31 See for example Vellinga and Grubb 1993; Mintzer and Leonard 1994; Nilsson and Pitt 1994; O'Riordan and Jager 1996; Paterson 1996.

32 First devised within the EC as a means of successfully concluding the Large Combustion Plant Directive (Nitze 1990: 24–5), it has provided a framework within which very different national requirements for greenhouse gas emission reductions (or in the case of the Southern members of the Union – increases) can be accommodated. Table 4.2 represents the burden sharing agreement as revised subsequent to the Kyoto negotiations. The accession countries also have Kyoto reduction targets in the range of 6 to 8 per cent but these are somewhat different because as 'economies in transition' they are allowed alternative baselines (Schreurs 2004: 47).

33 The points on developing country participation were contained in the Senate's Byrd-Hagel Resolution that made it very unlikely that the Clinton administration would ever achieve ratification of the Protocol. The Japanese position – a 5 per cent reduction on 1990 levels by 2008–12 – occupied the middle ground between the US and EU.

34 The agreement was finalized at the first post-enlargement EU–Russia summit in May 2004. There were a range of issues related to EU support for Russian WTO accession but the energy agreement appears to have been crucial. This involved an effective doubling of Russian domestic natural gas prices to industrial users by 2010 (www.europa.eu.int/comm/trade/issues/bilateral/countries/russia/pr210504_en.htm). While denying actual linkage, Russian President Putin was prepared to acknowledge that, 'The European Union has made concessions on some points during the negotiations on the WTO. This will inevitably have an impact on our positive attitude to the Kyoto process. We will speed up Russia's movement towards ratifying the Kyoto Protocol' (www.delrus.cec.eu.int/en/news_584.htm).

35 Under Directive 2003/87/EC of 13 October 2003, 'establishing a scheme for greenhouse gas emission allowance trading within the Community and amending Council Directive 96/61/EC'. There is also a 'linking directive' that relates the scheme to Kyoto's JI and CDM flexibility mechanisms.

5 The EU as development and humanitarian actor

1 In the 1980s food aid accounted for almost 50 per cent of all EU aid. However, despite an increase in its volume (from €3.2 billion in the 1980s to €4.2 billion in the 1990s), the proportion of food aid has fallen to approximately 10 per cent of total EU aid.

2 These products are subject to phased tariff reductions. Tariffs will be eliminated by 2009 for rice and sugar, and by 2006 for bananas.

3 Even provisions such as the GSP and EBA are subject to suspension in the case of countries deemed not to be respecting fundamental principles such as respect for human rights.

4 TEC Article 177 sets out the aims of development cooperation, which are to foster:

- the sustainable economic and social development of the developing countries, and more particularly the most disadvantaged among them;
- the smooth and gradual integration of the developing countries into the world economy;
- the campaign against poverty in the developing countries;
- the general objective of developing and consolidating democracy and the rule of law, and of respecting human rights and fundamental freedoms.

5 For a full discussion of the Millennium Development Goals see United Nations Development Programme (2003).

6 These are Afghanistan, Bangladesh, Bhutan, Cambodia, Laos, Nepal, Maldives, Myanmar

and Yemen. As a consequence of its record on human rights, EU preferences towards Myanmar have been suspended.

7 See Chapter 3 and, in particular, Table 3.1.

8 In 1957, in addition to the African colonies, France retained a number of small dependencies in the Pacific and Caribbean. Belgium also retained colonies in Africa (at that time Congo Brazzaville and Ruanda-Urundi). While the Netherlands retained a colonial presence in South-East Asia, and Italy had a UN mandate over Somaliland, neither had major colonial interests. Germany had no remaining colonial attachments.

9 Fuller treatment of the concept of association, its antecedents and implications, is provided by Grilli (1993).

10 There was, in particular, a need to accommodate UK arrangements with Commonwealth countries. However this was a source of controversy between the UK and French governments. Eventually, twenty African, Caribbean and Pacific countries were invited to participate in the new Convention. At French insistence, the UK's former colonies in Asia were excluded on the grounds that inclusion of these large countries would detract from the relationship with Africa.

11 While, as Figure 5.1 shows, the ACP is an artificial 'bloc' effectively created by the Community, the Group has separate legal status as an international organization, governed by the Georgetown Agreement of 1975. Thus the EU is unable to impose members upon the ACP nor, indeed, can it disband the Group.

12 The System for the Stabilization of Export Earnings (STABEX) provided for compensation payments, funded from the EDF, in respect of a range of specified agricultural products which fall outside the Common Agricultural Policy. A drop in price of more than 7.5 per cent triggered STABEX payments. In subsequent Conventions this threshold was both reduced and differentiated, so that by Lomé IV the STABEX trigger had reduced to 1 per cent for least developed ACP countries.

13 ACP debt doubled between 1981 and 1986, when it amounted to $130 billion, of which $102 billion was owed by sub-Saharan African countries. By the end of 1986 the overall ACP debt service ratio stood at approximately 34 per cent (Ravenhill 1993: 42).

14 The inclusion in Lomé II of the System for the Promotion of Mineral Production and Exports (SYSMIN) was new. Nevertheless it represented a defeat for the ACP negotiators, who had urged that STABEX be extended to include mineral exports. SYSMIN involved the financing of projects to enhance mineral output rather than compensation for falling prices, and hence was geared towards ensuring continuity of supply for EU importers.

15 This reflected not only ACP weakness but EU preoccupation with internal matters – the Single Market process and the Southern enlargement. Here, the accession of Spain and Portugal brought increased pressure for a broader approach to development policy to encompass Latin American and Mediterranean non-member countries.

16 Unlike previous Conventions, Lomé IV was to last for ten years, with provision for a mid-term review. The post-1995 revised Convention is referred to as Lomé IV *bis*.

17 The 1997 Libreville Declaration, adopted by a Summit of ACP Heads of State and Government, envisaged a 'new and even more vigorous relationship with the European Union and its Member States'. There was a commitment to 'strengthen the unity and solidarity of the [ACP] Group and retain it as a geographical entity' (http: //www.oneworld.org/acpsec/gabon, 7 November 1997).

18 Procedures for suspension of the Agreement are set out in Articles 96–8. They provide for fuller consultation between the parties than previously and institute a disputes settlement procedure that involves recourse to the Permanent Court of Arbitration in Den Haag. The procedures have been applied in the cases of Haiti, Fiji, Côte d'Ivoire and Zimbabwe (Overseas Development Institute 2004b: 4).

19 In a provision that reflects the Union's exclusionary identity (see Chapter 2), the ACP 'partners' are required to accept the return of their nationals found residing illegally in the EU 'without further formality' (Article 13.5).

20 To facilitate this, an additional institution, the ACP–EU Economic and Social Committee, has been created.

21 The regional groupings comprise West, Central, East and Southern Africa, the Caribbean and the Pacific.

22 Southern Africa was the region expected to benefit most from the EPA format: 'it is a relatively coherent and competent group and there are other political and economic factors in its favour' (Interview, ACP Mission, January 2003).

23 The Peace Facility was first used in 2004 to support the AU's peace-keeping efforts in the Darfur region of Sudan.

24 These regions are based upon existing groupings – the Economic Community of Western African States (ECOWAS) and the Central African Economic and Monetary Community (CEMAC).

25 In 2000, when the Cotonou Agreement was signed, €9.9 billion remained uncommitted from previous EDFs. In the case of the sixth EDF (1985–90) the last payment was made only in 2002 (ODI 2004a: 2).

26 Indeed several ACP representatives complained of closure of delegations. The Commission, it was alleged, had 'confused deconcentration with its own restructuring, which has involved cutting staff and downgrading delegations' (Interview ACP Mission, January 2003).

27 Integration, or 'mainstreaming', of gender issues across all policy areas has been an official policy of the EU since 1996. In relation to development policy, as elsewhere, assessments of the strategy's effectiveness have been mixed (Bretherton 2001).

28 Article 32 contains, in addition to general provisions, specific clauses relevant to the particular situations of ACP members – including protection of coral reefs and the threat posed by climate change to small island ACP states. As with gender, there is a requirement that environmental considerations are integrated across all policy areas. EU 'environmental conditionality' is dealt with more fully in Chapter 4.

29 There has been little growth in ACP exports over the past 30 years, while exports from Asia have increased significantly (ODI 2004c).

30 The Lomé *bis* financial protocol was for 12 billion ECU over a five-year period (1995–2000). Given an ACP population of approximately 6 million at that time, this provided little more than €5 per person per year (*The Courier* 1996: 23).

31 Lobbying in the complex policy environment of the EU has proved daunting even to Missions having large staffs and substantial financial resources. ACP Missions do not have these advantages. A typical ACP Mission has only three diplomats and is accredited to the Benelux countries and several other Member States in addition to the EU.

32 This proposal was strongly criticized by development NGOs as a further diversion of funds from the Union's proclaimed commitment to poverty eradication (*European Voice* 10–16 March 2005).

33 Here, there is concern that budgetization of the EDF (from 2008) would facilitate greater flexibility in the use of development funding (Interviews, ACP Missions, January 2003).

34 The EU market has been, and remains, Latin America's second largest export destination (after North America). Consequently, concerns over the operation of the common external tariff were well founded. In addition, the introduction of the Common Agricultural Policy in the 1960s severely restricted the market access of Latin American temperate products. Thus it is unsurprising that Latin American policy-makers have evinced suspicion, even antipathy, towards the EU.

35 In contrast with the EDF funded EU–ACP arrangements, these programmes are funded from the Community budget; moreover they fall within the responsibility of DG External Relations, not DG Development.

36 At this time the US government was openly 'advising' and covertly supporting the Contra rebel forces attempting to overthrow the Nicaraguan government.

37 Trade between the EU and Mercosur was valued at €40 billion in 2003 (*European Voice*, 14–20 October 2004: 14).

38 For a variety of reasons neither the EU nor Mercosur has been anxious to expedite conclusion of negotiations. For an interesting discussion of these matters, see Klom (2003).

39 Comprising Indonesia, Malaysia, the Philippines, Singapore and Thailand when created in 1967, ASEAN has expanded to include Brunei (1984) and, since the end of the Cold War, Cambodia, Laos, Myanmar (Burma) and Vietnam.

40 ASEAN members did not seek political integration and were reluctant to criticize the internal policies of fellow members.

41 The end of the Cold War nonetheless permitted the Union to conclude broadly focused cooperation agreements with Vietnam and Nepal in 1996. These agreements emphasize employment generation, primary health care and the role of women.

42 Throughout the 1990s ASEAN countries defended 'Asian values' in the context of the EU–ASEAN relationship. Myanmar's position on human rights issues, in particular forced labour, continues to cause great concern to the Commission and EU Member States, as does the detention of Aung San Sui Kyi, leader of Myanmar's democracy movement. Consequently Myanmar continues to be subject to a range of EU sanctions, including suspension from EBA arrangements.

43 Laos and Cambodia were also included at this time.

44 Participation in the EU's Galileo satellite navigation system is a further element of this enhanced cooperation.

45 For discussion of how the global needs assessment is calculated, see Commission 2003c. Areas of greatest need identified in ECHO's Aid Strategy for 2004 were Africa (Horn, Great Lakes, West Africa and Southern Africa), Asia (Afghanistan and Iraq) and the Occupied Palestinian Territories (ibid.: 7).

46 Other funding commitments in 2003 were to regions, such as the Western Balkans, where ECHO operations are being phased out, and various small allocations for measures such as training and enhancement of staff security in the field. Total expenditure for 2003 was €600,349,000.

47 The decision to combine the ECHO and Development portfolios under a single Commissioner, from 2000, represents an attempt to improve cooperation between ECHO and DG Development, which deals with ACP countries.

48 A central aim of the TEU is to give overall political direction, and hence consistency, to all aspects of external policy. The Council and Commission are jointly charged with ensuring such consistency.

49 In addition to this general inadequacy, key areas of shortfall in terms of the Millennium Development Goals were strategies to promote basic education, gender equality and environmental protection.

50 In 2002 the Commission was charged with monitoring Member States' progress towards attainment of the Millennium Development Goals.

51 A 1997 survey of Member State development policies found that seven (Austria, Finland, France, Italy, Portugal, Spain and the UK) had made no commitment to ensuring consistency with EU objectives. Only Denmark and the Netherlands had fully consistent policies, including mechanisms for implementation (van Reisen 1997: 175).

52 Despite this parallelism, competence problems of the type encountered in environmental negotiations are avoided (see Chapter 4) because the Commission enjoys full competence in relation to Community development policy.

53 While in 2001 Member States were said to 'vary in the level and reliability of information supplied' (Interview, ECHO, September 2001), refinements to the procedure in 2002 and 2003 are considered to have enhanced coordination of EU and Member State efforts.

6 Candidates and neighbours

1 The MNCs are considered to be Morocco, Algeria, Tunisia, Libya, Egypt, Israel, Jordan, Lebanon, Syria and the Palestinian Authority. Turkey also falls into this category, but has been accorded different treatment since attaining candidate status in 1999.

2 In anticipation of entry into force of the TEU (in November 1993) when the CFSP was formally activated, the June 1992 European Council identified the Southern and Eastern Mediterranean as a priority area for CFSP. The criteria for prioritization were geographical proximity, the political or economic stability of a state or region and potential threats to the Union's security.

3 At the 1999 Helsinki European Council it was decided that Cyprus would be permitted to accede to the EU even if the island, divided between Greek and Turkish Cypriots since 1974, was not reunited. This decision represented a quid pro quo for the Greek government's acceptance of candidate status for Turkey. In a referendum in April 2004, on the eve of accession, UN plans for reunification of the island were supported by the people of Northern Cyprus but rejected by Greek Cypriots in the South. In consequence the island remained divided on accession and Turkish Cypriots do not have access to the benefits of EU membership.

4 The *acquis communautaire* refers to the rights and obligations attaching to membership of the EU. It comprises:

  • The content, principles and objectives of the Treaties.
  • Legislation, statements and resolutions adopted.
  • The case law of the European Court of Justice.
  • International agreements, including those concluded by the Member States in relation to Union activities.

5 At this time 'rejoining Europe' denoted not only a desire for increased economic well-being, it also implied espousal of a set of ideas and values which could fill the political and ideological vacuum created by the demise of the Soviet system – 'participatory democracy, the market economy, the rule of law, constitutional order and social citizenship' (Kolankiewicz 1994: 481).

6 The designation of the association agreements as 'Europe Agreements' was intended to symbolize the Union's commitment (short of membership guarantees) to CEEC under-going transition.

7 See Chapter 2 for discussion of the discourses of 'responsibility' and 'return' that preceded the 1993 decision on CEEC membership.

8 To assist with this task the Commission issued detailed questionnaires to each candidate country, a practice that has continued. The responses, which comprise three thousand pages on average, relate to the work of all the Directorates General. One purpose of the questionnaire is 'to assess the ability of candidates to provide the type of information routinely required by the Commission' (Interview, [then] DGIA, September 1996).

9 The Commission's recommendation at that time was that accession negotiations should open early in 1998 with only five CEEC – the Czech Republic, Estonia, Hungary, Poland and Slovenia – deemed sufficiently prepared. However, in 2000 it was decided that the remaining five CEEC candidates – Bulgaria, Latvia, Lithuania, Romania and Slovakia – had advanced sufficiently in their preparation also to open accession negotiations.

10 Launched in 1993 as a CFSP Joint Action, the Stability Pact is an example of successful preventive diplomacy. It resulted in signature of numerous bilateral treaties regularizing intra-CEEC relations.

11 As late as February 2004 warning letters were issued to each of the candidates identifying specific concerns and measures to be taken.

12 At that time negotiations with Bulgaria on all 31 chapters of the *acquis* had been concluded. In the case of Romania four chapters – competition, environment, justice and home affairs and 'other' – remained to be closed.

13 The postponement clause can be invoked by the Council using QMV procedures in the case of Romania, while in the case of Bulgaria unanimity will be required. Romania has been characterized by high levels of corruption in both the public and private sectors. It is possible that the December 2004 election of Traian Basescu as President will promote

political pressure for Romania to accede in 2007. President Basescu adopted a populist, anti-corruption stance similar to that of Ukraine's Victor Yushchenko, to the extent of also adopting orange as his campaign colour.

Also of concern in the case of Romania are outstanding border issues with Moldova and the potential for instability in that country.

14 The Turkish constitutional court subsequently disbanded the Welfare Party on the grounds that its actions undermined the secular principles of the Turkish Republic.

15 In political terms, the Turkish government is obliged to implement decisions taken in EU fora, where it has no representation. Economically, too, the relationship has been unbalanced, with EU producers benefiting disproportionately from the liberalization of trade in industrial products.

16 Ambivalent attitudes towards Turkey within the EU, and the question of Turkey's identity as a European country, are discussed in Chapter 2.

17 Since 2003 the Turkish government has strongly urged that a settlement of the Cyprus conflict be achieved – supporting the UN (Annan) plan for a resolution and offering to significantly reduce the Turkish military presence in Cyprus. For a discussion of the positions adopted by various Turkish political groups on this and other issues in recent years, see Önis 2003.

18 A further requirement, that Turkey must formally recognize the Republic of Cyprus, was circumvented by Turkish agreement to extend the Customs Union to all new Member States. This can only provide a temporary solution, however.

19 See Chapter 2 for further discussion of these matters.

20 At the insistence of the Greek government, which considers that the identity of the Greek province of the same name would be usurped, Macedonia is traditionally referred to in full (within the EU) as the Former Yugoslav Republic of Macedonia (FYROM).

21 Following inter-ethnic conflict in 1999, Kosovo has been a *de facto* UN protectorate (under UN Resolution 1244). NATO has maintained peace-keeping forces in the province since 1999. The final status of Kosovo – as a semi-autonomous province of Serbia or an independent state – has yet to be determined.

22 Membership is very broad, participants including the UN, the World Bank, NATO, the Council of Europe, the USA, Canada, Russia, Japan and Turkey. For discussion of the creation of the Stability Pact see Friis and Murphy (2000).

23 Progress is reported in areas such as cross-border transport, trade, energy and infrastructure. Dialogue is also taking place on sensitive issues such as cross-border crime (Commission 2004f: 26).

24 Governments are required to apprehend indicted war criminals and send them to Den Haag for trial. Progress in this respect has been mixed, with particular reluctance to comply evident in Republic Srpska – the Serb dominated region of Bosnia and Herzegovina.

25 In practice, as has been the case with development cooperation (see previous chapter), the economic problems suffered by the West Balkans countries have limited their ability to benefit from trade concessions. See Commission 2004f: 29–33 for an analysis of the effects of the Union's trade measures.

26 The central issue was the continuing failure to apprehend General Ante Gotovina, who had been indicted as a war criminal by the ICTY. Nationalist opinion within Croatia regards General Gotovina as a war hero.

27 Member State governments were, in practice, divided upon the issue. Supporters of Croatia's case (Austria, Hungary, Ireland, Lithuania, Slovenia, Malta and Cyprus) argued that deferral of negotiations represented both an excessive reaction to events in Croatia and a signal to other aspirant members in the region that accession is a very remote possibility.

28 Following violent conflict between Albanian and Slav Macedonians in 2001, CFSP High Representative Javier Solana used the incentives of financial assistance and a membership perspective to persuade both sides to accept new constitutional and political arrangements

for power sharing between the communities, involving, *inter alia*, increased decentralization of authority. This comprises the Ohrid Framework Agreement.

29 Both politically and economically, Macedonia is less well prepared to undertake membership negotiations than Croatia. Indeed the Commission has reported (2004f: 36) that in Macedonia the reform process 'is still in its infancy'. While the political situation has stabilized considerably there are still tensions between ethnic groups and problems with implementation of the rule of law and excessive influence of the military.

30 The crisis was resolved following military intervention by an Italian-led 'Multinational Protection Force' – an operation which provided a precedent for the Union's ESDP.

31 At the June 2003 Thessaloniki Summit, for example, the government of Serbia and Montenegro announced that it was willing to participate in dialogue over the future of Kosovo.

32 Here a Stability and Association Tracking Mechanism is in operation. This, it is claimed, enables Union officials to support 'EU compatible reforms' and ensures that Kosovo is 'firmly anchored' in the SAP (Commission 2004f: 38).

33 Article 49 states that 'Any European State which respects the principles set out in Article 6(1) may apply to become a member of the Union'.

34 This was explicitly acknowledged in a speech in December 2004 by the External Relations Commissioner (Ferrero-Waldner 2004: 1). See Chapter 2 for further discussion of these matters in the context of the Union's inclusive and exclusive identities.

35 Action Plan negotiations were concluded, in 2004, with Ukraine, Moldova, Morocco, Tunisia, Jordan, Israel and the Palestinian Authority and commenced in early 2005 with Azerbaijan, Armenia, Georgia, Lebanon and Egypt. All of these countries already have in force 'association' agreements with the EU.

36 It is noteworthy that the European Security Strategy also prioritizes relations with neighbours – 'Our task is to promote a ring of well governed countries to the East of the European Union and on the borders of the Mediterranean with whom we can enjoy close and cooperative relations' (European Council 2003: 8).

37 This concept applies to the members of the European Economic Area – Norway, Iceland and Liechtenstein. In relations with Eastern neighbours, it was originally employed by Commission officials (prior to the development of the ENP) in the context of EU–Russia relations.

38 The dangers potentially emanating from the region are said to include – 'terrorism, cross-border organised crime, narcotics trafficking, direct migration, transit migration from other regions, transmission of HIV/Aids and other infectious diseases, environmental degradation and the proliferation of conventional and nuclear, chemical and biological weapons' (van Oudenaren 2004: 256).

39 Originally meaning 'Poland–Hungary: Aid for Reconstruction of the Economy', Phare became a generic term for assistance to CEEC candidates.

40 Tacis refers to Technical Assistance to the Commonwealth of Independent States. The current EU usage of 'NIS' reflects the poor performance of the CIS and the preference of NIS governments. The Tacis programme supports the transfer of knowledge and expertise, primarily through training programmes. Nuclear safety was an early focus but the programme has subsequently broadened in scope to include areas such as institutional, legal and administrative reform.

41 The PCAs are contractual in nature. They cover trade relations and impose obligations on partners in relation to economic and political reform. They also provide for political dialogue on security-related and JHA issues. Institutional arrangements include bilateral Cooperation Councils and Committees.

42 For a concise discussion of EU relations with Central Asian countries, see MacFarlane (2004).

43 All three countries are affected by border and/or ethnic conflicts. The Southern Caucasus has been the subject of several Joint Actions in the context of the Union's CFSP and in 2003 an EU Special Representative was appointed to coordinate these initiatives.

44 The strategic partnership notion originated in the CFSP Common Strategy on Russia (Council of the EU 1999). This was the first Common Strategy to be agreed following entry into force of the Amsterdam Treaty, which provided for this new instrument.

45 Institutional arrangements with Russia include twice-yearly summits, the Permanent Partnership Council which meets in various formats at ministerial level, a Cooperation Committee which meets at senior official level and nine Sub-Committees at technical level. There is nevertheless a sense, in Russia, that the PCA format does not sufficiently acknowledge Russia's importance in the region, and that new structures are needed (Interview, Russian official, January 2003). The priority for the Union, however, is to ensure that the existing institutions function effectively (Commission 2004g: 4).

46 Various attempts have been made by the Russian government to ameliorate this economic dependence through creation of partnerships with countries of the 'near abroad'. The most recent of these is the 2003 Single Economic Space agreement between Russia, Ukraine, Kazakhstan and Belarus. However this, like its predecessors, has yet to gain substance.

47 The situation in Moldova is of particular concern to the EU as a consequence of its border with Romania and hence, in the future, with the Union.

48 An example here is the EU–Russia summit in November 2004. Little progress was made as a consequence of EU criticism of the conduct of Ukraine's presidential election days previously (which was won by Russia's favoured candidate but subsequently overturned as fraudulent). Also a source of resentment were expressions of concern about further centralization of power by President Putin following a terrorist attack (reputedly by Chechen rebels) on a school in Beslan, North Ossetia in September 2004.

49 The new interest in Russia's 'near abroad' heralded by the ENP (and in particular its extension to the South Caucasus) is seen as 'particularly alarming' by Russia's Special Representative to the EU (*European Voice*, 9–15 December 2004: 12).

50 Ukraine remains a divided country, with a substantial minority of Russian speaking citizens maintaining an orientation towards the East, and a tradition of attempting to balance relations with Russia and the EU.

51 The first election in October was followed by sustained mass demonstrations in the capital in favour of the defeated candidate Victor Yushchenko. Perceived as popular expressions of support for democracy and a Western orientation, these came to be known as the 'Orange Revolution' – a reference to Yushchenko's campaign colour. International monitors confirmed that the election had been marred by widespread malpractice and a second election was held in late December.

52 The MNC are Morocco, Algeria, Tunisia, Libya (with which the EU currently has no formal agreements), Egypt, Israel, Jordan, Lebanon, Syria and the Palestinian Authority. Turkey, because of its candidate status, is not included in the ENP.

53 In 2000, 77 per cent of oil exports from North Africa were to the EU. The figure for gas exports was 96 per cent (Gault 2004: 179).

54 Tunisia and Morocco attained independence from France in 1956, while Algeria remained a French Department until 1962. In this latter case the complex and highly sensitive nature of Franco–Algerian relations has impinged upon the Union's relationship with Algeria. France also enjoys close relations with Lebanon and has consistently adopted a pro-Arab stance in relation to Middle East conflicts. Tense relations between Spain and Morocco, in the context of disputed territorial claims and the unresolved conflict in Western Sahara, also impinge on EU–MNC relations; and indeed upon relations between Spain and France.

55 With the exception of Egypt at 38 per cent, all MNC send more than 50 per cent of their exports to the EU. Tunisia is the most trade dependent, with 73 per cent of exports destined for the Single Market.

56 Cooperation Agreements having broadly similar features, in terms of trade, financial assistance and (bilateral) common institutions, were eventually concluded with Algeria, Morocco and Tunisia in 1976 and with Egypt, Lebanon, Jordan and Syria in 1977.

57 This was the situation at the commencement of the Single Market programme, which further threatened MNC market shares. A consequence of the concern among MNC governments was Morocco's 1987 application for EU membership. The application was rejected, on the grounds that Morocco is not a European country. See Chapter 2 for further discussion of this matter.

58 The context, here, is the 1993 Oslo Accord (or 'Declaration of Principles') which launched the, subsequently stalled, Middle East Peace Process.

59 MEDA stands for MEsures D'Accompagnement – referring to the financial and technical measures accompanying the Euro–Med Partnership.

60 The CSCE process, initiated in 1975 in the context of Cold War East/West relations, was intended to build confidence and security among the parties.

61 The political and security partnership aims to promote, *inter alia*, development of the rule of law and democracy; respect for human rights and fundamental freedoms; peaceful settlement of disputes. And to prevent, *inter alia*, terrorism; proliferation of nuclear, chemical and biological weapons; excessive accumulation of conventional arms. In one of the most contested areas of the Declaration, reference is made to the right to self-determination of peoples, within the context of international law and UN resolutions. Neither the Israeli nor the Turkish government was comfortable with this element of the Declaration (Barbé 1996: 39).

62 The third chapter includes: developing human resources through education and training; health promotion; promoting understanding between cultures and exchanges between civil societies; reduction of migratory pressures; joint action against drug trafficking. MNC governments were unhappy with the EU tendency to conceptualize migration in security terms and, at their insistence, matters relating to racism and xenophobia were added to this section of the Declaration (Barbé 1996: 35).

63 The Barcelona Process operates at various levels, including periodic meetings of Ministers for Foreign Affairs and *ad hoc* thematic meetings of Ministers, senior officials and experts. A 'Euro-Mediterranean Committee for the Barcelona Process' (at senior official level), comprising the EU Troika and one representative from each of the MNC, provides general oversight of the partnership process and carries out preparatory work for Euro–Med Ministerial Conferences.

64 MEDA II provides a further increased financial package for the period 2000–6 and was the first programme to be subject to EuropeAid's devolved management procedures (Commission 2004i).

65 Increased competition inevitably damages local enterprises. It has been predicted, for example, that, during the 12 year period envisaged for phased market opening, 2,000 Tunisian companies will be driven into bankruptcy (Marks 1996: 17). There will also be loss of customs receipts and other revenues from imports.

66 In the case of the negotiations with Morocco, for example, the Commission's position was constrained as much by Belgian, Dutch and German sensitivity over tomatoes and cut flowers as by Spanish preoccupation with fish (Marquina 1995; Barbé 1996).

67 In 2000, for example, a Common Strategy for the Mediterranean Region, with the aim of 'reinvigorating the Process and making it more action-oriented and results-driven' (European Council 2000: 1) was undermined by the outbreak of the Second Intifada only three months after its publication.

68 While tensions persist, both within the Commission and between Commission and Council, a satisfactory working relationship between External Relations Commissioner Chris Patten and CFSP High Representative Javier Solana ensured that the new arrangements from 2000 worked relatively effectively. These matters are discussed further in Chapter 7.

69 In addition to the concerns expressed by the governments of Austria, Germany and the Netherlands, the new Eastern members have a strong orientation towards their immediate neighbours and a lack of enthusiasm for Turkish accession.

70 The German government is a strong supporter of Croatia's candidacy and has shown a relaxed attitude to elements of political conditionality. The governments of the UK and the Netherlands, however, advocate strict adherence to the condition that Croatia cooperates with the ICTY.

7 Common foreign and security policy

1 At the height of this disagreement, for example, the Union's first ESDP mission (in Bosnia-Herzegovina) was launched and the planning for its second (in Macedonia) completed.
2 Michael E. Smith (2004) provides an excellent analysis of the evolution of EU foreign policy in terms of 'the institutionalization of cooperation'.
3 In 1961 the French government published the Fouchet Plan, which proposed an intergovernmental European Political Union which would coordinate foreign policy through a new institution, the European Political Commission, to be based in Paris. This proposal was rejected by the majority of Member States as a Gaullist ploy to undermine the EC.
4 The composition of the Troika has evolved over the years. It currently comprises up to four members – the Presidency, the High Representative, a Commission representative and the next Presidency.
5 Coreu transmissions have tended to be confined to relatively insignificant matters, due to Member State concerns about the security of the system. Coreu has been upgraded to a computer based messaging system, officially now called Cortesy, but the Coreu name has stuck. The upgrading was followed by increased use of the system by approximately 20 per cent annually (Interview, Council Secretariat DGE, July 1997).
6 In December 1994 the CSCE became known as the Organization for Security and Cooperation in Europe (OSCE).
7 This was reflected in the 1989 decision of the Western Economic Summit that the EC should be responsible for coordinating Western aid to Central and Eastern Europe. During the 1990s the view that 'European integration supports stability on the continent' was strongly emphasized by US diplomats (Interview, US Mission, January 1996).
8 The EC responded to the invasion of Kuwait by Iraq in August 1990 by agreeing to an oil embargo, freezing Iraqi assets and supporting United Nations sanctions. Serious divisions arose, however, when decisions had to be taken on recourse to military action, with each Member State ultimately adopting a different position (Salmon 1992).
9 The numerous Joint Actions and Common Positions adopted (which are specific in terms of aims and duration) are legal acts which together constitute the *acquis politique* of the EU. Details can be found in the Annual Reports on the operation of CFSP submitted by the Council to the European Parliament.
10 There are many examples of use of human rights conditionality, both in relations with neighbours and in the context of development cooperation. Exclusion of Myanmar from the Everything but Arms initiative is but one.
11 Martin Holland (1995) considers the CFSP Joint Action in South Africa to have been particularly successful.
12 Joint Actions included, amongst others, support for the Non-Proliferation Treaty, initiatives in relation to North Korea and appointment of a Special Representative to the Great Lakes Region.
13 TEU, Title I, Article 3 is worded thus:

> The Union shall in particular ensure the consistency of its external activities as a whole in the context of its external relations, security, economic and development policies. The Council and the Commission shall be responsible for ensuring such

consistency and shall cooperate to this end. They shall ensure the implementation of these policies, each in accordance with its respective powers.

14 A further disappointment of the TEU was its failure to accord legal personality to the Union; the power to conclude international agreements on behalf of its members remained solely with the EC, in its areas of competence. Thus, when matters fall under Pillar II (CFSP), it is necessary for individual, bilateral agreements to be made by each Member State according to national ratification procedures. Ratification by each Member State is also necessary on conclusion of 'mixed' Association Agreements with third countries, which can greatly delay entry into force of such Agreements.

15 Should QMV be used, Member States still have recourse to the so called 'emergency brake'. This is a right of veto over the taking of a decision by QMV on the basis of 'important and stated reasons of national policy' (TEU Article 23.2).

16 This would allow the Council to proceed with a decision even though one or more Member States (but no more than the Members whose votes would constitute one third of the total under QMV procedures) prefer to abstain. An abstaining Member State 'shall not be obliged to apply the decision, but shall accept that the decision commits the Union' (TEU Article 23.1).

17 The administrative duties previously attaching to the post of Secretary-General were transferred to a new post of Deputy Secretary-General.

18 The Treaty provision (TEU Article 26) states that the High Representative shall:

> … assist the Council in matters coming within the scope of the common foreign and security policy, in particular through contributing to the formulation preparation and implementation of policy decisions, and, when appropriate and acting on behalf of the Council at the request of the Presidency, through conducting political dialogue with third parties.

19 In this capacity he had, at the time of his appointment, been heavily involved with the 1999 Kosovo crisis, itself the trigger for renewed commitment to strengthen CFSP and build ESDP.

20 In terms of external representation, the Amsterdam Treaty also provided a formal basis for the practice of appointing 'Special Representatives', or envoys, with a mandate to represent the Union on particular issues (TEU Article 18.5). It was subsequently agreed that the Special Representatives should be responsible to the High Representative.

21 The arrangements were made in the context of an Inter-Institutional Agreement, which provided *inter alia* for an annual report from the Council to the European Parliament on the operation of CFSP.

22 The seniority of appointees varies between Member States, as does the extent to which Brussels-based diplomats are accorded responsibility for decision-making. Some PSC members, it is said, 'can be seen in corners frantically phoning capitals for direction' (Interview, Permanent Representation, October 2004).

23 During the crisis in Macedonia in 2001, for example, the PSC met almost daily. Members claim that the PSC is able, if necessary, to convene within thirty minutes.

24 Due to the supposed technical, 'apolitical' nature of its subject matter, the Military Committee has a permanent chair. See Chapter 8 for further discussion of this matter.

25 For a useful discussion of the agenda-shaping powers of the Presidency see Tallberg (2003).

26 The incorporation of the Development Council into the GAERC is seen by ACP and NGO representatives as denoting the subordination of development to political priorities and security concerns – a perception that is strengthened by the provisions of the European Security Strategy.

27 In passing communications to COREPER for transmitting to the Council, PSC officials try to avoid inclusion of unresolved (square-bracketed) items, thus obviating the need for COREPER to discuss PSC issues.

28 At the time of this interview, for example, the Balkans Working Group was meeting weekly in Brussels.

29 The output of Working Groups was criticized by Javier Solana following his appointment as High Representative. 'What is all this bumph? Can't we bin it?', he is said to have demanded (Interview, Council Secretariat, July 2001).

30 At the outset there were considerable differences in approach between CFSP officials and those responsible for Pillar I matters. To some extent, these have persisted. Trade officials are more content to function as a traditional secretariat, while CFSP staff are relatively eager to play a policy advice role. These differences reflect the fact that the Commission has sole right of initiative in most aspects of external economic relations, whereas policy initiation in the CFSP Pillar lies primarily with the Presidency and the Council.

31 To address this issue, an ENP Task Force has been created comprising officials from both DGs.

32 An example here is controversy, during the early months of 2005, over lifting of the Union's arms embargo against China.

33 G3 diplomacy in relation to Iran, for example, is accepted by the other Member States.

34 Shortly after accession to the EU, the Cypriot Government vetoed a package of aid and trade measures intended to assist the Turkish Republic of Northern Cyprus (TRNC) in the aftermath of the April 2004 referendum, in which Turkish Cypriots supported, and Greek Cypriots rejected, the Annan Plan for reunification of the island. This outcome prevented TRNC citizens from accessing the benefits of EU membership.

35 It has long been acknowledged that the Commission should be 'more proactive in CFSP and allow ideas to be subsumed within a Presidency paper. There must be a sense of the greater interest of the Union' (Interview, [then] Commission DGI, July 1997).

36 The RRM allows rapid disbursement of funds in crisis situations. Unlike the humanitarian assistance provided by ECHO it is not bound by the requirement to be politically neutral. The RRM has been used in a variety of situations, including provision of funding for reconstruction in Iraq in 2003 and measures to support the rule of law in Georgia in 2004.

37 The Council President would have been elected for an initial period of two and a half years, renewable once.

38 The Union as a whole would have been accorded legal personality (Article I-7), hence gaining the ability to enter into formal international agreements in political as well as economic aspects of policy.

39 It had been decided that the current High Representative, Javier Solana, would fulfil this demanding dual role.

40 These matters were the subject of contention, with strong opposition from the European Parliament to a joint proposal by Javier Solana and Commission President Barroso that the External Action Service be functionally independent of both the Commission and the Council (*European Voice*, 3–9 March 2005: 2). The future of the external delegations was a matter of particular concern.

41 Various practical problems also arise. Where, for example would Solana be seated at meetings of the European Council, with the Commission as Vice-President or alongside the President as Foreign Minister?

42 Common Positions were agreed, for example, on the imposition of sanctions or restrictive measures against third countries, on freezing of assets of persons suspected of terrorism and on support for the International Criminal Court.

43 In 2002 more than 200 Declarations were issued, on a wide range of topics (Council of the EU 2003).

44 Other areas where attention focused that year include the Middle East, Zimbabwe and weapons proliferation.

45 In 2002 dialogue with the USA involved one summit, two meetings at ministerial level, two meetings of senior officials and 35 meetings of experts. In the case of Canada there were two summits but relatively few (23) meetings of experts, and in the case of China only five meetings at expert level. In most other cases there were no or very few meetings at expert level (Council of the EU 2003).

46 EUSRs are responsible to the High Representative but also report to the PSC.

47 In the early years the Commission's suspicion of EUSRs extended to reluctance of EC Delegation staff to provide basic logistical support (Interview, Council Secretariat DGE, July 1997).

48 Here, Lord Ashdown is 'double hatted' as Special Representative of the EU and of the United Nations.

49 This applies to ACP and Euro–Med countries, the Balkans and NIS having Partnership and Cooperation Agreements in effect.

50 This reflects the provisions of the 'Roadmap' for the Middle East Peace Process, which accords to the European Commission principal responsibility for supporting democratic processes in the Palestinian authority.

51 This funding, as with development funding more generally, has tended to prioritize ACP members and neighbouring countries, including candidates for EU membership.

52 The list of those targeted has been subject to more than forty amendments. Information concerning sanctions or restrictive measures adopted under CFSP can be found at http://europa.eu.int/comm/external_relations/cfsp/sanctions.

53 For example the EU–Pakistan Cooperation Agreement of November 2001 included concessions to Pakistan explicitly related to the 'international campaign against terrorism'.

54 Prior to 2001 the EU was already a major donor of humanitarian assistance to Afghanistan, and to displaced persons outside the country (Commission 2001f).

55 Initially, priority was given to Indonesia, the Philippines and Pakistan as 'pilot countries' for the provision of technical assistance in developing counter-terrorism measures.

56 Matters of internal security are inevitably sensitive for Member State governments. A source of delay in implementing the European Arrest Warrant was concern on the part of the Italian government that its provisions might apply to Prime Minister Silvio Berlusconi.

57 Relations with Moldova, which borders Romania, are growing in importance due to Romania's projected accession to the EU in 2007.

58 The EU is the largest donor of assistance to the Palestinian Authority (PA). Funding has been provided for infrastructure, to support the development of political institutions and to pay the salaries of state employees. However, given the deteriorating situation in the PA since its isolation by Israel following the outbreak of the second Intifada, humanitarian relief has become a major focus of EU assistance.

59 In accordance with a CFSP Common Position, a group of Palestinians involved in the crisis were given refuge in EU Member States (Council of the EU 2003: 13).

60 The Union (in practice the EC) is a full member only of the World Trade Organization, the Food and Agriculture Organization and the European Bank for Reconstruction and Development.

61 In 2000 the EU made 22 verbal and 64 written statements to the UNSC (Laatikainen 2004: 9).

8 The EU as a security community and military actor

1 These debates are not in themselves new; although they are certainly a novel, post-Cold War concern for traditional security analysts. The concept of societal security has been developed by the Copenhagen Research Group over a number of years. It is intended to complement, rather than replace, analysis of state security and has consequently attracted

criticism both for departing too radically from, and for not moving sufficiently far beyond, traditional approaches. For debates about the validity and usefulness of the concept see Huysmans (1995); McSweeney (1996); Buzan and Wæver (1997).

2 It remained so, despite intermittent complaints from the USA about 'burden-sharing' by the European members and simmering resentment on the part of the French government at US dominance of the Alliance. Ultimately this resulted, in 1969, in French withdrawal from NATO military structures, although France remained a member of the political organization.

3 Monnet was then head of the French Planning Commission. His Memorandum was addressed to the French Foreign Minister, Robert Schuman, who subsequently launched the ECSC proposal (known as the Schuman Plan).

4 Thus the EC's role in coordinating the monitoring of ceasefires was undertaken at the request of the CSCE – whose own conciliation mechanisms, agreed only in 1990, were not yet operational.

5 Thus, in addition to the common defence provisions of the amended Brussels Treaty, the WEU was to develop a new role, in accordance with Chapter VIII of the UN Charter, as a 'regional arrangement' for the implementation of tasks at the request of the UN. The new tasks envisaged for the WEU – subsequently known as the 'Petersberg Tasks' – were humanitarian and rescue, peacekeeping and peacemaking.

6 Following the decisions to extend their roles beyond collective defence, both NATO and the WEU were anxious to demonstrate their usefulness in carrying out the new tasks. Accordingly, both organizations offered their services in monitoring (and subsequently enforcing) UN sanctions against Serbia imposed in May 1992. In 1995, the EU requested WEU support for the administration of Mostar, undertaken by the EU as its contribution to implementing the 1995 General Framework Agreement for Peace (the Dayton Agreement). In this case the WEU coordinated a deployment of approximately 180 police officers. This was the only occasion on which the WEU acted at the request of the EU in pursuance of a CFSP joint action.

7 In the context of considerable uncertainty over NATO's future, the TEU provisions on defence were originally greeted with some suspicion at NATO. The notion of a 'European security identity and defence role' was formally endorsed at the 1991 Rome Summit. However it was not until the 1994 Brussels Summit that the concept of a European Security and Defence Identity (ESDI) *within NATO* was developed. It was formally agreed at NATO's Berlin Council in June 1996, allowing European officers within NATO to occupy parallel positions in the WEU and making NATO structures and assets available for WEU-led missions. This agreement is still referred to in its amended version ('Berlin-plus') governing the availability of NATO assets to ESDP.

8 The Albanian intervention aimed to protect aid distribution and support the re-establishment of a viable police force. The relevance of the Albanian operation for future EU involvement in humanitarian/peacekeeping tasks is that it demonstrated the potential for combining EC/EU instruments and the WEU. Thus the Commission coordinated the international aid effort, the 'willing coalition' undertook measures to secure aid routes and the WEU coordinated civilian police support.

9 The notion of a coalition of the willing, tested in Albania, was clearly reflected in the Amsterdam Treaty – through inclusion of the 'constructive abstention' procedure among the revised CFSP provisions (Article J.23.1). The Treaty also specifically refers to the WEU Petersberg Tasks (Article J.17.2).

10 From a UK point of view the reference in the TEU is 'unfortunate', the 'French keep pointing this out but preventing this is a major red line' (Interview, Permanent Representation, 2002).

11 Article 25, concerning the PSC, was inserted into the TEU at Nice. The EUMC, EUMS and SITCEN were set up by a Council Decision of 22 January 2001 (2001/78/CFSP). The details are to be found in annexes to the Decision in *Official Journal* (*OJ*)L27, 30.1.2001: 1–9.

12 Cornish and Edwards (2001: 587) define such a culture as, 'The institutional confidence and processes to manage and deploy military force as part of the accepted range of legitimate and effective policy instruments'. It also represented a 'sea change' for the head of the enterprise, Solana, 'from a huge NATO structure to a very small tight structure and a Secretariat very different from NATO's international staff' (Interview, Brussels Permanent Representation, July 2001). Security procedures had to be revised and tightened, hence the move to the Cortenbergh building. As seconded national diplomatic and military staff moved in the early period there were turf battles and a feeling of 'irrelevance' by some of the military. This had changed markedly by 2003 with the prospect of real operations (Interview, Council Secretariat, July 2003). One aspect of militarization was the innovation of an 'armoire' in the Cortenbergh offices in order that military personnel could wear their uniforms at work but leave in civilian dress.

13 The text is in 'Laeken declaration on the operational status of the ESDP', Presidency Conclusions, Laeken European Council, 14–15 December 2001.

14 There is no official diagram of the crisis management system within the Council. We were told that the political sensitivities were such that some things were best left to 'constructive ambiguity' (Interview, Council Secretariat, October 2002)! Figure 8.2 is therefore our unofficial attempt to depict the organizational structure.

15 In an operation involving non-EU contributors the participating EUMC members would sit on the 'Committee of Contributors'.

16 The initial document proposing the creation of CIVCOM envisaged that it would operate 'on a flexible basis, so that necessary expertise is available to suit its agenda. Representatives from Permanent Representations as well as experts should attend as necessary' (Interview, Council Secretariat, October 2002).

17 In the *Artemis* operation in the Congo of 2003 a request from the UN Secretary General was dealt with directly and agreed by French President Chirac and UK Prime Minister Blair (Interview, Permanent Representation, October 2003).

18 EUJUST *Lex* had a budget of €10 million and involved 770 personnel (Council 8 March 2005, SO102/05).

19 Twenty per cent of the police participating in EUPM Bosnia-Herzegovina were from non-EU states. In *Proxima* invitations were extended to eight non-EU states to send participants (Lindstrom 2004: 112,121). The Committee of Contributors to the *Althea* military operation includes Albania, Argentina, Bulgaria, Canada, Chile, Morocco, New Zealand, Norway, Romania, Switzerland and Turkey (*OJ* L357, 2.12.2004: 39). In fact none of the military operations has had an exclusive EU character. *Concordia* involved 13 EU Member States, six NATO non-EU states including Turkey, and seven states not at the time members of either. *Artemis* involved forces from six EU Member States, plus limited initial involvement from Brazil, Canada and South Africa (Lindstrom 2004: 117–20).

20 In the case of Bosnia-Herzegovina a joint UN/EU Special Representative, Lord Ashdown. When, as in *Althea*, there is a police unit included in a military operation it is subject to the military chain of command.

21 The key points are Numbers 8, 9 and 10, Washington Summit Communiqué, 'An Alliance for the 21st Century' NAC-S(99)64, 24 April 1999. 'Berlin-plus' involves, (a) assured EU access to NATO planning capabilities able to contribute to military planning for EU-led operations; (b) the presumption of availability to the EU of pre-identified NATO capabilities and common assets for use in EU-led operations; (c) identification of a range of European command options for EU-led operations, further developing the role of DSACEUR in order for him to assume fully and effectively his European responsibilities; (d) further adaptation of NATO's defence planning system to incorporate more comprehensively the availability of forces for EU-led operations.

22 The arrangements were agreed at Nice and are to be found in Presidency Conclusions Nice 2000, Annex VIII. Five national Headquarters have so far been declared to the EU.

23 A comprehensive framework for EU–NATO permanent relations was concluded on 17 March 2003. This was necessary because *Concordia* took over from the existing NATO *Amber Fox* operation. The full negotiated relationship involves not only 'Berlin-plus' but provision for scheduled meetings (at least one per Presidency) between the PSC and the NATO North Atlantic Council and at lower levels, and crisis consultation arrangements. Also, a necessary element before the conduct of operations, a security of information agreement. It is also made clear that it is for the EU to request the NATO command option and the use of NATO assets and capabilities. A summary is provided in Council 2003, *Background – EU NATO: The Framework for Permanent Relations and Berlin Plus*.

24 This followed the difficult experience in Kosovo with accusations about intelligence sharing amongst allies, reliance on US airpower and the need to obtain political approval for 807 of the 976 sorties carried out. The unambiguous conclusion of the incoming Bush administration was that this would be the 'last NATO war' (Haine 2004a: 136). This conclusion can only have been reinforced by the Iraq experience when, on 6 February 2003, five EU Members (France, Germany, Belgium, Luxembourg and the Netherlands) blocked NATO support for Turkey in an Extraordinary meeting of the NACC.

25 The compromise, in a document entitled 'European defence: NATO/EU consultation, planning and operations', was agreed in the Summer of 2004 and endorsed by the December 2004 European Council. The operations centre will be available by January 2006 at the latest.

26 The Helsinki European Council of December 1999 called for a 60,000 strong force deployable within 60 days and sustainable for one year. Because of the need for rotation of units the real figure would have been an unwieldy 180,000 troops.

27 The 'battlegroup' concept involves high readiness force packages which can stand alone. A 'battlegroup' is composed of a combined arms battalion with combat support including relevant air and naval capabilities. It should be deployed no later than ten days after an ESDP launch decision (Council of the EU 2004a: 2).

28 Progress with the 'road map' now forms part of the Single Progress Report on ESDP presented by each Presidency (Military Capabilities Commitment Conference, Declaration on European Military Capabilities, 22 November 2004 at Annex I to European Council 2004a).

29 On the basis of the ECAP process, deficiencies exist in: deployability, with an average of 10–15 per cent of forces deployable abroad; mobility, with an absence of dedicated air and sea lift capability; sustainability, which requires much improved logistics to keep forces in the field; effective engagement, which includes shortages of precision guided munitions etc.; and C4ISR (command control, communications, computer intelligence, surveillance and reconnaissance) (Schmitt 2004: 95–6).

30 Council Decision 2004/197/CFSP, *OJ* L63/68, 28.2.2004.

31 There was a difficulty of this kind with the Canadian contribution to *Althea*. Canada would, under the formula, be required to pay more than any of the other third parties without being part of the decision-making for the operation (*European Voice*, 23–29 September 2004).

32 The Security Strategy (European Council 2003) should be read in conjunction with another document, approved by the Council in May 2004, which is the EU's submission to the UN High Level Panel (Council of the EU 2004c).

33 '… we should be able to sustain several operations simultaneously. We could add particular value by developing operations involving both military and civilian capabilities' (European Council 2003: 11).

34 The Security Strategy and submission to the High Level Panel identify a number of threats not involving direct armed attack. They are terrorism, proliferation of WMD and their possible combination, regional and ethnic conflict, state failure and organized crime.

35 Massive human rights violations and genocide represent a threat to international peace and security and the 'use of force may be needed to prevent or halt them' (Council of the EU 2004c: 12). However, the EU stresses the responsibility of the Security Council

here, and the consequent need to clarify principles under which humanitarian intervention may be justified (ibid.).

36 The wording was deemed too controversial for some members, especially Germany (Haine: 2004b: 19).

37 The relevant UNSC Resolutions are: EUPM Bosnia-Herzegovina, 1396, *Concordia* 1317, *Artemis* 1484, *Proxima* 1371, *Althea* 1575.

38 Between June and December 2003, according to Haine (2004b: 20–1), a compromise was found between the British insistence on 'effective' policies and the German traditional interest in UN multilateralism. A move towards Berlin's view was based upon a new French enthusiasm for the UN after the events of 2003, European public preference, and UK experience with *Artemis*.

39 This type of operation is described as very demanding and carrying 'considerable associated risks'. The 'battlegroup' concept is very relevant to the provision of appropriate forces. A number of issues are still to be resolved in the EU–UN relationship, including EU involvement in UN planning, command and control, situation awareness and the transfer of authority.

40 The 2004 Cooperation Agreement refers to 'in depth knowledge of each other's procedures, concepts and structures in military crisis management' and 'enhancing the network already established', along with UN access to EU satellite facilities and intelligence sharing (European Council 2004b). In April 2005 the EU and UN held a two day crisis management exercise (EST05) (*European Voice*, 7–13 April 2005).

41 In EUPM Bosnia-Herzegovina 5 of 18 participants were neither Members nor applicants, in *Concordia* 3, in *Artemis* 3 for the first month, in *Proxima* 7 from 35 and in *Althea* 8 from 34. Sources: Lindstrom: 2004, EUPOL *Proxima* Factsheet, http://www.eu.int/uedocs/ cmsUpload/ProximaBrochturre.pdf, also EUFOR website http://www.euforbih.org.

42 From within the EU all 25 countries participated in *Proxima*, and all but Malta in EUPM Bosnia. Denmark did not participate in *Concordia*, *Artemis* and *Althea* (the military operations) and Cyprus and Malta likewise. Ireland was not present in *Concordia*, and Luxembourg and Finland, along with all the applicants, were not represented in *Artemis*.

Bibliography

Aalto, P. (2004) 'EU, Russia and the Problem of Community', Paper presented at BISA Annual Conference, University of Warwick, 20–22 December.

ACP General Secretariat (2002) *Priority of the ACP Council of Ministers Ahead of the ACP–EU Economic Partnership Agreement: Maintaining and Strengthening ACP Unity and Solidarity*, Brussels, 26 September.

Adler, E. and Barnett, M. (eds) (1998) *Security Communities*, Cambridge: Cambridge University Press.

Aggarwal, V.K. and Fogarty, E.A. (eds) (2004) *EU Trade Strategies: Between Regionalism and Globalism*, Houndsmill: Palgrave.

Aho, C.M. (1993) 'America and the Pacific century: trade conflict and cooperation', *International Affairs*, 69,1: 19–38.

Allen, D. and Smith, M. (1990) 'Western Europe's presence in the contemporary international arena', *Review of International Studies*, 16, 1: 19–37.

—— (2003) 'External policy developments', *Journal of Common Market Studies*, Annual Review 2002/3, 97–114.

Andersen, M.S. and Liefferink, D. (eds) (1997) *European Environmental Policy: The Pioneers*, Manchester: Manchester University Press.

Andréani, G., Bertram, C. and Grant, C. (2001) *Europe's Military Revolution*, London: Centre for European Reform.

Asseburg, M. (2003) 'The EU and the Middle East Conflict: tackling the main obstacle to Euro–Mediterranean Partnership', *Mediterranean Politics*, 8, 2–3: 174–93.

Bail, C., Falkner, R. and Marquand, H. (eds) (2002) *The Cartagena Protocol on Biosafety: Reconciling Trade in Biotechnology with Environment and Development*, London: RIIA Earthscan.

Bailey, R. (1972) *The European Community in the World*, London: Hutchinson.

Banchoff, T. (1999) 'German identity and European integration', *European Journal of International Relations*, 5, 3: 259–89.

Barbé, E. (1996) 'The Barcelona Conference: launching pad of a process', *Mediterranean Politics*, 1, 1: 25–42.

Benedick, R.E. (1991) *Ozone Diplomacy: New Directions in Safeguarding the Planet*, Cambridge, MA: Harvard University Press.

Biscop, S. (2004a) 'The European Security Strategy: implementing a distinctive approach to security', *Sécurité et Stratégie*, Brussels Royal Defence College, Paper No. 82: March.

—— (2004b) 'Able and willing? Assessing the EU's capacity for military action', *European Foreign Affairs Review*, 9: 60–86.

Biscop, S. and Coolsaet, R. (2003) 'The World is the stage – a global security strategy for the European Union', *Groupement D'Etudes et de Récherches notre Europe*, Policy Paper No. 8: December.

Black, I. (2003) 'We don't do war', *The Guardian*, 25 March: 21.

Bretherton, C. (1998) 'Global environmental politics: putting gender on the agenda?', *Review of International Studies*, 24, 1: 85–100.

—— (2001) 'Gender mainstreaming and EU enlargement: swimming against the tide', *Journal of European Public Policy*, 8,1: 43–59.

—— (2004) 'Economic and monetary union: implications for the European Union's global role', in D. Morland and M. Cowling (eds) *Political Issues for the Twenty-First Century*, Aldershot: Ashgate, 193–218.

Bretherton, C. and Ponton, G. (eds) (1996) *Global Politics: An Introduction*, Oxford: Blackwell.

Bretherton, C. and Vogler, J. (2000) 'The European Union as a trade actor and environmental activist: contradictory roles?', *Journal of Economic Integration*, 15, 2: 163–94.

Bringezu, S. and Schütz, H. (2001) *Total Material Requirement of the European Union*, Copenhagen: European Environment Agency.

Brinkhorst, P. (1994) 'The European Community at UNCED: lessons to be drawn for the future', in D. Curtin and T. Heukels (eds) *Essays in Honour of H.G. Schermers,* Vol. II, Dordnecht: Niijhoff, 609–17.

British Petroleum (2004) *Statistical Review of World Energy 2004*, http://www/bp/com.

Buchan, D. (1993) *Europe: the Strange Superpower*, Aldershot: Dartmouth.

Bull, H. (1983) 'Civilian power Europe: a contradiction in terms?', in R. Tsoukalis (ed.) *The European Community: Past, Present and Future*, London: Blackwell, 149–70.

Burakovsky, I., Nemyria, H. and Pavlink, O. (2000) *Roadway into the Future – Roadway to Europe: Ukraine's European Integration*, Kiev: Centre for European and International Studies.

Burton, J.W. (1972) *World Society*, Cambridge: Cambridge University Press.

Buzan, B. (1991) *People, States and Fear: An Agenda for International Security Studies in the Post-Cold War Era*, Hemel Hempstead: Harvester Wheatsheaf.

Buzan, B. and Wæver, O. (1997) 'Slippery? Contradictory? Sociologically untenable? The Copenhagen school replies', *Review of International Studies*, 23, 2: 241–50.

Cameron, F. (2002) 'The European Union's growing international role: closing the capability–expectations Gap?', Paper presented at Conference 'The EU in International Affairs', Canberra Australian National University: 4–5 July.

—— (2003) 'The future of the CFSP', *Brown Journal of World Affairs*, IX, 2: 1–10.

Cameron, J., Nerksman, J. and Roderick, P. (eds) (1996) *Improving Compliance with International Environmental Law*, London: Earthscan.

Carmin, J. and Vandeveer, S.D. (2004) 'Enlarging EU environments: central and east Europe from transition to accession', *Environmental Politics*, 31, 1: 3–24.

Cecchini, P., Catinat, M. and Jacquemin, A. (1988) *The European Challenge, 1992*, London: Wildwood Press.

Chapman, J. (2004) 'The Real Reasons Bush went to war', *The Guardian*, 28 July: 27.

Checkel, J.T. (2001) 'Social construction and European integration', in T. Christiansen, K.E. Jørgensen and A. Weiner (eds) *The Social Construction of Europe*, London: Sage, 50–65.

Christiansen, J., Petito, F. and Tonra, B. (2000) 'Fuzzy politics around fuzzy borders: the European Union's near abroad', *Cooperation and Conflict*, 35, 4: 389–415.

Christiansen, T. (2001) 'Intra-institutional politics and inter-institutional relations in the EU: towards coherent governance?', *Journal of European Public Policy*, 8, 5: 749–69.

Christiansen, T., Jørgensen, K.E. and Weiner, A. (eds) (2001) *The Social Construction of Europe*, London: Sage.

Collier, U. (1996) 'The European Union's climate change policy: limiting emissions or limiting power?', *Journal of European Public Policy* 3, 1: 122–38.

Cornish, P. and Edwards, G. (2001) 'Beyond the EU/NATO dichotomy: the beginnings of a European strategic culture', *International Affairs*, 77, 3: 587–603.

Commission (1982) 'Memorandum on the Community's development policy', *Bulletin of the European Communities*, Supplement 5(82).

—— (1989) *Commission Opinion on Turkey's Request for Accession to the Community*, SEC(89), 2290, final.

—— (1990a) *Europe – A Fresh Start: The Schumann Declaration 1950–90*, Luxembourg: Office for Official Publications of the European Communities.

—— (1990b) *The European Community and its Eastern Neighbours*, Luxembourg: Office for Official Publications of the European Communities.

—— (1990c) *Redirecting the Community's Mediterranean Policy*, SEC(90), 812.

—— (1991) *Opening up the Internal Market*, Luxembourg: Office for Official Publications of the European Communities.

—— (1992a) *Development Cooperation Policy in the Run-up to 2000*, SEC(92), 915, final.

—— (1992b) 'Europe and the Challenge of Enlargement', *Bulletin of the European Communities*, Supplement 3(92), Luxembourg: Office for Official Publications of the European Communities.

—— (1993) 'Commission opinion on the application by the Republic of Cyprus for membership', *Bulletin of the European Communities*, Supplement 5(93).

—— (1995a) 'Strengthening the Mediterranean policy of the European Union: establishing a Euro–Mediterranean partnership', *Bulletin*, Supplement 2/95, Luxembourg: Office for Official Publications of the European Communities.

—— (1995b) *Report on the Operation of the Treaty on European Union*, Brussels: Office for Official Publications of the European Communities.

—— (1996) *Report from the European Commission to the UN Commission on Sustainable Development on the European Community's Progress Towards Sustainability*, prepared for the Fourth Session, Brussels: Office for Official Publications of the European Communities, April.

—— (1997a) 'For a stronger and wider Union', *Agenda 2000*, Volume I, Strasbourg: DOC(97), 6.

—— (1997b) *Green Paper on Relations Between the European Union and the ACP Countries on the Eve of the 21st Century: Challenges and Options for a New Partnership*, Luxembourg.

—— (1997c) *Agenda 21 The First Five Years: European Community Progress on the Implementation of Agenda 21: 1992–97*, Brussels: Office for Official Publications of the European Communities.

—— (1997d) *Climate Change: the EU Approach to Kyoto*, COM(97), 481.

—— (1998) *Euro–Mediterranean Partnership Short and Medium Term Priority Environmental Action Programme (SMAP)*, Brussels: Office for Official Publications of the European Communities.

—— (2000a) *The European Community's Development Policy*, Statement by the Council and the Commission.

—— (2000b) *The New ACP–EU Agreement: General Overview*, http://europa.eu.int/comm/development/cotonou/overview.

—— (2000c) *Communication from the Commission to the Council and the European Parliament of 6 September 2000 to Prepare the 4th Meeting of Euro-Mediterranean Foreign Ministers 'Reinvigorating the Barcelona Process'*, COM(2000) 497, final.

—— (2000d) *Communication from the Commission on the Precautionary Principle*, COM(2000) 1, final.

—— (2001a) *How Europeans See Themselves: Looking Through the Mirror with Public Opinion Surveys*, Luxembourg: Office for Official Publications of the European Communities.

—— (2001b) *Living in an Area of Freedom, Security and Justice: Justice and Home Affairs in the European Union*, Luxembourg: Office for Official Publications of the European Communities.

—— (2001c) *Communication from the Commission on Conflict Prevention*, COM(2001) 211, final.

—— (2001d) *European Distant Water Fishing Fleet: Some Principles and Some Data*, Brussels: Directorate-General Fish.

—— (2001e) *The European Union's Role in Promoting Human Rights and Democratisation in Third Countries*, COB(2001) 252, final.

—— (2001f) *Action by the European Union Following the Attacks on 11th September*, MEMO/01/327: 15 October.

—— (2001g) *Communication from the Commission: EU–Russia Environmental Cooperation*, COM(2001) 772, final.

—— (2001h) *Communication from the Commission on the Implementation of the First Phase of the European Climate Change Programme*, COM(2001) 581, final.

—— (2002a) *For the European Union: Peace, Freedom Solidarity. Communication of the Commission on the Institutional Architecture*, COM(2002) 728, final.

—— (2002b) *Towards an Integrated Management of External Borders*, COM(2002) 233, final.

—— (2002c) *Towards the Enlarged Union: Strategy Paper and Report of the European Commission on the Progress Towards Accession by Each of the Candidate Countries*, COM(2002) 700, final.

—— (2003a) *Flash Eurobarometer 151 'Iraq and Peace in the World'*, Brussels: Office for Official Publications of the European Communities, October.

—— (2003b) *Commission Policy Paper for Transmission to the Council and the European Parliament: A Maturing Partnership – Shared Interests and Challenges in EU–China Relations*, COM(2003) 533, final.

—— (2003c) *ECHO Aid Strategy 2004*, Brussels: Office for Official Publications of the European Communities, 18 December.

—— (2003d) *Wider Europe – Neighbourhood: A New Framework for Relationships with our Eastern and Southern Neighbours*, COM(2003) 104, final.

—— (2003e) *EU Agriculture and the WTO Doha Development Agenda*, http://europa.eu.int/comm/agriculture.

—— (2003f) *White Paper – Space: A New European Frontier for an Expanding Union. An Action plan for Implementing the European Space Policy*, COM(2003) 673.

—— (2004a) *European Neighbourhood Policy: Strategy Paper*, COM(2004) 373, final.

—— (2004b) *Communication from the Commission to the Council and the European Parliament: Building our Common Future: Policy Challenges and Budgetary Means of the Enlarged Union 2007–2013*, COM(2004) 101, final.

—— (2004c) *Report from the Commission Humanitarian Aid Office (ECHO): Annual Report 2003*, COM(2004) 583, final.

—— (2004d) *Communication from the Commission to the Council and the European Parliament: Strategy Paper of the European Commission on Progress in the Enlargement Process*, COM(2004) 657, final.

—— (2004e) *Communication from the Commission to the Council and the European Parliament: Recommendation of the European Commission on Turkey's Progress Towards Accession*, COM(2004) 656, final.

—— (2004f) *The Stabilisation and Association Process for South-East Europe: Third Annual Report*, COM(2004) 202, final.

—— (2004g) *Communication from the Commission to the Council and the European Parliament on relations with Russia*, COM(2004) 106.

—— (2004h) *Commission Staff Working Paper: European Neighbourhood Policy. Country Report: Ukraine*, COM(2004) 373, final.

—— (2004i) *Euromed Special Feature – MEDA II: Reinforced Effectiveness*, Brussels: Office for Official Publications of the European Communities, 18 October.

—— (2004j) *Bilateral Trade Relations: The European Union and its Main Trading Partners: Economic and Trade Indicators*, http://europa.eu.int/comm/trade/issues/bilateral.

—— (2004k) *Trade Policy in the Prodi Commission: An Assessment*, Brussels: Office for Official Publications of the European Communities, 19 November.

—— (2004l) *Bilateral Trade Relations: China*, http://europa.eu.int/comm/trade/bilateral/countries/china.

—— (2004m) *The Doha Development Agenda: General Statistics and Development Statistics*, Brussels: Office for Official Publications of the European Communities, 6 May.

—— (2005a) *Bilateral Trade Relations: USA*, http://europa.eu.int/comm/trade/issues/bilateral/countries/usa.

—— (2005b) *Bilateral Trade Relations: Africa, Caribbean, Pacific*, http://europa.eu.int/comm/trade/issues/bilateral/regions/acp.

—— (2005c) *The European Union and its Main Trading Partners: Economic and Trade Indicators*, http://europa.eu.int/comm/trade/issues/bilateral.

Cooper, R. (2004) *The Breaking of Nations: Order and Chaos in the Twenty-first Century*, London: Atlantic Books.

Coplin, W. (1965) 'International law and assumptions about the state system', in J.N. Rosenau (ed.) *International Politics and Foreign Policy: A Reader in Research and Theory*, 2nd edn, New York: Free Press, 142–52.

Cronin, D. (2004) 'Macedonian membership on the table', *European Voice*, 25–31 March: 19.

Cosgrove, C.A. and Twitchett, K.J. (eds) (1970) *The new International Actors: The UN and the EEC*, London: Macmillan.

Council of the European Union (1995) *Report on the Functioning of the Treaty on European Union*, Brussels.

—— (1999) *Common Strategy of the European Union of 4th June 1999 on Russia*, 1999/414/CFSP, L157/2.

—— (2003) *Annual Report from the Council to the European Parliament on the Main Aspects and Basic Choices of CFSP*, 7038/03.

—— (2004a) *Headline Goal 2010*, 6309/6/04.

—— (2004b) *Civilian Capabilities Commitment Conference: Ministerial Declaration*, Brussels, 22 November.

—— (2004c) *Paper for Submission to the High Level Panel on Threats, Challenges and Change*, May.

Cox, A. and Koning, A. (1997) *Understanding European Community Aid: Aid Policies, Management and Distribution Explained*, London: Overseas Development Institute.

Cox, R. (1986) 'Social forces, states and world orders: beyond international relations theory', in R.O. Keohane (ed.) *Neorealism and its Critics*, New York: Columbia University Press, 204–54.

—— (1993) 'Structural issues of global governance: implications for Europe', in S. Gill (ed.) *Gramsci, Historical Materialism and International Relations*, Cambridge: Cambridge University Press, 259–89.

Craig Nation, R. (1996) 'The Turkic and Other Muslim Peoples of Central Asia, the Caucasus, and the Balkans', in V. Mastny and R. Craig Nation (eds) *Turkey Between East and West:*

New Challenges for a Rising Regional Power, Boulder, CO: Westview Press, 97–130.

Damro, C. (2001) 'Building an international identity: the EU and extraterritorial competition policy', *Journal of European Public Policy*, 8, 2: 208–26.

Damro, C. and Luaces Méndes, P. (2003) 'Emissions trading at Kyoto: from EU resistance to Union innovation', *Environmental Politics*, 12, 2: 71–94.

Dannreuther, R. (2004) 'The Middle East: towards a substantive European role in the peace process', in R. Dannreuther (ed.) *European Union Foreign and Security Policy: Towards a Neighbourhood Strategy*, London: Routledge, 151–69.

Davenport, M. (1992) 'Africa and the unimportance of being preferred', *Journal of Common Market Studies*, 30, 2: 233–51.

Dedring, J. (2004) 'Reflections on the coordination of the EU member states in organs of the United Nations', *CFSP Forum*, 2, 1: 1–3.

Deighton, A. (2002) 'The European Security and Defence Policy', *Journal of Common Market Studies*, 40, 4: 719–41.

Den Boer, M. and Monar, J. (2002) 'Keynote article: 11 September and the challenge of global terrorism to the EU as a security actor', *Journal of Common Market Studies*, Annual Review: 11–28.

Dessler, D. (1989) 'What's at stake in the agency–structure debate?', *International Organization*, 43, 3: 441–73.

Deudney, D.H. and Matthews, R.A. (eds) (1999) *Contested Grounds: Security and Conflict in the New Environmental Politics*, New York: State University of New York Press.

Duchêne, F. (1972) 'Europe's Role in World Peace', in R. Mayne (ed.) *Europe Tomorrow: Sixteen Europeans Look Ahead*, London: Fontana, 32–47.

Egeberg, M. (1999) 'Transcending intergovernmentalism? Identity and role perceptions of national officials in EU decision-making', *Journal of European Public Policy*, 6, 3: 456–74.

Eide, E.B. (ed.) (2004) *Effective Multilateralism: Europe, Regional Security and a Revitalised UN*, London: The Foreign Policy Centre.

Elliott, L. (2004) 'What the WTO needs is a new reformation', *The Guardian*, 2 August: 19.

Erridge, A. (1981) 'The Lomé Convention: a case study', *World Politics*, Paper 12, D233, Milton Keynes: The Open University Press.

Esty, D.C. (1994) *Greening the GATT: Trade, Environment and the Future*, Washington, DC: Institute for International Economics.

European Convention (2003) *Draft Treaty Establishing a Constitution for Europe: Submitted to the European Council Meeting in Thessaloniki, 20 June 2003,* Luxembourg: Office of Official Publications of the European Communities.

European Convention Secretariat (2002) Note from Praesidium to Convention, *Delimitation of Competence between the European Union and the Member States – Existing Systems, Problems and Avenues to be Explored,* CONV 47/02, May.

European Council (1999a) 'Presidency Conclusions', Tampere, October.

—— (1999b) 'Common Strategy of 11 December 1999 on Ukraine', Helsinki, December.

—— (2000) 'Common Strategy of 19th June 2000 on the Mediterranean Region', Santa Maria de Feira, June.

—— (2003) 'A Secure Europe in a Better World: European Security Strategy', Brussels, December.

—— (2004a) 'Action Plan for Civilian Aspects of ESDP', Brussels, June.

—— (2004b) 'EU–UN Cooperation in Military Crisis Operations, Elements of Implementation of the EU–UN Joint Declaration', Brussels, June.

—— (2004c) 'ESDP Presidency Report', Brussels, December.

European Environment Agency (2004) *EEA Signals, 2004*, Copenhagen: EEA.

European Parliament (2002) *Report on the proposal for a Council Decision Concerning the Conclusion, on behalf of the European Community, of the Kyoto Protocol to the United Nations Framework Convention on Climate Change and the Joint Fulfilment of Commitments Thereunder*, A5–0025/2002 Final.

Eurostat (2003) *50 Years of Figures on Europe: Data 1952–2001*, Luxembourg: Office of Official Publications of the European Communities.

—— (2004) *EU Enlargement: The New EU of 25 Compared to EU 15*, News Release 36.2004, March.

Eurostep (2004) *Vision of a Responsible Europe*, http://www/eurostep.org.

Everts, S. and Keohane, D. (2003) 'The European Convention and EU Foreign Policy: learning from failure', *Survival*, 43, 3: 167–86.

Extraordinary European Council (2001) *Conclusions and Plan of Action*, Brussels, September.

Feldman, D.L. (1992) 'Institutions for managing global environmental change', *Global Environmental Change*, March: 42–58.

Feldstein, M. (1997) 'EMU and international conflict', *Foreign Affairs*, 76, 6: 60–73.

Ferguson, N. and Kolitikoff, L.J. (2000) 'The degeneration of EMU', *Foreign Affairs*, 79, 2: 110–21

Ferrero-Waldner, B. (2004) *Press Conference to Launch First Seven Action Plans under the European Neighbourhood Policy*, SPEECH/04/529, Brussels, December.

Fierke, K.M. and Jørgensen, K.E. (eds) (2001) *Constructing International Relations: The Next Generation*, Armonk, NY: M.E. Sharpe.

Fierke, K.M. and Wiener, A. (1999) 'Constructing institutional interests: EU and NATO enlargement', *Journal of European Public Policy*, 6, 5: 721–42.

Fogarty, E.A. (2004) 'Be careful what you wish for: the European Union and North America', in V.K. Aggarwal and E.A. Fogarty (eds) *EU Trade Strategies: Between Regionalism and Globalism*, Houndmills: Palgrave, 180–206.

Friis, L. and Murphy, A. (2000) 'Turbo-charged negotiations: the EU and the stability pact for South Eastern Europe', *Journal of European Public Policy*, 7, 5: 767–86.

Galloway, D. (2001) *The Treaty of Nice and Beyond: Realities and Illusions of Power in the EU*. Sheffield: Sheffield Academic Press.

Galtung, J. (1969) 'Violence, peace and peace research' *Journal of Peace Research*, 3: 167–89.

—— (1973) *The European Community: A Superpower in the Making*, London: George Allen and Unwin.

García, S. (ed) (1993) *European Identity and the Search for Legitimacy*, London: Pinter.

Gault, J. (2004) 'EU energy security and the periphery', in R. Dannreuther (ed) *European Foreign and Security Policy: Towards a Neighbourhood Strategy*, London: Routledge, 170–85.

Geddes, A. (2000) *Immigration and European Integration: Towards Fortress Europe*, Manchester: Manchester University Press.

Gegout, C. (2002) 'The quint: acknowledging the existence of a big four–US *Directoire* at the heart of the European Union's Foreign Policy decision-making process', *Journal of Common Market Studies*, 40, 2: 331–44.

Giddens, A. (1984) *The Constitution of Society: Outline of the Theory of Structuration*, Basingstoke: Macmillan.

Gilson, J. (2004) 'Weaving a new silk road: Europe meets Asia', in V.K. Aggarwal and E.A. Fogarts (eds) *EU Trade Strategies: Between Regionalism and Globalism*, Houndmills: Palgrave, 64–92.

Ginsberg, R.H. (2001) *The European Union in International Politics: Baptism by Fire*, Lanham, MD: Rowman and Littlefield.

Gnesotto, N. (ed.) (2004) *EU Security and Defence Policy: The First Five Years (1999–2004)*, Paris: Institute for Security Studies, European Union.

Gokay, B. (forthcoming) 'The US, world hegemony and Eurasia', *Perceptions*.

Goldstein, W. (2001) *The Euro Paradox: Will it Live?*, New York: New York University, New York Consortium for European Studies, February.

Gomez, R. (2003) *Negotiating the Euro–Mediterranean Partnership: Strategic Action in EU Foreign Policy?*, Aldershot: Aldgate.

Gouldner, A. (1971) *The Coming Crisis of Western Sociology*, New York: Heinemann.

Gowan, R. (2004) 'The EU, regional organisation and security: strategic partners or convenient alibis', in S. Biscop (ed.) *Audit of European Security Strategy*, Egmont Paper No. 3, Brussels: IRRI-KIIB, Academia Press.

Greco, E. (2004) 'South-Eastern Europe: the expanding EU role', in R. Dannreuther (ed.) *European Union Foreign and Security Policy: Towards a Neighbourhood Strategy*, London: Routledge, 63–78.

Greene, O. (1996) 'Environmental regimes: effectiveness and implementation review', in J. Vogler and M.F. Imber (eds) *The Environment and International Relations*, London: Routledge, 196–214.

Grilli, E.R. (1993) *The European Community and the Developing Countries*, Cambridge: Cambridge University Press.

Grubb, M. (1995) *The Berlin Climate Change Conference: Outcome and Implications*, Briefing Paper No. 21, London: RIIA

Grubb, M. and Yamin, F. (2001) 'Climate Collapse at The Hague: what happened and where do we go from here? *International Affairs*, 77, 2: 261–76.

Guild, E. (2002) 'Immigration in an area of freedom, security and justice, paper to 6th ECSA-World Conference, Brussels, December.

Guiraudon, V. (2004) 'Immigration and asylum: a high politics agenda', in M.G. Cowles and D. Dinan (eds) *Developments in the European Union*, Houndmills: Palgrave, 160–80.

Haas, E. (1958) *The Uniting of Europe*, Stanford, CA: Stanford University Press.

Haigh, N. (1996) 'Climate change policies and politics in the European Community', in T. O'Riordan and J. Jager (eds) *Politics of Climate Change: A European Perspective*, London: Routledge, 155–84.

Haine, J.Y. (2004a) 'ESDP and NATO', in N. Gnesotto (ed.) *EU Security and Defence Policy: The First Five Years*, Paris: Institute for Security Studies, European Union, 131–44.

—— (2004b) 'Venus without Mars: challenges ahead for ESDP', in S. Biscop (ed.) *Audit of European Security Strategy*, Egmont Paper No. 3, Brussels: IRRI-KIIB, Academia Press, 18–26.

Hansen, A.S. (2004) 'Security and defence: the EU police mission in Bosnia-Herzegovina', in W. Carlsnaes, H. Sjursen and B. White (eds) *Contemporary European Foreign Policy*, London: Sage, 173–85.

Haukkala, H. (2004) 'Is the EU ready for its new eastern neighbourhood?', *EuroFuture*, Winter: 44–7.

Hay, C. (1995) 'Structure and Agency' in D. Marsh and G. Stoker (eds) *Theory and Method in Political Science*, Basingstoke: Macmillan, 189–206.

Hayes-Renshaw, F. and Wallace, H. (1997) *The Council of Ministers*, Basingstoke: Macmillan.

Heidensohn, K. (1995) *Europe and World Trade*, London: Pinter.

Helvacioglu, B. (1996) '"Allahu Ekber", We are Turks: yearning for a different homecoming at the periphery of Europe', *Third World Quarterly*, 17, 3: 503–23.

Hession, M. (1996) 'The role of the EC in implementing international environmental law', in J. Cameron, J. Nerksman and P. Roderick (eds) *Improving Compliance with International Environmental Law*, London: Earthscan, 177–84.

Heugsen, C. (2004) 'Implementing the European Security Strategy', in S. Biscop (ed.) *Audit of European Security Strategy*, Egmont Paper No. 3, Brussels: IRRI-KIIB, Academia Press, 5–17.

Hill, C. (1993) 'The capability–expectations gap, or conceptualising Europe's international role', *Journal of Common Market Studies*, 31, 3: 305–25.

Hindley, B. (1992) 'Trade policy of the European Community', in P. Minford (ed.) *The Cost of Europe*, Manchester: Manchester University Press.

Hocking, B. and Smith, M. (1990) *World Politics: An Introduction to International Relations*, Hemel Hempstead: Harvester Wheatsheaf.

Hoekman, B. and Kostecki, M. (1995) *The Political Economy of the World Trading System: From GATT to WTO*, Oxford: Oxford University Press.

Holland, M. (1995) 'Bridging the capability–expectations gap: a case study of the CFSP joint action in South Africa', *Journal of Common Market Studies*, 33, 4: 555–72.

—— (2002) *The European Union and the World*, Basingstoke: Palgrave.

—— (2004) 'Development policy: paradigm shifts and the "normalization" of a privileged relationship', in M.G. Cowles and D. Dinan (eds) *Developments in the European Union*, Houndmills: Palgrave, 275–94.

Hollis, M. and Smith, S. (1991) 'Beware of gurus: structure and action in international relations', *Review of International Studies*, 17, 4: 393–410.

Homan, K. (2004) 'Building up EU military capabilities: an incremental process', in S. Biscop (ed.) *Audit of European Security Strategy*, Egmont Paper No. 3, Brussels: IRRI-KIIB, Academia Press, 33–6.

Hopkins, R.E. and Mansbach, R.W. (1973) *Structure and Process in International Politics*, New York: Harper and Row.

Horakik, W. (2004) 'Torn between Russia and the West, Ukraine must make crucial choice', *European Voice*, 29 July–1 September: 3–4.

Howorth, J. (2000) 'Britian, France and the European Defence Initiative', *Survival*, 42, 2: 33–55.

Huysmans, J. (1995) 'Migrants as a security problem: dangers of "securitising" societal issues', in R. Miles and D. Thränhardt (eds) *Migration and European Integration: the Dynamics of Inclusion and Exclusion*, London: Pinter, 53–72

Jachtenfuchs, M. (1990) 'The European Community and the protection of the ozone layer', *Journal of Common Market Studies*, XXVII, 3: 261–77.

Jacobsen, J.K. (2003) 'Duelling constructivisms: the ideas debate in IR/IPE', *Review of International Studies*, 29, 1: 39–60.

Jawara, F. and Kwa, A. (2004) *Behind the Scenes at the WTO: The Real World of Trade Negotiation*, London: Zed Books.

Jervis, R. (1991/2) 'The future of world politics: will it resemble the past?', *International Security*, 16, 3: 39–73.

Jessop, B. (1990) *State Theory: Putting Capitalist States in their Place*, Cambridge: Polity.

Jileva, E. (2003) 'Larger than the European Union: the emerging EU migration regime and enlargement', in S. Lavenex and E. Ucarer (eds) *Migration and the Externalities of European Integration*, Lanham, MD: Lexington Books, 75–91.

Johansson-Nogués, E. (2004) 'The fifteen and the accession states in the United Nations General Assembly, *CFSP Forum*, 2, 1: 10–12.

Jordan, A., Liefferink, D. and Fairbrass, J. (2004) 'The Europeanization of national environmental policy: a comparative analysis', in J. Barry, B. Baxter and R. Dumphy (eds) *Europe, Globalization and Sustainable Development*, London: Routledge, 123–58.

Kagan, R. (2002) 'Power and Weakness', *Policy Review*, June/July: 3–28

Keeler, J.T.S. (1996) 'Agricultural power in the European Community: explaining the fate of the CAP and GATT negotiations', *Comparative Politics*, January: 127–49.

Keohane, R.O. (2002) 'Ironies of sovereignty: the EU and the US', *Journal of Common Market Studies*, 40, 4: 743–65.

Keohane, R.O. and Hoffman, S. (1991) *The New European Community: Decision-Making and Institutional Change*, Boulder, CO: Westview.

Keohane, R.O. and Nye, J.S. (eds) (1973) *Transnational Relations and World Politics*, Cambridge, MA: Harvard University Press.

—— (1977) *Power and Interdependence: World Politics in Transition*, Boston, MA: Little, Brown and Co.

Kissinger, H.A. (1966) *The Troubled Partnership*, Garden City, NY: Doubleday.

—— (1982) *Years of Upheaval*, London: Weidenfeld and Nicolson.

Klom, A. (2003) 'Mercosur and Brazil: a European perspective', *International Affairs*, 79, 2: 351–68.

Knill, C. and Lenschow, A. (eds) (2002) *Implementing EU Environmental Policy: New Directions and old Problems*, Manchester: Manchester University Press.

Kolankiewicz, G. (1994) 'Consensus and competition in the eastern enlargement of the European Union', *International Affairs*, 70, 3: 477–95.

Koutrakos, P. (2001) *Trade, Foreign Policy and Defence in EU Constitutional Law*, Oxford: Hart Publishing.

Krasner, S.D. (1985) *Structural Conflict: The Third World Against Global Liberalism*, Berkeley, CA: University of California Press.

Kubálková, V. (ed) (2001) *Foreign Policy in a Constructed World*, Armonk, NY: M.E. Sharpe.

Kupchan, C. (2002) *The End of the American Era: US Foreign Policy and the Geopolitics of the Twenty-First Century*, New York: Alfred A. Knopf.

Laatikainen, K.V. (2004) 'Assessing the EU as an actor at the UN: authority, cohesion, recognition and autonomy', *CFSP Forum*, 2, 1: 4–9.

Laffan, B. (1996) 'The politics of identity and political order in Europe', *Journal of Common Market Studies*, 34, 1: 565–94.

Lahav, G. (2004) *Immigration and Policies in the New Europe: Reinventing Borders*, Cambridge: Cambridge University Press.

La Serre, F. de (1996) 'France: the impact of François Mitterand', in C. Hill (ed.) *The Actors in Europe's Foreign Policy*, London: Routledge, 19–39.

Lavanex, S. (2001) 'Migration and the EU's new eastern border', *Journal of European Public Policy*, 8, 1: 24–42.

Le Gloannec, A, (1997) 'Europe by other means?', *International Affairs*, 73, 1: 83–98.

Legg, T. and Egenhofer, C. (2001) *CESDP Commentary. After Marrakech: The Regionalization of the Kyoto Protocol*, Brussels: Centre for European Policy Studies.

Leitzmann, K.M. and Vest, G.D. (eds) (1999) *Environment and Security in an International Context*, NATO CCMS Report No. 232, Bonn: Ministry for the Environment.

Lenschow, A. (2004) 'Environmental policy: at a crossroads?', in M.G. Cowles and D. Dinan (eds) *Developments in the European Union*, Houndmills: Palgrave, 140–59.

Leonard, M. (1997) *Politics without Frontiers: The Role of Political Parties in Europe's Future*, London: Demos.

Liberatore, A. (1997) 'The European Union: bridging domestic and international environmental policy-making', in M.A. Schreurs and E.C. Economy (eds) *The Internationalization of Environmental Protection*, Cambridge: Cambridge University Press, 188–212.

Lindberg, L. and Scheingold, S. (1970) *Europe's Would-Be Polity*, Englewood Cliffs, NJ: Prentice Hall.

Lindstrom, G. (2004) 'On the ground ESDP Operations', in N. Gnesotto (ed) *EU Security and Defence Policy: The First Five Years (1999–2004)*, Paris: Institute for Security Studies, European Union, 111–29.

Lynch, D. (2004) 'Russia and ESDP: towards a Greater Europe', *EuroFuture*, Winter: 36–9.

MacFarlane, S.N. (2004) 'The Caucasus and Central Asia: towards a non-strategy', in R. Dannreuther (ed.) *European Foreign and Security Policy: Towards a Neighbourhood Strategy*, London: Routledge, 118–34.

Macleod, I., Hendry, T. and Hyett, S. (1996) *The External Relations of the European Communities: A Manual of Law and Practice*, Oxford: Oxford University Press.

Macrory, R. and Hession, M. (1996) 'The European Community and climate change: the role of law and legal competence', in T. O'Riordan and J. Jager (eds) *Politics of Climate Change: A European Perspective*, London: Routledge, 106–54.

Manners, I. (2002) 'Normative power Europe: a contradiction in terms?' *Journal of Common Market Studies*, 40, 2: 235–58.

Manners, I. and Whitman, R.G. (2002) 'The "difference engine": constructing and representing the international identity of the European Union', *Journal of European Public Policy*, 10, 3: 380–404.

Marks, J. (1996) 'High hopes and low motives: the new Euro–Mediterranean Partnership Initiative', *Mediterranean Politics*, 1, 1: 1–24.

Marquina, A. (1995) 'The European Union Negotiations on Partnership-building Agreements with Morocco and Tunisia', Paper presented to second Pan-European Conference on International Relations, Paris: 13–16 September.

Mason, T.D. and Turay, A.M. (eds) (1994) *Japan, NAFTA and Europe: Trilateral Cooperation or Confrontation?*, New York: St Martins Press.

McCormick, J. (2001) *Environmental Policy in the European Union*, London: Palgrave.

McGoldrick, D. (1997) *International Relations Law of the European Union*, London: Longman.

McGrew, A., Lewis, P. *et al.* (1992) *Global Politics*, Oxford: Polity.

McNamara, K.R. and Meunier, S. (2002) 'Between national sovereignty and international power: what external voice for the euro?', *International Affairs*, 78, 4: 849–68.

Mearsheimer, J.J. (1990) 'Back to the future: instability in Europe after the Cold War' *International Security*, 15, 1: 5–56.

Mensah, C. (1996) 'The United Nations Commission on sustainable development', in J. Werksman (ed.) *Greening International Institutions*, London: Earthscan, 21–37.

Merle, M. (1987) *The Sociology of International Relations*, Leamington Spa: Berg.

Meunier, S. and Nicolaïdis, K. (1999) 'Who Speaks for Europe? The Delegation of Trade Authority in the EU', *Journal of Common Market Studies*, 37, 3: 477–501.

Milward, A. (1992) *The European Rescue of the Nation-State*, London: Routledge.

Mintzer, I.M. and Leonard, J.A. (eds) (1994) *Negotiating Climate Change: The Inside Story of the Rio Convention*, Cambridge: Cambridge University Press.

Missiroli, A. (2004) 'The EU and its changing neighbourhood: Stabilization, integration and partnership', in R. Dannreuther (ed.) *European Union Foreign and Security Policy: Towards a Neighbourhood Strategy*, London: Routledge, 12–26.

Mitreva, I. (2004) 'Macedonia's way towards Europe', Speech by HE I. Mitreva, Minister of Foreign Affairs of the Republic of Macedonia, London, RIIA, March.

Monar, J. (2003) 'Justice and Home Affairs', *Journal of Common Market Studies*, Annual Review: 119–36.

Moravcsik, A. (2003) 'Striking a new transatlantic bargain', *Foreign Affairs*, 28, 4: 74–89.

Müftüler-Bac, M. (1997) *Turkey's Relations with a Changing Europe*, Manchester: Manchester University Press.

Neumann, I.B. (1996) 'Self and other in international relations', *European Journal of International Relations*, 2, 2: 139–74.

Neumann, I.B. and Welsh, J.M. (1991) 'The other in European self-definition: an addendum to the literature on international society', *Review of International Studies*, 17, 4: 327–48.

Nicolaïdis, K. and Howse, R. (2002) 'This is my EUtopia…: narrative as power', *Journal of Common Market Studies*, 40, 4: 767–92.

Nilsson, H.G. (2004) 'The Justice and Home Affairs Council', in M. Westlake and D. Galloway (eds) *The Council of the European Union*, London: John Harper, 133–42.

Nilsson, S. and Pitt, D. (1994) *Protecting the Atmosphere: The Climate Change Convention and its Context*, London: Earthscan.

Nitze, W. (1990) *The Greenhouse Effect: Formulating a Convention*, London: RIIA.

Nugent, N. and Saurugger, S. (2002) 'Organizational structuring: the case of the European Commission and its external policy responsibilities', *Journal of European Public Policy*, 9, 3: 345–64.

Nuttall, S.J. (1992) *European Political Co-operation*, Oxford: Oxford University Press.

—— (1996) 'The Commission: the struggle for legitimacy', in C. Hill (ed.) *The Actors in Europe's Foreign Policy*, London: Routledge, 130–50.

Obradovic, D. (1996) 'Political legitimacy and the European Union', *Journal of Common Market Studies*, 34, 2: 191–222.

Ockenden, O. and Franklin, M. (1995) *European Agriculture: Making the CAP Fit the Future*, London: Pinter.

OECD (2003) *Environmental Review of Poland*, http://www/oecd.org.

Önis, Z. (2003) 'Domestic politics, international norms and challenges to the state: Turkey–EU relations in the post-Helsinki year', in A. Çarkoglu and B. Rubin (eds) *Turkey and the European Union: Domestic Politics, Economic Integration and International Dynamics*, London: Cass, 9–34.

Ortega, M. (2004) The EU and the UN: strengthening global security', in E.B. Eide (ed.) *Effective Multilateralism: Europe, Regional Security and a Revitalised UN*, London: The Foreign Policy Centre, 11–21.

O'Riordan, T. and Jager, J. (eds) (1996) *Politics of Climate Change: A European Perspective*, London: Routledge.

Overseas Development Institute (2004a) *European Development Cooperation to 2010*, London, ODI: July.

—— (2004b), *Political Partnership with the South*, London: ODI, May.

—— (2004c) *EU Trade Partnerships with Developing Countries*, London: ODI, April.

Paemen, H. and Bensch, A. (1995) *From the GATT to the WTO: The European Community in the Uruguay Round*, Leuven: Leuven University Press.

Palan, R. (2000) 'A world of their making: an evaluation of the constructivist critique in international relations', *Review of International Studies*, 26, 4: 575–98.

Paterson, M. (1996) *Global Warming and Global Politics*, London: Routledge.

Patten, C. (2001) 'Commission Statement to the European Paraliament', Strasbourg, October.

People's Republic of China (2003) 'China's EU Policy Paper', Ministry of Foreign Affairs, October.

Peterson, J. (1996) *Europe and America: the Prospects for Partnership*, London: Routledge.

Piening, R. (1997) *Global Europe*, Boulder, CO: Lynne Rienner.

Pomfret, R. (1992) 'The European Community's relations with the Mediterranean countries', in J. Redmond (ed.) *The External Relations of the European Community: The International Response to 1992*, London: Macmillan, 77–92.

Randel, J. and German, T. (eds) (1997) *The Reality of Aid 1997/8: An Independent Review of Development Cooperation*, London: Earthscan.

Ravenhill, J. (1985) *Collective Clientelism: The Lomé Conventions and North/South Relations*, New York: Columbia University Press.

—— (1993) 'When weakness is strength: the Lomé IV negotiations', in W. Zartman (ed.) *Europe and Africa: The New Phase*, Boulder, CO: Lynne Rienner, 41–61.

Regelsberger, E. (2003) 'The impact of EU enlargement on the CFSP: growing homogeneity of views among the twenty-five', *CFSP Forum*, 1, 3: 3–7.

Reid, T.R. (2004) *The United States of Europe: The New Superpower and the End of American Supremacy*, London: Penguin.

Rifkind, J. (2004) *The European Dream: How Europe's Vision of the Future is Quietly Eclipsing the American Dream*, Cambridge: Polity Press.

Risse, T. (2004) 'Social constructivism and European integration', in A. Wiener and T. Diez (eds) *European Integration Theory*, Oxford: Oxford University Press, 159–75.

Risse-Kappen, T. (1994) 'Ideas do not float freely: transnational coalitions, domestic structures and the end of the Cold War', *International Organization*, 48, 2: 185–214.

Rontoyanni, C. (2003) 'So far, so good? Russia and the ESDP', *International Affairs*, 78, 4: 813–30.

Rosamond, B. (2001) 'Discourses of globalization and European identities', in T. Christiansen, K.E. Jørgensen and A. Wiener (eds) *The Social Construction of Europe*, London: Sage, 158–75.

Rosenau, J.N. (1990) *Turbulence in World Politics: A Theory of Change and Continuity*, New York: Harvester Wheatsheaf.

Royal Institute for International Relations (2003) *A European Security Concept for the 21st Century*, Brussels: IRRI-KIIB, October.

Rubin, B. (2003) 'Introduction', in A. Çarkoglu and B. Rubin (eds) *Turkey and the European Union: Domestic Politics, Economic Integration and International Dynamics*, London: Frank Cass, 1–3.

Ruggie, J.G. (1983) 'International regimes, transactions and change: embedded liberalism in the post-war economic order', in S.D. Krasner (ed.) *International Regimes*, Ithaca, NY: Cornell University Press, 195–232.

—— (1993) 'Territoriality and beyond: problematizing modernity in international relations', *International Organization*, 47, 1: 139–74.

Rumelili, B. (2004) 'Identity, difference and the EU', *Review of International Studies*, 30, 1: 27–48.

Ryborg, O. (2002) 'Wallström's green team', *E!Sharp*, March: 35–7.

Salmon, T.C. (1992) 'Testing times for European political cooperation: the Gulf and Yugoslavia, 1990–1992', *International Affairs*, 68, 2: 233–53.

Sbragia, A. (1996) 'Environmental policy: the "push–pull" of policy making', in H. Wallace and W. Wallace (eds) *Policy Making in the European Union*, 3rd edn, Oxford: Oxford University Press, 235–55.

Schimmelfennig, F. (2000) 'International socialization in the new Europe: rational action in an institutional environment', *European Journal of International Relations*, 6, 1: 109–39.

Schimmelfennig, F. and Sedelmeier, U. (2002) 'Theorizing EU enlargement: research focus, hypotheses and the state of research', *Journal of European Public Policy*, 9, 4: 500–28.

Schmitt, B. (2004) 'European capabilities – how many divisions?', in F. Gnesotto (ed.) *EU Security and Defence Policy: The First Five Years (1999–2004)*, Paris: Institute for Security Studies, European Union, 89–110.

Schreurs, M. (2004) 'Environmental protection in an expanding European Community: lessons from past accessions', *Environmental Politics*, 31, 1: 27–51.

Shemiatenkov, V. (2002) 'EU–Russia: The Sociology of Approximation', Paper to Sixth ECSA-World Conference, Brussels, December.

Singer, J.D. (1961) 'The level of analysis problem in international relations', in K. Knorr and S. Verby (eds) *The International System: Theoretical Essays*, Princeton, NJ: Princeton University Press, 77–92.

Singh Sidhu, W.P. (2004) 'Regionalisation of peace operations', in E.B. Eide (ed.) *Effective Multilateralism: Europe, Regional Security and a Revitalised UN*, London: Foreign Policy Centre, 32–7.

Sjöstedt, G. (1977) *The External Role of the European Community*, Farnborough: Saxon House.

Sjursen, H. (2002) 'The question of legitimacy and justification in the EU's enlargement policy', *Journal of Common Market Studies*, 40, 3: 491–553.

Skjaerseth, J.B. (1994) 'The climate policy of the EC: too hot to handle?', *Journal of Common Market Studies*, 32, 1: 25–45.

Smith, A. (1992) 'National identity and the idea of European unity', *International Affairs*, 68, 1: 55–76.

Smith, C.J. (1996) 'Conflict in the Balkans and the possibility of a European Union common foreign and security policy', *International Relations*, XIII, 2: 1–21.

Smith, H. (2002) *European Union Foreign Policy: What it is and What it Does*, London: Pluto.

Smith, K.E. (2000) 'The end of civilian power EU: a welcome demise or cause for concern?', *International Spectator*, 35,3: 11–28.

—— (2003) *European Union Foreign Policy in a Changing World*, Cambridge: Polity Press.

Smith, M. (2004) 'The European Union, the United States and the Asia-Pacific: a new trilateralism?', in M.G. Cowles and D. Dinan (eds) *Developments in the European Union*, Houndmills: Palgrave, 237–53.

Smith, M.E. (2004) *Europe's Foreign and Security Policy: The Institutionalization of Cooperation*, Cambridge: Cambridge University Press.

Solana, J. (2002) 'Europe's place in the world', address to the Danish Institute of International Affairs, Copenhagen, May.

Somsen, H. (1996) 'The European Union and the Organization for Economic Cooperation and Development', in J. Werksman (ed.) *Greening International Institutions*, London: Earthscan, 181–204.

Sondermann, F.A. (1961) 'The linkage between foreign policy and international politics', in J.N. Rosenau (ed.) *International Politics and Foreign Policy: A Reader in Research and Theory* 1st edn, New York: Free Press, 8–17.

Spence, D. (2000) 'Plus ça change, plus c'est la même chose? Attempting to reform the European Commission', *Journal of European Public Policy*, 7, 1: 1–25.

Swann, D. (1975) *The Economics of the Common Market*, Harmondsworth: Penguin.

Tallberg, J. (2003) 'The agenda-shaping powers of the EU Council Presidency', *Journal of European Public Policy*, 10,1: 1–19.

Taylor, P. (1996) *The European Union in the 1990s*, Oxford: Oxford University Press.

Teitelbaum, M.S. and Martin, P.L. (2003) 'Is Turkey ready for Europe?', *Foreign Affairs*, 82, 3: 97–111.

Thränhardt, D. (1966) 'European migration from East to West: present patterns and future directions', *New Community*, 22, 2: 227–42.

Töre, N. (1990) 'Relations between the European Community and Turkey' *European Access*, 3: 8–11.

Trondal, J. and Veggeland, F. (2003) 'Access, voice and loyalty: the representation of domestic civil servants in EU committees', *Journal of European Public Policy*, 10, 1: 59–77.

Tunander, O. (1997) 'Post-Cold War Europe: synthesis of a bipolar friend–foe structure and a hierarchic cosmos–chaos structure', in O. Tunander, P. Baev and V.I. Einagel (eds) *Geopolitics in Post-Wall Europe: Security, Territory and Identity*, London: Sage, 17–44.

United Nations (2002) *Report on the World Summit on Sustainable Development, Johannesburg, South Africa, 26 August–24 September 2002* A/Conf.199/20, New York: United Nations.

United Nations Development Programme (1995) *Human Development Report 1995*, Oxford: Oxford University Press.

—— (2003) *Human Development Report 2003*, Oxford: Oxford University Press.

—— (2004) *Human Development Report 2004*, Oxford: Oxford University Press.

Van Oudenaren, J. (2004) 'Policy towards the extended frontier: the Balkans and the Newly Independent States', in M.G. Cowles and D. Dinan (eds) *Developments in the European Union*, Basingstoke: Palgrave, 256–74.

van Reisen, M. (1997) 'European Union', in J. Randel and T. German (eds) *The Reality of Aid*, London: Earthscan, 160–78.

—— (2004) *2015 Watch – The EU's Contribution to the MDGs*, Brussels: European External Policy Advisers.

Van Schaik, L. and Egenhofer, C. (2003) *Reform of the EU Institutions: Implications for the EU's performance in Climate Negotiations*, Brussels: Centre for European Policy Studies.

Vaughan, R. (1976) *Post-War Integration in Europe*, London: Edward Arnold.

Vellinga, P. and Grubb, M. (eds) (1993) *Climate Change Policy in the European Community*, London: RIIA.

Vogler, J. (1995) *The Global Commons: A Regime Analysis*, Chichester: John Wiley.

—— (1996) 'The structures of global politics', in C. Bretherton and G. Ponton (eds) *Global Politics: An Introduction*, Oxford: Blackwell, 23–48.

—— (2002a) 'Environment and natural resources', in B. White, R. Little and M. Smith (eds) *Issues in World Politics*, London: Palgrave, 191–211.

—— (2002b) 'The European Union and the "securitisation" of the environment', in E.A. Page, and M. Redclift (eds) *Human Security and the Environment: International Comparisons*, Cheltenham: Edward Elgar, 179–98.

von Moltke, K. and Rahman, A. (1996) 'External perspectives on climate change: a view from the United States and the Third World', in T. O'Riordan and J. Jager (eds) *Politics of Climate Change: A European Perspective*, London: Routledge, 330–45.

Wæver, O. (1995) 'Identity, integration and security: solving the sovereignty puzzle in E.U. studies', *Journal of International Affairs*, 48, 2: 399–439.

—— (1996) 'European security identities', *Journal of Common Market Studies*, 34, 1: 103–32.

—— (2004) 'Discursive approaches', in A. Wiener and T. Diez (eds) *European Integration Theory*, Oxford: Oxford University Press, 197–216.

Wæver, O., Buzan, B., Kelstrup, M. and Lemaitre, P. (1993) *Identity, Migration and the New Security Agenda in Europe*, London: Pinter.

Walker, R.B.J. (2000) 'Europe is not where it is supposed to be', in M. Kelstrup and M.C. Williams (eds) *International Relations Theory and the Politics of European Integration*, London: Routledge, 14–32.

Wallace, A. (2004) 'Completing the Single Market: the Lisbon Strategy', in M.G. Cowles and D. Dinan (eds) *Developments in the European Union*, Houndmills: Palgrave, 100–18.

Wallerstein, I. (1984) *The Politics of the World-Economy*, Cambridge: Cambridge University Press.

—— (1991) *Geopolitics and Geoculture: Essays on the Changing World-System*, Cambridge: Cambridge University Press.

Waltz, K.N. (1979) *The Theory of International Politics*, Reading, MA: Addison Wesley.

Webber, M., Croft, S., Howorth, J., Terriff, T. and Krahmann, E. (2004) 'The governance of European Security', *Review of International Studies*, 30, 1: 3–26.

Weigall, D. and Stirk, P. (1992) *The Origins and Development of the European Community*, Leicester: Leicester University Press.

Weller, M. (2002) 'Undoing the global constitution: UN Security Council action on the International Criminal Court', *International Affairs*, 78, 4: 693–712.

Wendt, A. (1994) 'Collective identity formation and the international state', *American Political Science Review*, 88, 2: 384–96.

Werksman, J. (ed.) (1996) *Greening International Institutions*, London: Earthscan.

Westlake, M. and Galloway, D. (eds) (2004) *The Council of the European Union*, London: John Harper.

White, B. (2001) *Understanding European Foreign Policy*, Basingstoke: Palgrave.

—— (2004) 'Foreign policy analysis and the new Europe', in W. Carlsnaes, H. Sjursen and B. White (eds) *Contemporary European Foreign Policy*, London, Sage: 11–31.

White, S., McAllister, A. and Light, M. (2002) 'Enlargement and the new outsiders', *Journal of Common Market Studies*, 40,1: 135–53.

Winters, L.A. (1994) 'The EC and world protectionism: dimensions of the political economy', Discussion Paper 897, London: CEPR.

Woolcock, S. (1996) 'An agenda for the WTO: strengthening or overburdening the system?' GEI Working Paper, 17, ESRC.

Woolcock, S. and Hodges, M. (1996) 'EU policy in the Uruguay Round', in H. Wallace and W. Wallace (eds) *Policy-Making in the European Union*, Oxford: Oxford University Press, 301–24.

World Bank Group (2004) *Data and Statistics*, http://www.worldbank.org/data.

World Commission on Environment and Development (1987) *Our Common Future*, Oxford: Oxford University Press.

WTO (2002a) *Trade Policy Review: European Union Report by the Government*, WT/TPR/G/102: June.

—— (2002b) *Trade Policy Review: European Union Report by the Secretariat*, WT/TPR/S/102: June.

Wurzel, R.K.W. (1996) 'The role of the EU Presidency in the environmental field: does it make a difference which state runs the Presidency?', *Journal of European Public Policy*, 3, 2: 272–91.

Young, A.R. (2004) 'The EU and world trade: Doha and beyond', in M.G. Cowles and D. Dinan (eds) *Developments in the European Union*, Houndmills: Palgrave, 200–20.

Young, O.R. (1972) 'The actors in world politics', in J.N. Rosenau, V. Davies and M.A. East (eds) *The Analysis of International Politics*, New York: Free Press, 125–44.

—— (1989) *International Cooperation: Building Regimes for Natural Resources and Environment*, Ithaca, NY and London: Cornell University Press.

Youngs, R. (2004) 'Normative dynamics and strategic interests in the EU's external identity', *Journal of Common Market Studies*, 42, 4: 415–35.

Zagorski, A. (2004) 'Policies towards Russia, Ukraine, Moldova and Belarus', in R. Dannreuther (ed) *European Union Foreign and Security Policy: Towards a Neighbourhood Strategy*, London: Routledge, 79–97.

Zehfuss, M. (2001) 'Constructivism and identity: a dangerous liaison', *European Journal of International Relations*, 7, 3: 315–48.

Zielonka, J. (1998) *Explaining Euro-Paralysis: Why Europe is Unable to Act in International Politics*, Basingstoke: Macmillan.

Index